The Translation of Culture

CONTRIBUTORS

JOHN BARNES
University of Cambridge

T. O. BEIDELMAN
New York University

ELIZABETH COLSON
University of California, Berkeley

JAMES J. FOX
Harvard University

KATHLEEN GOUGH
Simon Fraser University

C. R. HALLPIKE
Dalhousie University

DAVID HICKS
State University of New York,
Stoney Brook

CLAUDE LÉVI-STRAUSS
Collège de France

JOHN MIDDLETON
New York University

RODNEY NEEDHAM
University of Oxford

JULIAN PITT-RIVERS
University of Chicago *and* École
pratique des hautes études, Paris

PETER RIGBY
Makerere University College

PETER RIVIÈRE
University of Cambridge

ERIC TEN RAA
University of Western Australia

VICTOR W. TURNER
University of Chicago

E. E. EVANS-PRITCHARD

The Translation of Culture

Essays to E. E. Evans-Pritchard

Edited by T. O. Beidelman

TAVISTOCK PUBLICATIONS

First published in 1971
By Tavistock Publications Limited
11 New Fetter Lane, London EC4
Printed in Great Britain
In 11 on 13 point Imprint
By Butler & Tanner Ltd, Frome and London

SBN 422 73410 1

Distributed in the USA by Barnes & Noble Inc

'I am not denying that the semantic difficulties in translation are great. They are considerable enough between, shall we say, French and English; but when some primitive language has to be rendered into our own tongue they are, and for obvious reasons, much more formidable. They are in fact the major problem we are confronted with in the subject we are discussing . . .'

E. E. EVANS-PRITCHARD
Theories of Primitive Religion

Contents

Contents

Editor's Preface

In these collected essays the various contributors have sought to present a tribute to Professor E. E. Evans-Pritchard in the year of his retirement from the Chair of Social Anthropology at the University of Oxford. Some of the contributors were his students; others studied elsewhere but were deeply influenced by his work, both in terms of the enormous theoretical and ethnographic contribution it has made to the discipline, and in terms of the unfailing example he has set for scholarship and dedication to professional achievement. It is hoped that the diversity of approach in these various essays in some way conveys the wide breadth of Evans-Pritchard's own interests.

The idea for this volume grew out of informal correspondence rather than out of any orderly canvassing of prospective contributors. I realize that there are many people who would have liked to present their respects to Evans-Pritchard; unfortunately, the number of contributions possible in a volume was limited.

The Righthand and Lefthand Kingdoms of God

A Dilemma of Pietist Politics

JOHN BARNES

Many people would say that the basic difference between Christianity and most tribal religions is that Christianity is an ethical and universal religion based on broad moral principles binding on all men at all times and places. By contrast a tribal religion is typically particularist, calling for specific performances by certain persons in delimited contexts; it does not specify how strangers should behave nor what they should believe, nor does it indicate how its followers should act outside the strictly religious situation. But if this is the basic difference, then expressed in these terms we have only a caricature of Christianity and of tribal religions as revealed by modern research. For just as in most tribal religions there are some actions that invite religious censure or activate mystical retribution, so in Christendom the form of the good life is shaped not only by ethical statements like the ten commandments and the Sermon on the Mount but also by cosmological beliefs about heaven and hell, the Trinity and the Atonement, as well as beliefs about postulated historical events such as the Incarnation and the Resurrection. The same is true of other so-called ethical religions. Buddhism provides a theory of re-incarnation and of escape from re-incarnation as well as 227 rules of conduct, and Islam has a hierarchy of angels as well as its duties of the faithful. Nevertheless many would argue, particularly in the present anti-theological and pro-ecumenical climate, that cosmological or metaphysical beliefs influence the behaviour of a believer primarily in specifically religious or liturgical contexts, in prayer and ceremonial, and do not directly determine how he behaves as a citizen in the marketplace or the factory or in parliament. In these areas of activity the righteous citizen is guided by ethical principles rather than by his beliefs about the structure of heaven.

I

Yet even in this modified form the disjunction between religious behaviour validated by metaphysics and secular behaviour determined by ethics has only limited taxonomic value. For within all the great world religions we see the historically persistent contrast between Faith and Works as roads to salvation. Max Weber has more than any other writer examined the sociological implications of the diverse forms taken by this contrast in the various religions, and in the light of his studies we should be alert to the probability that beliefs not only about the fate of the believer after death but about other aspects of the cosmological order as well may have a direct influence on behaviour that is ostensibly entirely mundane and secular.

In societies without writing, the past is encapsulated in the present in many ways – in legends, traditions, genealogies, the pattern of enduring social relations and the continual re-enactment of ostensibly unchanging rites. Continuity in the social life of literate peoples is maintained partly by the same devices, but in addition there are written records which endure unchanged even while they are forgotten, waiting to be rediscovered and put to new uses after centuries of oblivion. Although everywhere our perception of the past is continually being revised in the light of our changing present interests, in a literate society the past still remains accessible in the contemporary records that have been preserved unchanged through time. It is significant that in his phantasy of the new barbarism, *1984*, Orwell stresses both the perpetual revision of the history of the very recent past and the destruction of contemporary records; in *1984*, as in a non-literate society, the past is hidden and only the latest versions of the myth are in free circulation.

These considerations are particularly relevant to the study of social life in western Norway, where a long tradition of literacy, a well-developed system of public records, and a keen sense of historical continuity and development combine to make the recollected and documented past an essential element in the affairs of the present. In this context a fieldworker who necessarily spends only a limited period of time on his inquiries is at a permanent disadvantage. Under tribal conditions the ethnographer who sees the results of his investigations in comparative perspective and who can utilize evidence from archaeology, linguistics and other disciplines may well become better informed about the history and development of the people he studies than are the people themselves. In a literate and diversified society actively concerned with its own past and able to utilize the results of scientific inquiry the position is reversed. The ethnographer can never hope to read all the books all his informants have read and he cannot expect to absorb more than a fraction of the complex and diverse cultural background, partly myth and partly fact, that they have taken a lifetime to acquire. As Evans-Pritchard (1962: 64) puts it, 'Then history cannot be ignored.' The ethnographer has not only to observe and listen to his informants; he also has to use his abilities as a sleuth to pick his way through the jungle of archives and libraries to arrive at precisely those facts which impinge critically on the contemporary scene he is trying to understand. Yet this necessity is also a temptation. It is an attractive and peaceful jungle with many byways and it is easy to forget just what one has come to seek. Some ethnographers may never be seen again.

What follows is a description of one instance in which cosmological beliefs influence political behaviour. I shall discuss a contemporary situation in Bremnes, a district in western Norway where I have been making sporadic inquiries for a decade or so (Barnes 1954, 1957, 1960). By political behaviour I refer here to the way in which people vote in Parliament and on local councils and the support they give to national political parties. The cosmological belief is derived from the writings of Martin Luther who taught that there are two kingdoms or regimes or regiments ruled over by God, a lefthand kingdom and a righthand kingdom. I make no assumption about the primacy of this or any other religious belief but merely assume that whatever material, mental or genetic causes may promote or sustain any religious belief, the belief soon acquires an autonomy of its own.

In 1965, after twenty years of almost unbroken rule, the Labour government in Norway was defeated in a general election and was re-placed by a governing coalition of four right and centre parties, one of them being the Christian People's Party. This is the strongest political party in Bremnes. Throughout Norway the party is mainly supported by Christians who follow that version of Lutheranism introduced into Norway at the very end of the eighteenth century by the Pietist evangelist Hans Nielsen Hauge. Pietism has been dominant in Bremnes for the last seventy or eighty years and enjoys even more local support than does the Christian People's Party. The postwar Labour government clashed with the Pietist movement soon after it came to power over the control of a teachers' training college, but in its later years one of the strongest conflicts concerned subsidies for schools for adolescent boys and girls run by Pietist organizations. The Labour government refused

3

to provide funds for the schools. One of the first acts of the new incoming government was to provide this financial aid. During the Labour period, the Pietists argued that education, particularly the moral instruction and character-training provided for adolescents in these schools, was a function of the Christian community and not a matter that could be left to the state, which at that time they saw as being controlled by a government covertly if not openly anti-Christian in its sympathies. But it was only right, they claimed, that the state should encourage this good work for the community; work which was otherwise almost entirely dependent on the financial sacrifices made by individual Christians. Now that the Christian People's Party is part of the new coalition government, with the Minister for Church and Education a member of this party, many Pietists realize that the same arguments may be put forward by Catholics, Seventh Day Adventists, Mormons, Jehovah's Witnesses, and other smaller groups, each group demanding subsidies for its own schools. Pietists in Bremnes and elsewhere tend to regard with suspicion all non-Lutheran religious teaching and in particular recall Luther's identification of the Pope as an anti-Christ. Hence opinion in the party is divided. Some members argue that the secular state has no authority to discriminate in religious matters and that, to be fair, if it subsidizes the schools of one religious persuasion it must subsidize all; others argue that the state should aid only those citizens who preach the word of God and not those who preach false doctrines. Both opinions have their advocates in Bremnes but the majority of party members hold that accepting grants from the state for Pietist schools does not entail agreeing to financial grants to the schools of other denominations.

These are the facts I discuss. In this paper I am not concerned with the ethical problems they pose and my interest is limited to the evidence they provide about how the people of Bremnes participate in the national political system. To analyse the facts in terms of this system I have to range far afield over the historical development of church and state in Norway. In the context of this short paper I must necessarily treat this development very superficially, but my aim is to provide merely a brief analysis of contemporary events rather than an adequate historical and theological account of their antecedents.

To understand how this division of opinion within the party has come about, and why Bremnes party members incline to what we may call the particularist rather than the universalist alternative, we must look both

4

at the local scene in Bremnes, and at some of the distinctive features of Pietism and Lutheranism in Norway. These relevant features are the relations of the Norwegian state church to the secular government, to the Lutheran tradition, and to the Pietist movement. I mention how the Pietist movement, which is anti-clerical in sentiment, has become responsible for training priests, and why it runs schools of its own. In Bremnes, I sketch the local pattern of industrialization and the varying amount of local support for Pietism.

The first question to ask is, why does the Christian People's Party enjoy solid support in Bremnes? The party was founded in western Norway in 1933 and arose out of a feeling that the existing parties had all become inadequately Christian. Bremnes is a district which, within this region, has a reputation for being markedly Christian and it is not surprising that the new party attracted strong local support. However this salient interest in religion is a phenomenon that has changed with the passage of time. It seems probable that while Bremnes now stands out among the neighbouring districts of western Norway for the support given to prayer houses, missions, and other voluntary church activities, this prominence is due more to a recent decline in these activities in other districts rather than to an increase in Bremnes. The trend in Bremnes is in the same direction as elsewhere, but it is less pronounced. It seems that fifty years ago there was a greater degree of consensus throughout the region than there is now about the authority of the text of the Bible and the importance of regular attendance at religious meetings, saying grace before and after meals, and abstinence from alcohol. These traits constitute some of the distinguishing external characteristics of the present dominant culture in Bremnes but are not universally followed even there. There are many who go to church and the prayer house only infrequently, who go hunting on Sundays, and do not say grace. Apart from these people who accept the moral superiority of the dominant culture without meeting all its behavioural demands, there is now a substantial minority which actively rejects the dominant culture. In this local context support for the Christian People's Party in Bremnes is an expression of support for the dominant culture in the face of increasing local attack and erosion. On the national level, however, support for the party cannot mean, as it still does in Bremnes, opposition to cinemas, theatres, dancing, sex education in schools, and the building of the secular youth clubs. On the national scene these battles have already been lost and a minority party, even as part of a ruling coalition,

5

cannot hope to reopen the attack. The defenders of the old values can envisage Bremnes only as a remnant of Christian living in an un-Christian nation. If the coalition government is a success, and if the party increases its support, there may perhaps be talk of a national Christian counter-offensive; but this is merely a possibility for the future.

The programme of the Christian People's Party includes, as the second of its eight basic points, the improvement of primary schooling and the provision of state subsidies for independent schools for adolescents. The first of its points includes the preservation of Christian instruction as the core of primary school education and the denial of official support to all anti-Christian institutions (Bondevik 1965: 69–70). Other points deal with Christian social justice, temperance, support for agriculture and fisheries, disarmament, equitable taxation and prudent state spending, and impartial Christian democratic courts. Thus the party is distinguished from other coalition parties, as well as from the Labour opposition, in its advocacy of the application of Christian principles to the business of government. This is no new development in Norwegian Pietism, for Hauge, and Gisle Johnson after him, both stressed the importance of Christian witness in the secular world and were opposed to any withdrawal from it. The party gives a general and unspecific endorsement to economic free enterprise, coupled with a determination to improve the structure of the welfare state set up by the former Labour government; the main plank of the party is the protection of Christian values in private life. The public business of government and the private life of the individual meet most forcefully in the national schools. In Norway the great majority of primary and secondary school children, and in a country district like Bremnes all these children, attend schools that form part of the loose national system. The local district council is responsible for building schools, hiring and paying teachers, and choosing between alternative syllabuses offered by the central government. Education accounts for over half of the expenditure of the local district council, and parents take an active interest in what is taught to their children in the local schools. Furthermore the national school system, as we may call it, has always had a close link with the state church. In the mid-nineteenth century children were taught to read, and adults who were too old to go to school taught themselves to read, so that they could study the Bible. Apart from the three Rs, the only other subject of importance taught in school was Christian knowledge. The district parish rector was, and still is *ex officio* a member of the local school board, and instruction in school was linked with the instruction given by the rector to confirmation candidates. For many years compulsory schooling was limited to seven years, from age seven to age fourteen, and for many boys and girls confirmation during the last year of school marked the transition from childhood to the world of earning a living. The transition was often from the shelter of a Christian home and Christian school to the rough and tumble of life in the fishing fleet or in domestic service in the towns. During the twentieth century the school curriculum began to take in many new subjects. Even in Bremnes some children continued their schooling beyond age fourteen, sometimes going on to secondary school after a year with the fishing fleet to save a little money. A retired school teacher summed up the changes in the period 1900 to 1950 by saying: 'Christianity used to be the major subject and now it has become just a minor subject.' Thus the concern of the Christian People's Party with education is easy to understand, particularly at a time when post-Sputnik pressures, in Norway as elsewhere, have led to enlarged curricula, longer periods of schooling, overcrowded classrooms, and an acute shortage of school teachers.

This tradition of education based on the Bible goes back to the beginnings of Lutheranism, with the work of Francke at Halle University in Germany. In nineteenth-century Norway, at least in the countryside, literacy and piety went hand in hand. Many of those who were interested in religion became teachers, and the teachers who succeeded professionally were often lay preachers. As the syllabus came to include more subjects, the Christian component in teacher selection and training became less significant. In the last few years, the shortage of trained teachers has led to the employment in primary, and even in some secondary, schools of so-called 'students', young men and women who have recently passed the matriculation examination but who have not yet gone to teachers' training college or university. Thus the school can no longer be seen as primarily concerned with the transformation of Christian infants into Christian adults; it has become a school of skills rather than a school of values. In these circumstances we can understand why the Pietist movement seeks financial support for its own schools to supplement those provided by the state.

To understand the attitude of the party towards state aid we must also look at the relation between church and state. Here we are not specifically concerned with Bremnes, for the broad outline of the relation between local church and local organs of central government within the Bremnes arena is common to all districts in Norway, though there are some special features in Bremnes we shall look at presently. The Lutheran church in Norway is a state church in that there is a government department responsible for church affairs (it is significant that this is the Department of Church and Education); its clergy are civil servants and are paid from official funds; all citizens are members of the church unless they have formally registered themselves as non-members. These conditions have persisted more or less unchanged from the Reformation through the centuries of Danish and Swedish rule into the present era of independent nationhood. Not only is there a state church but all citizens, except registered non-members, are required under the constitution to bring up their children in the Lutheran faith. Hence at first sight it is surprising that the argument, familiar enough in other contexts, that the state should not concern itself with religion has any relevance for this particular state and this religion. Indeed, a simple identity of the interests of the Lutheran evangelical Christian church and the Norwegian state was implied in the article of the constitution, now amended, which used to read 'Jews and Jesuits must not be tolerated'. But in fact we are here dealing with a Lutheran church which has become in certain parts of the country strongly Pietist in sentiment, and not, say, with an Eastern Orthodox church constitutionally able to live in century-long harmony with a Byzantine Christian monarchy. Nor has there ever been in Norway a western medieval type of tension between church and state. The Reformation, and the new relationship between an Evangelical or Lutheran church and a Protestant prince, were hammered out in Germany and the results were imported ready-made via Denmark to Norway in 1537. During the three hundred years following the Reformation, the church in Norway became an Erastian state church, and was in fact the most pervasive instrumentality of the central government, with its clergy stationed farther out into the countryside than any other branch of the bureaucracy. In the eyes of country folk it became strongly identified with the Danish colonial establishment and urban elite and, eventually, with the dangerous doctrines of the Enlightenment and theological rationalism. It was with this church already in existence that the Pietist movement brought to the Norwegian countryside at the beginning of the nineteenth century not only its own version of the Lutheran tradition but also an interest in the basic tenets of Lutheranism which in

Norway seems not to have accompanied the Reformation itself. Hence it comes about that during the last hundred and fifty years Pietist arguments based on a Lutheran interpretation of the Scriptures have been advanced in radical criticism of the status and teaching of the manifestly Lutheran church and of the ostensibly Lutheran state. This fact, together with Hauge's forthright disapproval of sectarianism, helps to explain why, to such a substantial extent, Pietist dissent has been contained within the institutional fold of the state church. The position is well stated in the proud slogan of the principal organ of the Pietist movement, the Inner Mission: 'In, but not under, the state church.'

How is this relation between church and state derived from Luther's teachings? The Dano-Norwegian institutional arrangement of a national church with total membership and assimilated to the state public service follows one of the several solutions outlined by Luther for settling the problems of church and state. It was the solution followed throughout Protestant Germany. Nevertheless Luther's views on this matter shifted substantially in the course of his lifetime. It is difficult for the outsider to summarize his intellectual position, for some commentators argue that his teaching must be understood in the light of his conviction that the end of the world was imminent (e.g. Forell 1954: 15), whereas others argue that he looked back to primitive Christianity rather than forward to the millennium (e.g. Wolin 1956: 34–5). In these circumstances it is apparent even to the non-theological anthropologist that Luther did not develop a clear theory of worldly society. His voluminous writings provide authoritative ammunition for those advocating various other conflicting solutions for the worldly status of the church, particularly when the state can no longer be conceptualized as the prince who happens to be a Christian. Here I am concerned only with the interpretation of his teaching accepted by Pietists in Bremnes.

Luther discusses at length the duties of the Christian, as a 'world-person' rather than as a Christian, to obey the civil authorities, but he also criticizes these same authorities bluntly. He writes:

'The offices of princes and officials are divine and right, but those who are in them and use them are usually of the devil. And if a prince is a rare dish in heaven, this is even more true of the officials and court personnel' (LW 13: 212; cf. WA LI, 254, 10–13; Mueller 1954: 55).

This attitude of critical obedience was found in western Norway during the nineteenth century, where it was extended to the church and translated into action by Pietists who would gather at the church an hour before the service was due to begin, to pray for the rector who was to preach and whose theology they mistrusted.

The policies of the Christian People's Party are directly influenced by Luther's doctrine of God's two governments or regiments (cf. Cargill Thomson, cited in Fortes 1962: 58, fn. 2). I speak with hesitation on matters outside my competence, but it seems, according to Cranz (1959: 159–73), that in his 'Commentary on the sermon on the mount' (WA XXXII, 299–544; LW 21: 1–294), Luther argues that every Christian exists simultaneously in two realms or governments, a spiritual realm where he is subject to God's spiritual government and a worldly realm where he is under God's worldly government. The offices, or in modern terminology statuses, of prince, judge, lord, servant, wife, child, all belong solely to the worldly realm, even though the individuals who fill these offices may be Christians. In the worldly realm God rules through reason, whereas in the spiritual realm God rules alone. The temporal organization of the church on earth, with its offices of bishop and priest, is part of the worldly realm and while it, along with the family and the state, is ordained by God as part of the worldly realm, the church does not occupy any special position within that realm. The relative status of the two realms emerges clearly in a passage from a sermon preached by Luther on 15 December 1532. Here he says

> 'Likewise also secular government may be called God's kingdom. For he wills that it continue and that we be obedient to it. But it is only the kingdom of the left hand. His rightful kingdom where he himself rules and where he appoints neither father nor mother, emperor nor king, henchman nor policeman but where He is himself the Lord is this: where the Gospel is being preached to the poor.' (WA XXXVI, 385, 6–11 and LII, 26, 21–7, cited in Mueller 1954: 43; cf. Cranz 1959: 172, f. n. 195.)

The ambiguity in the word 'rightful' is present in Luther's original German text. Hertz (1960) seems to have overlooked this nice example of the pre-eminence of the right hand, in the field of religion itself. It is important to note that Luther does not equate God's left hand with damnation, as in Matthew 25, v. 31–46, but with secular life here on earth.

With this relationship between church and state in mind, we can look again at the distinctive features of the Norwegian social scene, remembering that these Lutheran doctrines form part of the contemporary thinking of Pietists in Bremnes and other parts of Norway. Most of the books and periodicals on the shelves in Bremnes homes are religious works, and these usually include expositions of Lutheran and Pietist doctrine. At the beginning of the nineteenth century the Pietist movement was introduced into Norway by Hans Nielsen Hauge, and gained much support in the west of the country, including Bremnes (Hamre 1964; Molland 1951; Straume 1960). The movement stressed the value of personal experience of Christian salvation and personal morality and minimized the distinction between clergy and laity. It became a movement of believers, the leaven within the larger body of members of the state church. It was opposed to the liberal interpretation of Christian doctrine then espoused by many clergy. In many parts of the country it was associated with the nationalist movement that followed the adoption of the 1814 constitution and the transfer of Norway from Danish rule to Swedish tutelage following the Treaty of Kiel. It was also associated with the movement to revive the indigenous dialects of the countryside in a composite country language in opposition to the Danish speech associated with former colonial rule. The history of Pietism and these related movements in Bremnes and elsewhere does not concern us here, except to note that by the beginning of this century this laymen's movement had gained sufficient support in the nation to challenge the liberal clergy on their own ground by setting up a theological college of its own in Oslo. During the twentieth century the supporters of liberal views have largely withdrawn from the church altogether, and at the present time the great majority of priests entering the Norwegian church receive their training in this college; yet Pietism remains essentially a laymen's movement and is referred to in these terms. It remains committed to the view that service as a priest is no higher a vocation than any other acceptable to God. The main body of the Pietist movement is no longer actively anti-clerical or against the state church, and a great deal of effort is made by influential Pietists to ensure that if possible priests appointed to churches where Pietists are numerous are themselves of Pietist persuasion or sympathy. Pietists often have an ambivalent attitude towards the church and its officials. This was well expressed in a speech given at a farewell feast in honour of the Bremnes-born man, a Pietist, who had become a priest and who, after completing a period of duty as curate in Bremnes, had been promoted to a rectorship in another parish. The chairman of the prayer house, where the feast was held, expressed the feelings of the neighbourhood by saying that all were very sorry that he was leaving, though they had to be pleased that he had secured promotion. The curate was admonished that however far his talents might take him in the ecclesiastical hierarchy, he must always remember that he was really a layman in priest's clothing. This remark was not only the highest tribute the chairman could pay, for the believing laity are the salt of the earth, but also a warning that the outward signs of ecclesiastical rank belong only to God's worldy regiment and not to his spiritual kingdom.

As well as a theological college, the Pietist movement founded many other enterprises, such as missionary societies and temperance hotels and daily newspapers, which do not come into our story. Two kinds of activity do however bear directly on the plight of the Christian People's Party that we are trying to analyse. Throughout the Norwegian countryside followers of the Pietist movement set up prayer houses where meetings for prayer and Christian witness were held, organized by the local group of believers and addressed by their own members or by itinerant preachers sent out by regional Pietist organizations. Meetings were arranged so as not to clash with the official services held in the church, and the local clergy, if sufficiently Pietist in their views, were often invited to speak in the prayer houses of their parish. They then spoke as personal Christians, speaking to their equals in the sight of God, and not as civil servants appointed by the king to preach God's word. The prayer houses came to be the local headquarters of a teritorially organized national movement, the institutional aspect of Pietism as it were, which paralleled the territorial organization of the state church. The church was official, included everyone, provided facilities for baptism, confirmation, and marriage, and was authoritarian in as much as clergy were appointed ultimately by the king on behalf of the central government. The prayer house was voluntary, was supported by those who had been born again in Christ, and was egalitarian, at least between men; women were inferior to men in both systems.

This combination of organizational strength and lack of commitment to the ideological institutions provided by the state led naturally to the decision to establish voluntary Christian schools for adolescents. Just as the prayer house supplements but does not replace the church, so the voluntary schools supplement but do not replace the schools provided by the state. Examples provided in Germany and Denmark, together with various practical considerations, dictate the choice of boarding-schools for adolescents, attended for six-month courses at the age of sixteen to eighteen or so. Whereas confirmation at the age of fourteen is a ceremony of the state church, embracing all children as a matter of course, the voluntary schools provide an opportunity for those beginning their lives as autonomous adults to demonstrate that they have decided, or are deciding, to be children of God rather than children of the world. In a sense it is the pervasiveness of Christian instruction and orientation in the state schools that necessitates the creation of voluntary Pietist Christian schools.

These general conditions have manifested themselves in specific form in Bremnes and have affected local attitudes to the recent dilemma. We have mentioned that until recently a high degree of conformity to Pietist principles was achieved in Bremnes, possibly to a greater extent than in neighbouring districts. In part this was probably because until the beginning of the century Bremnes remained an undifferentiated fishing and small-farming district, exporting to the towns of Norway and to the United States of America those who were ambitious or who would not conform. Casual labourers came to the district in connexion with fishing and mining and many of these were scarcely children of God, but no permament settlements of migrants were established. After the turn of the century industrial enterprises began to be established by local entrepreneurs whose managerial drive was matched by their steadfast faith in the tenets of Pietism. Indeed, the teachings of Hauge on the importance of commercial and industrial initiative in the Pietist way of life provided an ethical model for industrialization in Bremnes. The outward forms of Pietism were enforced with sanctions just as its inward manifestations were encouraged through prayer meetings and religious concerts. For example, under Norwegian law hard liquor can be bought only at the retail branches of the official Wine Monopoly, the nearest branch to Bremnes being sixty or seventy kilometres away in Bergen. This arrangement has been in force since the 1920s. Liquor ordered by workers in the largest factory in Bremnes was sent by coastal steamer from Bergen to its port of call nearest Bremnes and was there transhipped for delivery to the hamlet where the factory is located. The founder of this factory was also skipper of the boat used for transhipping goods. Stories are told of how, when he discovered a case of liquor addressed to one of his employees, he sank it in deep water, refunded the cost to the employee, and dismissed him forthwith. More generally, the high degree of local control in financial matters, including the granting of subsidies to voluntary bodies, enabled the Pietist majority, through the local district council, to protect Bremnes from the secularizing tendencies of the second quarter of the twentieth century. In other parts of Norway, and even in another part of the ecclesiastical parish that includes Bremnes, there have been various breakaway movements from Pietism that have led to the establishment of independent Lutheran churches or to sects that are not even Lutheran. Until about five years ago, none of these had gained a foothold in Bremnes. The only public buildings in the district where meetings could be held were the church, the prayer houses and the schools, and a single lodge belonging to a Christian temperance organization. Since assemblies out of doors are usually not feasible in the Bremnes climate, it was almost impossible for organizations openly hostile to the dominant culture to hold public meetings. Unapproved activities such as dancing by adolescents took place only clandestinely in boat houses or at the chilly cross-roads. It was therefore easy for the dominant group to be intolerant in matters of faith and morals.

In the last five years or so, the local battle has entered a new phase. The introduction of television has brought a keener recognition of the possibilities of other styles of life. Better communications have brought the cinemas and dance halls on neighbouring islands within easy reach of young people, who now drive cars from ferry to ferry whereas their parents went all the way by row-boat. More significantly, the economic prosperity that Norway has enjoyed during the last ten years and the provision of abundant electric power to Bremnes from the mainland have led to a shortage of workers in the expanding industrial enterprises in the district. Factories and workshops can no longer be run patriarchically and the proportion of the population attending the prayer houses seems to be declining. There is however still no youth club and no public dancing, and Pentecostalists are not allowed to use school buildings for their meetings. On the local front the supporters of the dominant Pietist culture are hard-pressed but have not yielded ground.

Diminution of local support has, as we have seen, been accompanied, somewhat unexpectedly, by national success. Bremnes supporters of the Christian People's Party, after long years in opposition, find themselves forced to discuss national political issues in a context that is unfamiliar and radically different from the one they face at home. There are some party members who do not accept that new tactics are necessary and who hold that the sole function of their representatives should be to preach the word of God in parliament to their colleagues in other parties. But the very existence of a Christian political party is based on the recognition that Luther's notion of secular government by a prince who happens to be a Christian no longer applies to Norway. The party must do more than preach; it exists to restore by legislation the distinction between God's spiritual government and his worldly government. In particular it endeavours to ensure that the worldly government does not intrude into what properly belongs to God's spiritual government. Its policy is that Christians shall render unto Caesar only those worldly external things that are his and shall render unto God those internal things that are his alone, particularly the minds of school children. The policy and tactics of the party while in opposition, resisting the efforts of an anti-Pietist government to further secularize the school system, were clear enough. Now that the party is in power, the correct course of action is not so easily determined. In opposition the party could hold uncompromisingly to its principles but in power it is faced with the common, political necessity of compromising if it is to translate any of its principles into practice. The difficulties are particularly great for the supporters of the party in rural areas like Bremnes who are faced with a sudden change of scale in the relationships they have to consider, and with an unfamiliar political arena where they cannot estimate in advance the likely profit and loss from compromise. One solution to these difficulties is to appeal to the second clause of the Norwegian constitution which establishes the evangelical Lutheran religion as the official religion of the state, and to argue that so long as this clause stands, Lutheran organizations, including those that are Pietist, have a special claim to state support. Yet to link the Pietist movement with the constitution in this way would seem to lead it into the trap that caught the church when it became an organ of the state. It would convert the laymen's movement into part of God's worldly government, the lefthand kingdom of God, and remove it from the righthand kingdom and the direct experience of salvation. But it is too much to expect Bremnes party members readily to abandon a claim for special treatment for Pietist organizations and to advocate state support for all schools, including those run by Catholics. This is a step that even the secular Labour government did not take. The dilemma remains.

The complex task of reconciling ideology and organization is met with in many contexts. Many situations can be found that parallel the one I have described. The similarities and differences between the

Bremnes dilemma and those faced in one-party states based on anti-institutional ideologies are particularly striking. These comparisons lie beyond the scope of this paper. All I hope to have demonstrated is that in order to understand political action in a literate society, with its past encapsulated not in the malleable material of genealogies and myths familiar to us from tribal societies but in the more refractory stuff of books and printed articles of belief, it may be necessary to go back even to the text of a sermon preached four hundred and thirty-five years ago. More important, in large-scale societies, political decisions have to be referred to the various arenas in which they are arrived at and to which they apply, and these do not always coincide. The criteria used to decide between alternative actions may be broad ethical principles or may be derived from specific cosmological beliefs. The goals or pay-off may be here on earth or in the realm of the spirit or, as in the present case, both at the same time.

NOTE

I am much indebted to my wife and my colleagues A. L. Epstein and W. E. H. Stanner for their comments on an earlier draft of this paper.

REFERENCES

BARNES, JOHN ARUNDEL 1954 Class and Committees in a Norwegian Island Parish. *Human Relations* **7**: 39–58.

— 1957 Land Rights and Kinship in Two Bremnes Hamlets. *Journal of the Royal Anthropological Institute* **87**: 31–56.

— 1960 Marriage and Residential Continuity. *American Anthropologist* **62**: 850–66.

BONDEVIK, KJELL 1965 Kristelig Folkesparti. pp. 67–74 in Øisang, Per (ed.), *De 7 Politiske Partier i Norge*. Oslo: Gyldendal Norsk Forlag.

CRANZ, FERDINAND EDWARD 1959 *An Essay on the Development of Luther's Thought on Justice, Law and Society*. Harvard Theological Studies 19. Cambridge, Mass.: Harvard University Press.

EVANS-PRITCHARD, EDWARD EVAN 1962 *Essays in Social Anthropology*. London: Faber.

FORELL, GEORGE WOLFGANG 1954 *Faith Active in Love: an Investigation of the Principles Underlying Luther's Social Ethics*. New York: American Press.

FORTES, MEYER 1962 Ritual and Office in Tribal Society. pp. 53–88 in Gluckman, Max (ed.), *Essays on the Ritual of Social Relations*. Manchester: Manchester University Press.

HAMRE, ALFRED 1964 *Haugiansk Frukt: Sunnhordland, Hardanger og Voss Indremisjonssamskipnad Gjennom 100 År 1864–1964*. Bergen: Sunnhordland, Hardanger og Voss Indremisjonssamskipnad.

HERTZ, ROBERT 1960 The Pre-eminence of the Right Hand: a Study in Religious Polarity. pp. 87–113 in *Death and the Right Hand*. London: Cohen and West.

LUTHER, MARTIN LW *Luther's Works*. American edition. St. Louis, Mo.: Concordia Publishing House; and Philadelphia: Muhlenberg Press. 55 vols. 1955– .

— WA *D. Martin Luthers Werke*. Kritische Gesammtausgabe. H Böhlaul 69 Vols. 1883– .

MOLLAND, EINAR 1951 *Fra Hans Neilsen Hauge til Eivind Berggrav: Hovedlinjer i Norges Kirkehistorie i Det 19. og 20. Århundre.* Oslo: Gyldenda. Norsk Forlag.

MUELLER, WILLIAM A. 1954 *Church and State in Luther and Calvin: a Comparative Study*. Nashville, Tenn.: Broadman Press.

STRAUME, JAKOB 1960 *Kristenliv i Handanger, Sunnhordland og Karmsund: eit Sogeskrift*. Bergen: A. S. Lunde (Haugesund-Sunnhordland og Hardanger Krins av Norsk Lutersk Misjonssamband).

WOLIN, SHELDON S. 1956 Politics and Religion: Luther's Simplistic Imperative. *American Political Science Review* **50**: 24–42.

Heroism, Martyrdom, and Courage

An Essay on Tonga Ethics

ELIZABETH COLSON

INTRODUCTION

Evans-Pritchard's contribution to anthropology is formidable, covering as it does most of the fields of social anthropology. Through most of his career, however diverse his interests may have been, he has shown a consistent concern with expanding our understanding of the terms in which men conceptualize their physical and social environments. He has been adept at finding ways to examine an alien system of thought in its own terms and in making explicit the postulates with which a people operate. In *Witchcraft, Oracles and Magic Among the Azande* (1937) he explored the rationale of Azande magical behaviour and showed the relationship between this portion of their mystical beliefs and their system of morality. The seemingly irrational became rational when he had succeeded in extracting from Azande beliefs a set of principles which governed their actions. Azande thought became the standard by which we came to understand the nature of magical thought in general.

In this paper I am attempting to follow Evans-Pritchard's lead by devoting attention to a body of thought intimately linked to social behaviour. For twenty years I have been trying to work my way to an understanding of the ideas of the Tonga of Zambia about the nature of social life. Here I propose to examine the nature and implications of their thought about appropriate human reactions to situations of threat and violence. In other words I shall be examining ideas that involve what for want of a better term may be called courage. For analytical reasons I shall need to distinguish between two forms of courage: valour and fortitude. I am using valour with an implication of positive force to cover a public assertion of a position. In Western thought it is epitomized in the figures of hero and martyr. Fortitude implies the

19

acceptance of danger and hardship, but has no connotations of defiance against persons or society at large.

These preliminary definitions do not entirely meet the problem of finding a neutral medium for the examination of alien concepts. Courage is not a simple attribute which men can be expected to have or know simply because they are men. It is a complex idea with a long history. It provides a set for the interpretation of action and a standard against which actions are judged. Interpretation and moral judgement are closely interlinked and are assumed to be shared views held by all reasonable men. Yet Western ideas on the subject of appropriate action in times of danger, summed up in the term courage, provide no universal statement about an inevitable human evaluation of such situations. Other ideas may be equally but no more reasonable. As Evans-Pritchard long since pointed out, we cannot assume the principles by which men live. They are a matter of patient inquiry. Only when we know what they are can we understand the nature of social action in whatever society we are examining. I start the discussion with Western ideas of courage only because they are familiar to the reader. My primary concern is with concepts used by Tonga to explain and justify their behaviour. The confrontation of the two disparate systems should also provide a starting-point for further work on the comparison of ethical systems.

Tonga concepts of courage are not simple givens ready to be supplied to the observer. I have had to abstract them from the mass of behaviour in which they are implicit; for Tonga ideas on this subject are no more likely to take explicit form than were Azande concepts of witchcraft. Evans-Pritchard noted,

'I hope I am not expected to point out that the Zande cannot analyse his doctrines as I have done for him. In fact I never obtained an explanatory text on witchcraft, though I was able to obtain in the form of texts clear statements on dozens of other subjects. It is no use saying to a Zande "Now tell me what you Azande think about witchcraft" because this subject is too general and indeterminate, both too vague and too immense, to be described concisely. But it is possible to extract the principles of their thought from dozens of situations in which failure is attributed to some other cause. Their philosophy is explicit, but is not formally stated as a doctrine' (1937: 70).

The Tonga had little formal philosophy in the past, a fact no doubt related to the general austerity of their ritual and symbolism, and to the lack of elaboration of their social and political life. Until recently their concern has been with the here and now, and with action rather than intellectual pursuits. In this century they have increased rapidly both in numbers and wealth. Today they probably number some 300,000, the majority of whom live within the southern province of Zambia, though a minority of Gwembe Tonga are settled on the Rhodesian side of the Zambezi River. In recent years Tonga migrants have taken up land elsewhere in Zambia or have found work in the towns and cities of southern Africa. Until the 1920s they were subsistence farmers, depending on hoe cultivation, with herds of small stock and cattle where tsetse fly were absent. Since then they have shared in the economic development of their country. The majority still cultivate the land, but increasingly as cash-crop farmers using the plough and sometimes the tractor. Some have become industrial workers, teachers, pastors, government officials, professional men and women. Some 57,000 Gwembe Tonga, in Zambia and Rhodesia, underwent a major uprooting in 1957–8 when part of their homeland was flooded by Kariba hydro-electric dam. They are therefore well aware of the implications of economic and political development.

The Tonga language was first reduced to writing late in the nineteenth century shortly before schools were introduced and literacy become possible. Since 1950 an increasing number of Tonga writers have begun to produce a literature in ciTonga, though most literate Tonga prefer to read and write in English. Even those who remain in the remote rural areas now find their views affected by ideas stemming from the schools and from Western literature. Christians know and quote the Bible; school children for some sixty years have listened to its stories and memorized its verses. Both old and young also hear the spoken words of those who reflect the values of the greater world, as they listen to the wireless or to political leaders who seek to fire their imagination with the oratory of the political rally.

It would be foolish to maintain that a single view of life is common to all contemporary Tonga from university graduate and high government official or professional man to the illiterate man and woman who try to preserve old virtues in the face of rapid change. This paper reflects a philosophy which is probably rapidly disappearing. Much of what I have to say is probably now invalid even of those who live in remote villages. These too are becoming imbued with a larger patriotism as they become involved in the new nation whose leaders urge upon them the ideal of self-sacrifice in the interests of the general good or for the abstract idea of nationhood. In writing this paper I am not attempting to provide a guide to contemporary or future action. I am attempting to understand a point of view which seems to have pervaded much of Tonga life as I have known it, during periods of fieldwork among the Plateau Tonga of Mazabuka and Choma Districts, 1946–7 and 1948–50, and among the Gwembe or Valley Tonga of Gwembe District, 1956–7, January 1960, 1962–3, and July–August 1965.[1]

In the attempt to construct a systematic analysis of Tonga ideas of courage I have looked for consistencies in many different aspects of their life. I have also used many kinds of evidence: casual comments upon behaviour, discussions which somehow involved the subject of behaviour under stress, observation, the themes of tales and proverbs, the usage of words, and general impressions culled over a period of years from a great many parts of Tonga country on many different occasions.[2] I am following a method common to anthropologists who seek to understand a complex range of behaviour. In the hands of such a craftsman as Evans-Pritchard it has given us at least one masterpiece in the study that still dominates current work on the significance of magical thought and the relationship between it and morality: *Witchcraft, Oracles and Magic Among the Azande* (1937).

'HEROISM' AND 'MARTYRDOM'

For two thousand years and more, Western writers have glorified valiant deeds and given recognition to the hero and the martyr. *The Shorter Oxford English Dictionary* (1959) defines the one as requiring 'exalted courage or boldness', the other as involving the voluntary acceptance of death or great suffering 'on behalf of any belief or cause, or through devotion to some object'. Western concepts of courage are permeated with ideas associated with these two figures and thereby given a heroic cast. Currently intellectuals may be bemused by the non-hero or anti-hero, as an earlier generation delighted in the picaresque hero. Both provide a measure of the world's decay through their ability to survive by compromise and shabby dealing. Whatever their origins as existential characters in contemporary life, anti-hero and picaresque hero derive their significance as the polar opposites of the heroes and martyrs who dominate so much of Western literature and the tales still told to children. Political and social action, if it involves a challenge to authority or seems likely to lead to violent reprisals, is seen in terms whose emotional impact derives from the traditional glorification of unyielding resistance in a good cause: Leonidas and the Spartans in the pass of Thermopylae, the Maccabees in their revolt, Roland at Roncevaux, Daniel in the den of lions, Socrates drinking the hemlock, Peter who quailed and later chose the cross. Western ideals and Western idiom are imbued with this tradition. No one may know what actually happened at Thermopylae, but Greek imagination used an already formulated ideal to cast the event in an enduring form which still holds sway over Western imagination. Men are always being urged to resist to the end against aggression or to demonstrate the truth of their opinions by their sacrifice. Current happenings are interpreted in the form provided by the model.

Tonga imagination does not play upon valorous deeds. It provides other interpretations of events. Since neither heroes nor martyrs exist in their tradition, they examine what is happening by an appeal to standards which have little to do with any concept involving valour. Those of their actions which the Westerner would be likely to interpret as high points of valour, worthy of heroes and martyrs, are seen in a very different light by the Tonga themselves. They find no virtue in the last-ditch defence and no shame in cowardice. For them, as for the rest of humanity, life is not always good nor is it always preferable to death. But they do not expect others to choose death as a protest against the force of an opponent or as witness to the rightness of a cause, or to court death or serious injury for reputation's sake. This does not make them into anti-heroes; they have no feeling that they are reacting against an impossible ideal.

At first glance, their recent history seems to belie this characterization and to underline their willingness to die for a cause. They have frequently defied authority and opposed government programmes, particularly in the latter days of colonial rule. They have faced government officials with shouts of defiance and a shower of stones. In 1958 Gwembe Tonga of Chipepo Chieftaincy defied the government order that they move from their homes in the Zambezi valley which was soon to be flooded by the Kariba hydroelectric dam. Most villagers did not believe that the dam could create a vast lake. They thought they were being forced to move to clear the region for European settlement. Leaders of the newly formed political party, the African Nationalist Congress, encouraged them in their resistance. Eventually a large body of men gathered at Chisamu Village, charged the government forces, spears and knobkerries against rifles. Eight Tonga were killed; an unknown number were wounded. One might well argue that a people who can rise to heroic action must value heroes; that people who can die as martyrs must understand martyrdom.

The Tonga do not see events in this light. My appreciation of their perspective began to develop as I pondered a conversation overheard in 1963. A group of Chipepo men were angrily discussing a recent meeting with the European District Commissioner, who still administered their affairs in those days just before independence. He had urged them to dispose of many of their goats before these destroyed the vegetation of the resettlement areas. The Tonga regard their small stock as a valuable investment against lean years. They do not slaughter an animal lightly and part with one reluctantly. But the discussion was crystallized by the man who said, 'What can we do? It is just like the Kariba resettlement. The chiefs agree to what they are told and then they come and say we must do it. Well, I do not think we are going to stand up and be shot to keep our goats.' The others agreed. Who indeed, they said, would stand and be killed for his goats.

This led me to ponder their willingness to be shot for other causes and thus to their probable views on the heroic gesture or the martyr's stance. They had charged the police at Chisamu in defence of their right to remain in their homes. In 1963 the 'War of Chisamu' was still a favourite topic of conversation, much discussed in all its aspects. Now whatever the motives of those who died may have been, it was obvious that they had not become folk heroes. They received no honours, and they were not spoken of as having given their lives for their people or as having set an example of resistance. Instead the common complaint was that the government had been deceitful and men had died as a result. None of them, so it was argued, would have been so foolish as to take part in the charge if they had thought the government forces would open fire. They had called what they regarded as a monstrous bluff, trusting in the restraint of the Europeans. The Chisamu dead, five years after their death, were regarded as the unlucky victims of miscalculation rather than as men who had preferred death to compliance.

Survivors of the charge counted themselves as fortunate and were bitter against the government for encouraging them to risk their lives.

The Tonga view of the 'Chisamu War' thus described innocent victims caught in a violence they thought they had no reason to expect. Survivors expanded upon their fear when they discovered this was a real battle. They amused one another by arguing the honour of being the first to run and the first to reach home. Those who had not been present talked about fleeing at the sound of distant guns and how they had hidden in reeds or bushes until all danger seemed over. They admitted to two emotions, fear and anger. The latter was aimed perhaps equally at government and at their own leaders who had encouraged them into danger. Violent resistance to resettlement collapsed immediately after the Chisamu shooting. In succeeding years, until independence, a resentful morose people found considerable pleasure in needling European officials and their own chiefs by the display of their disaffection, but they did so with a keen eye for the limits to which they could press their attacks. People avoided protest that would again endanger their lives and property. Each government demand or order was examined for the likelihood that it would be backed by force.

The defeat of the African Nationalist Congress in the elections of 1964 produced a similar rapid retreat from fierce political opposition. Most Plateau and Gwembe Tonga were strong supporters of the ANC while they had little to fear from the violence of other parties. They were particularly fervent in their opposition to the United National Independence Party whose organizers and few local supporters they were not at all loath to attack. UNIP's victory brought a quick ending to this open hostility. Active ANC officials vanished into the obscurity of village life and tried to forget their former boasts, rather to the amusement of those whom they had once sought to inspire with fervour. Even before this happened most villagers had usually repudiated the idiom of heroic action in the cause of party and people which the leaders had acquired from European radical protest. An ANC leader who attempted to rally support in a speech wherein he called upon the people to die in defence of their party's cause got the ready retort, 'If you want to be killed, that is your affair. We want to live.' This was regarded as the appropriate attitude for the sensible man. Even village political leaders were likely to regard their heroic phrases as part of a political style and were either entertained or annoyed if I tried to discuss political intentions in terms of political speeches.

In the least politically active parts of the country, discussions of the relative merits of various political parties and policies usually revealed the determination to survive whosoever should be the winner. An elder expressed the common view when he told a politically active foreigner, 'All right, we agree to have independence. None of us is saying we refuse

25

to have it. We agreed to let the Europeans look after us. Now we agree to have independence. We are not objecting. We agree. We always agree to what is wanted.'

Tonga proverb emphasizes the wisdom of compliance: ' "Who surrenders is not speared in the hands" ' (Fell, n.d.: 247). A folktale in which leopard battles lion for supremacy ends with the leopard saying: ' "All right, I will fear you now, because I lack strength to fight with a great one like you." Then the lion said, "That is as it should be" ' (Fell, n.d.: 47). The leopard surrenders, but appropriately he surrenders only to force and does not argue that the lion is otherwise superior to himself. Tonga acquiescence to force does not imply support or approval or any willingness to continue in agreement if power should wane.

Willingness to compromise is a common enough human trait and reflects the basic concern of mankind with the need to survive however difficult the conditions. Before overwhelming force or in the face of certain defeat, what purpose is there in protest? Who would be silly enough to start a battle which must be lost? Most people most of the time would agree with the Tonga, but those nourished on tales of splendid defiance may need to justify their surrender by idealizing the force to which they submit.

The Tonga feel no such need. The man who comes to terms with superior strength is behaving according to accepted standards. His neighbours expect no more from a reasonable man. Both he and they agree that it is as foolish to brave the strong as it is reasonable to enforce one's claims against the weak. In the absence of chiefly office or centralized government in pre-colonial days, Tonga expected men to back their claim with a resort to force when necessary. It was considered legitimate to attack either the offender or some other member of his matrikin who might be more easily available. Whatever the abstract justice of the claim, men were likely to use force only if they expected to be successful in attack or immune to retaliation. A man with a strong body of supporters could ignore most claims against him and his dependants and could exact what he would from lesser neighbours for minor wrongs. Weaker men fled or found a protector. They waited to press a claim until they had found a vantage point from which to strike, hiding their anger beneath a show of acquiescence. The unaccompanied stranger was fair game to all unless he found a local protector.

Heroism, Martyrdom, and Courage

'MUKALI' AND 'MUKANDU'

The Tonga do not have a highly developed vocabulary to deal with the subject of courage. They have no terms which approximate the English 'valour'.[3] Torrend (1931) seeking a term for 'hero' had to settle for the phrase *u cita milimo mibotu a nguzu zinizini* (he who does a good work with all his strength). Several word lists cite *silubinda, mukozu,* or *sicamba* as translations for bravery or courage.[4] I have not found them in common use. The common term which in some contexts has the connotation of courage is *bukali* but this is better translated as 'fierceness' or 'anger'. Animals that attack, such as lion or leopard, and poisonous snakes have *bukali*. So does the man who ignores danger or is quick to anger. The fighter or the person who imposes his wishes on others is called *mukali*, 'a fierce person'. A man and woman who defied morality by living together in an incestuous union were said to have *bukali*. The drum beat associated with raids and danger is called *lyabukali*. *Bukali* and *mukali* though frequently spoken in tones of admiration can be used as reproaches, as in rebuking a child who hits out at others. It is said to be regrettable for boys to be born without a sister since they are then more likely to have *bukali*.

Since *bukali* is associated with violence, Tonga are likely to fear it as they do violence, perhaps because they are so familiar with its dangers. Axes, clubs, hoes, and spears are close at hand. Angry men who lose control cause great injury. Beer drinks, when inhibitions are low, may be the occasion for grudge fights of considerable intensity. Some men are notoriously dangerous when drunk, but any person under stress may give way to *bukali*.

Those who are persistently *mukali* are to be avoided. Either they are fools who do not count the cost, and therefore dangerous because uncontrollable, or they must have acquired powerful medicines which allow them to set others at naught with impunity. Court messengers who had to journey into other neighbourhoods were exposed to the violence of angry men smarting from a recent verdict of the court or indignant at being summoned to a hearing. Since the Tonga have little respect for authority, the messengers were not protected by the fact that they summoned people in the name of a chief. Those who survived in their posts for any length of time were likely to be tough men reputed to have taken medicine for strength such as *mangoloma*, made from stones found in an elephant's stomach, which gave both immunity to

27

blows and the strength to beat down one's opponent. Some of these medicines are said to involve the possessor in procuring the life force of his kin, who are thus a sacrifice to his search for strength. In the long run, the possessor must also expect to pay for his power with his own strength; for his medicine will eventually turn against his body and destroy him. A man who has such medicines need not become a public danger to those of other kin groups unless he also has malice or envy (*munyono*). Then he is almost certainly a sorcerer (*mulozi*) who uses his power to kill.

Fierceness and hardihood may thus be admirable qualities in some contexts, but for a man to be outstanding in either implies that he has acquired strong medicines and has at least incipient powers for sorcery.

Perhaps the converse of *mukali* is *mukandu*, which has some of the same connotations as the English word 'coward'.[5] The hyena which will not face the challenger but lurks in the bushes waiting his chance is *mukandu*; so is the man who shirks his duty in the face of danger or complains of pain. Children nearing puberty were once taunted into submitting to the removal of their upper incisors, the old mark of Tongahood and of maturity, by being accused of being *mukandu*. Women in childbirth are told to stifle their outcry lest they be known as *mukandu* to their shame. But in other circumstances no one feels that it is shameful to be *mukandu* or to have *bukandu*, which may be translated as the quality of physical fear which is regarded as common to both men and animals. Men say they avoid fights because of *bukandu*. They ascribe their preference for work above ground, even at lower pay, to their *bukandu* which leads them to avoid the mines. Those who ran at Chisamu thought their *bukandu* appropriate and amusing.

Mukali and *mukandu* therefore are not simple oppositions of good and bad as the English 'brave man' and 'coward' tend to be. *Bukali* is a quality which is always suspect but sometimes useful. *Bukandu* is a common reaction which becomes despicable only when it leads people to cringe from the inevitable demands of ordinary life.

I have never asked Tonga which is better, *bukali* or *bukandu*. I suspect that at heart they have some preference for the former though they do not glorify it in oral history or in folklore. On occasion they dramatize *bukali* in a public context. Gwembe Tonga still pride themselves on their neighbourhood Drum Teams (*Ingoma*) which compete against one another at funerals and occasionally at other times. Team display includes mimic warfare, replete with boasts, taunts, and fierce challenges. When opposing teams are traditional enemies or relations are tense from recent clashes, the mimic war is likely to erupt into a general mêlée in which men are sometimes badly injured since dancers are armed with spears and axes. Teams may depart for a funeral spoiling for a fight, boasting of how they will intimidate this or that opponent. Despite this, active participants do not thereby acquire a local reputation for valour. Drum songs as well as other dance songs which comment on events of enduring interest memorialize scandal or personal foibles rather than deeds of prowess. If a man wishes his deeds to be recorded favourably he must compose his own song which he sings perhaps more to himself than to an audience. I suspect, though here I am not sure, that most such songs would recount journeys and observations on life rather than displays of courage. Whatever their burden, narrative songs are personal to the singer and are not preserved as a form of communal history.

The Tonga may sometimes say that they had more *bukali* in the precolonial days than at the present time, but they do not think that they were ever great warriors. Plateau Tonga still told stories of the old days of raid and warfare in the 1940s when a few eyewitnesses were likely to be found in any village. They made no attempt to claim for themselves any heroism in battle or in defence. When they talked of Lozi raids, they sometimes awarded themselves the victory, but this was always due to sorcery or to the superior medicine (*bwanga*) of a local leader who was thereby able to send the raiding party away bemused. Of Ndebele raids they said only that they had been killed without being able to resist. Those who could, ran; those who could not, were killed or enslaved. It may be that Hopgood's informant was thinking of these raids when he gave the sentence, ' "Do not laugh at him. Don't you know that the cowardly hyena is the one who lives longest" ' (1953 : 103). One of the earliest accounts we have of the Tonga shows them as evading battle. This appears in the text dictated by a Tonga lad in the 1880s who was describing conditions on the Zambezi: ' "The Karange submit . . ., the Shukulumbwe fight, the Tonga neither submit nor fight, but they cross [the Zambezi] in canoes, and come to live on this side [the southern bank of the Middle Zambezi], returning [afterwards] to their homes, when they no longer fear the Lumbu" ' (Torrend 1891 : 286).

Interneighbourhood raids are said to have been fairly common at this period, but fifty years later few were interested in recalling any particular raid. None seems to have entered into folklore or become the subject for an elaborated narrative. The folktales still told around the evening fires between harvest and the next planting season evince the same lack of stress upon warfare or open resistance. In the tales stupidity is punished, as is evildoing. Generosity is encouraged, as is respect for kinship obligations. The tales also approve the clever person who uses trickery to rescue himself from a stronger enemy or to gain his ends. Crafty hare regularly wins his encounters with the powerful but guileless lion. Hare is described approvingly as being *ulicenjede*, i.e. having an eye to his interests. The term is used of anyone regarded as crafty, intelligent, and quick. A man who hastens to leave a scene of violence is *ulicenjede*, so is one who provokes his enemies to fight one another. The folktales openly show a preference for the man who is *ulicenjede* over one who is *mukali*. Indeed, the clever man uses *bukali* or *bukandu* as serves his purpose.

FORTITUDE

The Tonga may not have the hero and the martyr as types upon which to model themselves; they value intelligence above ferocity; cowardice is of the accepted nature of man. It might seem then that the Tonga scheme of life which gives so little emphasis to valour holds little place for courage. I would argue that the form of courage which they expect of their fellows is that best termed 'fortitude', which has been defined as 'Firmness in the endurance of pain or adversity'[7] or as 'the strength or firmness of mind that enables a person to encounter danger with coolness and courage or to bear pain or adversity without murmuring, depression, or despondency: passive courage: resolute endurance'.[8]

The hunter, who in the past pitted himself against large and dangerous animals with only spear or harpoon, showed great daring and was respected and emulated. The Tonga were notable hunters of elephant, hippo, rhino, and buffalo, showing a cool courage which aroused the admiration of early observers. Such men, however, worked with the aid of powerful medicines and with the shades of dead hunters to encourage them and to protect them. Those who lack medicines and shades (*mizimu*) are not expected to risk themselves in this fashion and would be considered foolhardy if they did.

Fortitude is a matter of daily living and a standard which everyone must meet, whether they have medicines or not. People again and again display such courage without question and quite incidentally as part of the normal course of events. The man who jumps from his bed in the dark to cope with a possibly venomous snake because his children are asleep on the floor may or may not think to mention the incident the following morning; if he does, he is likely to be interested in the possibility that the snake was sent by a sorcerer rather than with his own display of courage. Darkness is feared for many reasons, but those who call for help in the middle of the night to announce a death or a sudden emergency can expect their neighbours to cross the village to their assistance. Those who drive hyenas from their stock pens after dark may have little to fear from the hyenas but they also expose themselves to the attacks of sorcerers and ghosts who use the night to cover their raids. Men, and even women, have also pitted themselves against the lion attacking their stock, driving off the marauder with spear and axe. Only the latter would be likely to be called *mukali*.

It is also expected that people will bear pain without complaint. Women proudly boast that they have not cried out in childbirth though they say the pain is like a flame. Men and women brutally injured by some accident and those wretchedly ill bear their pain with stoicism. Babies wail and scream in minor discomforts, small children rend the air with their protests, older children have already learned to suppress signs of acute distress, even though they have a searing burn or a limb swollen with infection. Adults half-mad with pain still refuse to cry out. They also seek to cause as little trouble as possible to those who must care for them, dragging themselves to work while they can, lying quietly to one side when they cannot. When they have no hope of recovery, and the illness is such that they find their dependence unendurable, they have a further resource. For a few days they refuse to accept food or drink; then, having arranged their affairs, they pass into a coma which presages death.

Those who have sought to protect themselves against accident or sorcery by acquiring *mangole* medicine are said to be unable to die no matter how broken or decayed their bodies. The Tonga regard it as wrong for a person to use this medicine because it leads to trouble for his kin when he can no longer care for himself. 'It is right for a person to die quickly without causing all this trouble to others.' Someone who has succumbed to a desire to preserve life at any cost may still find in old age or helpless misery that he no longer wants his bargain. Then he tells his kin where to cut upon his body so that the medicine may flow out with his blood and release him into death. Extreme old age is seen as evil, bought at the cost of the living, and often by the use of medicine which drains the life from the young into the old.

The Tonga respect men and women who meet daily life with fortitude avoiding violence and contention, earning their own living, giving assistance when need be to their kin and neighbours. Of them they say, *balamoyo muyumu*, 'they have strong hearts'. These are the people they describe as *balilomene* 'upright people' or 'those to be respected'. Their virtues are the standard virtues which give no special renown outside one's own small community. Their attainment comes not with medicines but rather with conscious endeavour. Parents may advise their children to acquire medicines as a sensible precaution against the mischances of life and the malice of others. They insist upon the need to acquire fortitude as they insist upon the need to learn to work and to be able to take one's place in society. When men and women can no longer take an active part and their continued survival is a burden to themselves and others, then they should accept death with dignity even though the spirit world has few joys or comforts in comparison with this life. As spirits, however, they will again be able to help their kin and again become worthy of respect.

With this we return to the question posed early on in this discussion: 'For what is a man prepared to die?' The answer seems clear. In the interests of his kin, a man should be prepared to die, but only as a last resort when he can no longer serve them in any other way. He accepts death therefore on behalf of the only people with whom he has a long-term identification; for in the past at least Tonga society did not foster the development of a wider loyalty. Death in the interests of one's kin is a private matter which does not admit a flamboyant display of valour such as is associated with the Western hero. Nor does it require the passionate defence of principle associated with the martyr, since the principle involved is accepted by all.

I am not attempting to argue here that the form of Tonga society has engendered the attitudes described; there are too many instances of societies with much the same ideals but differing social forms.[9] I argue only that Tonga ideas of courage are congruent with the loyalties required of them by their society. In life and in death they are expected to practise the quiet virtue of fortitude.

Often enough the Tonga must feel that it would be a relief to forget the quieter virtues and to indulge in a display of *bukali* at whatever cost. On occasion they find in physical violence a welcome outlet to their resentments against the impositions of others. They admire as well as resent the forceful action of others. Yet on the whole they would agree that the fearless man is likely to be a danger to his fellows. They would appreciate Montaigne's dictum, 'Valour has its limits like other virtues, and these once transgressed, we find ourselves on the path of vice, so that we may pass through valour to temerity, obstinacy, and madness, unless we know its limits well – and they are truly hard to discern near the borderlines' (1965 edition: 47). The Tonga would add sorcery to Montaigne's list of evils here associated with the potentiality for valour, thus indicating their belief that men can excel in a defiance of danger, as in other directions, only at the expense of ordinary social morality.

NOTES

1. All field research save that in 1965 was financed by and under the auspices of the Rhodes-Livingstone Institute, now the Institute for Social Research in the University of Zambia. In 1965 the Institute provided hospitality and assistance but the research was financed by a grant from the African Studies Committee of the Social Science Research Council, New York City. Grants from the African Studies Program of the University of California at Los Angeles and from the research funds of the University of California at Berkeley have provided research and clerical assistance since 1964. The National Institute of General Medicine awarded me the fellowship which has made possible a year's residence at the Center for Advanced Study in the Behavioral Sciences, Stanford, where this paper was written 1968. Colleagues at the Center (Morton Bloomfield, Robert Levy, and David Sills) criticized an early draft of the paper. My colleague, Dr. Thayer Scudder, has made available all his field data from the Gwembe, including that from his most recent visit in 1967. A great many Tonga friends and acquaintances gave assistance over the years. I owe a special debt to my field assistant with the Plateau Tonga who also worked with me on the first visit to the Gwembe Tonga. This is Mr Benjamin Shipopa, now of Gwembe.

2. Full-length studies of the Tonga are to be found in Colson 1958 and 1962 (Plateau Tonga); and in Colson 1960 and Scudder 1962 (Gwembe Tonga).

3. No Tonga–English dictionary has been published. Torrend (1931) provides an English–Tonga dictionary which is badly in need of revision. Hopgood (1953) and Collins (1962) are grammars with word lists and

33

grammatical texts. Torrend (1891), a comparative grammar on southern Bantu languages, is largely based on Tonga. Torrend (1930), Joppe and Hobby (1950), and Nkazi (1957) are English–Tonga phrase books. Torrend (1891; 1921) and Fell (n.d.) provide folklore texts with extensive vocabularies.

4. Torrend (1931) and Nkazi (1957) gave *silubinda*, which must mean not a quality but the person who has the quality. I am unable to interpret further. Torrend (1931) gives *mukozu*. Collins (1962) gives *sicamba* which seems derived from *camba* 'chest' and to have the literal meaning 'the chesty one'.

5. Hopgood (1953) gives *mowa* or *moa* as another synonym for 'coward'.

6. *Oxford English Dictionary.*

7. *Webster's Dictionary.*

8. E.g. Smith and Dale (1920, v. 1: 170) comment of the Ila, close neighbours of the Tonga, 'To die in the last ditch would appear to almost all of them the height of folly. They themselves hold the view, and act upon it, that courage is shown, or a man's heart is strong, as they put it, under certain circumstances only.' The Ila are noted for their fearless defence of their cattle in the face of lions and for their pursuit of buffalo (ibid.: v. 1: 170; v. ii: 188).

9. Yet the Ila had more formal organization associated with small chieftaincies, large villages, and age-sets than did the Tonga.

REFERENCES

COLLINS, B. 1962 *Tonga Grammar.* London: Longmans.

COLSON, E. 1958 *Marriage and the Family among the Plateau Tonga of Northern Rhodesia.* Manchester: Manchester University Press.

— 1960 *The Social Organization of the Gwembe Tonga.* Manchester: Manchester University Press.

— 1962 *The Gwembe Tonga.* Manchester: Manchester University Press.

EVANS-PRITCHARD, E. E. 1937 *Witchcraft, Oracles and Magic among the Azande.* Oxford: Clarendon Press.

FELL, J. R. n.d. *Folk Tales of the Batonga and Other Sayings.* London: Holborn Publishing House.

HOPGOOD, C. R. 1953 *A Practical Introduction to Tonga.* London: Longmans, Green.

JOPPE, LEVI P., AND ALVIN HOBBY 1950 *English-Tonga Phrase Book.* London: Macmillan.

MONTAIGNE, M. de 1965 *The Complete Essays of Montaigne.* Translated by Donald M. Frame. Stanford: Stanford University Press.

NKAZI, L. 1957 *CiTonga Note Book*. London: Longmans.

SCUDDER, T. 1962 *The Ecology of the Gwembe Tonga*. Manchester: Manchester University Press.

SMITH, EDWIN, AND ANDREW DALE 1920 *The Ila-Speaking Peoples of Northern Rhodesia*. London: Macmillan and Co.

TORREND, J., S.J. 1891 *A Comparative Grammar of the South-African Bantu Languages*. London, Kegan Paul, Trench, Trubner.

— 1921 *Specimens of Bantu Folk-lore from Northern Rhodesia*. London, Kegan Paul, Trench, Trubner.

— 1930 *An English-Tonga Phrase-book for Rhodesia (North and South)*, 2nd edition. Natal: Mariannhill.

— 1931 *An English-Vernacular Dictionary of the Bantu-Botatwe Dialects of Northern Rhodesia*. London: Kegan Paul.

A Rotinese Dynastic Genealogy

Structure and Event[1]

JAMES J. FOX

INTRODUCTION

Since Robertson Smith, anthropologists have been concerned with the political use of genealogical statements. *Kinship and Marriage in Early Arabia* (1885) was the first extensive examination of genealogical fictions. Writing of various tribes of Arabia, Robertson Smith argued that the tribal genealogies were of practical interest because they 'had a direct bearing on the political combinations of the time . . . To make a complete system out of such materials it was necessary to have constant recourse to conjecture, to force a genealogical interpretation on data of the most various kinds, and above all to treat modern political combinations as the expression of ancient bonds of kinship' (1885: 7–10).

Among social anthropologists, Professor Evans-Pritchard has been foremost in developing the ideas of Robertson Smith. At first briefly in 'Nuer Time-Reckoning' (1939) and later at length in *The Nuer* (1940), Professor Evans-Pritchard proposed that genealogical time be considered as an expression of structural distance directly related to forms of lineage segmentation: 'the social distance between any two existing agnates is always strictly in proportion to the social distance that separates them from a common ancestor' (1939: 212). Nuer lineages and clans show a remarkable formal constancy. Minimal lineages generally consist of four to five generations, main clans have ten to twelve generations, and the ancestral founders of other significant segments must be placed between these points of reference. To achieve this, irrelevant ancestral names are obscured and finally forgotten, links in the direct lines of descent are dropped and collateral lines merge (1939: 211–16; 1940: 105–7, 198–203). Nuer tribes, like Nuer clans, segment to form structurally relative units and, by personifying the tribes and giving them a kinship value, tribes are assimilated to their dominant

37

clans (1940: 237). What is retained in Nuer genealogies is minimal in comparison to what must necessarily be neglected and obscured to maintain a political order, and even this is subject to reinterpretation as shifts in power occur among dominant groups.

This first major analysis of the political use of genealogies in the formation of an African segmentary lineage system has given rise to a considerable literature which has repeatedly confirmed Professor Evans-Pritchard's initial insight.[2] With recourse to a wealth of detailed Tiv genealogies, Laura Bohannan (1952) demonstrated this most clearly. 'Genealogies validate present relationships; these relationships prove the genealogies; and the form of the genealogy is modelled on the form of present relationships.' Moreover, a lineage system like that of the Tiv requires genealogical uncertainty and lack of rigidity for its own proper maintenance and continued survival (1952: 314).

Leach, among Asianists, has advanced a similar argument in reference to Kachin genealogies. Citing Evans-Pritchard's 1939 article on 'Nuer Time-Reckoning', Leach writes:

'Every Kachin chief is prepared to trace his descent back to Ninggawu Wa, the Creator. To do this some groups are prepared to put forward genealogies of forty or more generations. It is quite impossible to assert at what point such descent lines become purely fictional. My point of view is that Kachin genealogies are maintained almost exclusively for structural reasons and have no value at all as evidence of historical fact . . . it seems to me that all Kachin genealogies must be regarded as equally fictional. Undoubtedly they have *some* historical content but no one can say how much or how little' (1954: 127–8).

This tradition of genealogical interpretation is so well established within anthropology as to be unassailable. No one would now contend that genealogies are not subject to manipulation nor that their primary significance is not dependent upon structural requirements. Similarly there is no one form of genealogy; what is encoded within genealogies is dependent upon the selective criteria of particular forms of social classification.

Yet this situation is not entirely satisfactory. Historians and scholars have, since before the time of Robertson Smith, utilized genealogies, primarily dynastic genealogies, in the search for some form of chronologically relevant sequence. In the study of literate Asian societies, historians are inevitably forced to rely upon the extant genealogies recorded in inscriptions, genealogy books, chronicles, and court records and these scholarly endeavours cannot be completely dismissed.[3]

Whereas anthropologists have concentrated upon what is obscured and lost within genealogies and upon the principles for such exclusion, historians have had no choice but to concentrate upon what remains – what is retained and recorded. Initially, an anthropologist, too, has no choice – as Leach has argued – but to consider genealogies as part of a structural system, on their own right within the categorical order of the people he studies. To do otherwise would be to confound systems of classification. Yet it would seem that the anthropologist has little right to assert, without having first examined the historical evidence, that his genealogies are fictional and offer no evidence of historical interest. In the majority of instances with which anthropologists deal, this question must be left unconsidered because of the lack of historical records. It is the intention of this paper, however, to demonstrate that in at least one instance the genealogies of a non-literate people do retain historical evidence. Although genealogies are certainly structured, they are often far more than a simple rationalization of present structural relations.

My procedure and basic argument, in brief, are as follows. I examine the use of genealogy among the Rotinese, an island people in the Timor area of eastern Indonesia. I then consider, in some detail, the political use of dynastic genealogy in one autonomous domain of the island. Accompanying every dynastic genealogy is a traditional political narrative, a sequential commentary on the achievements of named royal personages. An integral part of this narrative is – of necessity – a commentary on the events of succession. I attempt to demonstrate (1) how, by means of this dynastic narrative, genealogically unrelated clans are brought into political association with the royal line and (2) how even contrary events of succession—the temporary loss of rule – are used to confirm the prestige of a single royal line. Finally, I turn to an assessment of Dutch historical records dating from 1653 and consider how these accord with Rotinese dynastic traditions. What is remarkable about these records is that they name – with only a few exceptions – all the Lords of Termanu from 1681 to 1965 and that these names are the very names remembered in the oral traditions of the domain.

Rotinese genealogies are unlike Nuer or Tiv genealogies. Similarly Rotinese lineages segment in a fashion different from those of the Nuer or Tiv. Consequently, I have adopted the term 'status lineage' (Gullick 1958: 69) to refer to the core of the Rotinese lineage system and, throughout this paper, I use the term more generally as a convenient means of distinguishing this system from that of the more classic African segmentary systems. Above all, I follow Professor Evans-Pritchard in maintaining that political systems based upon different forms of lineage segmentation yield dissimilar forms of structural time.

THE STRUCTURE OF THE ROTINESE DOMAIN

The Rotinese, who number some 100,000,[4] recognize no common ancestor. Their island is divided into eighteen autonomous states or domains (*nusak*), each ruled by its own Lord (*manek*) whose major task is to hear disputes and to give judgement at his court. Each domain maintains its own variant form of customary law, cultivates its own dialect and prides itself on its distinctive manners and dress. By 1662 twelve of the present domains of the island were already recognized by the Dutch East India Company. Despite a brief and unsuccessful attempt at consolidating the domains in the early part of this century, the island has retained much of its traditional political system and the government of the Republic of Indonesia has incorporated this traditional system in its administrative structure. The Lords of the domains, who are now recognized as government officials, hear court cases, collect taxes, and convey national directives to their peoples.

Each Rotinese domain is comprised of a number of named clans which constitute its traditional political units. Clans are confined to a single domain; there is no island-wide system of clanship. Every clan is ideally headed by a clan lord or court lord (*manesio*) who represents the clan at court and assists the Lord in rendering judgements.

Persons are divided into the classes, noble and commoner. Nobility resides in two clans, the clan of the Lord, the Manek, and the clan of his complementary and executant lord, the Fetor.[5] The title of Lord is derived from the root *mane*, meaning 'male'; the title *fetor* is found among several peoples of the Timor area and may be of Portuguese origin. The Rotinese, however, by native folk etymology derive this title from their own word, *feto*, meaning in certain contexts 'woman' and in others 'female'. And they see in the relationship of the clans of the Manek and Fetor a symbolic sexual polarity. In most domains these two clans are united in reciprocal affinal alliance.[6]

Lordship is the source of nobility. The greater nobles (*mane-ana*: lit., 'minor lords' or 'children of the manek') are 'agnatically' related and

40

ranked according to their genealogical distance from the line of the Lord; the lesser nobles (*feto-ana* or *mane-feto-ana*) are similarly related to the line of the Fetor. It is more suggestive of Rotinese usage to differentiate the descendants (both male and female) of the Manek as 'male nobles' and the descendents (again both male and female) of the Lord Fetor as 'female nobles'. [Henceforth I refer to the Lord Manek simply as Lord and the Lord Fetor as Fetor.]

All other clans in a domain are commoner clans. Commoners (*laus* from the root *lau-* which in other contexts has the sense 'rotten', 'filthy', 'ugly', 'illness', 'misfortune', and forms a verb meaning 'to do servile labour') are not ranked among themselves in any hierarchical order nor do they commonly claim genealogical ties one to another.[7] Each is, ideally, a singular unit and claims its own constellation of ritual privileges. Most of these entitlements are to distinguishing non-utilitarian symbols (i.e. the right to perform a lesser harvest ritual, the right of a certain clan to fire the first shot in battle, or the right to exchange horses – of equal value – with the Lord on the death of a member of his descent line, etc.). In Rotinese tradition, clan ancestors possessed or were given by their Lord land and water. Today clans retain the right to appoint a ritual sacrificer at sources of irrigation water, but land and other forms of property are held individually by clan members rather than by the clan as a whole.

One commoner clan in every domain is the clan of the Head of the Earth (*dae langak*). The Head of the Earth claims spiritual authority over the entire domain, including the clan of the Lord. He has the right, in certain instances, to contravene the judgements of the Lord, and claims various rights to rituals affecting the earth. It is reported (Jackstein 1873: 353) that until the 1870s when a Dutch Resident enforced a change, the Lord of the Earth alone had the right to keep, within his house, the staff of office conferred upon the Lord by the Dutch. At present throughout Roti, the Heads of the Earth, always elders, are looked upon as the most knowledgeable exponents of customary usage. There exists the belief in a formal antagonism between the Head of the Earth and the Lord of the domain. Each domain has its own legend to justify this antagonism.

Clans are comprised of named lineages (*-teik*). In contrast to the formal political order of the clans, lineages are subject to the full developmental processes of fission and segmentation. Lineages, not clans, become exogamous segments and marriage remains the acceptable

41

criterion for the determination of lineage segmentation. Lineages within noble clans are ranked in status and the genealogical connexions ordering these lineages are generally known and accepted. The lineages of the Lord and Fetor are the highest-status lineages of their respective clans; other lineages within these clans are ranked in accordance with their descent relation from these highest lineages; there are usually, however, a number of non-noble lineages incorporated within noble clans. Although they recognize their existence, noble lineages acknowledge no formal genealogical connexion with these other lineages and attribute their lowly status to dubious origins.[8] The lineages that make up the common clans are rarely ranked; the genealogical connexions among them are difficult to discover and, when such connexions are proposed, they are frequently confused and disputed. Some commoner clans have within them a prominent – but by no means dominant – lineage.

It is possible to make finer social discriminations in Rotinese, dividing lineages into *bobongik* (descent lines, literally 'birth groups') and ultimately houses (*uma*). Lineages like clans are ideally 'patrilineal' but women may in certain instances provide the vital links within a line of named male ancestors.

With this brief summary, it is possible to examine the use of genealogy in Rotinese society. I intend, however, to go beyond this simple formal statement when I consider the complexities of a single domain, that of Termanu in north central Roti.

THE USE OF GENEALOGY

Genealogies consist of ancestral names. An ancestral name is composed of two parts: two separate names. The first name of a person is determined by divination and selected from a wide range of father's or mother's ancestors' names,[9] but as a last name, a person assumes the first name of his father. Hence ancestral descent names (what Rotinese call 'hard names') form a simple system of patronyms.[10]

A genealogy is therefore an ordered succession of names, with a first name repeated in a succeeding generation as a last name. In reciting a genealogy, a Rotinese begins with the name of an apical ancestor and proceeds in a *direct line* to the name of the father of the individual for whom the genealogy is intended. (It is improper and highly offensive to mention the ancestral descent name of a living individual.) Recitation may be a simple succession of names or it may be given more stately form using the verb, *bongi*, 'to beget' or 'to give birth'. Thus, for example, *Fala Kai bongi Nggomi Fala, Nggomi Fala bongi Dulu Nggomi, Dulu Nggomi bongi Solu Dulu* . . . 'Fala Kai begat Nggomi Fala, Nggomi Fala begat Dulu Nggomi, Dulu Nggomi begat Solu Dulu . . .' In the proper recitation of a genealogy, there is no mention of collateral lines, no branching effect, simply a direct uninterrupted line of succession. A well-born Rotinese begins with his oldest known ancestral name and proceeds through the name of his clan's ancestor, his lineage ancestor, and eventually to the name of the ancestor of his descent line. Older ancestral names are shared with several lineages and possibly even several clans—for most nobles, these are beyond dispute; later names become progressively more private. The genealogy of an entire nobility in any domain presents a ramifying rank structure, a structure which is not extended to the majority of commoners. Yet from the viewpoint of any noble, his genealogy is represented as a single line of descent names. It is the anthropologist, not the Rotinese, who assiduously assembles all names to construct an all-embracing network.[11]

The recitation of ancestral names is described as *lona bei-bai*, 'bringing down the male and female ancestors'. The recitation of a genealogy is, in fact, an invocation of the ancestors. And Rotinese are extremely reluctant to invoke their ancestors without proper sacrifice. For those who are proud of their ancestral names and wish them to be known, there exist a variety of means. It is possible for a Rotinese to risk the recitation of his ancestral names if he is at a safe distance from his home or his domain. (One literate Rotinese who had for over a year promised to tell me the names of his ancestors finally gave me the names on a tattered sheet of paper just before I was about to board a perahu to leave the island.)

The customary method is, however, to request a chanter (*manahelo*) to recite one's ancestral names publicly. Chanters are specialists in Rotinese ritual language and they possess knowledge of the significant genealogies of their domain. They are not an established class of individuals and may be either nobles or commoners. There is always considerable rivalry among chanters and some argument as to who ought deservedly to be called a chanter. Yet there is no institutionalized means of according this popularly conferred title. Traditionally there were competitions between chanters at important rituals and these were judged by the Lord of the domain and his nobility. Folktales record similar chanting contests between domains. It is sufficient here to acknowledge the long-standing existence on Roti of ritual figures who have specialized in the memorization of genealogies and whose knowledge has been subject to the public scrutiny of the noble class.

Nobles, not commoners, possess significant genealogies. It is enough for most commoners to know the ancestral founder of their lineage and at most, the names of the ascending three or four generations above their own. Some Rotinese commoners, when questioned, claimed that others might know their genealogies but this rarely proved the case. Many lineage lords of commoner clans knew no more than the other members of their lineages. For eminent chanters, knowledge of these genealogies was unimportant and, in many cases, useless. For Rotinese of client origin, genealogies are often best obscured and forgotten. The mere suggestion that certain commoners might possess genealogies was itself considered laughable. The implication was simply that only nobles had significant ancestors.[12]

Noble genealogies centre upon the genealogy of the status lineage of their clan. Since in most domains, the genealogies of the Lord and the Fetor merge in some higher ascending generation, there is a single prestige genealogy for all the nobles of the domain. Furthermore the Lord's genealogy is the only wholly public genealogy of the domain.

Beyond the level of the domain, there is no accepted genealogy which unites the nobility of the entire island.[13] Each domain has its own separate prestige genealogy. The Lords and nobles of Roti are united among themselves, not by recognized descent, but by specific affinal alliances. Although the two noble clans in any one domain are genealogically connected, commoner clans are often neither linked among themselves nor related to the noble clans. The question, therefore, is how is political unity achieved within the domain. The answer is simply that all the founders of the commoner clans are associated, according to traditional political narrative, with one or another of the ancestors named in the prestige genealogy of the Lord. For this reason, commoners frequently know the genealogy of their Lord better than they do their own particular genealogies. The Lord, above all, possesses the significant political genealogy.

The ancestors of the Lord are credited with the political formation of the domain. Before the Lords, there were no domains; these were not created immediately but were formed by succession of noble personages who united, allied, and conquered the separate independent clans to form a single domain. To the genealogy of a Lord are attached dynastic

44

traditions which chronicle the political development of the domain. These traditions are 'mythic' in form. They have a structural rather than probable order. Yet they do refer to what are regarded as specific events in time.

I consider now the domain of Termanu and the genealogy of its Lord. I then summarize the dynastic traditions associated with it.

THE DOMAIN OF TERMANU

The domain of Termanu consists of nine commoner clans and two noble clans. The Lord's clan is Masa-Huk; the Fetor's clan is Kota-Deak. The nine commoner clans are as follows:

1. Meno	4. Ingu-Beuk	7. Ingu-Fao
2. Suï	5. Nggofa-Laik	8. Ulu-Anak
3. Kiu-Kanak	6. Dou-Danga	9. Ingu-Naü

Meno is the clan of the Head of the Earth. Formerly the Rotinese claim there existed the clan Leli and the clan Ndeko-Ndao. Remnants of the former clan, Ndeko-Ndao, have been incorporated as a small adherent lineage of Kota-Deak.

These clans are the named political units of the domain. Their existence as such is the result of former recognition by a Lord of Termanu. Consequently their clan status has little to do with present size or membership. The commoner clan, Kiu-Kanak, is the largest in the domain and its membership is probably equal to membership of all the other commoner clans together. Its constituent lineages are larger than some of the smaller clans. With the death of its last clan lord, Ulu-Anak is approaching extinction. Dou-Danga, Ingu-Fao, and Suï are of approximately equal size while Meno and Ingu-Naü are considerably smaller. Ingu-Beuk and Nggofa-Laik, long united in reciprocal affinal alliance, have now diminished to the point where they act not as affines but as a single exogamous unit.

In comparison with commoner clans whose lineages possess few status distinctions, noble clans are highly segmented.[14] The clan Masa-Huk is composed of – at present – nine noble lineages and seven adherent lineages of dubious origin whose status is only marginally noble. The lineages of unmistakable noble descent are ranked in their relation to the royal lineage. This rank order is given recognition by explicit formal statements about the minimum bridewealth that may be demanded for women of these lineages. Bridewealth in excess of this minimum establishes finer shifting gradations in the hierarchy.

At the core of the clan of Masa-Huk is the royal lineage, Fola-Teik, the status lineage from which all other noble lineages derive their status. The royal lineage embraces several lines of descent, including one important client line. Within the royal lineage the single most prestigeful line is the line of the present Lord of Termanu. His genealogy consists of thirty-one generations of ancestral names. The whole of this genealogy is as follows:

1. Paki Dae	17. Kila Muskanan
2. Hu Paki Paki	18. Kelu Kila
3. Dae Hu	19. Leki Kelu
4. Ndesi Dae	20. Amalo Leki
5. Edo Ndesi	21. Tola-Manu Amalo
6. Damai-Do Edok	22. Seni Tola
7. Paliko Damai-Do	23. Kila Seni
8. Sain Paliko	24. Sinlae Kila
9. Nggeo-Nggeo Sain	25. Fola Sinlae
10. Putu Nggeo-Nggeo	26. Muda Fola
11. Bui Putu	27. Amalo Muda
12. Kilo Bui	28. Keluanan Amalo
13. Kai Kilo	29. Pelo Keluanan
14. Bula Kai	30. Keluanan Pelo
15. Ma Bulan	31. Napu Keluanan
16. Muskanan Mak	

To this prestige line of names is attached nearly the whole of Termanu's traditional political narrative. Any event of significance for the domain is always 'dated' by reference to a name in the dynastic genealogy. Here I propose to summarize major events told in this narrative and related to the prestige line of the Lord. Necessarily, I reduce long 'legends' to their barest outlines and emphasize their 'charter' aspects. Many of these legends are, in fact, largely charters; clan legends, in particular, lay claim to a variety of rights and privileges. These legends, however, make highly complex symbolic statements and proceed by a number of recognized Rotinese means of argumentation. (One such means of argumentation involves 'proof by folk etymology'. A variant of this is 'proof by place name'.) The following commentary does little justice to the liveliness of the narratives. I begin with the first ancestor of the Lord and proceed through the genealogy to the present Lord's father. Not all names receive commentary nor are they all associated with specific events. In general, events tend to cluster around key ancestral names.

THE EXEGESIS AND COMMENTARY ON ANCIENT NAMES

Of the first twelve names of the royal line, little is said. These names are the subject of etymological exegesis and speculation rather than of full native commentary. Christian Rotinese, including many of the high nobles of Termanu, prefer to interpret their early ancestry in Biblical terms. Thus, it is explained, that since Paki Dae [1] initiates the sequence, his name must be regarded as an ancient Rotinese reference to *Allah*. By conflating Malay and Rotinese, the name Paki Dae may be interpreted as 'Earth Fastener', a suitable appellation for Creator. The name, Hu Paki-Paki [2], is left unexplained, but Dae Hu [3] (lit.: 'Earth Origin') is taken as an obvious Rotinese name for Adam. Further on in the genealogy, Nggeo-Nggeo Sain [9], a name whose closest literal translation might be 'Darkness on the Sea' but whose figurative translation suggests a 'Host (of Men) upon the Sea', is interpreted as a reference to Noah. The royal genealogy of the domain of Bilba has gone further in the development of this form of interpretation. Lasi Noa ('Old Noah') is included among the first ancestors of the Lords of Bilba.[15]

Kai Kilo [13] is the first of the significant names in the royal genealogy. His sons represent the first bifurcation in the genealogy, a bifurcation that is said to have occurred before the arrival of the ancestors on the island. Bula Kai [14] is a pivotal ancestor for the entire nobility, but especially the clan, Masa-Huk. Fala Kai, another son of Kai Kilo, is regarded as the ancestral founder of the large commoner clan Kiu-Kanak.[16]

For the clan, Kiu-Kanak, this common descent through Kai Kilo is in itself insufficient to establish the clan's complete political incorporation within the domain. The giving of a woman of the royal lineage of Masa-Huk, ten generations later, to one of the major lineages of Kiu-Kanak is more often cited as the specific event that led to the political incorporation of Kiu-Kanak. Thereafter the royal lineage and several of the high noble lineages of Masa-Huk have continued to maintain a special reciprocal affinal alliance with this particular lineage of Kiu-Kanak.

47

James J. Fox

Whereas it is nearly impossible to discover accepted genealogies for the other divisions of this large clan, the nobles of Masa-Huk are as much concerned with preserving the integrity and 'correctness' of the genealogy of their affinal lineage in Kiu-Kanak as they are with maintaining their own genealogies. They justify their marriage alliance with a commoner clan by deriving this clan's origin from any ancient bifurcation of their own prestige line.[17]

Four generations after Bula Kai [14], there occurs the name, Kelu Kila [18]. This juncture is not particularly significant for the Lord's clan, Masa-Huk, but rather for the Fetor's clan, Kota-Deak. Just as Masa-Huk is linked in affinal alliance with Kiu-Kanak, Kota-Deak is linked in alliance with the commoner clan, Ingu-Naü. The nobles of Kota-Deak, too, are concerned with preserving a genealogy for their affines. Hence the clan, Ingu-Naü, is acceptably derived from a brother of Kelu Kila, named Lai-Talo Kila.

In the telling of Termanu's traditional history, Ma Bulan [15] is the first of the royal ancestors to arrive on Roti. Landing on the south coast and wandering the island in a counter-clockwise direction, Ma Bulan eventually arrived in Termanu where he encountered Pada Lalais ('Heavenly Pada'), the founding ancestor of clan Meno. The two vied with each other to establish a personal priority between themselves. Ma Bulan won three symbolic contests; two he won by deception and one by demonstrating his knowledge of the sea and its tides, but since neither could establish a convincing superiority, the two agreed to a division of roles. Pada Lalais claimed rights over the earth and was given a series of ritual privileges, while Ma Bulan claimed rights to nobility and Lordship. The telling of these events is a long, structurally important tale. It is also the charter for the primary political division of the domain between the spiritual authority of the Head of the Earth and the temporal power of the Lord.

THE CYCLE OF THE DEEDS OF TOLA MANU

There is little commentary associated with the names from Ma Bulan [15] to the single most important royal ancestor, Tola Manu or Tola-manu Amalo [21]. Some elders insist that certain of the deeds attributed to Tola Manu were actually performed by an earlier ancestor, Leki Kelu [19].[18] In general, however, Tola Manu's prestige is such that events are given significance by their association with his name. To

48

men of other domains, Tola Manu's name is commonly known and used almost as if it were a title for all early Lords of Termanu. Even the present name of the domain, Termanu, is regarded as a Malay corruption of Tola [Tora] Manu.

It is noteworthy how the name Tola Manu has undergone, within the royal genealogy, what appears to be a slight adaptation. On the insistance of the Dutch, most Rotinese have adopted, in addition to their other names, an official last name (a *fam* name, possibly from the Dutch word, *familie*). The *fam* name of the present Lord of Termanu is Amalo, a name which occurs later in the royal genealogy [Amalo Muda: 27]. In all popular legends, Tola Manu is simply Tola Manu. When, however, the royal genealogy is recited in the presence of members of the royal lineage, Tola Manu invariably becomes Tolamanu Amalo, making explicit the royal connexion with this eminent ancestor. To permit this adaptation Manu Leki must appear as Amalo Leki.

Tola Manu is credited with expansion of the nobility (conceived of as still a single clan), the foundation of the domain and the incorporation, by conquest and alliance, of most of its clans. The tales of Tola Manu constitute what might be considered a cycle, an idyll of an ideal founder who concludes, in his lifetime, the formation of a domain. Yet the Rotinese frequently make the distinction that Tola Manu, though he prepared the Lordship, was not himself a Lord (*manek*) but only a warrior (*pelani*). Prior to his conquests, each clan dwelt separately and retreated, at the threat of attack, to its own defensible walled redoubt, perched upon some hilltop. The tales are richly specific. They refer to specific clans and specific places. In recounting them, I can here give only the briefest indication of their content.

Tola Manu's first alliances were with the clan lords of the related clans Ingu-Beuk and Nggofa-Laik. These clans were given the task of guarding the centre of Tola Manu's territory and his eastern flank while he waged war to the west. His first war was with the clan Leli on his western border and arose over a disputed source of water. He allied himself with the ancestor of Dou-Danga, a wandering goldsmith who had access to Leli's impregnable redoubt and with this ancestor's aid he was able to overcome the clan Leli. In recognition of his aid, Tola Manu bestowed a portion of Leli's land, rice fields, and water sources on the ancestor of Dou-Danga, thus accomplishing the incorporation of the clan within the domain.

The next war was with another clan, Ndeko, on Tola Manu's western border. The tradition parallels that of the conquest of Leli: an alliance, this time with the ancestor of the clan Suï, a stratagem, the conquest and destruction of Ndeko and the bestowal of the better portion of Ndeko's land upon Suï. (There are also further legends – all of them charters for present ritual exchanges – concerning Tola Manu and clan Suï.)

In another tradition of this cycle, Tola Manu conquers the clan Ingu-Fao to his east through the devices of his allies, the clans Ingu-Beuk and Nggofa-Laik. A further legend tells of Tola Manu's attempted conquest of the tiny island of Ndao; another of Tola Manu's rape of the two daughters of the then powerful ruler of Bokai and the expansion of the domain to the southeast to incorporate much of Bokai territory. Tola Manu also figures in Termanu's version of a popular legend of Korbaffo, a neighbouring domain: in this legend, Tola Manu bequeaths land – even now disputed – to Korbaffo on his eastern border. Interestingly, Tola Manu sometimes figures in a legend common to all of Roti. The legend recounts Tola Manu's subjugation of the domains of western Roti; the intervention of the Dutch, and a massacre by Tola Manu of the first visiting Dutchmen to the island. This same legend is also told in Termanu but these events are not attributed to Tola Manu but rather his great-great-grandson, Ndao-Manu.

Besides asserting claims to all of Termanu's present borders, these traditions account for the political incorporation of the commoner clans: 1. Ingu-Beuk, 2. Ngoffa-Laik, 3. Suï, 4. Dou-Danga, 5. Ingu-Fao and for the subjugation (and now virtual disappearance) of the clans: (1) Leli and (2) Ndeko-Ndao.

The final political act associated with the traditions of Tola Manu is the complementary division of his realm between his two sons. The eldest son, Lusi Tola, became Fetor and founder of the clan, Kota-Deak (lit. 'Outside the Walls') in which this title is vested. The youngest son, Seni Tola (22), became Lord and the crucial ancestor in the foundation of the clan, Masa-Huk. Thereafter the prestige line of the domain consists in what is claimed to be a direct succession of youngest sons.

From Seni Tola [22] to Napu Keluanan [31], the ancestral names are represented as an unbroken line of succession of youngest sons. Elder sons descended of Seni Tola are the founders of the principle noble lineages of the clan.

After Seni Tola, the commentary on the royal genealogy is no longer concerned with the foundation of new clans. Rather it is concerned with the formation of noble lineages within the clan, Masa-Huk.

A Rotinese Dynastic Genealogy: Structure and Event

Of the two sons of Seni Tola [22], the youngest Kila Seni [23] continued the prestige line; his elder brother, Edo-Seni was the founder of the noble lineage Hailiti-Tein. In the next generation, Pelo Kila, the elder brother of Sinlae Kila [24], was the founder of the noble lineage Nelu-Tein. The five elder brothers of Fola Sinlae [25] founded five similarly named noble lineages: Ndaomanu-Tein, Edo-Tein, Kila-Tein, Loe-Tein.[19] Muskanan Fola, the elder brother of Muda Fola [26], was the founder of the lineage Muskanan-Tein. Muda Fola is credited with giving his name to the present royal lineage Fola-Tein. Together the noble lineages of Masa-Huk, as opposed to the non-noble adherent lineages of the clan, comprise what is called *Faloa Saon*, its politically significant division.

The successors of Muda Fola continue the prestige line within the royal lineage. Elder brothers have founded a number of recognized but as yet unnamed descent lines. With the exception of one eminently successful client line (Fox 1968: 243–55), the lineage forms a large but strictly exogamous unit.

The whole of Termanu's political history may be represented graphically in relation to the prestige line as follows:

Ancestral Names			Clans and Lineages
1. Paki Dae	[Allah]		
2. Hu Paki-Paki			
3. Dae Hu	[Adam]		
4. Ndesi Dae			
5. Edo Ndesi			
6. Damai-Do Edok			
7. Paliko Damai-Do			
8. Sain Paliko			
9. Nggeo-Nggeo Sain	[Noah]		
10. Putu Nggeo-Nggeo			
11. Bui Putu			
12. Kilo Bui			
13. Kai Kilo			
14. Bula Kai	brother of	Fala Kai	Kiu-Kanak
15. Ma Bulan	contest with	Pada Lalais	Meno
16. Muskanan Mak			
17. Kila Muskanan			
18. Kelu Kila	brother of	Lai-Talo Kila	Ingu-Naü
19. Leki Kelu			
20. Amalo Leki	[Manu Leki]		

Ancestral Names			Clans and Lineages
21. Tolamanu Amalo	[Tola Manu]		
	alliance with	Kuüpana Telik	Ingu-Beuk
	alliance with	Bobo Telik	Nggofa-Laik
	conquest of		Ingu-Fao
	alliance with	Tule Nara	Dou-Danga
	conquest of		Leli
	alliance with	Baä Anin	Suï
	conquest of		Ndeko
22. Seni Tola (y)	brother of	Lusi Tola (e)	Kota-Deak
23. Kila Seni (y)	brother of	Edo Seni (e)	Hailiti-Tein
24. Sinlae Kila (y)	brother of	Pelo Kila (e)	Nelu-Tein
25. Fola Sinlae (y)	brother of	Ndaomanu Sinlae (e)	Ndaomanu-Tein
	brother of	Edo Sinlae	Edo-Tein
	brother of	Kila Sinlae	Kila-Tein
	brother of	Muloko Sinlae	Muloko-Tein
	brother of	Loe Sinlae	Loe-Tein
26. Muda Fola (y)	brother of	Muskanan Fola (e)	Muskanan-Tein
27. Amalo Muda (y)			
28. Keluanan Amalo (y)			
29. Pelo Keluanan (y)			
30. Keluanan Pelo (y)			
31. Napu Keluanan (y)			

Here a simple genealogical model forms the basis, the skeletal structure, for the political order of the domain. By a combination of descent, conquest, and alliance, all the clans of the domain and all the significant lineages of the noble clan are brought into relationship with the prestige line of the royal lineage. Its simplicity and order would argue that it is a direct expression or reflexion of present political relations in the domain. Its 'orthodoxy' is assured by the power of the present royal lineage and by the Lord of the domain. By fulfilling the contracts established through his distant ancestors and embodied in the genealogical narratives – in short, by affirming legendary clan privileges, the Lord receives, from the clans, their assent to his unique status position. He alone is recognized as the bearer of the prestige line.[20] As a structural model reflecting political relations, the royal genealogy appears no different than the genealogies of the Arabs, the Nuer, the Tiv, or the Kachin.

A Rotinese Dynastic Genealogy: Structure and Event

SUCCESSION AND EVENT: THE EVIDENCE OF THE NARRATIVES

Commentary on the royal genealogy, after Seni Tola [22], does more than detail the divisions of the clan, Masa-Huk; it recounts the vicissitudes of succession to the Lordship of Termanu. Lordship has not followed the ordered sequence of youngest sons portrayed in the royal genealogy. Yet deviation from this ideal order has nevertheless been used by the bearers of the prestige line to affirm their right of succession.

To begin with, the Rotinese claim no formal rule of succession by ultimogeniture. The closest approximation to such a rule is the unalterable rule that, in any otherwise equal inheritance of property, the youngest son inherits his father's house. In contrast to this rule, an eldest son alone has the right to replace his father as ritual participant in the ceremonies of former affines. In the succession to political office, all sons are considered equal. In succession to a lineage office, all members of the lineage are said to be eligible.

In the royal genealogy, the political ordering of the commoner clans ended with Tola Manu [21]. The political division between the clans of the Lord and Fetor was achieved by his sons, Seni Tola [22] and Lusi Tola. Kila Seni [23] succeeded his father as Lord and ruled jointly with the Fetor, Kiu Lusi, son of Lusi Tola. His elder brother, Edo Seni, founded the lineage Hailiti-Tein. In the commentary, nothing more is told of Kila Seni. The question of succession arose in the following generation. Pelo Kila, an eldest son, succeeded to the Lordship. Only after a long reign, was Pelo Kila succeeded by his youngest brother, Sinlae Kila [24]. In terms of the ideal order, the line of succession was temporarily broken yet returned to the youngest son.

At this juncture, the narrative is troublingly unsatisfactory. The only explanation suggested for this form of succession is that Pelo Kila, supposedly childless, was obliged to adopt a son to continue his line. Since this son could not succeed to royal office, the Lordship passed to his youngest brother. The implication is that Pelo Kila, had he been able to retain the rule in his line, would have done so. In Rotinese ideology, there is a deep antagonism between eldest brother and youngest brother.

By present standards, the explanation is questionable. Rotinese accept clients; they rarely adopt children. To this day, Pelo Kila is credited with founding the noble lineage, Nelu-Tein. His recognized descendants are important nobles in the domain. There is no suggestion that Pelo Kila ruled as regent until his youngest brother was mature enough to accede to the Lordship nor the suggestion of a rule that the Lordship should pass from father to eldest son and from eldest son to youngest son. Such a rule would explain many of the events of later succession but as an ideal, it would compromise the exclusive claims of the prestige line of youngest sons. What is striking is that the commentary on the royal genealogy fully admits the fact of Pelo Kila's rule. There is no attempt, for the sake of affirming an ideal order, to deny this rule, but only to disparage its legitimacy.

In the following generation, the same form of succession recurs. Ndaomanu Sinlae, an eldest son, succeeded his father Sinlae Kila [24]. He, in turn, was succeeded by his youngest brother, Fola Sinlae [25]. Unlike the commentary on the previous generation, the events of this succession are told in great detail. The narrative involved is long and complicated. It recounts Termanu's attempted conquest of neighbouring domains, a Rotinese request for Dutch intervention, the 'purchase' of Christianity, and finally the massacre of some of the first Dutchmen to arrive on the island. Ndaomanu Sinlae is accused of having treacherously slaughtered these Dutchmen.[21] As a result, he was removed from office and all his former subjects swore an oath of cat's blood that thereafter his descendants could never succeed to the Lordship. Again Lordship was restored to the line of youngest sons. The implication of the commentary is that the calamitous events surrounding the rule of an eldest brother belie any claim to legitimacy. The Dutch are represented as impartial arbitrators of right order who intervened to restore the rule to Fola Sinlae.

For two generations the succession of youngest sons is orderly. Fola Sinlae [25] was followed by Muda Fola [26]; Muda Fola was followed by Amalo Muda [27]. Thereafter an eldest son, Mauk Amalo, once again succeeded to the Lordship. In Termanu's legends, Mauk Amalo is credited with the wholly deceitful invasion of Dengka, a domain in west Roti. His rule is represented as disastrous but the cause for his dismissal by the Dutch is not entirely clear. The usual explanation involves Mauk Amalo's refusal to release war prisoners from Dengka and his branding these men and women as slaves. (The explanation is phrased in terms of the customary proof by folk etymology and reference to place name.)

At his dismissal, the Lordship of Termanu left the royal lineage, Fola-Tein and was given to the lineage Hailiti-Tein, founded by Edo Seni, the other son of Seni Tola [22]. Kiuk Pelo succeeded to the Lordship and was followed by his son, Fangidae Kiuk. After a relatively short reign by these Lords, the office again reverted to the legitimate line. Mauk Amalo's youngest brother was Keluanan Amalo [28]. He never held the Lordship. But his youngest son, Pelo Keluanan [29] restored the Lordship to Fola-Tein. (At this point, the rulers of Termanu began to use Dutch/Christian *fam* names. Pelo Keluanan took the Christian name Michiel, and was known both as Michiel Keluanan and as Michiel Amalo.) The explanation for the return of the Lordship is couched in traditional terms. A woman of Fola-Tein, Tali Hanik, daughter of Hanik Amalo, was given in marriage to a European and through the intercession of this powerful ally, the Lordship was returned to its rightful claimant.

But again the Lordship left the line of youngest sons and was held by another member of the royal lineage, Kila Muskanan (who used the Christian name Stephanus Paulus Amalo.) There are various humorous tales told of this Lord. Educated as a sailor, he is said to have known little of Termanu custom and to have had great difficulties with the native language. To this day, he is jokingly referred to as *Mane Makabebek* and *Mane Lela Foe*. Both nicknames involve Rotinese puns. *Mane Makabebek* might be rendered either as 'The Lord who acted like a duck' (the sound of a duck being *bek, bek*) or 'The Lord who was always asking what? what?' (*bek* is 'what' in Rotinese). The nickname *Mane Lela Foe* compares the Lord to a water buffalo with white markings. According to the chants, these water buffalo emerged from the sea and were the gift of the crocodile and shark. According to present day Rotinese the Lord had, from his youth, white whiplash scars on his person. His personal inabilities rendered him incapable of proper rule.

In Termanu's traditions, after Kila Muskanan the Lordship was to have passed to Keluanan Pelo (Jeremias Michiel Amalo) [30], but he died suddenly in Kupang on Timor where he had gone to receive the formal recognition of the Dutch government. Again for want of a proper successor, the Lordship was held by a member of Hailiti-Tein, Dama Balo (who had the Christian name Salmun Pela).

At this point the royal genealogy enters the realm of living memory. Those cited in the genealogy or concerned with succession are the fathers of prominent noble Rotinese. Keluanan Pelo had three sons: Funu Keluanan (Christofel Jeremias Michiel Amalo), Muku Keluanan (Christian J. M. Amalo) and Napu Keluanan (Johannis J. M. Amalo). Napu

Keluanan succeeded to the Lordship; he, in turn, was succeeded by his brother Funu Keluanan who held the native title of Lord through the period of attempted Dutch administrative change on Roti. His Dutch title varied. These administrative changes were abruptly ended by the Japanese invasion. Two sons of Funu Keluanan ruled in turn during the Japanese occupation. After the Japanese occupation, the structure of the old political domains was continued and the youngest son of Napu Keluanan succeeded to the Lordship, once again restoring the prestige line of the youngest son. Ernst Amalo's accession once again marked the end of a period of disruptive rule. Order and legitimacy coincided.

It is possible to compare diagramatically the prestige line of the royal genealogy with the longer and more complicated line of succession as recounted by the Rotinese elders.

Prestige Line	*Lords of Termanu*
21. Tola Manu	Tola Manu
22. Seni Tola	Seni Tola
23. Kila Seni	Kila Seni
	Pelo Kila [e]
24. Sinlae Kila	Sinlae Kila [y]
	Ndaomanu Sinlae [e]
25. Fola Sinlae	Fola Sinlae [y]
26. Muda Fola	Muda Fola [y]
27. Amalo Muda	Amalo Muda [y]
	Mauk Amalo [e]
28. Keluanan Amalo	
	Kiuk Pelo [Hailiti-Tein]
	Fangidae Kiuk [Hailiti-Tein]
29. Pelo Keluanan	Pelo Keluanan (M. Amalo)
	Kila Muskanan (S.P. Amalo)
30. Keluanan Pelo (J. M. Amalo)	
	Dama Balo [Hailiti-Tein]
31. Napu Keluanan	Napu Keluanan (J. J. M. Amalo) [y]
	Funu Keluanan (C. J. M. Amalo)
	G. J. Amalo
	A. Ch. Amalo
32. Ernst J. J. Amalo	Ernst J. J. Amalo [y]

The genealogy of the Lord of Termanu is an oversimplification. It is, however, an assertion of a moral order, the way in which things *ought* to be. The fact that repeatedly succession has returned to the youngest son is taken as proof of this line's moral superiority—its right to succession. The events of succession are an integral part of the royal narratives. Certain of these events are deviations from proper order. The fact that proper order has always been restored is convincing proof of its validity.

SUCCESSION AND EVENT: THE DUTCH EVIDENCE

The earliest European references to Roti are Portuguese. These date from the late sixteenth century, when the island was known as Savu Pequeno. The island was the subject of a dispute between the Dominican and the Jesuit orders. The Dominicans were the first to establish a mission. This mission was short-lived, and in 1621 the Jesuits attempted to install themselves on the island, whereupon the Dominicans asserted their prior mission right and briefly (around 1630) replaced the Jesuits (Leitão 1948: 161–72). On the basis of present Portuguese archival material, it is difficult to assess the degree of Portuguese involvement on the island to the middle of the seventeenth century. All indications are that this was slight. Thereafter from approximately 1650 to 1750 the island was disputed by the Dutch East India Company and a small group of Portuguese-speaking sandalwood traders of mixed descent who were centred first on Solor, then on Flores, and eventually on Timor. In the literature of the period, these independent Portuguese are known as the Topassen or 'Black Portuguese' (Boxer 1947). In Rotinese, they are remembered as the *Sina Nggeo*, the 'Black Chinese'.

There are few Dutch references to Roti before 1653. When, however, traders of the East India Company had firmly established themselves at Castle Concordia in Kupang on Timor, they sought alliances with the local rulers of Roti and in their attempt to secure and maintain these alliances against the incursions of the Black Portuguese, they were able, for a period of well over a hundred years, to report (sometimes in considerable detail) on the political developments of the island. The bulk of these reports were entered in the Company's Daily Log Book (*Daghregister*) in the Castle of Batavia. Other valuable information is to be found in the Register of General Resolutions passed by the Castle of Batavia and especially in the four separate treaties of contract signed by the Company with rulers of Roti in 1662, 1691, 1700, and 1756 (*Corpus Diplomaticum Neerlando-Indicum* Part I–VI: 1907–1955). Relations between the Company and the Rotinese were secure enough in 1656 for a general resolution to be accepted (but never acted upon) to destroy Castle Concordia and to remove the Company's settlement from Kupang to Roti: 'The island', it was argued, 'is fruitful, well-peopled, already for the most part under our control and very well positioned against the trouble and damage of the Portuguese' (*Daghregister* 1656–1657, 1904: 11).

Rather than discuss in detail the complexities of Rotinese local history, I would like to indicate – for the purposes of this paper – (1) the relative stability of the Rotinese domains over the past 300 years and (2) the relative stability of the clans of Termanu over the past hundred years. I would then like to examine those events recorded by the Dutch which concern the domain of Termanu and the genealogy of its Lord.

DUTCH EVIDENCE ON THE DOMAINS OF ROTI

The eighteen present-day domains of Roti are roughly from west to east: 1. Delha, 2. Oenale, 3. Thie, 4. Dengka, 5. Loleh, 6. Lelain, 7. Baä, 8. Termanu, 9. Keka, 10. Talae, 11. Bokai, 12. Lelenuk, 13. Diu, 14. Korbaffo, 15. Bilba, 16. Oepao, 17, Ringgou, 18. Landu.

The East India Company never attempted to treat the island as a whole nor did it recognize a paramount ruler. All treaties were with specific rulers. The Company's early punitive expeditions were mainly directed against specific domains which were allied with the Black Portuguese or against those domains which refused to honour their contracts. By their treaties of contract, the Company appears to have frozen what might otherwise have continued to be a fluid political system of conquest and alliance. Legally, Dutch involvement with the island until the twentieth century was based exclusively upon early trading treaties (Resink 1968: 129). In fact, these treaties were interpreted as allowing the Company, and later the Dutch government, the right to act as an external arbitrator in local political disputes. The Dutch frequently acted to end hostilities between warring domains, to return conquered territories and to restore 'legitimate' rulers.

In 1653, the Lords of the four easternmost domains – Landu, Oepau, Ringgou, and Bilba – swore allegiance to the Company's officer in Kupang and, in the following year, 'to strengthen his allies there against their enemies', this officer with a contingent of Rotinese and Kupangese attacked and burned the neighbouring domain of Korbaffo which had remained allied with the Portuguese (*Daghregister* 1653, 1888: 154; *General Missiven*, II, 1639–1655: 750). Although no mention

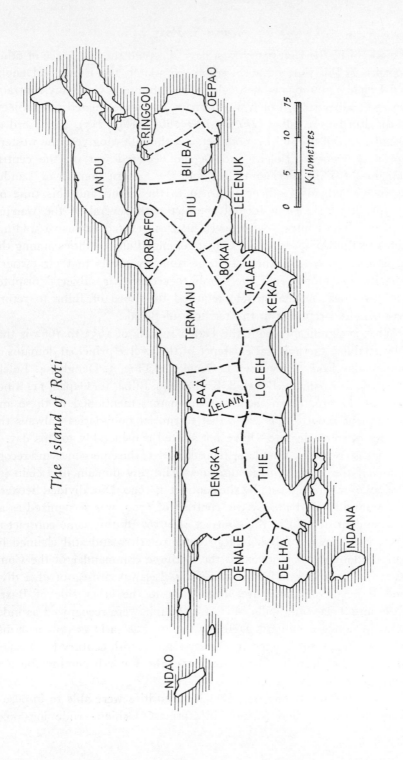

The Island of Roti

LANDU

RINGGOU

OEPAO

BILBA

DIU

LELENUK

KORBAFFO

BOKAI

TALAE

TERMANU

KEKA

LOLEH

BAÄ

LELAIN

DENGKA

THIE

NDANA

OENALE

DELHA

NDAO

Kilometres

0 5 10 15

is made of it, the Company must have accepted the allegiance of other domains at this time because, seven years later, the Lords of Dengka and Loleh were reported as negligent in fulfilling a Company contract. On 19 October 1660, Loleh was overrun, and an estimated 500 subjects of the Lord were killed (*Daghregister* 1661, 1889: 217). The Lord of Dengka agreed to fulfil his contract, but the following year the western Lords of Dengka, Loleh, and Oenale declared war on the central domains of Thie, Termanu, Baä, and the eastern domain of Landu. Again a Company's officer returned to the island and this time on 27 July 1662 signed a formal contract with several of the warring domains. The contract with seven articles granted exclusive trading-rights to the Company's representative, ended all hostilities among the signatories, called for the return of runaway slaves to their owner's domain, and empowered the Lords to settle their subjects' disputes over livestock. A final article required the Lord of Bilba to return prisoners and refugees to the territory of Bokai.

What is significant about the Dutch reports of 1653 to 1662 is that they establish the political existence of the twelve principal domains of present-day Roti. These are: 1. Oenale, 2. Thie, 3. Dengka, 4. Loleh, 5. Baä, 6. Termanu, 7. Bokai, 8. Korbaffo, 9. Bilba, 10. Oepao, 11. Ringgou, 12. Landu. From the few place-names mentioned in these and subsequent reports it is clear that territorial boundaries – always the subject of some dispute – have not shifted considerably to this day.

It is also possible, from later reports, to date the emergence and recognition of the island's other domains. The tiny domain of Lelain (or Ossipoko) was recognized by the contract of 1690. Diu, divided between Termanu and Korbaffo by the contract of 1700, was recognized as an independent domain in the contract of 1756. By this same contract of 1756, the domain of Bokai (apparently rulerless and still claimed by various domains) was given to the Rotinese commander of the Company's native mercenaries or *mardijkers*. Lelenuk arose out of a division of Bokai sometime after 1756 while to the other side of Bokai, Keka and Talae, originally part of Termanu, were recognized as independent domains in 1772. Delha (mentioned as early as 1665 as a distinct territory) was created in the early nineteenth century by division of Oenale between its Lord and Fetor, the Fetor becoming the new Lord of Delha.

It was not until 1887 that Dutch authorities were able to impose a common demarcation (using – in Rotinese fashion – rude log poles carved in human effigy) of all domain borders on Roti. To this day, this boundary demarcation is unacceptable to some domains. Nevertheless, the Company's recognition of a number of independent, autonomous states, each with a legitimate Lord and Fetor (the earliest Dutch documents refer to both: *koning* or *regent* and his *tweede* or *tweede regent*) fixed and established the pattern of Rotinese state for subsequent centuries. This is a major factor in understanding Rotinese political systems.

DUTCH EVIDENCE ON THE CLANS OF TERMANU

Clans are the ideal political units of a domain. In a formal sense, the Lord of a domain creates the clans by his royal recognition, by bestowing certain rights and privileges upon a clan, and by permitting each clan representation at his court. Thus all clans exist by royal charter and, as I have attempted to demonstrate in the case of Termanu, the creation of each clan must be accounted for in the narrative that accompanies the Lord's genealogy.

In Termanu, in the course of time, some clans have disappeared, others have diminished considerably, while others have grown and now have membership equal to three or four of the smaller clans. Segmentation continues within the clans; the marriage and alliance of lineages and lesser descent groups is adapted to this continual segmentation. To far lesser extent, the court has adapted to these developments (Fox 1968: 175–275). But for a clan to segment and a new clan to come into existence requires the recognition of the Lord. In Termanu, no new clan has been recognized in the past hundred years. As evidence of this, it is possible to cite several Dutch sources.

The Baron van Lynden, the Dutch resident on Timor, concluded a report on Roti in 1851 with a list of the names of the 'radjas' and 'fetors' and – what he called – the 'principal villages' (*voornaamste kampongs*) of each domain of the island. This list for Termanu names eleven clans. Another list of the clans of Roti was published in a curious short article by F. S. A. de Clercq in the year 1874. In this article de Clercq, who gathered his information from Rozet, the Dutch *posthouder* on Roti, gives a long catalogue of village names and he adds to this a further list of what he identifies – quite properly – as descent groups (*geslachten*). This list of clans is more inclusive than that of Baron van Lynden. A third list of Termanu's clans is to be found under the word *leo* (clan) in Jonker's dictionary of ordinary Rotinese (1908: 300). The texts for this dictionary were gathered at about the turn of the century and the list is virtually identical to the list of clans named by the Rotinese today. The three lists are as follows:

van Lynden (1851)	*de Clercq (1874)*	*Jonker (1908)*
1. Masa hoek	Masa hoek	Masa-Huk
2. Kioek anak	Kioek anak	Kiu-Kanak
3. Soe iek	Soei	Suï
4. Inggoe naoeh	Ingo naoe	Ingu-Naü
5. Dan dangah	Dodanga	Dou-Danga
6. Inggoe faoh	Ingo fao	Ingu-Fao
7. Oeloe anak	Oeloe anak	Ulu-Anak
8. Menoh	Meno	Meno
9. Inggoe beoek	Ingoe Beoek	Ingu-Beuk
10. Gofa-laik	Gofa laik	Nggofa-Laik
11. Lelik	Leli	[Leli]
12.	Kota-deak	Kota-Deak
13.	Deko	[Ndeko]
14.	Ingo ndaoes	[Ingu-Ndao]
15.	Boto-kameng	
16.	Endae [?]	

In present traditions, Termanu is composed of eleven clans: nine commoner clans and two noble clans. Leli and Ndeko (usually referred to as the amalgam Ndeko-Ndaos) are no longer recognized as clans. The remaining members of Leli are said to have been pressured into migrating to the domains of eastern Roti and to Timor. The remnants of Ndeko and Ndaos now form a single small lineage incorporated within Kota-Deak. The clan Ulu-Anak presents a serious challenge to this ideal order. The last Lord for this clan died prior to my arrival in Termanu; his son is incapable of replacing him and the clan is all but extinct. It is noteworthy that while Leli and Ndeko figure prominently in the royal narratives, there is no legend linking Ulu-Anak to the royal line. I was assured by several elders that such a legend existed but no one was able (or willing) to recount it. Ingu-Beuk and Nggofa-Laik also deviate from this ideal order. These tiny allied clans are regarded, in certain contexts, as separate clans and, in others, as a single amalgamated clan.

Van Lynden's list differs therefore from present ideals in that it includes Leli but fails to name the clan Kota-Deak. Interestingly, van

A Rotinese Dynastic Genealogy: Structure and Event

Lynden records eleven clans, as do present-day Rotinese. De Clercq's list includes Kota-Deak as well as Leli. It also lists Ndeko and Ingu-Ndaos as separate clans. Boto-Kama is a diminished non-noble lineage (with special court privileges) now incorporated in the clan Masa-Huk. It is intriguing to speculate that Boto-Kama may once have been a separate clan. Only Endae is unrecognizable as a descent group in Termanu. Jonker records the names of the same eleven clans cited to this day. Elsewhere in his dictionary (1908: 204, 295, 417) he does, however, enter the names Leli, Ndeko, and Ingu-Ndao.[23]

It would appear that in the face of contrary reality, the Rotinese of Termanu have continued to assert an ideal structure based upon two ruling clans and nine ruled clans. Nine is a ritual number symbolic of fullness and it is relevant that the court lords representing the commoner clans are still referred to as *manesio*, Lords of Nine.

DUTCH REFERENCES TO EVENTS IN TERMANU

The events I recount here are fragments. They are given form by the fact that they all refer to Termanu and they are cited in chronological order. Their further value – for the argument of this paper – is that they allude to events of significance in the royal narratives. I record these events in a strict chronology, confining my commentary to brackets.

1661 This is the first Dutch mention of Termane [Termanu]. The 'Kings' of Dengka, Loleh, and Oenale swore a war oath against Thie, Termanu, Baä, and Landu (*Daghregister* 1661, 1889: 217).

1662 Commissaris Cuylemburg signed, on Roti, the first formal Company contract with the rulers of Roti: Kieu [Kiuk] was the signatory for Termanu. There is no indication of his rank or title. [Throughout the 1660s and 1670s, the domains of east and west Roti were several times in revolt and suffered savage punitive expeditions. Termanu remained loyal. By the fact that it never suffered reprisal raids, Termanu appears to have been – throughout its history – a staunch Company ally.]

1681 The *Daghregister* reports that Thie, Oenale, and Dengka rebelled against the Company and its allies Ossipoko [Lelain] and Termanu; the rebellious domains were laid waste by an expedition of 600 men. Dam in his *Beschryvinge van de Oostindische Compagnie* (Vol. II: 258–259) recounts that shortly before this time the 'territory Leli' was punished for its rebellion, was overrun, and suffered the loss of 'about 500'. This caused such fear throughout Roti that the other rebellious 'Kings' sought peace.

1681 The *Daghregister* contains a letter from radja Pelo, his second, Zadeck or Saocq [Saduk], and other radjas of Timor to the Governor General in Batavia (*Daghregister* 1681, 1919: 617–18). All radjas requested a quantity of gold as a sign of loyalty and in addition, Pelo and Saduk requested a drum and a flag. [In the genealogy of Kota-Deak, Sadu Kiu is named as the Fetor who was contemporary with Pelo Kila (and later Sinlae Kila). His father, Kiu Lusi (son of Lusi Tola, the founder of Kota-Deak) was Fetor to the Lord Kila Seni. The 'Kieu' who was signatory to the contract of 1662 would appear to have been Kiu Lusi.]

1682 The *Daghregister* records a letter of reply from Cornelis Speelman, the Governor General, to the radjas and heads of Roti and Timor granting, along with other gifts, a flag and drum to 'Radja Pelo' and his '*mede-regent* Sadok'. (The letter also urged the radjas to be less brutal and destructive in putting down subsequent rebellions) (*Daghregister* 1682, 1928: part 1, 262–4).

1682 Again the *Daghregister* contains a letter, this time of thanks, from the radjas of Roti and Timor to the Governor General which concludes with the passage '. . . Radja Pelo of Termane and Poughoulou Sadok heartily thank their Excellencies for their great and evident friendship and are prepared to remain under the protection of the Company as long as the sun and moon shall give their light and will never forget the Company's name by the day or night, morning or evening to all eternity. Radja Pelo and Poughoulou Zadok[24] also request two muskets as a sign that the Company is disposed to send affection to us' (*Daghregister* 1682, 1931: part II, 1188). [The passage – originally written in Dutch – follows the formal phraseology which the Rotinese and Timorese still utilize today.]

1691 The second formal treaty concluded between the Company and the rulers of Roti was signed with the mark of 'Pelo Kina [Pelo Kila], King of Termane'.

1700 The third formal treaty between the Company and the rulers of Roti was signed in Castle Concordia with the mark of 'Sinlay Kiera [Sinlae Kila], King of Termane' and 'Sadok-Kieuw [Sadu Kiuk], second regent of Termane'. [In Rotinese traditions, Sinlae Kila succeeded his elder brother Pelo Kila while Sadu Kiuk continued to rule as Fetor.]

1737 In a report prepared by Commissaris Paravacini in 1756 on the problem of succession to the Lordship of Landu, there is mention of the fact that the youth recognized as Landu's Lord in 1737 was under the influence and control of his 'uncle, the noted Regent of Termano, Doumano' [Ndaomanu Sinlae] (Leupe 1877: 439). [In the narratives, Ndaomanu Sinlae, as eldest son, succeeded his father Sinlae Kila.]

1746 On 11 October, Jan Anthonij Meulenbeek, the Company's chief officer at Kupang, visited Termanu with a contingent of twelve Europeans and nineteen native soldiers. Three 'tumukungs' [clan lords] from Landu had escaped from block arrest and Meulenbeek demanded their return. Instead, he was offered one hundred slaves as compensation. Meulenbeek became enraged at this offer and abused the assembled Lords. The Lord of Thie is said to have fired upon Meulenbeek but to have missed. He, in turn, was shot down by Meulenbeek's servant. At this, the Rotinese attacked Meulenbeek and his company, massacred them, and 'burnt the bodies on the shore'. Only one European, a man named Gonst, managed to save himself and it was he who returned to Kupang to report the incident (Roo van Alderwerelt 1904: 197). Retaliation for this massacre was directed not against the entire population of the island, nor against Termanu, but only against the population of Landu. In 1750, the domain of Landu was devastated and 1145 of its inhabitants were captured and sent as slaves to Java. [Rotinese traditions represent this same event from a different perspective. The massacre of the Dutch at Kota Leleuk in Termanu forms the concluding episode of the long legend on the coming of the Dutch and the acceptance of Christianity. Ndaomanu Sinlae alone is blamed for these treacherous murders as well as the murders of the Lords of Thie and Loleh. He and his descendants were thereafter excluded from the Lordship and he was succeeded by his youngest brother, Fola Sinlae.]

1756 The fourth formal treaty between the Company and the rulers of Roti – the contract of Paravicini – was signed in Castle Concordia by 'Fora Sinlay [Fola Sinlae], regent of Termano'.[25]

1771 War broke out between Termanu and Dengka, but the intervention of the Company was unable to settle the dispute because the 'grievances on both sides were too great' (Roo van Alderwerelt 1904: 213).

1772 The territories of Keka and Talae were separated from Termanu and were assigned to native mercenaries of the Company (Roo van Alderwerelt 1904: 215).

1785 There is mention of unrest in Termanu. Some men near Ingu-Fao asserted their independence and attempted to establish a separate domain. [This attempt appears to have failed. For the next thirty years, there are few references to Roti. Between 1797 and 1815, acting on alliances formed in Europe during the Napoleonic Wars, the British twice held control of Castle Concordia at Kupang.]

1815–16 The Dutch regained control of Roti and Timor and initiated a policy of transporting Rotinese to the plains surrounding Kupang to form a buffer zone between the town and the hostile Timorese. Niks (1888: 96–7) reports that the first 600 Rotinese who resettled in Babauw and Pariti came from Termanu. The emigrants left willingly because of disputes within the domain. The first party to Babauw was composed of dissident villagers from the area of Ingu-Fao and was led by nobles of the lineage Ndaomanu-Tein. Niks records that the reason for this emigration was a long-standing feud in the royal clan (*radja-geslacht*) between the Amalo's and the Ndaomanu's. [One of the individuals Niks mentions by name was – according to the present genealogy of Ndaomanu-Tein – the grandson of Ndaomanu Sinlae. Interestingly, the second party to leave Termanu was composed of villagers from the area of Hoiledo (written 'Holledo'), the traditional village of the clan of Ndeko.]

1832 This was the year of the invasion of Dengka by the combined forces of the other domains of Roti. E. Francis (1832) reports Kiwpeloh [Kiuk Pelo] as ruler in Termanu. [In the traditions of Termanu, this invasion was led by Mauk Amalo, who is said to have been removed from the Lordship for his refusal to free war prisoners from Dengka. Succession to the Lordship passed from the royal lineage Fola-Tein to that of Hailiti-Tein. The first Lord from Hailiti-Tein was Kiuk Pelo. He was succeeded by his son, Fangidae Kiuk.]

1851 Henceforth it is possible to date the reigns of all the Lords of Termanu.

1851–9 Fanggidai Kioek [Fangidae Kiuk] (van Lynden 1851: 397; van Dijk 1925, II: 622).

1860–75 Michiel Keloeana (van Dijk 1925 II: 622). [Michiel Keluanan is the combination of a Christian first name and a Rotinese last name. In Rotinese traditions, this individual is also known by the Christian name, Michiel Amalo. The subsequent Lords of the royal line have retained all Christian names of their predecessors. Hence the present Lord of Termanu has the full name: Ernst Johannis Jeremias Michiel Amalo. Michiel Keluanan's proper Rotinese name was Pelo Keluanan, In the genealogy of the prestige line, he is the son of Keluanan Amalo, the youngest brother of Mauk Amalo who was removed from the Lordship after the war with Dengka.]

1876–87 Stephanus Paulus Amalo. In 1887, N. Graafland, during a tour of the island, recounts his somewhat unhappy impressions of a visit to this royal person in Feapopi (1889: 275–277). At the time, Graafland reports the Lord was under accusation by his subjects but was still able to maintain a modicum of prestige. He spoke the best Malay of the Lords of Roti and wore European clothes which 'suited him . . . he had something of the appearance of an English tourist'. As a youth, he had sailed to Menado, Singapore, Hongkong, and England and eventually became captain of a small coaster. His household was cluttered with the remains of his youth: Indo-european tables, stools, sofas, 'easy-chairs' without upholstery, broken mirrors, stopped clocks, 'a chronometer with thermometer and barometer' – all defective – pictures of ships in storm, others safely in the harbour of Hongkong, Napoleon beside the Pyramids, all manner of pipes and smoking equipment, a violin without strings, and, hung all about, pictures of women 'of questionable beauty'. The missionary Graafland's disapproval was hardly limited to the disarray of the royal household but impugned the very character of the Lord, who 'on account of his seaman's life had brought with him horribly shameful habits: cursing which shows no indication of refinement and an addiction to strong drink'. [I have already recounted various anecdotal tales about Stephanus Paulus Amalo. His Rotinese name was Kila Muskanan, and he was a member of the royal lineage but not of the prestige line within this lineage. Stephanus Paulus Amalo was to have been succeeded by Keluanan Pelo (Christian name: Jeremias Michiel Amalo), the youngest son of the previous Lord, Pelo Keluanan. But, according to tradition, Keluanan Pelo died in Kupang where he had gone to be recognized by the Dutch authorities. Stephanus Paulus Amalo was succeeded instead by a man of Hailiti-Tein, Damo Balo (Christian name: Salmon Pella).]

1888–92 Salmon Pella (van Dijk 1925, II: 622).

1894–1912 Johannes Jeremias Michiel Amalo (van Dijk 1925, II: 622). After 1908, under the 'intensification of rule' programme of the Netherlands' Indies Government, there were various administrative attempts to consolidate the domains (cf. Fox 1965: 55–60). Johannes Jeremias Michiel Amalo was succeeded by his brother, Christofel Jeremias Michiel Amalo, who ruled Termanu and various amalgamated divisions of middle Roti until the Japanese invasion. Two sons of Christofel Amalo ruled during the Japanese occupation and shortly thereafter. Then Ernst Amalo, a son of Johannes J. M. Amalo, was chosen Lord in 1947 and continued as Lord through 1965, the time of my field research in the domain. Since 1961, Ernst Amalo had served as district officer of middle Roti and resided for much of his time in the administrative headquarters of Baä. His weekly court was presided over by a *Wakil*, an Acting Lord, Frans Biredoko, the youngest son of the man who had served as *Wakil* to his father Johannes. For the sake of completeness, I list the Lords of Termanu and the dates of their reign.

1912–41 Chr. J. M. Amalo.

1942–3 G. Chr. J. M. Amalo.

1944–6 A. Chr. J. M. Amalo.

1947–66 E. J. J. M. Amalo.

What does this exercise in historical identification demonstrate? It demonstrates that in all likelihood at least nine of the thirty-one ancestors named in the royal genealogy were historical individuals. This span of ancestors carries the genealogy back approximately three hundred years. But it demonstrates even more clearly that the genealogy *alone* is not intended purely as historical record. The royal genealogy, on its own, is an assertion of a moral order, a claim to the right of succession. Of the nine ancestors who link the present Lord with his pivotal ancestor Seni Tola [22], seven are regarded as having ruled Termanu. And of these seven, only four ancestors are specifically named in the Dutch records. These seven ancestors may be compared with the twelve historically documented successors to the Lordship or to the seventeen successors to the Lordship who are named in Termanu's traditional narratives.

But the royal genealogy, together with its accompanying oral narratives, provides a remarkable representation of succession within the domain, the order and events of which are corroborated by independent sources. To sever the genealogy from the narratives would structure succession to the point of misrepresentation. Similarly, were the narratives ever to become unanchored from their reference genealogy, their coherence would be destroyed or, at least, rendered virtually incomprehensible, although individual symbolic episodes would still yield a persistent logic.

More specifically it may be observed that neither the historical records nor the traditional narratives indicate that the Lordship has ever left the clan Masa-Huk. In terms of present structures, the Lordship has been held by only four lineages: Hailiti-Tein, Nelu-Tein, Ndaomanu-Tein, and Fola-Tein. And of these four, the present royal lineage Fola-Tein, since the time of its ancestor Fola Sinlae, claims to have actually held the Lordship ten times. Seven of these reigns are confirmed in the historical records.

Had not the present Lord of Termanu ruled for nearly twenty years and were he not repeating the twenty-year rule of his father and the less successful thirty-year rule of his father's brother, it is unlikely that his descent line would now enjoy so unrivalled a status in his clan and, more important, in his own large lineage. The historical records attest to the clear emergence and establishment of this line in the late nineteenth century after a long period of less certain succession.

For Termanu, the historical records confirm a considerable stability of rule by Fola-Tein of Masa-Huk. On Roti, only the Lords of Thie and Bilba claim a greater continuity of rule by one line of Lords and this, too, appears confirmed by Dutch historical evidence. I list, once again, the ancestral names of the prestige line as well as the names of the Lords of Termanu as told in the narratives and I cite the dates of their rule as given in or inferred from the historical records. Inferential dates are in brackets. (A full citation of the names of all the Fetors would involve an extended discussion of the vicissitudes of succession in this line. Disappointingly, apart from the early Fetors – Kiu Lusi: 1662+; Sadu Kiuk: 1681–1700+ – there are few Ducth references to the names of the Fetors.)

Prestige Line	*Lords of Termanu*	*Dates of Rule*
22. Seni Tola	Seni Tola	
23. Kila Seni	Kila Seni	[1662+]
	Pelo Kila	1681–1691+
24. Sinlae Kila	Sinlae Kila	1700+
	Ndaomanu Sinlae	1737 [–1746]
25. Fola Sinlae	Fola Sinlae	1756+
26. Muda Fola	Muda Fola	
27. Amalo Muda	Amalo Muda	[1817+]
	Mauk Amalo	[–1832]
28. Keluanan Amalo		
	Kiuk Pelo	1832+
	Fangidae Kiuk	1851–1859
29. Pelo Keluanan	Pelo Keluanan	1860–1875
	Kila Muskanan	1876–1887
30. Keluanan Pelo		
	Dama Balo	1888–1892
31. Napu Keluanan	Napu Keluanan	1894–1912
	Funu Keluanan	1912–1941
	G. Chr. J. M. Amalo	1942–1943
	A. Chr. J. M. Amalo	1944–1946
32. Ernst J. J. M. Amalo	Ernst J. J. M. Amalo	1947–1966+

CONCLUSIONS

Genealogies by their inherent selectivity are poor codes for recording past events. In segmentary societies like the Nuer and Tiv, there appears to be a relatively constant rate of information loss in the form of ancestral names among all segments of the society. This permits the flexibility necessary for the maintenance of formal political relations between segments. It has the effect of contributing to the cohesion of the society by diminishing the inexorable separation incurred by each successive generation.

In status societies, like the Rotinese, genealogical information loss is not constant throughout the entire society. Many commoners evidence acute 'genealogical amnesia'. The genealogical connexions between acknowledged lineage segments of commoner clans are difficult or impossible to establish and are, furthermore, of little concern to lineage members because they carry no status significance. Consequently commoners are permitted a 'marriage laxity' wholly unacceptable to the nobility. The nobility, on the other hand, retains such an astonishing wealth of genealogical information that it has had to rely on ritual specialists, the chanters, for its preservation. As a result, the nobility continues to separate, its segments proliferate, and only marriage temporarily reunites these diverging segments.

It would be a distortion to assert that genealogy serves a single purpose in Rotinese society. Clearly, the royal genealogy defines and orders the clans and noble lineages in the domain. It 'models' ideal political relations. It also establishes the legitimacy of certain rulers. It justifies itself. But more than this, it anchors a narrative of autonomous symbolic structures (each of whose logic may be analysed separately) and it utilizes past events within these structures.

Historiography, like genealogy, is a form of classification. Both the Dutch records and the Rotinese narratives relate the same events. In October 1746, for example, twelve Europeans were massacred at Kota Leleuk in Termanu. In the Dutch archives, this report is a mere fragment but were it to be related in some structure, it might evidence, for example, the expansion of the Company in the East Indies and perhaps the initial native reaction to this expansion. In a revolutionary historiography, this same event might suggest early native resistance to Dutch colonization. When told outside of Termanu, this event is used to discredit Termanu's claim to superiority by demonstrating the domain's resistance to Christianity and Dutch rule. In Termanu itself, the event serves to discredit one line of potential rulers in the domain.[26] In this sense, events are meaningless without their explanatory structures and it is vain to hope that Western histories and native histories – where they exist – should coincide in their 'use' of past events.

The structure of the Rotinese narratives bears, in some instances, a certain similarity to the narratives of the neighbouring Atoni of Timor (Middelkoop 1939, 1968). Significantly, these narratives attest to a common form of historiography throughout the Malayo-Polynesian world. Whether it be the *Tantaran'ny Adriana* of the Merina Kings of Madagascar, the *Malay Annals*, the *Nagara-Kertagama*, *Pararaton*, or *Babad Tanah Jawi*, the chronicles of the rulers of Java, or the simpler folk histories of the clan chiefs of Tikopia (Firth 1961), these narratives serve to legitimize and extol native rulers and provide an order which superficially resembles Western chronological historiography because of its own 'internal chronology' of genealogical sequence. What these 'histories' allow us to examine on occasion is the dialectic interrelation of structure and event.

NOTES

1. The research on which this paper is based was supported by a Public Health Service fellowship (MH-23, 148) and grant (MH-10, 161) from the National Institute of Mental Health and was conducted, in Indonesia (1965–6), under the auspices of the Madjelis Ilmu Pengatahuan Indonesia and the Departemen (Lembaga) Urusan Research Nasional.
2. The literature on African genealogies is considerable. E. Peters (1960) has examined the use of genealogies in the proliferation of tertiary segments among the Bedouin of Cyrenaica; I. Cunnison (1957) their use among the heterogeneous Luapula. I. Mayer's recent article (1965) on Gusii genealogies discusses the kinship limits of a variety of African genealogies. More generally, J. Barnes (1967) has surveyed the usages to which anthropologists have put genealogical data. He advocates the term 'pedigree' for long dynastic genealogies but this term is still insufficiently established in the literature and carries with it (to my mind) a connotation of the stock-breeder's chart. The article also provides references to an extended debate on the validity and significance of Maori genealogies (Roberton 1956, 1957, 1958; Piddington 1956; Pei Te Hurinui 1958; Sharp 1958, 1959) in the *Journal of the Polynesian Society*. For a recent study of genealogy among an Indonesian people, see B. Sandin's earnest scrutiny (1968) of complex Iban *tusut* in tracing Dayak migrations in Sarawak.
3. For a discussion of the attendant difficulties facing Southeast Asian historians in this approach, it is useful to consult various contributions in D. G E. Hall (ed.): *Historians of South East Asia* (particularly Shorto: 'A Mon Genealogy of Kings', pp. 66–72) or in Soedjatmoko (ed.): *An*

Introduction to Indonesian Historiography (particularly Koentjaraningrat: 'Use of Anthropological Methods in Indonesian Historiography', pp. 299–325).

4. There are over 70,000 Rotinese on the island of Roti itself and an additional 25,000–30,000 Rotinese on the northeast plains area of Kupang. Their economy is varied. A large proportion of their subsistence is derived from tapping and cooking to a sugar syrup the juice of the lontar palm (*Borassus flabellifer* Linn). In a dry region of Indonesia, they are remarkably capable wet-rice cultivators but they also depend on maize, millet, and sorghum grown in dry-fields and household gardens. They keep herds of horses, water buffalo, goats, and sheep and most households raise pigs and chicken. Offshore fishing is important in the dry season.

5. Three small domains, Delha, Oenale, and Lelenuk, traditionally have no Fetor. These domains were formed originally from the division of a larger realm between Manek and Fetor. In another small domain, Talae, the Fetor has displaced the Manek and rules the domain – as Fetor – in what amounts to a state of permanent interregnum.

6. In two domains of south-central Roti, Thie and Loleh, this marriage ideal is given a more systematic expression. All clans are divided into moiety groupings which affect marriage. One moiety is that of the Lord; the other is of the Fetor. A consequence of this is that the genealogical links connecting Lord and Fetor are extended to embrace the other clans of their respective moieties. These genealogical connexions are not, however, all encompassing and definitely do not include the group of clans associated with the Head of the Earth within the moiety of the Lord.

7. It was commoners – never nobles – who pointed out to me the various attributes of the commoner class. Occasionally there exist recognized genealogical connexions between certain commoner clans in a domain. Where these connexions are recognized, they are utilized 'to justify' later affinal connexions between the same clans.

8. The imputation is that these lineages are descended from slaves attached to the royal household or are royal descendants of slave concubines. There exists some indication – I cite some evidence later in this paper – that certain of these lineages are the remnants of former clans incorporated, as clients, in the noble clan.

9. Failure to obtain a name by divination indicates that a person is to be given one of a set of – what might be translated as – 'heavenly names'. A comprehensive article on Rotinese naming systems is planned in the near future.

10. The child of a client or one for whom bridewealth has not been paid

takes as his last name the first name of his mother. Since women as well as men normally take their last name from their father, a child, in this case, is ultimately grafted – through the mother – to the ancestral line of the grandfather. It is this system of patronyms that underlines the Rotinese claim to 'patrilineal' descent.

11. Sahlins has written cogently on the contrast between ramified and descent-line systems of social organization in Polynesia (1958). But the social structure of a Rotinese domain would appear to fit neither of these types exactly. Commoners are divided among independent and usually unrelated clans composed of descent lines of insignificant status, whereas the nobility presents a ramifying structure centred upon a status core. Ultimately, the system would appear to be a descent-line system with noble impositions.

12. Geertz in his essay *Person, Time, and Conduct in Bali* (1966) has argued persuasively that the Balinese have both a 'depersonalizing concept of personhood' and a 'detemporalizing concept of time'. On Roti, the experience of time and the definition of person varies considerably between noble and commoner. A noble, and especially a Lord, has his genealogy and identifies himself with the exploits of his ancestors. On the other hand, a commoner lacks a developed genealogy, suffers to some extent from what Geertz has described as 'genealogical amnesia', and furthermore lacks tales about the exploits and peculiarities of his ancestors. A commoner is thus an 'ill-defined' person without a 'history' and his experience of time may not be unlike that of the Balinese commoner.

13. In Termanu, there exists the myth that the Lords of the other domains are descendants of other sons of the ancestor Bula Kai, whose principal son, Ma Bulan, was the first ancestor of the Lord of Termanu to arrive in Roti. This is an entirely local myth which gives precedence to Termanu's Lord among all the Lords of the island. It appears that each domain may have its own explanation to account for the nobility of the other domains.

14. Compared with Masa-Huk's present sixteen constituent lineages (Kota-Deak has six lineages), the large clan Kiu-Kanak has only five named lineages, Suï six, Dou-Danga, and Ingu-Fao have five, while Meno, Ingu-Beuk, Nggofa-Laik, and Ulu-Anak are unsegmented. Ingu-Naü has two lineages.

15. Seznec in *The Survival of the Pagan Gods* (Chapter I: The Historical Tradition) has described similar dynastic preoccupations of rulers in the late Middle Ages in tracing their descent from Biblical figures, mythological heroes, and Greek and Roman gods. Charles IX of France, for example, personally supervised the composition of Ronsard's *Franciade* which established the genealogical connexion between the sixty-three sovereigns of his own line and the fabulous heroes of antiquity.

16. Since the recitation of names is a form of ancestral invocation, names must be recited in direct sequence. Consequently in the normal recitation of the royal genealogy, no mention would be made of Fala Kai. A recitation of the ancestral names for the clan Kiu-Kanak does, however, include the first thirteen names of the royal genealogy and then continues on through Fala Kai. This genealogy contains a further sequence of nine names before any of the founders of Kiu-Kanak's five major lineages are named.

17. Descent and marriage on Roti are closely associated. Acknowledged common descent admits the possibility of reciprocal marriage. Commoners, except for the Head of the Earth, would, I suspect, willingly claim descent from noble ancestors (as a few commoners actually do *in secret*) were the nobility to allow them these presumptions. But this is precisely what the nobility denies the commoner because this would imply the opportunity of marriage with the nobility without the compensating payment of exorbitant bridewealth. Only in south-central Roti with its moiety systems are genealogical connexions extended to most clans to permit marriage between the moieties.

18. The elders of the clan Dou-Danga claim their incorporation within the domain was effected by Leki Kelu. If this were fully acknowledged, it would give their clan precedence of incorporation over other clans of the domain, Ingu-Beuk, Nggofa-Laik, Suï, and Ingu-Fao.

19. It is at this point, some insist, that at least two of the distinctly non-noble adherent lineages of Masa-Huk originated. They are given the status of ignoble sons of Sinlae Kila.

20. Were a Lord to fail to honour the ritual privileges of the clans, he would in effect deny his own direct descent from the ancestor who bestowed these privileges and would leave his position open for another to claim.

21. The events in this legend, when it is told outside Termanu, are sometimes attributed to Tola Manu rather than Ndao Manu.

22. My research into the Dutch and Portuguese historical materials on Roti is still in progress. The information I have been able to assemble to date is probably still incomplete. Eventually I hope to publish a monograph on Rotinese history, paralleling traditional narratives with Portuguese and Dutch records.

23. Off the coast of Roti, there exists the tiny island of Ndao whose population speaks a language closely related to Savunese. The Ndaonese traditionally emigrate to Roti and each Rotinese domain has a clan or lineage composed of the descendants of Ndaonese immigrants. For a number of reasons Kota-Deak, in Termanu, is the clan that customarily accepts Ndaonese clients.

24. In the same letter, the name Saduk is spelled Sadok and Zadok as pre-

viously it was spelled as Zadeck or Saocq. The manuscripts of this period, especially those of the Company's lesser officers, are not noted for their consistency of spelling. Pelo Kila is written in one instance as Pelo Kina.

25. One of the protagonists in the Rotinese legend about the massacre of the Dutch is Tou Dengalilo, Lord of Baä, who escaped Ndaomanu Sinlae's treachery by hiding in the loft of the house of his mother's brother, a member of Kiu-Kanak. The *Corpus Diplomaticum* records the fact that 'Touw Denkoliloe, regent of Baka' was a signatory of the contract of 1756.

26. This makes no judgement as to the relative accuracy or the interpretative qualities of these various forms of historiography. Thie's version of this legend claims its Lord was treacherously slaughtered by the Lord of Termanu whereas the Dutch version specifically reports that the Lord of Thie himself provoked the hostilities and was shot down by Meulenbeek's servant.

REFERENCES

BARNES, J. 1967 Genealogies. Pp. 101–27 in Epstein, A. (ed.), *The Craft o Social Anthropology*. London: Tavistock.

BOHANNAN, LAURA 1952 A Genealogical Charter. *Africa* **22**: 301–15.

BOXER, C. R. 1947 *The Topasses of Timor*. Koninklijke Vereeniging Indisch Instituut, Mededeling LXXIII, Afdeling Volkenkunde no. 24.

CLERCQ, F. S. A. DE 1874 Allerlei over het eiland Roti. *Bijdragen tot de Taal-, Land- en Volkenkunde* **21**: 291–312.

COOLHAAS, W. PH. 1964 *General Missiven van Gouverneurs-Generaalen Raden aan Heren XVII der Verenigde Oostindische Compagnie*, vol. II: 1639–1655. 's Gravenhage.

Corpus Diplomaticum Neerlando-Indicum. *Bijdragen tot de Taal-, Land- en Volkenkunde.*

— 1907 Part I, vol. 73.

— 1931 Part II, vol. 87.

— 1934 Part III, vol. 91.

— 1935 Part IV, vol. 93.

— 1938 Part V, vol. 96.

Corpus Diplomaticum Neerlando-Indicum, Part VI (1753–1799) 1955 (ed.) Stapel, F.W. 's Gravenhage.

CUNNISON, I. 1957 History and Genealogies in a Conquest State. *American Anthropologist* **59**: 20–31.

Daghregister gehouden in 't casteel Batavia, anno 1624–1682. 1896–1931 31 vols. Batavia.

DAM, P. VAN 1927–54 *Beschryvinge van de Oostindische Compagnie*. Stapel, F. W. (ed.) 7 vols. 's Gravenhage.

DIJK, L. J. VAN 1924–34 De zelfbesturende landschappen in de Residentie Timor en Onderhoorigheden. *De Indische Gids*, **47**: i, 528–40; ii, 618–23; **61**: 708–12.

EVANS-PRITCHARD, E. E. 1939 Nuer Time-Reckoning. *Africa* **12**: 189–216.
— 1940 *The Nuer*. Oxford: Clarendon Press.

FIRTH, R. 1961 *History and Traditions of Tikopia*. The Polynesian Society, Memoir 33. Wellington, New Zealand.

FOX, JAMES J. 1965 *Roti and Savu: A Literary Analysis of Two Island Societies in Eastern Indonesia*. Unpublished B.Litt. thesis, Oxford University.
— 1968 *The Rotinese: A Study of the Social Organization of an Eastern Indonesian People*. Unpublished D.Phil. thesis, Oxford University.

FRANCIS, E. 1832 Verslag van den Kommissaris voor Timor. Unpublished manuscript, Koninklijk Instituut voor Taal-, Land- en Volkenkunde.

GEERTZ, C. 1966 *Person, Time and Conduct in Bali*. Cultural Report Series no. 14, Southeast Asia Studies, Yale University, New Haven.

GRAAFLAND, N. 1889 Het eiland Rote. *Mededeelingen van wege het Nederlandsch Zendeling-genootschap* **33**: 239–77.

GULLICK, J. M. 1958 *Indigenous Political Systems of Western Malaya*. London School of Economics Monographs on Social Anthropology no. 17. London: Athlone Press. Oxford University Press.

HALL, D. G. E. (ed.) 1961 *Historians of Southeast Asia*. London:

JACKSTEIN, A. 1873 Eenige notizen over Rotti en de Rottinezen. *Tijdschrift voor Indische Taal-, Land- en Volkenkunde* **20**: 350–6.

JONKER, J. C. G. 1908 *Rottineesch-Hollandsch Woordenboek*. Leiden.

LEACH, E. 1954 *Political Systems of Highland Burma*. London: Bell.

LEIT O, H. 1948 *Os Portugueses em Solor e Timor de 1515 a 1720*. Lisbon.

LEUPE, P. A. 1877 Besognes der Hooge Regeering te Batavia gehouden over de Commissie van Paravccini naar Timor 1756. *Bijdragen tot de Taal-, Land- en Volkenkunde van Nederlandsch-Indië* **25**: 421–94.

LYNDEN, D. W. C. 1851 *Bijdrage tot de kennis van Solor, Allor, Rotti, Savoe en omliggende eilanden. Natuurkundig Tijdschrift voor Nederlandsch-Indië* **2**: 317–36; 388–414.

MAYER, I. 1965 From Kinship to Common Descent: Four Generation Genealogies Among the Gusii. *Africa* **35**: 366–84.

MIDDELKOOP, P. 1939 Amarasisch Timoreesch Teksten. *Verhandelingen van het Koninklijk Bataviaasch Genootschap van Kunsten en Wetenschappen*, **74**, Part II: 1–107. Bandung.

MIDDELKOOP, P. 1968 Migrations of Timorese Groups and the Question of the Kase Metan or Overseas Black Foreigners. *International Archives of Ethnography*, **51**: 49-142. Leiden.

NIKS, J. F. 1888 De Rottineesche nederzettingen op Timor. *Mededeelingen van wege het Nederlandsch Zendeling-genootschap* **32**: 95-7.

PETERS, E. L. 1960 The Proliferation of Lineage Segments among the Bedouin of Cyrenaica. *Journal of the Royal Anthropological Institute* **90**: 29-53.

RESINK, G. J. 1968 Independent Rulers, Realms, and Lands in Indonesia, 1850-1910. Pp. 107-47 in *Indonesia's History Between the Myths*. The Hague.

ROO VAN ALDERWERELT, J. DE 1904 Aanteekeningen over Timor en Onderhoorigheden, 1668 tot en met 1809. *Tijdschrift voor Indische Taal-, Land- en Volkenkunde* **47**: 195-226.

SAHLINS, M. 1958 *Social Stratification in Polynesia.* Seattle: The American Ethnological Society.

SANDIN, B. 1968 *The Sea Dayaks of Borneo.* East Lansing: Michigan State University Press.

SEZNEC, J. 1954 *The Survival of the Pagan Gods.* New York: Pantheon.

SMITH, W. ROBERTSON 1885 *Kingship and Marriage in Early Arabia.* Cambridge.

SOEDJATMOKO *et al.* (eds.) 1965 *An Introduction to Indonesian Historiography.* Ithaca: Cornell University Press.

Nuer Kinship

A Re-examination

KATHLEEN GOUGH

In *Kinship and Marriage among the Nuer* (1951) Professor Evans-Pritchard drew together in a single analytic framework concepts and information scattered in earlier papers on kinship, while also adding new data and interpretations. I shall concentrate on an examination of this book, drawing where necessary for additional information from the companion volume on social structure, *The Nuer* (1940), and from some of the author's numerous articles on the Nuer.

Thanks to Evans-Pritchard, the Nuer are one of the best-described societies in anthropological literature. The book to be considered is, in particular, a brilliant exposition of the salient features of Nuer kinship. The author's achievement, both in *The Nuer* and in *Kinship and Marriage*, is all the more remarkable when we consider the dates at which they were written, the short time that he was able to spend in the field, and the difficulties under which he worked. In this essay I shall draw attention to certain problems in the analysis of the data and at some points shall suggest alternative hypotheses. I do so with full admiration of the author's achievement in both books. Such an approach is, I think, one that Professor Evans-Pritchard would especially advocate, for he has always encouraged his students to question theories and to push their own analyses as far as the data will go.

Kinship and Marriage among the Nuer starts with the relation of kinship to the local community, proceeds to exogamic and incest prohibitions, and then to a discussion of marriage. This is followed by analysis of interpersonal relationships within the simple legal family and the several forms of domestic union brought about by alternative types of marriage, and finally by an account of interpersonal relationships in the wider kinship system, and by a summary of the argument.

Kathleen Gough

KINSHIP AND THE LOCAL COMMUNITY

The first chapter poses a number of related questions which recur at other places in the book and are, I think, not completely answered. I shall therefore consider it in some detail.

Evans-Pritchard reminds us that in *The Nuer* he focused on relations between lineages of the dominant clan in each tribe, since these are fused with other elements to form local communities and so have political significance. There live, however, in each tribal territory representatives of many clans not dominant in that tribe, who altogether considerably outnumber the dominant clanspeople. The members of these non-dominant clans fall into 'small lineages with fewer branches and less depth than the dominant clans' (1951: 1). These lineages may or may not be associated with local communities smaller than primary sections, but if associated with local communities, they are associated with them in terms of the tribal structure as a whole through some relationship to its dominant clan.

The wet-season village is the smallest political unit. It may comprise anything from a few families congregated on a riverside mound, to several hundreds of people occupying a ridge or scattered on high ground over several miles. It invariably includes members of several clans all related to each other through interpersonal kinship ties. It is a corporation owning cultivated plots, fishing pools, and grazing grounds, although ownership is 'spoken about in terms of the lineage with which the village is socially identified' (ibid.: 2). Villagers cooperate in occasional work such as building, clearing gardens, and harvesting. They fight side by side in defence and attack and support one another in feuds. At a dance attended by persons from several villages, men of one village assemble together in a war-line and fighting may break out between groups from different villages.

In large villages groups of kin occupy separate sections of the village and there is rivalry between them. Such a group may be a single homestead (*gol*) with its attendant cattle byre; a composite homestead with several byres but sharing a common kraal; or a hamlet of several homesteads whose members are close kin. The word *cieng* may be used of any of these local groups, of a village, or of any larger territorial unit up to a primary section. Members of several adjacent villages camp together in a dry-season camp, but some spatial segregation of homesteads, hamlets, and village groups is maintained. Occasionally, members of the same village may in one season drift to different camps, but this is unusual.

Cooperation in labour between homesteads is greater in camps than in villages: the cattle are kept in larger kraals and are herded together by different households in turn.

Having considered these local units, Evans-Pritchard turns to his distinction between lineage and kinship relationships. Lineage relationships are relationships between groups of the same order of segmentation. Between lineages of the same clan, the relationship is called *buth*; between lineages of different clans there may be a relationship which subsequent writers on African societies came to call 'perpetual kinship',[1] one lineage being 'children of the mother's brother' or 'of the father's sister' to the other. What are spoken of by Nuer as relations between lineages are however in fact relations between territorial sections, stated in terms of the lineage relationship between the segments of the clan that is dominant in the tribe. The lineage as an agnatic group is abstracted from its territorial context only 'on certain ritual occasions and in connection with feuds and rules of exogamy'.

Kinship relationships, by contrast, are relationships between persons; the Nuer call them *mar*, kinship, as distinct from *buth*. *Mar* includes not only relationships with close agnates and cognates but also with affines, after a child has been born to the relevant married couple to create kinship between their respective kin. The relations between agnates change from *mar* into *buth* when three to four generations have elapsed between the agnates and their common ancestor; when, that is, neither can claim bridewealth at the marriage of the other's daughter. But all agnates descended from the bride's father's father's father can in theory claim part of her bridewealth, and their relationship is therefore *mar*. *Rul*, finally, refers to relationships between lineages which are strangers to one another, that is to say between lineages which have no *buth*.

Within one village all members have *mar* with each other, for all are in some way kin. There can be no *buth* between villagers and therefore, Evans-Pritchard says, all relationships between villagers are interpersonal and not intergroup relationships. All villagers have *mar*, but each man's *mar* extends uniquely through matrilateral, conjugal, affinal, and agnatic links with persons in other villages of the district, in other districts and sections of the tribe, and sometimes in other tribes.

The author here analyses the kinship composition of two villages and one cattle camp: Konye village of the Lou tribe on the Anuak boundary, Nyueny village in the Leek tribal territory of western Nuerland, and Yakwac cattle camp, again on the boundary of Nuerland, where the Lou tribe faces the Balak Dinka people. The two border sites had to be chosen through circumstances beyond Evans-Pritchard's control; this is, however, perhaps unfortunate, for their composition may not be typical of encampments well within the Nuer area.

At Konye there are present members of the Lou aristocratic clan, but the chief 'bull' or powerful man of the village, with his agnates, belongs to the non-dominant Gawaar clan, and this man's son is the chief 'bull' of four outlying homesteads which form a hamlet on the edge of the village. At Yakwac, again, the chief 'bull' is a *woman* of the dominant clan, and in the wet season, when the site houses a small village, her son of a non-dominant clan is the most powerful figure in the village. In the dry season, however, this village apparently turns into a large camp and there flock to it members of other minimal lineages of the same minor lineage of the dominant clan, who arrive from inland villages. Nyueny, the interior village, has as its agnatic core and chief 'bulls' Nuer of the aristocratic clan of the tribe.

One is led to wonder whether the situation in which leadership of a village falls to non-dominant clansmen may be particularly characteristic of sites near the boundary between a Nuer tribe and a foreign people. Unfortunately, Evans-Pritchard does not deal with this problem. It must be noted, however, that in all three settlements, members of the aristocratic clan are present, although they are chief bulls in only one. Evans-Pritchard uses the analysis of these communities to point to certain recurrent principles of local and kinship grouping. Every village has as its core a group of agnates, often of the dominant clan. These appear always to look to a common ancestor some three to four generations back from the oldest living members, and they form a minimal lineage in opposition to collateral minimal lineages of other villages of their district. Attached to these agnates within the village are a number, usually a larger number, of their cognates and affines of other clans, who are related to the core of agnates by various kinds of ties through women. Many of these attached affines and cognates stay in the village for only a short period and then drift away from it to other villages, where they are able to establish residence by virtue of other affinal or cognatic ties to the dominant agnatic groups of these villages. Members of a village's agnatic core may, it seems, also wander away to other villages, but a majority of them are said to be present at any one time. Evans-Pritchard states that at some time in their lives most men turn again to the village of their legal fathers, wherever they were brought up.

Sometimes, however, the agnatic core attaches to itself certain other elements as more permanent residents of the village, some of whose descendants stay there over several generations. Such persons are descended, usually in the male line but sometimes through both males and females, from a woman of the agnatic core. They are collectively called 'children of the father's sister' or 'children of girls'. Many of these attached groups are persons whose male ancestor was a captured Dinka married to a woman of the village's agnatic core. The agnatic descendants of such Dinka, who are numerous, in time come to be regarded as true agnates of the dominant core, and in time they take on full membership of the dominant clan. Other Dinka men and girls are actually adopted by their captors' close agnates, and at once assume full membership of their captors' agnatic groups as daughters or as sons. Small agnatic groups of Nuer of non-dominant clans may also, moreover, become permanent residents in the village of an ancestress who was a member of the dominant clan, and their descendants in time claim partial membership of the dominant clan through treating their ancestress as if she were a man.

This more or less permanent attachment to an agnatic lineage of other groups classified as the 'children of girls' is so fundamental that we must look further into the process of their attachment. The first case is one in Nyueny village, where Jany, a Nuer of the non-dominant Juak clan whose mother was of the dominant Gaatbol clan, has settled with eleven of his children, who occupy ten out of the twenty-six homesteads in the village, in two of its four hamlets. These persons are collectively called 'children of the paternal aunt', since their father's mother was the son's daughter of the village ancestor. Evans-Pritchard says, 'In course of time a maternal link of this kind may be treated as though it were a paternal link and therefore within the genealogical structure of the principle lineage of the community. Jany's mother Duai is so treated. Nuer says of a woman who has this relationship that "she has become a man". Cognation becomes regarded for ordinary social purposes within community life as equal to agnation' (ibid.: 16).

Later in the chapter Evans-Pritchard notes that when elements of a non-dominant clan settle in a village to whose dominant lineage they are linked through an ancestress, they call themselves the *cieng* of this

83

ancestress so as to link up to the dominant lineage through her. Elsewhere, he states that unless the names of such linking ancestresses are
clearly distinguished by a feminine prefix, 'they may even become men'
(1945: 65). He ends this paper by stating: 'Individuals and family
associations of one kind and another seem to float about, as it were,
and have an independent existence. But they are anchored to some
lineage, or, if they break away from it, sooner or later attach themselves
to another lineage, take root in its stem, and become part of its growth'
(ibid.).

It seems, however, from other statements of Evans-Pritchard that
while the descendants of a Dinka husband can come in time to be
regarded as agnates of the lineage of their ancestress, Nuer of non-
dominant clans can never become so merged as true members of the
dominant clan. Thus in *The Nuer* (1940: 227) it is stated that while the
'children of girls' relationship is frequently brought into play in order
to attach non-dominant clansmen to some lineage of the dominant clan
so that they 'consider its members, rather than their father's lineage, as
their true kin', nevertheless, 'Nuer of [these] other clans [unlike Dinka]
can never *more* closely identify themselves with the dominant lineage
because, for ritual reasons, they must remain autonomous units' (my
italics). Likewise in *Kinship and Marriage*, Evans-Pritchard states that
'a very great number, I venture to say the vast majority, of people
tracing descent from the dominant lineage through a female, are Dinka.
If they are not Dinka, they are likely to be Nuer of clans not dominant
in *any* tribe, and these clans too, judging from myth, may originally be
of foreign origin. But the assimilation of course is never as complete
as that of Dinka, because these have their own clan symbols and *buth*
relationship to lineages of their birth (1951: 25).

Evans-Pritchard next discusses the several factors which tend to make
the residence of some Nuer other than patrilocal and thus bring about
the mixed kinship composition of individual villages. These include
widow-concubinage, in which the widow may sometimes live in her
lover's or her father's village, and her children, although acknowledging
as pater the woman's dead husband, may remain in this village. Similarly,
the child of an unmarried concubine, although legitimatized by his
genitor through payment of cattle, may live in the village of his mother.
Again, many Dinka live uxorilocally, and so do some Nuer whose
fathers are dead and who have quarrelled with their agnates, or who are
poor men whose fathers-in-law can help them with cattle. Still other

Nuer whose fathers are dead, and who are poor, may live with a mother's brother or with some affine who offers to help them to start a herd. There is, finally, a rule, sometimes broken, by which the eldest child of a marriage is brought up until initiation or marriage in the home of his mother's father. An eldest son who has been happy there may later decide to return from his pater's home to the home of his maternal grandparents.

Two other important points are made by Evans-Pritchard in this chapter. One is that every village has as its leaders certain powerful men or bulls, who are usually, but need not necessarily be, of the aristocratic clan. He adds that 'it is the ambition of every man, of the dominant clan especially, to become a "bull" and the centre of a cluster of kin, and Nuer say that it is for this reason that families often break up and cousins and brothers part, each to seek to gather his own community round him' (1951: 28).

The second point is that 'It would seem it may be partly just because the agnatic principle is unchallenged in Nuer society that the tracing of descent through women is so prominent and matrilocality so prevalent' (ibid.).

Three sets of problems arise for me out of this chapter and related writings, which I should like to consider in turn.

1 *The Feud*

The first problem concerns the relative significance of agnation and territoriality in the prosecution of feuds. Evans-Pritchard says that villagers support one another in feuds, and in *The Nuer* he states that feuds take place between territorial sections of like order (1940: 159). Yet in the first chapter of *Kinship and Marriage* he also states that the lineage as an *agnatic* group becomes *abstracted* from its territorial context 'on certain ritual occasions and in connection with feuds and rules of exogamy'. Later in the book we learn that a man's close agnates (his father, father's brothers, and their children – those who would help to pay bridewealth for him) must pay compensation if he kills or injures another, and that these close agnates and also the corresponding maternal kinsfolk, who would normally receive bridewealth for a girl, receive compensation if a man is killed. It is the close agnates of the slain, to a depth of not more than three generations, who are bound to attempt vengeance on his behalf. A man is not, however, legally obliged to support his mother's brother in feuds.

85

These various statements are to some extent reconciled in *The Nuer*, where Evans-Pritchard explains that it is the *ritually* sanctioned duty of a slain man's lineage to avenge his death, and that they may by ritual rules slay in return only a man of the minimal lineage of the slayer, and not any of the slayer's close cognates or affines; but that in fact the prosecution of blood feuds often leads to larger-scale fighting between the appropriate villages or larger territorial sections whose members flock to the support of the feuding minimal lineage (1940: 158).

These statements also, however, raise certain problems. For since the Nuer are individually so mobile, it must often happen that members of a minimal lineage are scattered in several villages of a district or even in several larger sections of a tribe. Presumably in that case it is only those living near the slayer who actively participate. It is not clear what would happen if close agnates of the slayer were living in the village of the slain, in which case they would have loyalties to both sides. It may be, as Gluckman has argued, that it is the very fact of dispersal of many minimal lineages, leading to conflicts between residential and agnatic loyalties, together with other conflicts that may arise between maternal and patrilineal, or maternal and residential ties, that permits feuds to be settled easily inside the smaller tertiary tribal sections within which most marriages occur (Gluckman 1955: 18–20). In *The Nuer* (1940: 156–7), indeed, Evans-Pritchard himself indicates that it is the general closeness and multiplicity of ties within the tertiary section that accounts for the rapid settlement of feuds, although he does not spell out the precise implications of dispersal of the minimal lineage.

Even in the case of the battles between larger sections, however, which Evans-Pritchard indicates often spring out of blood feuds, several persons may be placed in difficult positions, for both slain and slayer may have cognates, if not close agnates, living in the enemy section. Since battles between such larger sections are said to be ended with greater difficulty, one must conclude that, when they are at cross-purposes, residence rather than agnatic loyalties determine a Nuer's allegiance. This would, however, mean that territorial allegiances are stronger, and agnatic allegiances weaker, than Evans-Pritchard, through-out most of *Kinship and Marriage*, is inclined to suggest.

The paramountcy of residential over agnatic ties is, however, clearly stated in *The Nuer*, where Evans-Pritchard notes: '. . . though lineages maintain their autonomy, the lineage value only operates in the restricted field of ceremonial and is, therefore, only occasionally a determinant of

behaviour. Community values are those which constantly direct behaviour, and these operate in a different set of social situations to lineage
values. While lineage values control ceremonial relations between groups
of agnates, community values control political relations between groups
of people living in separate villages, tribal sections and tribes. The two
kinds of value control distinct planes of socal life' (1940: 211).

Later in the same book he states still more strongly, 'in our view the
territorial system of the Nuer is always the dominant variable in relation
to the other social systems. Among the Nuer, relationships are generally
expressed in kinship terms, and these terms have great emotional content, but living together counts more than kinship and, as we have seen,
community ties are always in one way or another turned into, or assimilated to, kinship ties, and the lineage system is twisted into the form
of the territorial system within which it functions' (ibid.: 265). In
Kinship and Marriage, however, emphasis is placed on 'the supremacy
of the agnatic principle' rather than of 'the territorial system' in determining the content of kinship relationships. I suggest that this may be
an oversimplification of the heterogeneity of kinship ties among the Nuer.

At this point I should like to digress briefly to take up another topic
in connexion with feuds. It seems doubtful whether the recent large-
scale battles that had occurred between primary and secondary sections
of certain tribes ought to be regarded as outgrowths of private blood
feuds of the kind traditionally handled by the Leopard Skin Chief.
For in several cases these battles had apparently been actual battles of
conquest, in which one side drove the other out of its territory and
forced it to migrate elsewhere. Thus Evans-Pritchard states in *The Nuer*
that within the Gaagwang primary section of the Gaajak tribe, the
Kwoth and the Bor secondary sections were defeated by the Gai
secondary section and forced to migrate south into Rengyan territory.
Later, the Gai secondary section themselves did battle with the Reng
primary section of the same tribe, and were expelled by the Reng and
forced to move to Karlual territory in the Leek tribe. Similarly, in the
Leek tribe the Karlual primary section was defeated by two other
primary sections, the Cuaagh and the Deng, who forced it over to the
left bank of the Bahr-el-Ghazal. After this defeat and resettlement, the
two conquering sections even pursued their enemies, the Karlual, into
their new territory where better grassland was to be found, but were
driven back again across the river (1940: 146). Following this, an agreement was reached that members of the Karlual section should not be

permitted to build permanent cattle byres in the territory already conquered by the Cuaagh and the Deng, and vice versa.[2]

This last fact indicates that the mobility of individual Nuer is not always so free as we are elsewhere led to believe, and that there is considerable competition for rights in land. More important, these battles between sections, which result in large displacements of population and in expansion of the Nuer territory as a whole, must surely create structural changes in the relations between tribal sections, and also, presumably, between segments of the aristocratic lineages of those sections. One wonders whether the genealogies of the dominant clans in these tribes have already been changed to fit the recent ousting of some sections and their replacement by others. At all events, such battles seem to be of a different order from the more private blood feuds waged by minimal lineages with the help of their fellow-villagers. The latter, which are most common within the district or tertiary tribal section could, by contrast with the former, take place and be settled without any major changes in the structural relations of sections.

These related problems concerning the feud lead to a general criticism. This is that although Evans-Pritchard gives us historical background on the Nuer, and clearly indicates that they have expanded their tribal territory and have undergone a series of social and legal changes during the past century (1940: 126–7); nevertheless, by ascribing Nuer actions to various 'structural principles' as if they were timeless, he gives at other times the impression of a society in a state of stable equilibrium. The same criticism has, of course, been levelled against many of the 'structural functional' monographs of the 1940s and 1950s. My purpose here will be to suggest that some of the features of Nuer kinship that Evans-Pritchard ascribes to the operation of seemingly unchanging and homogeneous structural principles – notably the 'agnatic principle' – can be better explained as features of an unstable, expanding, and above all an internally differentiated society.

2 The Children of Girls

The second set of problems arising from Chapter I concerns the 'children of girls'.

It is necessary first to stress a point that I think the author in *Kinship and Marriage* sometimes leads us to forget: that the dominant lineages of a tribe, whose segmentation in theory follows the lines of territorial segmentation, are seldom all of one clan. Thus two out of three secondary sections of the Reng primary section of the Gaajak tribe have 'foreign' lineages as their dominant lineages (1940: 140, 232). In the Lou tribe, two out of three secondary sections of the Mor primary section have dominant lineages of stranger clans, while in more of the tribes that Evans-Pritchard analyses in detail several tertiary sections have dominant lineages of stranger origin. Similarly, we know from both major works on Nuer social structure that, within any tertiary section, individual villages are often dominated by lineages not of the aristocratic clan.

It is not made clear whether these established stranger lineages, varying in depth from three to some ten generations, are all drawn into the genealogical structure of the aristocratic clan as the children of fathers' sisters. We may, however, perhaps safely assume that this is usually so, since Evans-Pritchard frequently remarks how common this practice is. Whatever the case may be, it is clear that the relationships between the lineage segments that are dominant in the various sections of a given tribe are seldom if ever all seen as agnatic relationships.

It is also apparently the case that Nuer tribes are not all equally 'agnatic' in this respect. Thus, tribes in the western and longer established part of Nuerland, according to the available evidence, are said to display a greater heterogeneity in the clan affiliations of the lineages that are dominant in the various sections of a tribe. Evans-Pritchard also thought that the status of aristocrats was less pronounced in the tribes to the west of the Nile. In the Karlual area of the Leek tribe, for example, 'the aristocratic prestige of a *dil* is recognized, but there are clans of strangers so well and long entrenched in the districts and villages in which they are found today that a *dil* has no legal privilege'. The author thought that conditions were much the same in the rest of western Nuerland, with the possible exception of the western Jikany (1940: 215-16).

This absence of a single strongly dominant clan among the western Nuer resembles the tribal structure among the non-expanding and much preyed-upon Dinka, who have been described by Lienhardt (1958) since the publication of the Nuer works. The situation is different in the larger tribes of the eastern portions of Nuerland, where certain groups of Nuer have more recently conquered territory that used to belong to the Dinka, and where, in so doing, conquering Nuer have absorbed into their own tribal structure larger numbers both of Dinka and of displaced Nuer. In this region, according to Evans-Pritchard, the prestige of aristocrats is more pronounced and a larger proportion of the dominant lineages of major tribal sections tend to be agnatically related as branches of the same dominant clan.

These points are made because it seems to me that in *Kinship and Marriage* the author has overstressed and 'over-homogenized' the significance of the 'agnatic principle' and has used it to explain some facts which it does not explain. Thus I disagree with his final statement in Chapter I, that it is just because the agnatic principle is unchallenged that the tracing of descent through women is so prominent and matrilocality so prevalent.

I would suggest rather another line of argument, which finds support in the author's data. This is that the expansion of the Nuer in historic times, and the conquest and absorption of Dinka and perhaps, also, of less powerful Nuer groups, has created a marked 'skewing' or unevenness in the operation of the agnatic principle among different layers of the population, especially in the eastern or more recently settled tribes. Thus it seems probable that agnation has become (at least fictionally) a *more* pervasive principle of *political* organization in these tribes for the conquering aristocrats than it is for the more homogeneous and longer-established western Nuer or for the Dinka. For in the eastern Nuer tribes, especially the larger ones, the aristocrats (who are presumably for the most part the descendants of conquerors) have been able, by fact or fiction, to establish a single agnatic clan as strongly dominant in most sections of each of these tribes. On the other hand, agnation seems to have become a *less* constant and pervasive principle of organization for the conquered, captured, immigrant, or otherwise absorbed Dinka and for the many Nuer who do not belong to the dominant clan in each tribe. In the case of such persons, who 'greatly outnumber the dominant clanspeople', residential ties, which are based on cognatic or affinal ties to segments of the dominant clan, far outweigh agnatic ties in the establishment of day-to-day obligations and loyalties.

The situation is complicated, for there are evidently (as Evans-Pritchard emphasizes) no permanent class or caste distinctions among the Nuer. There is rather a ready absorption of Dinka and of Nuer immigrants, either through adoption into the dominant agnatic groups themselves, or else through the continual establishment of new, small lineages, which are residentially linked to the dominant clanspeople as 'the children of girls'. Over time, moreover, with the consolidation of conquered regions, some of these latter groups seem to be themselves in process of becoming dominant in some tribal sections, so that a more traditional clan-heterogeneity among dominant lineages, comparable to that of the western Nuer, is gradually being restored. There is, therefore, among both aristocrats and non-aristocrats, an evident attempt to maintain or to restore 'the supremacy of the agnatic principle' at all levels of the population whenever possible. This attempt is most clearly seen in the insistence that every man of any consequence, whether living or dead, ought to have a legal son to carry on his agnatic line, and that every child ought to have a legal pater, however fictionally and loosely affiliated to him. In this sense, indeed, the ideal of agnation appears to be unchallenged.

In practice, however, I would argue that in the larger eastern tribes especially, both among the aristocrats and among the non-aristocrats, at the level of domestic relations, the context of expansion and conquest has caused a great variety of infringements of the normal rules of patrilineal descent. It has also caused a variety of modes of property transmission, group affiliation, and residence. Among the conquerors, this variety seems to have been brought about mainly by treating many women of the dominant lineages legally as if they were men. Among the recently conquered or the immigrant, the alternate modes seem to have been brought about by many men's being obliged to sacrifice both the claims of 'normal' legal fatherhood and also those of sonhood, and instead to occupy the roles of adoptees, co-resident sisters' sons, resident affines, or stand-in lovers, in relation to members of the dominant groups. In short, it is not that the tracing of descent through women is so common and matrilocality so prevalent, *because* the agnatic principle is unchallenged, but rather that an ideology of patrilineal descent, most strongly although not completely maintained by the aristocrats, has persisted *in spite of* frequent departures from agnatic norms – departures themselves necessitated by expansion and conquest.

To return to the 'children of girls', the strength of the agnatic principle would be clearer if we knew the precise relationships that these smaller attached stranger lineages have to the main body of the aristocratic clanspeople. When, in a single village, the chief bulls happen to be of a stranger clan, we know that the stranger minimal lineage is not regarded as aristocratic but is referred to as the 'children of girls'. But when, over a longer period of time, a larger stranger lineage has occasionally become dominant in a tertiary or secondary tribal section, do its members gradually come to be regarded as aristocrats strictly comparable to the true aristocrats of collateral tribal sections, even though

of different clan? And is the relationship of these odd sections dominated by strangers, with each other and with the sections dominated by
aristocrats, identical with the relationship between sections of the same
order dominated by aristocratic lineages?

The history of Thiang, a small subtertiary section of the Nyarkwac
tertiary section of the Lou tribe, suggests that this may not be the case
(1940: 144–6). The Thiang section was dominated by a stranger lineage
collectively called 'sisters' sons' both by the dominant lineage of its
collaterial subsection of the Nyarkwac tertiary section, the Yol, and also
by the dominant lineage of the Leng, a tertiary section collateral to
Nyarkwac. When the Yol and Thiang subsections fought, the Thiang
fled into the territory of the Leng, who supported them on the grounds
that they were sisters' sons, and with them fought off the Yol. The
case history is interesting because it shows that in fact, some tribes'
territorial sections are far from isomorphic with the genealogies of their
dominant lineages, and that the opposition between tribal sections has not
always been as balanced as Evans-Pritchard's paradigmatic presentation
would suggest. One wonders also whether the Leng would have supported the Thiang had the dominant lineages of Thiang and Yol both
stood to them in the relationship of distant agnates. We must, however,
leave aside this question, as the author does not discuss it. I would
argue in general, in fact, that in both books, both on a tribal and on a
village scale, Evans-Pritchard does not quite adequately explore the
specific intergroup relations between aristocratic lineages and the lesser
lineages of 'children of girls', nor does he explain their significance in the
total context of territorial and genealogical relationships.

This leads to a more general consideration of the author's distinction
between intergroup and interpersonal relationships as set forth in
Kinship and Marriage. Intergroup relationships, he states, are political
relationships; they are relationships between territorial sections of like
order, the smallest of which is the village, and they take their form
from the *buth* relationships between lineages of the dominant clan.
Interpersonal relationships are kinship relationships, the relationships of
mar. Within the village, it is stated, all social relationships are interpersonal kinship relationships, and each individual has many comparable interpersonal relationships stretching outside into other villages,
tribal sections, or even tribes (1951: 8).

The usefulness of a general distinction between interpersonal kinship
ties and durable relations between territorial sections is not disputed.

But it is clear that between these two there is another layer of social organization. Thus the village, although it may be nothing more than an expanded domestic unit, is itself divided into factions, ephemeral indeed but significant for intra-village organization. These factions are spatially separate units. In a small village, each comprises a composite homestead or group of homesteads; in a large village they form separate hamlets. Each faction appears to centre upon one 'bull' to whom the other members are linked, either transitorily or permanently, by a variety of kinship or affinal ties. Sometimes, the 'bulls' of different factions are close agnates. At Konye, for example, the two factions are headed respectively by a father and son, while at Nyueny, two pairs of aristocratic full brothers are found living far apart; in one case this results from a quarrel between their wives. Sometimes, however, there seems to be a tendency for the aristocratic agnates to set themselves up in one hamlet in the village with their attached affines, while another hamlet is occupied by a group categorized as 'children of daughters', together with some of *their* immediate affines. Thus at Nyueny two out of four hamlets of the village were occupied permanently by the children of daughters, one only by most of the aristocrats and their immediate attachés, huddled together in the south, while two, at opposite ends of the camp, were dominated by widows, one of whom (through the institution of widow-marriage) had a large congeries of wives and children. In the wet season at Yakwac, again, the two halves of the camp were dominated respectively by two 'bulls', both attached through the female line to the aristocratic lineage, but distantly related to each other; while in the dry season, each 'bull' was joined by a cluster of aristocratic kin of different minimal lineages of the minor lineage of the district (1951: 17–19).

Evans-Pritchard says little about the internal structure of these groupings, the relations between them, or the rise to power of their bulls. In *Kinship and Marriage* he merely states that there are rivalries between them. In *African Systems of Kinship and Marriage* he gives an interesting anecdote about how he once gave spears to some men living at the opposite end of Konye village. Later, 'a man at our end protested to me in private: – "When you have gone they will think nothing of killing us with your spears". When I expostulated that they were all members of the same village, he replied: "Have you not noticed that between our end and their end there is a wide gap?" ' (1950: 362). It is a pity we hear nothing more about this or other such gaps. For had the author explained more about the development of factions – had he in fact explored small-scale political relations within the village instead of presenting it as organized only on the basis of interpersonal kinship ties 'of equal weight' (1951: 9), it would have been easier to see how the kinship system is articulated to the political structure and to assess the different roles played by aristocrats and strangers (and by agnation and cognation) in each.

3 *Movement among the Nuer*

The existence of localized factions headed by 'bulls' each surrounded by various types of kin brings up the question of the extent and kinds of movement among the Nuer. Chapter 1 of *Kinship and Marriage* gives the impression at several points that all Nuer tend to wander freely in the course of their lives.[3] At other points, however, it becomes clear that it is immigrant or first-generation Dinka, or poorer Nuer (who are seldom of aristocratic lineage, and are often of 'foreign' lineages not dominant in any tribe) who have the greatest tendency to move permanently or to remain away from their patrilineal kin.[4] By contrast, the author notes that although not all members of a dominant lineage live in the area associated with it, 'very many of them may do so'. These statements indicate that the chances of residence for a long period away from the village of one's legal father and agnatic kinsmen are by no means even for the various categories of the population. This in turn suggests that it is chiefly among the aristocrats, who are the owners and in some cases the conquerors of tribal territories, that the agnatic principle predominates. Because of their land rights, and also because of a tendency to own more cattle (since most 'bulls' are aristocrats and 'bulls' must have cattle to be powerful), it appears that the aristocrats emphasize agnatic as against maternal and conjugal links and tend to live patrilocally. By contrast the strangers, and particularly of course immigrant, captured, or first-generation Dinka who have not been directly adopted into aristocratic lineages, tend to place a greater emphasis on maternal and conjugal links to persons of aristocratic lineage. Where circumstances are favourable, stranger Nuer, as 'children of girls', dig in their toes and develop a small lineage which may eventually oust the aristocrats of one village, or even, over time, of a tertiary or larger tribal section, and themselves develop a stronger agnatic bias. Descendants of Dinka may in time do the same thing by actually merging into the lineage of their Nuer ancestress, who comes to be regarded in the genealogy as if she had been a man. But for a majority of the population, who have as we are told only very shallow minimal lineages, and these often dispersed over several villages, this does not seem to be possible. Such persons apparently wander about, attaching themselves for convenience to villages through maternal or affinal links. Some aristocrats, too, must wander, even into other tribes. But for most aristocrats the greater pressure seems to be to perpetuate the pater's lineage in the natal village, or, as 'bulls', to move in lineage groups in order to become the leaders of newly occupied hamlets of their own tribal territories or of newly conquered hamlets in the territories of neighbouring tribes.

These interpretations are supported by various statements of the author about the position of Dinka, and of Nuer of stranger clans, in the society as a whole. In *African Systems of Kinship and Marriage* (1950), in particular, Evans-Pritchard notes the extensive use Dinka make of conjugal and maternal links and the fact that Dinka and persons of Dinka descent often have experiences which would be impossible for Nuer, moving from one village to another with no minimal lineage to support them, and attaching themselves wherever they can by virtue of conjugal and matrilateral ties. He also mentions in this paper and elsewhere that the lovers of unmarried women or widow-concubines, and of wives married to female husbands, are often poor strangers or Dinka, many of whom never marry a wife for themselves. In short, it seems apparent that the Nuer kinship system, with its curious features of frequent concubinage, woman-marriage, and the turning of ancestresses into men, depends at least partly on the continuous incorporation of immigrant and captured Dinka and stranger Nuer of lower rank; in other words that Nuer kinship is to a considerable extent a result of the Nuer's rapid expansion and conquests of the past hundred years or so, and needs to be explained in that context.

Although these facts are apparent from the author's own writings, I would argue that they are not sufficiently stressed and integrated into the argument. In particular, there is a tendency in much of *Kinship and Marriage* to present the kinship system as if it operated similarly for all categories of the population, whereas it is clear that its biases are of one type for the aristocrats and of quite another type for most other tribesmen. We must therefore question Evans-Pritchard's assumption of an 'unchallenged agnatic principle' in Nuer society. Instead, what we apparently have at any one time is a relatively small proportion of

95

the population (the aristocrats) who are oriented chiefly towards their agnates. Even this is not entirely true, for many aristocrats are of course also oriented towards the children of their sisters, some of whom live in uxorilocal marriage with low-ranking husbands and some of whom 'father' children for their brothers' lineages through the fiction of woman-marriage. On the other side, the stranger Nuer and the Dinka are chiefly oriented towards the aristocrats, which means towards their own matrilateral, mixed cognatic, or conjugal kin.

EXOGAMIC AND INCEST PROHIBITIONS

1 *Outline*

A Nuer may not marry into his own clan, into the maximal lineage or in some tribes the clan of his mother, nor with any cognate who shares with him a common ancestor or ancestress up to five or six generations ago. He may not marry into his genitor's maximal lineage, if his genitor was other than his pater, and he may not marry any natural kinswoman related to him through ancestors up to three or four generations ago. He may not be married to a woman and to any of her close kinswomen at the same time. He may not marry his dead wife's sister or other close kinswoman if his dead wife had children. Two brothers or close paternal cousins may not marry two sisters or close paternal cousins. A man may not marry the daughter of an age-mate. In general, except in the case of ego's own distant clanswomen or distant clanswomen of his mother, marriage prohibitions are stated in terms of bridewealth. A man may not marry any woman at whose marriage he himself or his close kinsfolk have the right to claim bridewealth, for it is forbidden for a person both to provide and to receive bridewealth for the same marriage.

Incest prohibitions extend in theory to all women whom it is forbidden to marry, with the exception of the daughter of an age-mate. Sexual relations with this girl are not incestuous unless there is kinship between the two; only marriage is prohibited, because, it is stated, this would bring into the respectful relationship of father-in-law a man with whom the bridegroom, as an age-mate, ought to be on terms of joking familiarity.

In addition to kinswomen prohibited for marriage, however, incest prohibitions are also extended to various living kinsmen's wives with whom it would not be incestuous and might even be obligatory to cohabit after their husbands' deaths. Thus, although Nuer may and occasionally do cohabit with the widows of their full brothers, fathers, mother's brothers, mother's brother's sons, and father's sisters' sons, it is incest of the gravest kind to have relations with these women while their husbands are alive. It is, however, only slightly incestuous to have relations with the wives of the father's paternal half-brothers, own paternal half-brothers, and first paternal cousins (some of the men on whose behalf a man may marry a woman in ghost marriage, or with whose widow he may be required to cohabit in the levirate); and it is not incestuous at all to have relations with the wives of more distant agnates.

Incest prohibitions vary in their strength and in the direness of the punishment with which they are thought to be visited. The worst forms of incest would be with the mother, sister, daughter, with a woman related to one through the mother, with the wife of a man related to one through the mother, with any woman with whom the father might subsequently have relations and so carry the son's sexual contact to the mother, or with the daughter or mother of a woman with whom one had previously had relations. These forms are of an order far more grave than is incest with a woman related to one through the father and not through the mother, because Nuer say that all of these in some way remind them of incest with the mother, which they believe would mean instant death.

2 *Exogamy and Territorial Groups*

Nuer marriage prohibitions are in harmony with their residential patterns and support the structure of their territorial groups. In two insightful passages (Evans-Pritchard 1940: 225–8; 1951: 46–7), Evans-Pritchard explains how prohibitions of marriage with cognates and affines, as well as with agnates, bring about virtual exogamy of the local community and hence also necessitate links between territorial sections of the tribe, which become less numerous as the territorial scale widens. The author also points out how the combination of clan exogamy with the prohibitions of marriage to cognates and affines separates out the dominant lineages of a tribe, thus providing the tribe with its segmentary genealogical framework, while at the same time fusing each dominant lineage of a local community with its own attached small lineages of 'children of girls'.

Kathleen Gough

Evans-Pritchard draws somewhat different conclusions from these facts in *Kinship and Marriage*, however, from those he draws in *The Nuer*. In *The Nuer* (1940: 228) he notes: 'A lineage remains an exclusive agnatic group only in ritual situations. In other situations it is merged in the community, and cognation (*mar*) takes the place of lineage agnation (*buth*) as the value through which people living together express their relations to one another. The agnatic structure of the dominant lineage is not stressed in ordinary social relations, but only on a political plane where relations between territorial segments are concerned, for the assimilation of territorial segments to segments of the dominant lineage means that the interrelations of the one are expressed in terms of the other.' This passage suggests that whereas the agnatic structure of the dominant clan provides a framework for the relations between territorial sections, in everyday social life cognation takes precedence over agnation.

In *Kinship and Marriage*, by contrast, the author writes (1951: 47–8) 'The Nuer make any kind of cognatic relationship to several degrees a bar to marriage, and, at least so it seems to me, it is a bar to marriage because of the fundamental agnatic principle running through Nuer society. In any Nuer residential group . . . the warp of the texture is the agnatic lineage and to it everyone attaches himself locally. If a man is not a member of the lineage with which he lives, he makes himself a member of it by treating a maternal link as though it was a paternal one or through affinal relationship.'

The section in *The Nuer* is to me the more enlightening in that it simply describes the state of affairs. In the passage in *Kinship and Marriage* we are burdened with an unnecessary paradox when we read that cognatic relationships are a bar to marriage because of the fundamental agnatic principle. This is a variant of the earlier paradox, that it is because the agnatic principle is unchallenged that the tracing of descent through women is so common and matrilocality so prevalent. In both cases I would argue rather that it is because of the incipient social stratification of Nuer society and the prominence of dominant clan groups, that other members of the society stress their cognatic links to the dominant lineage of the community rather than their own agnatic ties; and that the dominant lineages themselves make room in their structure for cognatically attached branches of lower rank. In the society at large, agnatic descent has thus given way to the requirements of conquest, absorption, and a fluid kind of social stratification, while

98

still providing the main (although not the sole) basis of organization of the dominant layer in each tribe.

I should like now to point to some more detailed ways in which it seems to me that exogamic rules buttress the political system. First, the rules bring into each village attached affines of many different clan groups who are not related to, and have no unity with, one another, but who are bound to the village through their individual ties to its 'bulls'. Further, such attached affines may not become related by intermarriage while they stay in the village. Even though some of them may stand outside the prohibited degrees to one another, their common kinship with the aristocrats and common residence in one village is apparently thought sufficient to prevent their intermarriage, although it does not prevent occasional concubinage among them.

Second, if the descendants of a woman of the dominant lineage should happen to remain in the village over several generations, they are prohibited from marrying back into the minimal lineage of their ancestress. They therefore temporarily attach themselves to the local exogamic group of the aristocrats and with it form part of the village's core, as against more recently arrived affines. Thus, all over Nuerland, small localized minimal lineages of aristocrats often have, attached to them, children of daughters whose descendants temporarily form one exogamic unit with them in each of their villages. Each of these small attached groups of 'children of girls' may, however, intermarry in *other* villages with people belonging to collateral lineages of aristocrats. Their status as affines of the aristocratic lineage is thereby maintained and they cannot merge with the aristocrats as a whole. The marriage prohibitions thus for a few generations make Nuer 'children of daughters' something like honorary members of the aristocratic clan in their own village, while permitting them to provide spouses for collateral lineages of aristocrats. Even the descendants of Dinka 'children of girls', although they may in time merge completely into the lineage of their Nuer ancestress, do not acquire membership in her whole clan, but may continue to marry into collateral lineages of it in other communities. In this way the rules of exogamy isolate the dominant lineages within each tribe as a whole and permit their segmentary structure to provide a rough framework for the segmentary oppositions between territorial sections, while at the same time each local lineage of the dominant clan is fused with other elements to form a solidary community.

99

Kathleen Gough

3 The Relationship of Exogamy to Incest Prohibitions

Evans-Pritchard states that the Nuer say that certain marriages are forbidden because they are incestuous. By contrast, however, he says that speaking sociologically, *we* may say that certain unions are incestuous because marriage is forbidden between the parties, that is to say, that incest prohibitions are derived from marriage prohibitions. The marriage prohibitions in turn exist because such marriages would bring the persons concerned into two sets of roles which conflict with one another.

I am not sure what Evans-Pritchard means by the statement that incest prohibitions exist because of marriage prohibitions and are derived from them. He refers to the fact that incest prohibitions are sociologically defined, that is, they are not innate in men (1951: 44). This is of course clear, since their range varies so greatly and can be shown to be in harmony with other aspects of social structure. It is not, however, the same as saying that incest prohibitions derive from marriage prohibitions. The author can scarcely mean that the marriage prohibitions preceded and led to the incest prohibitions historically, for this would be impossible to validate. His point that marriage prohibitions are related to the fact that, if they did not exist, conflictful social relationships would arise is, I think, a correct one, but this also applies to incest prohibitions in themselves, so it does not prove that the one type of prohibition derives from the other. He gives as a further reason the fact that Nuer regard as incestuous many relationships between persons who are not blood-kin. But this again proves nothing about the derivations of incest prohibitions, since it would be an adequate explanation to say that such incest prohibitions exist because incest itself, let alone marriage, would bring the parties or their kin into conflictful relationships. Perhaps all that can be said is that incest prohibitions and marriage prohibitions are intimately related to one another, that both derive from a need to avoid conflictful relationships, and that both are related to the political system and to the kinship system as a whole.

There is, however, positive evidence against the view that Nuer incest prohibitions exist solely because of marriage prohibitions. Some persons, for example the daughters of age-mates, are prohibited for marriage, yet extramarital relations with them are not incestuous and frequently occur. The reason for this is that marriage with an age-mate's daughter would bring the bridegroom into permanently conflictful relations with her father, whereas fleeting sex relations with her in contexts in which her father is not involved conflict with neither party's more permanent roles.

A further argument against the derivative character of incest prohibitions is that, among the Nuer, incest prohibitions and marriage prohibitions are given somewhat different emphases. The former relate equally to agnatic and maternal kinship, or, if anything, stress agnatic as against maternal kinship. Marriage with any clanswoman is unthinkable, whereas marriage to a distant clanswoman of the mother or to a cognatic kinswoman related to ego through an ancestor only five or six generations back, is sometimes permitted. The prohibitions on marriage, which is a durable institution setting up links between local groups and between lineages, are therefore more intimately related to the large-scale political structure than are incest prohibitions on casual sexual relationships, which pertain more to life within the local community or to temporary visits elsewhere. Incest prohibitions, by contrast, stress maternal kinship much more than agnatic kinship. The most dangerous forms of incest, bringing mystical retributions, are those which in any way suggest contact with the mother or with a person comparable to or closely linked with her. Relations with distant agnates, or with the wives of agnates not also related through the mother, are, by contrast, scarcely incestuous at all.

The 'uterine emphasis' of Nuer incest prohibitions is apparently in harmony with certain differences in both legal and emotional content between agnatic and cognatic kin. Thus, for example, as Evans-Pritchard points out, one reason why a Nuer may with comparative ease cohabit with his father's brother's wife but not with his mother's brother's wife is that agnates have a right to share a home and cattle. They marry wives with each other's cattle, and have residual rights in each other's wives. But a sister's son has no legal rights in any of the property of his mother's brother, who belongs to another agnatic group. If he lives with him, it is somewhat as a guest, by courtesy of the mother's brother, and always his relationship is one of ambivalence. He may demand things of the mother's brother by virtue of their close relationship through the mother, but can demand nothing as of legal right and dare not too much infringe on the privacy of his mother's brother or of the mother's brother's agnatic group. He has the licence of a guest in their village but is dependent on their generosity; he cannot claim this as a right. The same difference extends to the relations with more distant agnatic and matrilateral kinsmen and with their wives.

Kathleen Gough

4 Incest Prohibitions and Relations with Uterine Kin

This emphasis on incest prohibitions with the wives of uterine kinsmen is in harmony with a number of other observances. Thus, a man may not joke obscenely with men related to him through the mother. By contrast, male agnates make a habit of obscene joking, especially with reference to each others' maternal kinswomen; and 'bulls' who are not also uterine kin may share each others' sweethearts.

Aberle's analysis of avoidant and joking relationships among the Navaho sheds light on this distinction. 'The jokes seem to be a play on the ambiguities of group loyalty established by descent and marriage', so that 'Members of a clan joke about things that divide them: different paternal [in the Nuer case, maternal – K.G.] affiliations.' In addition, jokes between members of the same clan centre upon delicate relationships with close kinsfolk in other clans or through other channels of relationship, where such joking is not permitted: 'Every delicate relationship is a joke for someone else; every joke is about someone else's delicate relationship' (Aberle 1961: 156–7).

As Evans-Pritchard points out, differences of descent group affiliation are also at the heart of the relationship with the mother's brother (1951: 162–5). On the one hand he is the tender supporter. He indulges his sister's son in childhood; he makes gifts and commonly provides his nephew with cattle at marriage; he owes him special perquisites such as a bull-calf at initiation; if the youth's father dies or he does not get along with his paternal kinsmen, the mother's brother may provide him with a home and cattle. On the other hand, there are special prohibitions suggesting delicacy, ambivalence, and social separation between mother's brother and sister's son. The two may not tether their cattle in the same kraal, may not sleep in the same hut, or use the same sleeping-hide. Neither may bury the other after his death. If the uncle is wounded, the sister's son must go to him and put some of the blood on his own foot. A man may not skin a dead beast of his mother's brother. An uncle may not give his sister's son a spear-shaft, for the gift might cause him serious injury. Unlike the father, the mother's brother may curse a youth's cattle, his crops, fishing, and hunting, and his curse may prevent the nephew from begetting male children.

While the prohibitions relating to the mother's brother, and the usually strict ban on incest with the wives of matrilateral kinsmen, reflect a general distinction between patrilineal and matrilateral kin found in

102

all patrilineal societies, it seems to me that they have special point among the Nuer because of the residential patterns of local communities and the existence of dominant clans. Among the Nuer, residence with the maternal kin is not merely a special alternative of which a small number of disadvantaged people avail themselves. It is a common, indeed customary pattern in the case of many Dinka and 'stranger' Nuer, especially those of clans not dominant in any tribe. In spite of the egalitarian approach to life of the Nuer, the relationship of dominant clansmen to their sisters' husbands or sisters' sons is often one of superordination on the one side and dependency on the other, particularly if the latter are co-resident Dinka, poor Nuer, or men without a tribal 'home'. It is, however, a special kind of dependency. The mother's brother is usually glad to incorporate his sisters' children into his local community. They form part of his personal following, add to his strength, and may help him to set up a separate hamlet or village. They are also bound to him and to his uterine brothers through personal ties, in a way that the mother's brother's agnates, who 'belong' in the village, are not. This gives the mother's brother a great assurance of their loyalty as long as they remain with him.

On the other hand, a man's co-resident sisters' sons or sisters' husbands can be a burden to him. They may make claims on his generosity and his herds that he may be unable or unwilling to fulfil. Presumably, his own sons may become jealous of them. If he is a member of the dominant lineage it seems probable that circumstances could arise in which other aristocrats might resent the intrusion of strangers on village lands or might resent their bid for leadership in the community. The rules that separate a man and his sister's son, and the beliefs that centre upon their mutual ambivalence and power to harm each other serve, I suggest, to structure this delicate and potentially conflictful situation, in which sisters' sons have a right to live with their mothers' brothers but do not have a right to usurp the privileges of sons. The strength of incest prohibitions in relation to matrilateral kinswomen and to the wives of matrilateral kinsmen seems also to be appropriate to this frequent asymmetry of lineage rank (and often of cattle wealth) between the men of a dominant lineage and the co-resident 'children of girls'.

It is perhaps especially significant that his mother's brother's curse may prevent a man from begetting sons. While it may have other functions too, the belief sanctions the role of the mother's brother as one who permits his sister's son to settle as a dependent in his community.

If the youth transgresses the limits of hospitality, however, his mother's brother (and perhaps also, any classificatory 'mother's brother' of the community), while he may not be able to get rid of him directly, may curse the youth to prevent him from developing his own agnatic lineage there.

MARRIAGE

1 *Bridewealth*

Nuer marriage and incest prohibitions stress equally but in a different manner the paternal and maternal sides of an individual's kin. The same is true with regard to the payment of bridewealth, which Evans-Pritchard discusses in his third chapter on marriage. Ideally, forty cattle should be paid as bridewealth, of which twenty go to the bride's father's and twenty to her mother's side. Ten are distributed between the mother's brothers and mother's sisters and ten between corresponding kin of the father, while twenty go to the bride's elementary family. The bride's full brothers share seven cattle since they are both agnatic and uterine kin, while her paternal half-brothers receive only two. The father, however, receives eight as against the mother's three, so that the overall division is equal between these two halves of the elementary family.

Payment of cattle is obligatory to maternal as well as paternal kin. But the provision of cattle is legally the responsibility only of the bridegroom's immediate agnates (his father and father's brothers), although his mother's brother and sometimes his mother's sister are asked to contribute, and usually do so from affection. This legal difference in the provision and reception of bridewealth relates, I think, although Evans-Pritchard does not mention this, to the difference in status of an unmarried girl and of a wife. An unmarried girl, like a boy before initiation, belongs in a sense to both paternal and maternal kin. For it is the birth of children which changes the maternal and paternal kin from affines into cognates and, as Evans-Pritchard often stresses, sets up what is regarded as blood kinship between them. The mother's parents even have the right to bring up an eldest child until initiation or (in the case of a girl), betrothal. Both sides of kin are therefore recompensed for the partial loss of an unmarried girl.

A wife, by contrast, is the wife of a *gol* or small agnatic group. The close agnates, but not the maternal kin of the husband, have residual rights in her. One of them, for example, may become the levir of the

husband if he should die, and the agnates as a collectivity have the right
to divorce a young widow if she refuses to live in leviratic marriage with
one of them. It is therefore fitting that only the agnates should be
legally responsible for the payment of bridewealth at a marriage.

In this chapter Evans-Pritchard makes a statement about the nutritive
and marital value of cattle which seems to be a direct reversal of his
earlier view, expressed in *The Nuer*, of the importance of economic
determinants of social structure, and a foreshadowing of his later views
on the autonomy of values. Evans-Pritchard states (1951: 90): 'It is not
that having great nutritive value cattle acquire through it a general
social value, become a standard of worth, and are therefore employed
in ritual, for indemnification of injury, and as a means of acquiring a
mate. It is rather that their use as bridewealth gives them their supreme
value in Nuer eyes.' I very much doubt this statement, although I think
it would be impossible to measure the nutritive as against the marital
value which Nuer ascribe to cattle. But that their nutritive value certainly looms large for Nuer when bridewealth is being paid appears
from their scornful remark, quoted in the preceding paragraph, about
the Anuak payment of beads and spears at a marriage. 'Of what use are
these things? Can people live on them?'

A similar inversion occurs, I believe, with reference to the significance of the sexual play of Nuer children. Because it is associated with
playing at marriage and with imitation cattle byres, mud oxen, and huts
of sand, the author states (1951: 50): 'In its earliest expression therefore,
sex is associated with marriage, and the first sexual play occurs in
imitation of one of the domestic routines of married life. It occurs in
response to a cultural and not to an instinctual urge.' This interpretation seems unlikely, for children's sexual play has been recorded for a
large number of societies under varying cultural conditions. Psychoanalytic research suggests, moreover, that genital motives are probably
universal in children from the age of four or five, although of course
they receive varying cultural expressions. In both of these instances I
would argue that an unwarranted precedence has been given to symbolic
values over material and biological wants.

2 Forms of Marriage and Domestic Union

It is in the discussion in this chapter of the several forms of Nuer marriage and domestic union that I think Evans-Pritchard is at his best. I
find his analysis brilliant and can think of no questions to ask which are

not answered in his material. He advances here beyond Radcliffe-Brown's simple distinction between the genitor as physical father and the pater as legal father, for he points out that the Nuer genitor, too, can have various legal rights in his child, especially if he is acting as the pro-husband of a dead man.

In briefly mentioning the several types of marriage, I would, however, like to classify the rights of men as husbands, lovers, and fathers slightly differently from Evans-Pritchard, for I think that my classification throws light on some aspects of marriage and paternity that he has left obscure. I would divide the legal roles of persons in relation to wives or concubines and to children into three, namely those of the genitor, the pater, and what I shall call 'the legal marital partner'.

A genitor as mere genitor has no rights in nor duties to the woman by whom he begets a child. His rights in his children are confined to the right to receive the cow of begetting at the marriage of a daughter. This right, however, he may not or rather does not exercise if he begot the daughter by an unmarried girl whom he then refused to marry. Such a genitor, who is despised, in this case fades from the scene and the child belongs to its mother's lineage or else, later, has as pater the man who eventually marries its mother with cattle. A genitor of any kind is, however, believed to have a mystical connexion with his child and to be capable of harming it by wishing it ill. If a child is on good terms with his genitor he may later propitiate the ancestors of this man.

A pater, as pater, whether dead or living, gives his legal name to a child. The child belongs to his lineage and clan, and has the right to marry from any cattle the pater owns or has left behind, and to inherit further cattle if there are any. The pater, or his heir, has the right to receive the cattle of the pater at the marriage of a daughter. His son must communicate with the pater's ghost after death. By custom a boy ought to be initiated in the village of his pater, but this rule is not always observed and apparently cannot be enforced. Even a living pater, apparently, cannot legally force his children to live in his village, although he may steal them away or beguile them through promise of cattle. An unmarried boy or girl and a married man have, however, the right to live in the house and with the close agnates of the pater, and this right may not be refused. The rights of a pater are acquired through payment of cattle, either as bridewealth or as legitimization fee, and can be acquired in no other way. Further, once bridewealth has been paid for a woman, the person on whose behalf the cattle were paid is the pater of all children born to her unless she is divorced and the bridewealth cattle are returned. The rules regarding a female pater are the same as those for a male.

By 'legal marital partner' I refer to the person who, although he or she may or may not be the legal husband of a woman and the pater of her children, has by law exclusive rights in the woman's sexuality and rights in her domestic services. The legal marital partner is the person who may sue an adulterer for damages. A female legal marital partner holds these rights in the same manner as a male, except that she delegates sexual privileges to a lover of her choosing. She may however dismiss the lover at will, and it is she and not the lover who claims damages from an adulterer.

I now mention briefly the several forms of domestic union with reference to these three roles. In simple legal marriage all three roles are held by the husband and father by virtue of payment of cattle. In ghost-marriage, the dead man is the pater. The pro-husband is often a younger brother or brother's son of the ghost, occasionally his legal son, and rather more often his natural son. If the deceased has no agnates or natural sons, the pro-husband may be his sister's son. The pro-husband in ghost-marriage is both genitor and legal marital partner. The same distribution of roles occurs in the uncommon circumstance in which a man marries a wife to his dead barren sister or father's sister, and in the slightly more common circumstance in which a barren woman marries a wife to her dead agnate, except that in the latter case the female legal marital partner delegates the sexual role of genitor to some man who becomes the lover of the wife.

In ordinary woman marriage to a woman, the female husband, usually a barren woman, holds the roles of pater and legal marital partner. She takes on a man's role, manages her own herd and cattle byre, and is treated as husband and father by her wife and children. The lover to whom she delegates her sexual role has the role of genitor but not of legal marital partner.

In leviratic marriage the dead husband is the pater, and the pro-husband is both the legal marital partner and the genitor. His rights as legal marital partner are, however, weaker than in ghost-marriage, for if, after having two or more children by him or by the dead man, the wife goes away to a lover, he is unlikely to be able to exact damages and may not divorce her. He is then obliged to waive his right as legal marital partner, and the right lapses.

Kathleen Gough

Widow concubinage occurs when a woman refuses to cohabit with, or leaves, the levir of her dead husband, and goes to live with a lover. If she is young and has no children or only one child, her husband's agnates may divorce her and reclaim the bridewealth if necessary, leaving only sufficient cattle to legitimize the single child. The woman's subsequent children are then legitimized by their several genitors, each of whom thus also becomes a pater. The role of legal marital partner is absent in this union. The husband's agnates have surrendered it at the divorce, and the woman's subsequent lovers do not acquire it, for they have no exclusive rights in her sexuality and services and she may leave them at will. If the widow had two or more children by her dead husband or by his levir, the levir may not divorce her if she chooses to live with a lover. In this union, therefore, the dead husband is the pater of the woman's children, the role of legal marital partner lapses, and the widow's lover is merely the genitor of any children she bears to him.

A similar situation occurs in the concubinage of a wife. Here, a wife leaves her legal husband or pro-husband and goes to cohabit with a lover. The husband or pro-husband, as legal marital partner, may succeed in claiming damages for adultery, but if the woman refuses to return to him he cannot coerce her. If she has several children he may not divorce her, but must be content to allow her to 'bear in the bush'. The woman's legal husband is in this case the pater of all children born to his wife. Her lover is the genitor of any children she may bear to him, and the right of the legal marital partner lapses.

Unmarried concubinage is the concubinage of a woman who has never been married or who is divorced. If a man impregnates a girl who is willing to marry him and then refuses to marry her, he may not legitimize the child, nor may he later claim the cow of begetting if it is a girl. He is thus a mere genitor without any legal rights. The woman usually marries later and her husband becomes the pater of her formerly illegitimate child. A man who has impregnated an unmarried girl but who has no cattle may, however, promise to marry her with cattle later, and for the time being pay only the legitimization fee of the child. He is then both its pater and genitor and, if the child is a girl, may claim the cattle of the pater at her marriage, even if he has not fulfilled his promise to marry the mother. If a woman, as is not uncommon, refuses to marry and prefers to bear children in the bush, the several genitors legitimize their children by payment of a fee in cattle and become the respective paters of these children. The same situation arises in the case

108

of a divorced concubine. Occasionally, however, a young divorced woman who gives promise of fidelity to her lover may later be married by him, when she enters again into simple legal marriage. The role of legal marital partner is, however, lacking in all forms of unmarried concubinage.

Thus women living in widow concubinage, unmarried concubinage, and concubinage of a wife, are under the legal guardianship of no man in respect of their work and domestic services. Often, in fact, they own cattle, and always they are separate legal personalities. Further, in woman marriage to a woman, the female pater is not only a separate legal personality but also the legal guardian of a family, with male rights to receive bridewealth, to manage a homestead and cattle, and to inherit from her agnatic kin.

At Nyueny village, twenty out of thirty-three adult women had no legal marital partners, since they were living as concubines, as female paters, or as elderly independent widows. Nine of these women were, however, old, so that it is perhaps more relevant to point out that out of twenty-four women of childbearing age, eleven had no legal marital partners. If it is safe to assume from this that, in Nuerland as a whole, just under half the women of childbearing age are under the legal guardianship of no man, this surely has important implications for the 'strength of the agnatic principle'. One is that the rights of men over women, as against their rights over their children, are in this society very weak. Further, the rights of men in their legal children are also to some extent weakened when the mother is not legally subordinate to the father, for it is difficult for a pater to coerce the children of such women either to live with him or to fulfil the moral responsibilities of children towards him.

Speaking of the strength of the agnatic principle among the Nuer, Evans-Pritchard observes that the forms of domestic union other than simple legal marriage *strengthen* the units of the group of close agnates, for they weaken the unique bond with the father and thus undermine the exclusiveness of the elementary family, while at the same time attaching a child, through his pater, to his minimal lineage as a whole. This is indeed true of leviratic marriage, and also of ghost-marriage when the pro-husband is an agnate of the deceased. In this case the child is doubly bound to his agnatic group through both pater and genitor. Something of the same process may perhaps occur in the case of some children born in widow concubinage, for if, as Evans-Pritchard says often happens, the child eventually returns to his agnatic kin, he is, in the absence of his pater, bound to them as a group. It seems, however, from the genealogies that many sons born in widow concubinage do not, in fact, return to their pater's village, so that widow concubinage as a whole can hardly be said to strengthen agnatic ties. I doubt much, moreover, whether this process of strengthening of the agnatic group occurs in the case of children born in transitory unmarried concubinage, concubinage of a wife, or in those forms of ghost-marriage in which the pro-husband is a natural son or sister's son of the deceased. Here it would seem rather that the agnatic tie is greatly in danger of being weakened, for the son of such a union may opt to live with a foster-father who is not his pater, or with his maternal or conjugal kin. Since, at Nyueny, forty-two out of one hundred and nine children of thirty-two women were born in such unions, as against sixty-seven children born in the former type of unions more likely to give them strong bonds with their pater's agnates, it may be doubted whether, as a whole, unions other than those of simple legal marriage contribute greatly to the strengthening of agnatic ties.

These problems are further elucidated if we consider, from the house lists detailed in *Some Aspects of Kinship and Marriage*, the residence of married men and women at Nyueny. Out of the sixteen married men living at Nyueny at a particular point in time, seven lived in the village of their paters, five lived in the village of their genitors, one in the wife's village, one in the mother's brother's village, one in a concubine's village, and one in that of his sister's husband. Less than half of the men, therefore, lived in their pater's village, and it is most interesting to note that, of these seven, six were aristocrats. This supports my earlier argument that it is primarily for Nuer aristocrats that the agnatic principle is strong, but that it is much less strong for unadopted Dinka and for Nuer strangers. Out of a total of thirty-three adult women at Nyueny, fourteen lived in the village of their legal husbands in simple legal marriage, in ghost-marriage, or in leviratic marriage; ten lived in the village of their lovers, two in their pater's village, two old widows in the daughter's husband's village, and two other old unattached widows in a village where, apparently, they had no close kin. Thus considerably fewer than half the women of Nyueny lived in the village of their legal husbands, and of those fourteen women, it may be noted that eight of them were married to aristocrats. This again supports my view that the agnatic group is stronger, and the wives more closely bound to it, in the case of aristocrats than of others. Incidentally, the only female husband in this village was also an aristocrat; she lived in the village of her pater, controlled her own large cattle byre, and had accumulated three wives. These and their children lived with her and were visited by Dinka or stranger Nuer lovers from other villages.

Evans-Pritchard ends his analysis of marriage with the conclusion: 'Hence it follows that agnatic descent is, by a kind of paradox, traced through the mother, for the rule is that in virtue of payment of bride-wealth all who are born of her womb are children of her husband and therefore paternal kin, by whomsoever they may have been begotten. It is the fertility of the womb which a lineage receives by payment of bridewealth' (1951: 122).

This statement is of profound significance, for it focuses on the key characteristic of a particular kind of patrilineal kinship system which should, I think, be distinguished from various other patrilineal systems in comparative research. It is one which, by separating the rights in a woman as sexual partner and domestic worker from the rights in her as genetrix, affords a certain personal autonomy to women while retaining, at least in theory, the legal principle of agnatic descent. This feature is apparently widespread among the non-Muslim patrilineal peoples of Africa, but perhaps not commonly found elsewhere. Among the Nuer, I suggest that the separation between the rights *in uxorem* and the rights *in genetricem* has been carried to unusual lengths because of Nuer terri-torial expansion and the absorption of foreigners. In general, however, systems which permit the separation of rights *in uxorem* and *in genetricem* are radically different from various patrilineal kinship systems which are also what we may call patriarchal, in which a woman is legally subor-dinate to one man, or to one at a time, who controls at once the sexual, procreative, and domestic rights in her. The Brahmins of India exem-plify such a system. Here, unless he is born in adultery (when, if detected, both wife and child are expelled from the community), a man's legal son is always his natural son or else one he has, as an individual, legally adopted from among his agnatic kin. In this system, therefore, agnatic descent is traced through the father and not through the mother, for women are merely the procreative instruments of their husbands, and, after death, their names may be forgotten.

There is a second sense in which, among the Nuer, agnatic descent is traced through women. This arises from the fact that marriage is ideally, although it seems not very often in fact, polygynous. Collateral aristocratic lineages of varying depth are therefore frequently thought to have stemmed from paternal half-brothers, and each then traces its descent to the mother from whom it sprang. Such systems, also widespread in Africa, again contrast with that of the Brahmins, among whom polygyny is forbidden unless the first wife is barren, and among whom mothers do not therefore create points of fission within the agnatic lineage.

There are yet two other ways in which, indeed by a kind of paradox, agnatic descent among the Nuer may be traced through women. The first is the case of the female husband, and the second that of a woman, I suggest usually of the aristocratic clan, whose descendants claim a kind of honorary membership of her minimal lineage by continued co-residence with it, and, if their ancestor was a Dinka, may actually become incorporated as a branch of its clan. Both circumstances point to the unusual autonomy of women, especially of aristocratic women, and both, as I have said, reflect a weakening of what would normally be regarded as the agnatic principle. The prominence of both arrangements among the Nuer is connected, I suggest, with the social dominance of the aristocrats, probably resulting from conquest, and with the heavy rate of male mortality in warfare, a fact that Evans-Pritchard stresses (1945: 38). These conditions foster matrilocal residence among displaced and conquered strangers as one important means of reintegrating them into the society through cognatic attachment to the conquerors. The same conditions also appear to have reinforced a practice, no doubt of long standing among Nilotic peoples, of compensating for an unbalanced sex ratio by transferring childless women into the social roles of men.

Thus among the Nuer, I suggest, conquest and the systematic absorption of the conquered created a form of fluid social stratification in which it was primarily women of the conquering groups who were transferred into male roles through woman-marriage, or who were otherwise used to create points of attachment between each locally dominant group and its following of captives and strangers, classified as 'children of girls'. In so doing these women not only acted as social replacements for men of their own conquering groups who had been killed in warfare, but also served to oust from their marital and paternal roles numerous male captives or refugees, many of whom, apparently, never gave their name to a lineage or acquired a wife of their own. While, therefore, the separation of sexual and procreative rights in women may be a widespread feature in African societies, among the Nuer conditions of conquest and expansion gave it an unusual autonomy.

THE 'AGNATIC PRINCIPLE'

Considerations of space oblige me to leave aside Evans-Pritchard's analysis of relationships within the family and the wider kinship system. Bearing these in mind, I shall comment only on his main conclusion. This is that 'the supremacy of the agnatic principle which the lineage system embodies, by subordinating the roles of the family and the father to the interests of the wider groups of paternal kin and of the lineage, allows the many variants of forms of the family which are so common in Nuerland, and also the widespread adoption of Dinka, the easy translation of affinal and age-set ties into the values of the kinship system, a considerable social mobility, and high status of women. All these features seem to be interconsistent' (1951: 179).

Recapitulating, I would suggest rather that all these features are consistent, not with the supremacy of the agnatic principle in the society as a whole, but only with its supremacy among the aristocrats, and only then by virtue of the fact that the aristocrats, too, place such a high value on links through their women as a means of acquiring local adherents that they are willing to convert some of their women socially into men. For the aristocrats, and for those few lineages of stranger Nuer origin which have somehow managed to become dominant over a section of tribal territory and have acquired a certain depth, the agnatic principle is indeed strong. Through it, they acquire membership not only of a clan but also of a series of lineages of varying depth each associated with a segment of tribal territory. Through agnation they also acquire rights in the land of their lineages, prestige in the society at large, political affiliation to a territorial section, the legal support of a localized minimal lineage, and cattle for bridewealth and inheritance.

To the man who is not an aristocrat, however, the agnatic principle offers much less. It affiliates him to a dispersed exogamous clan (unless, indeed, he is an unadopted Dinka, when he is clanless and his descendants may take the clan of his wife). Agnation affiliates such a man to a minimal lineage usually only three generations deep or less, whose members may be scattered through one or more tribes, and who are therefore of little use to him in disputes, when he must rely for assistance on local matrilateral, conjugal, or natural ties. Agnation gives him little

prestige, which he derives rather from cognatic attachment to aristocrats of his locality. Agnation is unlikely to determine the non-aristocrat's residence, for the figures suggest that, at any one time, six out of
seven Nuer men residing in their paters' villages are aristocrats. Agnation gives the non-aristocrat no rights in land, for these he acquires
from aristocrats in whose locality, by virtue of cognatic ties, he resides.
Agnation may provide him with cattle to marry and establish a family
and the foundations of a lineage, but on the other hand it may not.
Out of twelve adult non-aristocrats at Nyueny, only five were either
legal husbands or pro-husbands for an agnatic ghost. Two, by contrast,
were pro-husbands respectively for their mother's brother and genitor's
brother, while three were the lovers of concubines and two had no
domestic union at all. Similarly, a non-aristocrat may in theory inherit
cattle through agnation, but it seems from the case histories that he is
more likely to obtain them, if at all, through the charity of maternal or
natural kin.

Since, as Evans-Pritchard says, non-aristocrats form the great majority of the population in any Nuer tribe, we most conclude that the
agnatic principle is far from supreme in its operation among the Nuer
although the ideal undoubtedly persists. It may be suggested that, in
Kinship and Marriage, Evans-Pritchard obscured this point because of
two tendencies in the presentation of his field material.

The first is that although he so brilliantly analysed the forms of
domestic union, the author tended at times to present the kinship
system as if it operated uniformly for a homogeneous population. In
the later chapters especially, Evans-Pritchard tends to abstract from
his material ideal norms of behaviour for the several sets of kin. Some
of these conflict with earlier evidence. His account of the unity of the
composite patrilineal homestead and the tendency of children of all
kinds of domestic unions to return to their paters' villages conflicts,
for example, with earlier evidence of the frequency with which men
reside with matrilateral, affinal, or natural kin.

Second, the analysis is somewhat distorted by being presented largely
from the point of view of men. Pages are devoted to the relationships
between male kinsmen, paragraphs to those between men and women,
and a few lines only to relationships among women. In particular, we
learn little of the relations between a man and his sister and daughter,
or between a woman and her daughter. We are told still less about the
relations between sisters, although it appears that a widow, or a wife

whose husband is lazy, may go to live with her sister, and that the relationship with the mother's sister's son is 'of all relationships, the one of most unadulterated benevolence' (1951: 168). It is sometimes argued by male anthropologists that relations with and between women are of only minor relevance to an analysis of the political aspects of kinship. This argument scarcely, however, holds good, at all events for a society where men are prohibited from cooking and so must attach themselves to some kinswoman's hearth, where some women may own cattle and live, legally autonomous, where they choose, where women may provide men with their local and political affiliations, and where, if all else fails them, some may turn themselves into men.

NUER KINSHIP IN ITS HISTORICAL SETTING

Kinship and Marriage among the Nuer exemplifies a tendency among British social anthropologists of the 1940s and 1950s to lift the social structure out of its historical setting and, at the point of interpretation, ascribe it to general principles as if it were in timeless equilibrium. In general, I question the value of such general principles as explanations of social structure, for they fail to take account of change and tend to explain away, rather than to explain, variability. Specifically, the Nuer case seems to be one in which the peculiar features of residence, marriage, and descent rules cannot be understood except in terms of a society until recently undergoing territorial expansion. It seems also to be one in a state of structural change such that the actual domestic relations of a large proportion of the population, especially with regard to male rights over women, do not fit the ideals of patrilineal descent, but are nevertheless continually reinterpreted, through a series of customary legal fictions, so that the ideals are preserved.

This preservation of the ideals through legal fictions may have occurred because the Nuer and the Dinka whom they conquered were patrilineal peoples of common origin and culture, surrounded by other patrilineal societies. They also had a pastoral mode of livelihood and a correlated sexual division of labour which, other things being equal, is conducive to patrilineal descent. The facts of conquest, high male mortality, and usurpation of land and cattle brought about, however, I suggest, an asymmetry in kinship relations such that both the men and the women in the conquering groups were advantageously placed in the business of owning and transmitting cattle, controlling land use, and thus of building up a local following in each community from among the less advantaged and the captive.

These suggestions are tentative. Two lines of further inquiry are needed to confirm or disprove them. One is into Nuer and Dinka history since the early nineteenth century. It would involve an attempt to correlate successive phases of Nuer expansion and consolidation with the formation of particular tribal structures and perhaps with the emergence of particular kinship usages. The other line of inquiry involves comparison of Nuer and Dinka kinship systems in recent times.

If it is true, as Howell asserts (1954: 7–9), that the Nuer and the Dinka were one people until the early nineteenth century, and if the Nuer have consistently preyed upon and absorbed the Dinka while the Dinka have as consistently been the victims of conquest and absorption, a comparison of their kinship systems might throw light on differences that are relevant to Nuer expansion. The comparison is complicated because most Dinka today live in a different ecological zone from that of most Nuer, so that, as Lienhardt points out, ecological influences on social structure have also to be considered (1958: 106, 112, 114). Nevertheless, useful insights could be gained from an investigation of the frequency of matrilocal residence or residence with affines in Dinka communities, as contrasted with Nuer, as also of the incidence of widow-concubinage, woman-marriage, unmarried concubinage and concubinage of a wife, the extent of female emancipation from male controls over sexuality and domestic services, and the connexions, if any, between these practices and the local dominance of particular lineages or clans. Such evidence as is available to me at present suggests that, while the forms of domestic union and patterns of residence of the Nuer are all present among the Dinka, their significance and frequency may be different. Thus, Lienhardt's account of the western Dinka suggests more regular adherence to the norm of patrilocal residence among the Dinka than among the Nuer, a multiplicity of small lineages in most Dinka communities, often with no one lineage clearly dominant, and a lower incidence of woman-marriage and of concubinage (ibid.). The Seligmans note that the Dinka, like the Nuer, do practise ghost-marriage, leviratic marriage, widow-concubinage, concubinage of wives, and divorce. These institutions therefore probably predate the separation of Nuer and Dinka and the Nuer conquests of Dinka over the past one hundred years. It is noteworthy, however, that the Seligmans describe woman-marriage by childless widows among the Dinka as being marriage on behalf of the widow's dead husband, rather than of her brother or other agnatic kinsman (Seligman and Seligman 1932: 161–5, 220–1). This suggests that although woman-marriage exists among the Dinka as one means of substituting women for men killed in battle, it does not, perhaps, play the same role as among the Nuer, who seem to use it to provide extra, female 'fathers' belonging to dominant lineages, and to absorb Dinka or 'stranger' Nuer in lower-ranking roles as lovers of these 'fathers', wives. These hints support my hypothesis that Nuer expansion brought about greater dominance by particular lineages, high residential variability among the displaced and the captive, and an increase, if not a development *de novo*, of domestic unions which freed some women, especially 'aristocratic' women, from the continuous legal guardianship of men. A more detailed comparison is, however, desirable.

With regard to Nuer history, Howell's and Evans-Pritchard's brief *résumés* suggest that the expansion of the Nuer, or of some tribal sections, in the nineteenth century, was in part stimulated, if not initially prompted, by Arab slave-raiding and the slave-trade. The first period of rapid Nuer expansion east of the Nile occurred before 1860 (Evans-Pritchard 1940: 124–7), followed by periods of consolidation, then of fission among Nuer tribes and tribal sections, then of Nuer resistance, under prophets, to Dervish slave-raiders, and finally of resistance to the Anglo-Egyptian government (Howell 1954: 8–9). Raiding of Dinka tribes by the Nuer continued, however, until the British subdued them in 1928, two years before Evans-Pritchard first visited Nuerland.

During the 1930s when Evans-Pritchard's studies were made, Nuer absorption of newly captured or immigrant Dinka, and the kind of fluid social stratification that resulted, appear to have been sufficiently recent phenomena for the actual domestic relations of a large proportion of the people, especially in relation to male rights over women, to fail to fit the norms of patrilineal descent. Nevertheless, absorption of Dinka, and reconsolidation of Nuer tribes, had apparently gone on over a sufficiently long period for a series of customary legal fictions to have become established which preserved the patrilineal ideals and legal forms and enabled the more successful layers of the population to adhere more or less closely to patrilineal descent. The less successful layers had to abandon strict patrilineal principles and adhere to the former through cognatic and affinal ties in order to reintegrate themselves into the society.

I would argue that Evans-Pritchard has somewhat understressed the extent of this social stratification and the significance of tribal leadership.[5] In emphasizing the absence of hereditary offices and the egalitarian outlook of the Nuer, he has tended to underplay matters such as the unequal distribution of land rights and cattle, the fact that bloodwealth for aristocrats, (especially in the eastern regions of more recent conquest) is higher than for 'stranger' Nuer, and higher for Nuer than for captured or immigrant Dinka, and the importance of leaders who united whole tribes or tribal sections in wars against the Dinka, the Arabs, and the British.

At the same time, Nuer society did remain tribal and did not advance to the level of the chiefdom.[6] Correspondingly, there was continuous social mobility and continual absorption of the conquered into the descent groups of the conquerors. The society was thus one in which leadership of local communities, sections, and tribes derived partly from hereditary advantages and partly from personal ambition and talents; and in which the raiding of other peoples provided avenues to upward mobility. Once the main conquest of Dinka had been accomplished in the nineteenth century, Nuer born into dominant lineages had the best chance of becoming prominent 'bulls' because they had superior land rights and tended to inherit more cattle than other men. A Nuer not of the dominant clan, or the son of a Dinka, could, however, achieve leadership by attaching himself to a locally dominant lineage, by acquiring cattle through heading raiding parties, and by establishing a reputation as a 'bull' through his bravery, wealth, generosity, or skill as a mediator (Howell 1954: 31).

The kinship mechanisms which allowed ambitious men, especially aristocrats, to gather a dependent following round them appear to have included the adoption of captives into established Nuer lineages, the acceptance of Dinka and indigent Nuer as lovers of kinswomen and genitors of their children, the use of some agnatic kinswomen as 'female husbands' who could inherit cattle and build up their own sub-following, the customary allocation of land use and grazing rights to people classified as 'children of girls', and the sponsoring by mothers' brothers of less fortunate sisters' sons. On the other hand, these same mechanisms seem to have provided avenues whereby the more forceful and competitive followers might, if they were fortunate in obtaining cattle, themselves succeed to positions of local prominence and eventually establish themselves in new small settlements, as 'bulls'.

Nuer Kinship: a Re-examination

CONCLUSION

Although I have ventured to modify some of Evans-Pritchard's interpretations and to suggest some alternatives, no other anthropologist has impressed me more deeply by the clarity and detail of his ethnography, the dignity of his style, his devotion to the subject, and his humane concern for his informants. His works have, especially, the merit that, while one may occasionally disagree with the conclusions, it is possible to go back to the description of facts and events and to find there either answers to problems or important clues to their solution. Professor Evans-Pritchard's works will therefore endure, both as classics for students of East African society and as sources of comparative data and inspiration for scholars in many lands.

NOTES

1. The term appears to have been coined by Ian Cunnison to describe relationships between villages of the Luapula Valley.
2. One wonders by whom, since Evans-Pritchard emphasizes the acephalous character of Nuer society. Howell argues that Evans-Pritchard tended to underestimate the authority of traditional tribal leaders (1954: 33).
3. For example, 'Nuer frequently change their place of residence' (1951: 24), and 'Nuer have great affection for their homes, and, in spite of their wandering habits, men born and bred into a village are likely to return to it even if they live elsewhere for some years', or 'Nuer move about their country freely, and reside for some years with one lot of kin and then for some years with another' (ibid.: 20).
4. See, for example (1951: 26): 'A true Nuer usually returns to his own people, eventually. As I have explained, sons-in-law who live with their wives' people are often Dinka, and Dinka are likely to remain with their affines, as they may have no kin of their own to return to; but one also finds Nuer in the same position. These may be persons who for one reason or another prefer to live apart from their paternal kin, or they may be poor men who cannot afford to pay full bridewealth, part of which is foregone by the wife's family in view of the fact that the man who has married their daughter has joined their community and is bringing up his children as members of it.'
5. See, for example, Fortes and Evans-Pritchard (1940: 296) quoted by Howell (1954: 33). Again, Evans-Pritchard suggests that aristocratic clans

exist because of the need for 'conceptual consistency and a certain measure of actual cohesion' within the structure of the tribe (1940: 235–6). I would argue, rather, that they exist by right of conquest, as, indeed, some of the case histories show. See, for example, the history of the conquest of the Lou country by the Jinaca (ibid.: 212).

6. See Service (1962: 111–77) for some of the structural features of chiefdoms as distinct from those of tribes. Sahlins has noted that the rise of prophets among the Nuer at the turn of this century, in response to Arab aggression, brought about a degree of political unification and strength of leadership different from anything the Nuer had known previously, and might have culminated in the development of fully fledged chiefdoms if the British had not subsequently conquered the Nuer. Sahlins's paper is, of course, an attempt to show that the segmentary lineage system of the Nuer dominant clans is itself an instrument of predatory expansion. My own tries to show that not only the large-scale political framework, but the peculiarities of interpersonal kinship relationships, are in large part traceable to Nuer expansion (cf. Sahlins 1961).

REFERENCES

ABERLE, DAVID F. 1961 Navaho. In Schneider, D. and K. Gough (eds.), *Matrilineal Kinship*. Berkeley and Los Angeles: University of California Press.

EVANS-PRITCHARD, E. E. 1940 *The Nuer*. Oxford: Clarendon Press.

— 1945 *Some Aspects of Marriage and Family among the Nuer*. Lusaka: Rhodes-Livingstone Institute Paper No. 11.

— 1950 Kinship and the Local Community among the Nuer. In Radcliffe-Brown, A. R., and D. Forde (eds.), *African Systems of Kinship and Marriage*. London: Oxford University Press (for the International African Institute).

— 1951 *Kinship and Marriage among the Nuer*. Oxford: Clarendon Press.

FORTES, MEYER, AND E. E. EVANS-PRITCHARD (eds.) 1940 *African Political Systems*. London: Oxford University Press (for the International African Institute).

GLUCKMAN, MAX 1955 *Custom and Conflict in Africa*. Oxford: Blackwell.

HOWELL, P. 1954 *A Manual of Nuer Law*. London: Oxford University Press (for the International African Institute).

LIENHARDT, R. G. 1958 The Western Dinka. In Middleton, John, and David Tait (eds.), *Tribes Without Rulers*. London: Routledge & Kegan Paul.

SAHLINS, MARSHALL D. 1961 The Segmentary Lineage: an Organization of Predatory Expansion. *American Anthropologist* **63** (2), part 1 (April): 322–45.

Nuer Kinship: a Re-examination

SELIGMAN, C. G. AND B. 1932 *Pagan Tribes of the Nilotic Sudan*. London: Routledge.

SERVICE, E. R. 1962 *Primitive Social Organization*. New York: Random House.

Some Problems in Cross-cultural Comparison[1]

C. R. HALLPIKE

Professor Evans-Pritchard, towards the end of his lecture *The Comparative Method in Social Anthropology*, remarks that

'. . . it is over two hundred years since *L'Esprit des Lois* was written, and, we may well ask once more what has been achieved by use of the comparative method, in whatever form, over this long period of time. Certainly little which could be acclaimed as laws commensurable with those which in the natural sciences have been reached in the two centuries' (Evans-Pritchard 1963: 24–5).

And in a forthcoming review[2] of the whole range of cross-cultural studies in the United States and elsewhere, a noted American specialist in the field concludes that only about half the findings have any significance, and even that is purely at the level of association, not causation. Certain general conclusions of this type of research, such that there is an association between kinship terminologies, residence rules, and descent rules, or that technologically simpler societies tend also to be simpler politically, less socially stratified, less urbanized, and to occur earlier in time than technologically advanced societies, may be true, but in the latter case especially will not come as a surprise to any educated person. While there is everything to be said for providing empirical evidence for what we had already surmised to be the case, success in this narrow range of endeavour can hardly be said to justify the hopes of the many scholars who have seen cross-cultural comparison as the royal road to true scientific status for social anthropology.

In this paper therefore I shall examine the general problems of cross-cultural comparison, of the statistical variety, and try to show where its major limitations lie. Köbben (1952, 1967), Naroll (1961, 1962), Blalock (1961), and others have pointed out at length, and in scholarly detail, the technical statistical problems of elucidating significant correlations, which are great, but not necessarily insuperable. But the main purpose of this paper is to argue that the belief that we shall be able to reach a thorough understanding of human society through the amassing of correlations, however valid these may be individually, is unfounded, and, secondly, that establishing correlations is not the only form of cross-cultural comparison, and that other, potentially more fruitful types have long been practised, though not under this name.

There are at least two major kinds of objective in cross-cultural comparison: these are the establishment of universals, and the explanation of differences. Like all dichotomies, this is of course rather too simplistic, but it has a large measure of truth. Early speculators about man have supposed that there might exist tribes without any kind of beliefs in the supernatural, who could only communicate with the most rudimentary sounds and gesticulations, or in which there was no marriage, but only coupling like beasts, or that the primitive life was the war of all against all, in which the human passions raged unchecked. The subsequent researches of ethnographers over the whole range of human societies as they exist today at all levels of technological development, have established beyond doubt that there is no people without a sophisticated and well-developed language, in which the social roles of the sexes are reversed or interchangeable, in which age status is unimportant, where the disposal of the dead is ignored, which lacks rites of *passage*, without some means of controlling agression or settling disputes, in which the parents of a child are ignored in the child's nurturance and upbringing, without incest taboos, and many other such findings could be adduced. It should be stressed, however, that findings of this sort require explanations which will originate as much in ethology, biology, psychology, and communication-theory as in social anthropology. As Evans-Pritchard has said, 'The more the universality claimed, not only the more tenuous does the causal interpretation become, but the more it loses its sociological content' (Evans-Pritchard 1963: 17).

For social anthropologists, now that we are aware of the general range of variation of human society, the problem is to elucidate the differences between societies, and to attempt to reduce these to certain principles of order. The exponents of the comparative method, especially Radcliffe-Brown and G. P. Murdock, have taken it as axiomatic that the business of any reputable social science is the establishment of laws.

'. . . the Cross-Cultural Survey has a special theoretical objective. It is organized so as to make possible the formulation and verification, on a large scale, and by quantitative methods, of scientific generalizations of a

Some Problems in Cross-cultural Comparison

universally human or cross-cultural character. Sociologists and most other social scientists regard the establishment of generalizations or "laws", i.e. verified statements of correlations between phenomena, as their primary aim' (Murdock 1940: 364).

Moreover, in a celebrated passage he regards these objectives as attained. At the conclusion of Chapter VII of *Social Structure*, on the determinants of kinship terminology, he says

'. . . the data of cultural and social life are as susceptible to exact scientific treatment as are the facts of the physical and biological sciences. It seems clear that the elements of social organization, in their permutations and combinations, conform to natural laws of their own with an exactitude scarcely less striking than that which characterizes the permutations of atoms in chemistry or genes in biology' (Murdock 1949: 183).

That these statements are over-exuberant will be made plain in a moment, but what is even more striking about them is their adulation of the natural sciences, a trait which was notable also in Radcliffe-Brown, and appears in the writings of many of the American cross-cultural researchers. It is an unfortunate fact, however, that few social anthropologists have any real knowledge of the procedure of the natural sciences above a secondary-school level; statements such as those quoted above are more typical of popularized accounts of science than of the manner in which working natural scientists actually appear to conduct their day-to-day research. Anyone who has friends working in laboratories, or who reads accounts of their research, will be struck in particular by the absence of any reference to the nature of 'science' and 'scientific method', or, for that matter, with any overriding concern with discovering 'laws'. Natural scientists simply get on with the job and leave speculation about method to philosophers, and other dilettantes. Just as one does not become a great man by reading biographies, but by being true to oneself, the social sciences might do better to concentrate on applying appropriate methods to their own data, which are significantly different from those of the physical world, rather than trying to imitate the half-understood techniques of physicists and biologists.

It is, I suggest, the obsession with 'laws', in particular, which represents one of the most damaging consequences of the attempt to apply what are supposed to be the methods of the natural sciences to human society. The nature of scientific laws, moreover, especially as understood by the modern cross-cultural researchers, seems to be restricted in practice to 'verified correlations between two variables', a conception

125

which is bound up with the statistical techniques used in their presentation. The problems involved in the establishment of significant correlations and, even more, of drawing causal inferences from them, are of course well known and have been discussed in the literature previously; the aspect of them which I wish to stress here is the peculiar unsuitability of statistical correlations for the establishment of sophisticated explanations of social phenomena.

One of the most recalcitrant of these problems has been that first raised by Galton, of how to distinguish correlations between phenomena which have arisen independently as a result of principles basic to human society, from correlations which are the result of diffusion from a common source. Naroll (1961) has suggested an ingenious method of distinguishing between correlations which are the result of diffusion, and those which are explicable in functional terms; he assumes that traits whose association together is causally produced will tend to diffuse together, while traits whose association is purely historical will tend not to diffuse together. On the assumption that 'the closer in space societies are, the more likely they are to resemble each other in any trait subject to diffusion', he selects two arcs across the globe which are cross-sections of the world's cultures (without being random samples) and tests for the co-presence of the same levels of political organization and social stratification, to see whether these traits are historically associated, by diffusion only, or if there is a functional relation between them. The results of his tests show that these two traits do tend to cluster far more than would be expected by random distribution, while lack of association between levels of political organization and levels of social stratification do not tend to cluster, which he considers validates the hypothesis that the traits in question are functionally related. But unfortunately this technique, subtle and original though it is, does not take us very far in the explanation of the phenomena in question. Not only, of course, as Naroll admits, is it incapable of telling us why the correlation exists, but it depends on a meaningful identification of the traits in question, that is, levels of political organization and social stratification, and this is a major problem in cross-cultural research. It is perhaps fairly easy to decide if a society has totemic clans, is grouped in villages or scattered homesteads, or cultivates rice or millet as its staple crop, but as soon as we are confronted with more subtle types of phenomena, the coding we employ in the tables becomes more arbitrary. For example, Murdock has, as Column 34 in the Ethnographic Atlas (Murdock 1967:160)

'High God'. 'A high god is defined, following Swanson, as a spiritual being who is believed to have created all reality and/or to be its ultimate governor, even though his sole act was to create other spirits who, in turn, created or control the natural world.' The range of beliefs is indicated by the following symbols:

A. A high god present but otiose, or not concerned with human affairs.
B. A high god present and active in human affairs but not offering positive support to human morality.
C. A high god present, active, and specifically supportive of human morality.
O. A high god absent or not reported in substantial descriptions of religious beliefs.

Yet it is easy to find examples of deities in the literature which cannot be fitted into this exiguous classification. For example, in the case of the Lugbara as described by Middleton (1960), God or Spirit is the creator, and the means by which men and society outside that of the Lugbara can be brought within a common frame of reference. Yet God has two aspects, transcendent and immanent. In his transcendent aspect, the creator of the world and universe, he is aloof from men, but in his immanent aspect he comes into direct contact with men, but as an anti-social force. In the light of examples of this type it becomes clear that Murdock's categories are quite inadequate to deal with the subtleties of the data. There are many other examples of categories in the Ethnographic Atlas that are either too crude to be useful, or so elaborate that they are completely arbitrary divisions of the data. This is not to say that any other scholar would perform the task better than Murdock; rather, it reveals a basic dilemma of such procedures, namely, that one must often choose between categories of such generality as to lack much diagnostic significance, or, on the other hand, one will in doing justice to the facts, be forced to multiply categories to the extent that one is in danger of creating a new category for each society. Categories cannot therefore be derived from the data in many cases, but must be imposed by the investigator, and in proportion as the subject-matter becomes more complex will become increasingly arbitrary.

Moreover, when rather vague phenomena such as social complexity or anomie, values or belief systems, are being investigated, some kind of index is often required, thus removing us yet a stage further from the data. A good example of this is to be found in Swanson's *Birth of the Gods* (1960) in which he attempts to demonstrate a correlation between type of social organization, as indicated by the degree of complexity and organization of what he defines as 'sovereign groups', and belief system, as characterized by the predominance of monotheism, polytheism, ancestor worship, witchcraft, and some other beliefs. Apart from the obvious fact that belief in such supernatural beings tells us precisely nothing about the cosmology of the peoples in question (which, since Swanson tells us he has no specialized knowledge of religion or anthropology, he might not be expected to know) his indexes of what constitute 'sovereign groups' are also open to serious doubt. For he tells us that he had his ratings of societies on the variables of sovereign groups checked by two graduate students in anthropology, and the correlations between their ratings and his were almost non-existent (Swanson 1960: 223). Even in the hands of more competent investigators than Professor Swanson, the use of indicators for complex traits is exceedingly difficult, and probably always open to doubt. This objection has greatest force in the case of value and belief systems, which are of the greatest significance in understanding the workings of any society, yet which are very difficult to break down into elements of a type suitable for cross-cultural comparison.

Even where we may accept that the units of measurement are correctly identified – and the equations of kinship are among the most specific kinds of data – the laws which Murdock has alleged to govern them seem less than exact on close inspection. Though he states 'To a valid scientific principle there are no exceptions; apparent exceptions are always due to the intrusion of another countervailing principle' (Murdock 1940: 370), the realities as displayed in *Social Structure* are very different. For example, let us take his alleged validation of what he calls 'Theorem 11', 'Bilocal residence tends to be associated with kinship terminology of the generation type,' accompanied by the table. But whatever may be the statistical significance of these findings, the plain fact remains that, in instances of bilocal residence there are 52 cases which support the hypothesis, and 55 which do not, while of cases without bilocal residence there are 163 exceptions to the theorem. If we are to accept that 'to a valid scientific principle there are no exceptions' then this supposed principle, like all the others that Murdock proposes, is a long way from being valid.

One of the chief assumptions in cross-cultural research of this type

Trios of relatives	Bilocal residence		Other residence		Q	χ^2
	Generation terms	Other	Generation terms	Other		
FZ-MZ-M	9	11	33	187	+·65	100
MBW-FBW-M	6	10	16	121	+·64	20
FZD-FBD-Z	13	7	46	168	+·75	1000
MBD-MZD-Z	13	7	46	158	+·73	1000
ZD-BD-D	7	12	16	176	+·73	1000
WBD-WZD-D	4	8	6	62	+·38	10
	52	55	163	872		

is that statistical significance is in itself evidence for some important relationship in the real world. But as Kish points out,

> 'Statistical "significance" is often confused with and substituted for substantive significance . . . These attempts to use the probability levels of significance tests as measures of the strengths of relationships are very common and very mistaken. The function of statistical tests is merely to answer: Is the variation great enough for us to place some confidence in the results; or, contrarily, may the latter be merely a happenstance of the specific sample on which the test was made' (Kish 1959: 336).

Yet a further problem in establishing correlations is that of attempting to demonstrate relationships between phenomena which are fairly widely separated in human society. We might expect there to be some relationship between economy and settlement patterns, and some between settlement patterns and political organization, but there is no reason to expect any link between cosmology and kinship system, or between family organization and the presence or absence of craftsmen. In other words, correlations become of progressively smaller meaning to the extent that the variables become more disparate. This is for the simple reason that the nexus of relationship between them must involve increasingly large numbers of unknown factors, which cannot be controlled for, and hence a proliferation of possible explanatory hypotheses. In our own society, for example, it is not difficult to see how a marked and swift increase in unemployment could significantly be correlated with a fall in the popularity of the government, but it is unlikely that the latter could be related to an increase in vegetarianism. Yet a number of cross-cultural studies, such as Swanson's *Birth of the Gods*, Spiro's and Andrade's 'Cross-Cultural Study of Some Supernatural Beliefs', and especially attempts to relate behaviour patterns to general features of social organization, are indefensible on this ground.

Indeed, even when one is dealing with such closely related phenomena as ecology and settlement patterns, the number of variables involved is likely to be quite large. For example, in an extremely stimulating analysis of the slash-and-burn agriculture of a central Brazilian tribe, and its relation to their settlement pattern, Carneiro (1956: 229–34) uses six variables to show that it is possible for this type of cultivation to support permanent settlements of the existing or larger size, and that the periodic construction of new villages is therefore culturally (in this case supernaturally) motivated, and not economically. These variables are (1) the area of cultivated land required to provide the average individual with the amount of food he ordinarily derives from cultivated plants per year, (2) the population of the community, (3) the number of years that a plot of land continues to produce before it has to be abandoned, (4) the number of years an abandoned plot must lie fallow before it can be recultivated, (5) the total area of arable land that is within practicable walking distance of the village, (6) the length of time (in years) that a village can remain in a single location in so far as the requirements of agriculture are concerned.

Reality is, in fact, a great deal too complicated to be reduced to correlations between two variables, yet this is the only statistical presentation available to cross-cultural research. For establishing correlations between more than two variables becomes very much more complicated, and, as I have already suggested, even to do justice to fairly simple situations half a dozen or more are likely to be necessary. But even if it were possible to produce more sophisticated correlations, the problem of how to interpret them would become greater not less. The root of the matter is that, as everybody knows, correlations do not elucidate patterns of relationships, nor even, in most cases, distinguish between dependent and independent variables. Of course, there are certain phenomena, such as basket-weaving designs, architecture, or music, which would certainly fall into the class of dependent variables, but to identify the independent variables affecting them is quite another matter. The whole concept of independent and dependent variables, or cause and effect, is based on an essentially linear model, in which each stage of the process is identifiable. More precisely, it makes at least five basic assumptions: (a) that the cause and effect can be empirically distinguished, (b) that the cause precedes the effect, (c) that the effect does not in turn modify the cause, (d) that the effect does not have an autonomous power of action, and (e) that the effects of different causes can be separately identified. For example, in the case of such a chain of interaction as that illustrated below, none of these conditions, except perhaps (d) is satisfied:

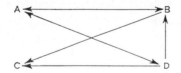

In such cases it is pointless to attempt to elucidate the nature of the process by correlating pairs of variables. Two conceptually more powerful approaches are the formation of equations from all the variables, though this is likely to be inappropriate in the majority of problems which are dealt with by social anthropologists, and secondly the use of simulations, either by computer or by hand, in which the essential elements or rules are reproduced, but these methods of course do not lend themselves to the statistical type of cross-cultural research.

Cross-cultural research is also frustrated by the fact that, for ease of coding among other things, it tends to focus upon the institutions of a society, and less upon the functions these institutions have within the society, or in other words, it concentrates on the elements of the system rather than on the modes of their relationship. But, for example, an age-grading system can control political relations, or working parties, or military organization, or education, or status relations, in various combinations, but its function in these respects need not be reflected in its formal structure. While it is true that certain basic processes and functions are common to all societies, such as the ecological, social control, education, the allocation of authority, the settling of disputes, and the diffusion of information, it is not the case that these functions are always performed by specific social institutions, nor do we find that residence groups, descent groups, age-grading systems, political officers, and so on, perform any characteristic functions that cannot be performed by any other institutions. Thus the descent system may have essential economic, juridical, and political functions, or the dissemination of information may be mainly accomplished by markets, by sermons, at the courts of nobles, by trading parties, or by the chance meeting of wayfarers. Institutions are multi-faceted, in fact, and there need be no relation between the formal nature of an institution and the basic processes of the society. To use a biological analogy, it would be as though an organism could as well use its stomach as its brain to think, its eyes to smell, and its skin to provide locomotion, or a combination of such functions. Once it is realized that form and function are largely dissociated in human society it becomes apparent that, even though there are many universals, in both institutions and functions, the way these are interrelated can be enormously varied, and cannot be disentangled by a statistical procedure involving the correlations of two or more variables.

Let us suppose, however, that we could establish several thousand correlations, with sufficiently few exceptions to allow their being dignified with the term 'laws'. Where precisely would this get us? Not, certainly, to any deeper understanding of how total societies operate, of the extent to which they are functioning systems, of the Radcliffe–Brownian type, on the one hand, or heterogeneous collections of institutions held together by a few general rules, on the other; of the significance of values and belief systems; of the extent to which the modes of production determine, and are determined by, the other major social institutions, and so on. These are the fundamental questions which social anthropology has to answer, and without understanding these principles any number of correlations are meaningless.

This brings us to the central difference between the cross-cultural specialists and those, especially in the British tradition, who concentrate on the analysis of single societies. For it can be fairly argued that the cross-culturalists have no coherent theory of society. To be sure, they believe there are certain basic similarities in all societies, but upon examination these turn out to be so general as to be explanatorily impotent. Murdock, for example, states (Murdock 1940) that these uniformities are (1) that culture is learned, 'and must obey the laws of learning which psychologists have now worked out in some detail', (2) that culture is social, and therefore all cultures should reveal certain similarities because they have all had to provide for societal survival, (3) that culture is ideational (conceptual) and will therefore reveal similarities derived from 'the universal laws governing the symbolic mental processes', (4) that culture always satisfies basic biological needs and secondary needs derived therefrom. 'Its elements are tested habitual techniques for gratifying human impulses in man's interaction with the external world of nature and fellow men', (5) culture is also adaptive to the environment, and the biological and psychological demands of the human organism, and integrative. But while it is undoubtedly true that culture is learned, borne by society, governed by certain general characteristics of the human mind, and adaptive to the environment, these platitudes scarcely amount to a theory of society. It will also be noted that they are phrased entirely in terms of 'culture' and not 'society', and indeed this is one of the greatest differences between current cross-cultural ideology and that of the British school, or, as Köbben phrases it, between the hologeistic and the Gestalt. Murdock believes that

> 'The special province of anthropology in relation to its sister disciplines is the study of culture . . . Having chosen to investigate culture, most anthropologists find themselves committed to studying the processes by which it grows (culture change), is transmitted from one generation to

another (education and socialization) and is spread geographically (diffusion or culture borrowing) and are thus driven irresistibly to an interest in history, psychology, and geography (Murdock 1951: 471).

With this conception of the aims of anthropology, which seems to be widely accepted, it is not surprising therefore that cross-cultural research, especially that done in America, is heavily oriented towards studies of individual behaviour, and personality structure, with a corresponding tendency to draw upon psychology for explanatory concepts. Studies of divorce rates, sex taboos, crime, alcoholism, child-training, food-sharing, artistic style, suicide, and romantic love are typical of many of the published studies. As Murdock realizes, the British anthropologists in particular are sociologists, and not anthropologists, in *his* definition of the term, in so far as they are interested primarily in social groups and their relationships. This being established, it is nevertheless relevant to ask how it is possible to study the workings of culture without basing such an analysis on an understanding of the nature of the societies with which it is intimately bound up. Correlations of traits can never be added together to produce higher-order generalizations, and consequently a basic understanding of human society, yet paradoxically cross-cultural research is also oriented towards understanding society, and not just culture.

This brings us to the problem of how it can be claimed that intensive study of a few societies, unrepresentatively selected, can illuminate our knowledge of society as a whole. The claim can in fact be defended by the same assumption as that made by the cross-culturalists – that all societies have certain fundamental similarities – and that a detailed study of some basic feature of primitive societies such as magic or leadership is likely to be relevant to all. Of course, this will depend on the extent to which the hypothesis being examined relates to fundamental social processes, or to more variable phenomena. It is clear that the intensive study of whole societies is the ideal, and in fact the only way to understand fundamental social processes, and the cross-culturalists give tacit admission to this fact by being forced to supplement their correlations with speculative explanations which relate their data to what they believe to be the basic processes of society. Therefore because (a) it is very hard to codify such basic variables as values, belief systems, law, etc., and (b) more importantly, because processes and rule systems cannot be reduced to correlations, or combinations of correlations, least of all of a two-variable type, we must depend for our understanding of basic social organization and process on intensive studies of whole societies. Some classis examples of this are Evans-Pritchard's study of the relationship between ecology and political organization in *The Nuer* (1940), which also contributed invaluably to our understanding of the work of acephalous political organization, Lienhardt's analysis of the relation between supernatural beings and the experience of the people in *Divinity and Experience* (1961), Evans-Pritchard's exposition of the logic of witchcraft and magic in *Witchcraft, Oracles and Magic among the Azande* (1937), Leach's work on the diverse political models of the Kachin, in relation to our concepts of social structure in *Political Systems of Highland Burma* (1954), and Spencer's study of gerontocracy and social control in *The Samburu* (1965), and so the list could be extended. For example, if I may be permitted to refer to my own work among the Konso, I was attempting to show the significance of values in giving coherence to a society; that certain institutions, such as the generation-grading system, should be explained not as political institutions or means of social control, but as rooted in their cosmology; and that the cosmological principles of God, Earth, and the Wild were the parameters according to which the crucial social categories of elders, women, and priests and diviners were related to the total social order, and in the course of this analysis the concepts of structure and function were necessarily subjected to a close critical scrutiny. In short, therefore, it is obvious that such intensive studies of single societies as those I have mentioned are relevant to all societies because they deal with fundamental social processes.

Of course, this does not mean that we are forced to choose between cross-cultural research of the statistical type, and intensive ethnographic studies reported in monographs. It is a curious fact that the literature on cross-cultural research almost, if not entirely, fails to consider the brilliant work of the *Année sociologique* school, which produced, among other masterpieces, Mauss's *The Gift* (1954), Hubert and Mauss's *Sacrifice: Its Nature and Function* (1964), Durkheim and Mauss's *Primitive Classification* (1963), and Hertz's essays on death and on the right hand, all of which are essentially cross-cultural, centred on a particular phenomenon, and not on a single society or even a few societies. Lévi-Strauss's *Totemism* (1963) and Mary Douglas's *Purity and Danger* (1966) are more modern works of the same seminal type. The chief and unique contribution of studies of this type is their elucidation of structural forms basic to human thought and social organization. One of the greatest contributions in this field was of course van

C. R. Hallpike

Gennep's *Les Rites de passage* (1909), in which he showed that a common theme of a great deal of primitive ritual was that of transition from one ritual or social status to another, in which the concept of liminality was crucial. Van Gennep's theory is about the structure of social and ritual relations, but does not say that all rituals must be of such and such a form, or even that transition must be a central element, or even present at all in a majority of rituals. What it does is to provide a conceptual scheme which allows us to perceive a common element in many cere-monies surrounding birth, initiation, marriage, and mortuary cere-monies. But it cannot be broken down into a series of correlations, nor can it be statistically validated, since its explanatory significance does not require it to be the sole explanation of any particular ritual, or even that it be relevant to a majority of rituals. In the same vein, Needham has shown in his paper on 'Percussion' (1967) that percussive sounds are frequently used to mark transition and designate liminality at the aural level, in the same way that boundary stones or lines do in the three-dimensional world. Or, if I may refer to a recent paper of my own on the symbolic significance of long and short hair (Hallpike 1969), I suggested that in many cases long hair signified standing outside society, in some capacity, while short hair signified re-entering society, or being subject to a particular disciplinary régime within society, and I also pointed out the frequent association between long hair and animality. Whether this explains only a majority of even a minority of cases of the ritual use of hair is beside the point; its value if it is correct is in showing how the basic categories of society/nature are brought into a relation-ship, as follows:

$$\left.\begin{array}{l} \textit{long hair} \\ \text{nature} \\ \text{animality} \\ \text{freedom} \end{array}\right\} \quad : \quad \left\{\begin{array}{l} \textit{short hair} \\ \text{society} \\ \text{social being} \\ \text{control} \end{array}\right.$$

Statistical verification is thus irrelevant. This is not to say, of course, that the theory has no empirical significance, since it is always possible to ask if it fits any particular case, and also an hypothesis which can only explain a very limited range of phenomena is obviously less satis-factory than an hypothesis which can explain a wide variety. This does not mean, however, that an hypothesis which can only explain a few cases is less *true* than one which can explain many, but merely that it is less useful. It is in this sense that I am saying that statistical verification is irrelevant.

Some Problems in Cross-cultural Comparison

To give another example of useful cross-cultural research based on intensive study of a few cases, if we were trying to explain why craftsmen in East Africa have a low status, and perhaps in most primitive societies are treated as a group apart, it seems likely to me on the basis of my Konso experience of this phenomenon that the following factors will be highly relevant: (1) they will tend to depend on trade and bargaining rather than herding or agriculture to produce food and the basic necessities of life, (2) that lack of demand for their products in any one location may enforce a higher degree of mobility upon them than other members of society, (3) whether they work as free agents or as clients of a particular group, (4) they socialize natural objects; by this I mean that they turn raw cotton into cloth, iron-ore into weapons and tools clay into pottery vessels, and so on. (1), (2), and (3) are clearly relevant to social status, and especially that of outsiders, while (4) will probably have some relevance to their magico-religious status, since nature and society are basic cosmological categories. I am not suggesting that these will be the only explanatory factors, or that some may not be unimportant in particular societies but that the interrelationship of these factors, in particular, is likely to be highly significant. Whatever the final explanation, the status of craftsmen is a complex matter which cannot be broken down into correlations, but can only be treated by the sort of structural analysis I have suggested here.

Many of the arguments against statistical cross-cultural comparison which I have made so far are well expressed by Raser in *Simulation and Society*.

'The conventional, logical positivist, inductive approach to science involves gathering isolated, punctiform bits of data in a specific area of interest, fitting them together into part-theories, and, in one-step-at-a-time fashion, trying to construct more comprehensive theory. In an illuminating discussion of pattern-matching as a scientific approach, Donald Campbell contrasts the "quest for punctiform certainty" with "distal" knowledge derived from "a prior identification of the whole". "Both psychology and philosophy", says Campbell,

are emerging from an epoch in which the quest for punctiform certainty seemed the optimal approach to knowledge. To both Pavlov and Watson, single retinal cell activation and single muscle activations [punctiform data] seemed more certainly reidentifiable and specifiable than perceptions of objects or adaptive acts.

But, says Campbell, we can identify any single "particle", or bit of data only because we have previously identified the complex phenomenon "perception". Rather than recognizing and identifying the complex whole through identification of its particles and establishment of their relationships, it is the complex whole about which we have the more certain knowledge, and that enables us to know something about elements or particles of which it is composed' (Raser 1969: 34–5).

CONCLUSIONS

The basic objections to cross-cultural research of the statistical type are therefore not so much that the data are vast, uneven in quality, difficult to codify without making arbitrary distinctions, that similar phenomena may be produced by different factors, or by diffusion, and that it is very difficult to obtain genuinely random samples, but rather, that social reality is not susceptible to being meaningfully broken down into correlations between two variables. Not only is there an important difference between statistical significance and substantive significance, but even more fundamentally, societies are processes and rule systems in which interactions are of a very complex type involving large numbers of variables, and this type of entity has to be analysed by more sophisticated methods, by equations or simulations if we are dealing with certain types of social phenomena, or more usually by intensive studies of particular cases by trained observers. A body of knowledge which claims to be explanatory as well as descriptive must be basically oriented to understanding the fundamental processes of the phenomena it is studying, and this cannot come from assembling large numbers of individual correlations; science is not a pastiche of elementary propositions, but a way of looking at things, and in social anthropology our chief inspiration has always been the study of the total society, and comparison of the structural characteristics of particular institutions and beliefs.

NOTES

1. I am obliged to Dr David Elliott for a number of valuable discussions on the problems raised here.
2. This review is at present being circulated privately in draft form and not for quotation.

Some Problems in Cross-cultural Comparison

REFERENCES

BLALOCK, H. M. 1961 *Causal Inferences in Nonexperimental Research.* Durham: University of North Carolina Press.

CARNEIRO, R. L. 1956 Slash-and-Burn Agriculture: a Closer Look at its Implications for Settlement Patterns. Pp. 229–34 in Wallace, A. (ed.), *Men and Cultures, Selected Papers of the 5th International Congress of Anthropological and Ethnological Science.* Philadelphia: University of Pennsylvania Press.

DOUGLAS, M. 1966 *Purity and Danger.* London: Routledge and Kegan Paul.

DURKHEIM, E., AND M. MAUSS 1963 *Primitive Classification* (trans. R. Needham). London: Cohen and West.

EVANS-PRITCHARD, E. E. 1937 *Witchcraft, Oracles and Magic among the Azande.* Oxford: Clarendon Press.

— 1940 *The Nuer.* Oxford: Clarendon Press.

— 1963 *The Comparative Method in Social Anthropology.* London: Athlone Press.

HALLPIKE, C. R. 1969 Social Hair. *Man* **4** (2) (June): 256–64.

— 1971 *The Konso of Ethiopia. A Study of the Values of a Cushitic People.* Oxford: Clarendon Press.

HUBERT, H., AND M. MAUSS 1964 *Sacrifice: Its Nature and Function* (trans. W. D. Halls). London: Cohen and West.

KISH, L. 1959 Some Statistical Problems in Research Design. *American Sociological Review* **24** (3): 328–38.

KÖBBEN, A. J. F. 1952 New Ways of Presenting an Old Idea: the Statistical Method in Social Anthropology. *Journal of the Royal Anthropological Institute* **82**: 129–46.

— 1967 Why Exceptions? The Logic of Cross-Cultural Analysis. *Current Anthropology* **8**: 1–37.

LEACH, E. R. 1954 *Political Systems of Highland Burma.* London: University of London Press.

LÉVI-STRAUSS, C. 1963 *Totemism* (trans. R. Needham). Boston: Beacon Press; London: Merlin Press.

LIENHARDT, R. G. 1961 *Divinity and Experience.* Oxford: Clarendon Press.

MAUSS, M. 1954 *The Gift* (trans. I. Cunnison). London: Cohen and West.

MIDDLETON, J. 1960 *Lugbara Religion.* London: Oxford University Press.

MURDOCK, G. P. 1940 The Cross-Cultural Survey. *American Sociological Review* **5** (3): 361–70.

— 1949 *Social Structure.* New York: Free Press.

— 1951 British Social Anthropology. *American Anthropologist* **53**: 456–89.

— 1967 Ethnographic Atlas: a Summary. *Ethnology* **6** (2): 109–236.

C. R. Hallpike

NAROLL, R. 1961 Two Solutions to Galton's Problem. *Philosophy of Science* **28** (1): 15–39.

— 1962 *Data Quality Control—a New Research Technique*. New York: Free Press.

NEEDHAM, R. 1967 Percussion and Transition. *Man* **2** (3): 606–14.

RASER, J. R. 1969 *Simulation and Society*. Boston: Allyn and Bacon.

SPENCER, P. 1965 *The Samburu*. London: Routledge and Kegan Paul.

SPIRO, M., AND R. G. ANDRADE 1958 A Cross-Cultural Study of Some Supernatural Beliefs. *American Anthropologist* **60** (3) (June): 456–66.

SWANSON, G. E. 1960 *The Birth of the Gods*. Ann Arbor: University of Michigan Press.

VAN GENNEP, A. 1909 *Les Rites de passage* (trans. M. Vizedom and G. Caffee, 1960). London: Routledge and Kegan Paul.

A Structural Model of Aweikoma Society

DAVID HICKS

In this essay earlier interpretations of Aweikoma social structure are criticized and an explanatory model which has certain novel features and embraces a wider range of social and symbolic fact than any hitherto suggested is propounded.[1]

The Aweikoma belong to the southern branch of the Gê-speaking peoples of Brazil which, unlike the central and northern groups, is currently wallowing in a slough of undeserved neglect. This is unfortunate since not only do the two chief representatives of the southern Gê, the Kaingang and Aweikoma, have social forms and symbolic features of fascination in themselves, but details of their social and symbolic structures are apposite to the comparative studies now in progress among the other Gê.[2]

Of these two southern tribes the Aweikoma in a sense command more interest than the Kaingang since many of their social forms are untypical of Gê culture in general. This singularity is particularly evident in what might be termed the 'social structure',[3] the isolation of which forms the theme of the present analysis.

My procedure is as follows. After a brief adumbration of the ethnographic background all data pertinent to an analysis of Aweikoma society have been collated from every source, the previous interpretations of this material are described and evaluated, and a new model is proposed. This is then assigned a place in a symbolic dimension of Aweikoma society which is considered in as much depth as the published ethnography permits. Finally, several consequences of the new model are predicated.

ETHNOGRAPHIC BACKGROUND

The Aweikoma are a tribe of hunters, food-collectors, and agriculturalists who, before their pacification by the Brazilians in 1914, were forest nomads inhabiting the State of Santa Catarina in southern Brazil.

In that year one subtribe[4] was settled into the Duque de Caxias reservation in eastern Santa Catarina. During 1934 a second subtribe was reported living south of the Posto da União which lies to the west of the Duque de Caxias reservation but as nothing ethnographically substantial has ever been published on this group this analysis refers to the former only.

Linguistically, and in certain other cultural respects, the Aweikoma are related to the neighbouring Kaingang with whom they have often been confused,[5] but though both tribes are members of the same Gê branch they are quite distinct, and in view of the quantity of pertinent comparative data available such a confoundation is astonishing.

ETHNOGRAPHIC EVIDENCE

The earliest generally useful source of information on Aweikoma social organization is provided by Jules Henry[6] in a 1936 note based upon thirteen months' fieldwork at the Duque de Caxias village from December 1932 to January 1934. According to this report there are no moieties or descent groups but six named, exogamous, alineal, dispersed groups each owning a different body-painting design. Their names, however, are not disclosed by the ethnographer. Each group also possesses an exclusive set of personal names so that if an individual's name is known his group affiliation can be inferred. These names, up to four, are bestowed by one of the child's parents and are typically those of one or more relatives of the latter, though parent's names may also be given. These need not be the names of only one group, for a child can receive those belonging to as many as three and so wear a combination of up to three designs, but it is unclear whether or not such a person is considered to be a member of all three groups. A child's group is not known until it receives a name and parents usually have children belonging to different groups.

A couple wearing the same design and who thus belong to the same group theoretically are forbidden to marry unless they have other designs which differ, but in practice little restriction is placed on a person's choice of spouse, only children and siblings being prohibited. Henry records ten such design combinations though he notes that a large number of permutations are theoretically possible. The population of the community varied between 1932 and 1941 from about 100 to 200, of which 62 per cent at the time of Henry's study belonged to two particular groups combined but these are unspecified by our authority.

A Structural Model of Aweikoma Society

A synoptic description of Aweikoma social organization is relegated to five pages of an appendix (pp. 175-9) of Henry's fieldwork monograph, *Jungle People*, which was first published in 1941 and reissued with an additional 'note to the reader' in 1964.[7] Except for this supplement both editions are essentially identical, and despite the publication of two subsequent interpretations of Aweikoma social structure by Nimuendajú (1946: 83, 98) and Métraux (1947), both of whom provide facts and an analysis strongly at variance with Henry's, the latter in the new edition does not even mention them, so one can only presume that he remains firmly wedded to the 1941 interpretation.

According to this, the subtribe is composed of *five* groups[8] to each of which pertains a distinct body-painting design accompanied by a set of personal names. Every design has a name describing its objective character but two designs, the disc (which will be subsequently termed 'spot'[9]) and the horizontal bar with vertical lines (which I subsequently describe as 'a horizontal stripe over vertical ones'), are not denoted by the type of designation applied to the other three groups, whose names are those of three respective eponymous culture-heroes. In summary form the details of the groups can be schematized thus:

Group name	Design name	Translation	Design
Wanyekí *kôika hë*	mêvídn	scattered all over	dots
Klendó *kôika hë*	kalébm	coming down	stripes
Kainlé *kôika hë*	kuikên	in a ring	circles
(none)	kaktêng kụ kalébm	horizontal and coming down	a horizontal stripe over vertical ones
(none)	kanêm	placed there	spots

From male ego's viewpoint a man having the same design as himself is termed *kôika hë*, good people, real people, (*kôiká* = relative; *hë* = whole, serviceable, entire, good) (p. 209). A man with a different design is called *wamộ* (*wa* = formal prefix; *mộ* = dative), a woman with the same design is *yôktë* (*yôk* = formal prefix; *të* = woman), and a woman with a different design is *plụ*, sexual partner, wife.

From female ego's viewpoint a woman or man having the same design as herself is termed *kôika hë*, a woman with a different design is *wamộ*, and a man with a different design is termed *mbâdn*, sexual partner, husband. The term *kôika hë* is also applied in a wider sense to include all persons regardless of sex who have the same painting as ego. Since a large number of persons have names from at least two groups and a relatively large number from three, the ethnographer concludes that 'the groups are not separate' (p. 176).

There is no fixed means by which names are given to children and designs do not descend systematically from parents or any other relative to members of the following genealogical level, but close relatives commonly choose the name of a close relative to give a baby, and an individual may have from one to eight names.

A rather vague association links names and specific designs, for while informants might agree on the names of a person they often disagreed as to the designs appropriate to those names, but certain names were related to the same design by everyone. These are what Henry terms the 'basic ones' of Wanyekí, Klendó, and Kainlé (p. 176) out of a total of 193 such names 49, i.e. about 25 per cent, were one of these.

'Extensive checking' led the ethnographer to conclude that the scheme of designs does not regulate marriage and 'has nothing to do with' the composition of hunting bands, food and property distribution, or with the cremation of the dead (pp. 176–7). Although theoretically individuals with the same design cannot marry, in practice no shame attends marrying someone with the same painting as oneself and such marriages occur.

The only function of the design group is what Henry calls 'magical' (p. 177). When a person dies everyone in the village paints himself with his design so as to frighten away the dead person's soul (*kuplêng*) but a widowed individual puts on designs other than his own upon returning from his ritual isolation (*waikômáng*) in the forest in order that the soul cannot recognize him. About 1927 a number of persons added the circle motif to their other paintings because when Kemblén[10] died he told all the people to change their designs 'so that the *kuplêng* would see it and go away' (p. 177).

Henry's second and final model of Aweikoma social structure is thus that of five groups each of the same structural order but he takes pains to stress their irrelevance for an understanding of Aweikoma society. The Aweikoma are described as 'a people with no sense of social form' (p. 33), they 'have no interest in social forms of any kind' (p. 33), the 'very formlessness' of the society 'makes us wonder what gave it coherence' (p. 49), and on page 175 he remarks on 'the theoretical social structure, which has been largely so much cultural flotsam for at least two hundred years and probably much longer . . .'

In structural respects the most valuable source of information is a letter dated 17 November 1933 written by Eduardo Hoerhan and published in part on pages 83 and 98 of Curt Nimuendajú's 1946 monograph, *The Eastern Timbira*. Hoerhan, an agent of the Indian Protection Service, concluded the 1914 peace treaty with the Aweikoma and since, according to Métraux (1947: 150), he experienced twenty years' 'close association' with this subtribe may be presumed to have been thoroughly familiar with the ethnographic material he describes.

On page 83 the following facts are set forth. The Aweikoma are divided into three exogamous, patrilineal, dispersed 'major clans' whose members 'claim kinship' with the three respective legendary heroes Uvanhêcü, Crên-ndô, and Zêit-tscha-cá-i-lê. The clansfolk call themselves 'kin' of the heroes, Uvanhêcü-*caïcá*, Crên-ndô-*caïcá*, and Zêit-tscha-cá-i-lê-*caïcá*. But the 'true clan names seem to be' mê-vídn, mê-cálêbn, and mê-cúi-ken.

Each has a different body painting: the mê-vídn uses two parallel rows of dots on the forehead, chest, and back; the mê-cálêbn has vertical stripes on the forehead; while the mê-cúi-ken employs circles on the forehead, cheeks, chest, and back. The three heroes created the animals which bear similar designs but the sun and moon are irrelevant to this classification.

Each clan contains a 'subclan' whose painting is a variation of that of the clan itself. The mê-to páa-pa subclan of the mê-vídn clan substitutes 'broad patches' (which I term 'spots') for the dots but retains the same pattern on the wearer's body. The zôo-zí subclan of the mê-cálêbn clan adds a horizontal stroke (my 'stripe') above the vertical forehead lines, and the cúi-kent subclan of the mê-cúi-ken clan inserts a central dot into each of its circles.

Less precise information is provided on page 98 where, after describing the hierarchy and functions of the Kaingang classes, Nimuendajú notes that a comparable 'institution', i.e. structure, is said by Hoerhan to exist among the Aweikoma referring the reader back to page 83, which contains the information given above.

So as to appreciate the significance and facilitate an understanding of Nimuendajú and Métraux's interpretations of the Aweikoma social structure some knowledge of the essential Kaingang social order is desirable. A few words on the latter are thus pertinent at this stage.

Among the Kaingang there are at least three classes, the pai, votoro, and penye. The moiety division bifurcates each class so that half of a class belongs to the Kanyerú moiety and the other half to the Kamé.

145

Each class and moiety has a distinctive design so that the subclass painting is a combination of class and subclass designs. Its name is likewise duplex.

Dots are worn by members of the Kanyerú moiety and stripes by Kamé persons. If they are Kanyerú, members of the pai class wear small dots but if they are Kamé they wear stripes. Persons of the penye class paint themselves with either large dots, i.e. spots, or large stripes, while votoro individuals wear either circles with central dots or circles with stripes. As an inspection of the representation below reveals, Nimuendajú's diagrammatic depiction is inexact.

A subclass is verbally denoted by an expression which commences with the moiety designation, concludes with that of the class, and connects both by the copulative '*ag*'. The Kanyerú-ag-pai, for instance, is that section of the pai class in the Kanyerú moiety and its design consists of small dots. Although recruitment to a moiety is by patrilineal descent a father may assign his child to whatever class he wishes, the latter's affiliation being symbolized by the name he bears.

Nimuendajú offers no explicit criticism of Hoerhan's account but in his comparison of the system of Aweikoma groups with that of the Kaingang moieties, classes, and subclasses the suggestion that there is something structurally anomalous in Hoerhan's interpretation of the Aweikoma social order is implicit; thus he leaves a gap in the Aweikoma (or, as he calls them, Botocudo) set of subgroups opposite that of the Kaingang Kamé-ag-votoro reproduced below. He writes on page 83:

'*Accordingly* [my italics], the votō'ro of the Kaingang *obviously* [my italics] corresponds to the Botocudo-mê-cúi-ken; the mê-to-páa [sic] subgroup of the mê-vídn (B.) to the pénye subgroup of the kanyerú moiety (K.); the zôo-zí subgroup of the mê-cálêbn (B.) to the pénye subgroup of the kamé moiety (K.); the cúi-kent (B.) to the votō'ro of the kanyerú moiety (K.).'

The correspondence, as he conceives it, between the social organization of the Kaingang and that of the Aweikoma he represents diagrammatically in the following manner.[12]

	Botocudo		*Kaingang*
Exogamous units			
Dot decoration	mê-vídn	=	kanyerú
Lines	mê-cálêbn	=	kamé
Rings	mê-cúi-ken	=	— (see subgroup votō'ro)

A Structural Model of Aweikoma Society

?	$\begin{cases}\text{kanyerú-ag-paí}\\\text{kamé-ag-paí}\end{cases}$	
?		
cúi-kent	$\begin{cases}\text{kanyerú-ag-votō'ro}\\\text{kamé-ag-votō'ro}\end{cases}$	Rings
mê-to páa-pa	$\begin{cases}\text{kanyerú-ag-péñye}\\\text{kamé-ag-péñye}\end{cases}$	Patches
zôo-zí		

Our final source of information and the most recent analysis of Aweikoma social structure is the 1947 article by Alfred Métraux, who was evidently unaware of the fact that Hoerhan's data had already been published by Nimuendajú since he reiterates almost every Aweikoma fact which the latter gives but his contribution is nevertheless useful for the additional scraps of data provided and because the author propounds a radical, originally significant interpretation of the social facts.

This supplementary material consists of the observations that the term for the 'major clan' is *uvain hodn*, a denotation which also signifies 'marks'; that three legendary heroes were former chiefs, and that the word applied to their relation with the members of their respective groups is *caïcá* (p. 149).

Métraux claims that some of Hoerhan's facts are wrong, as can be seen 'from a comparison of the two systems [i.e. the respective social structures of the Kaingang and Aweikoma] and especially of the traditional paintings . . .' (p. 150). He challenges Hoerhan's model which, he asseverates, is 'open to question' especially since its triadic form would be 'unique in Brazil' (p. 150), adding that Nimuendajú's impression is that Hoerhan's mistake was to regard as an independent clan one of the classes of the mê-cálêbn, i.e. the mê-cúi-ken which Métraux considers corresponds to the Kaingang Kamé-ag-votoro.

He asks us to note the resemblance between the name of 'this so-called clan' and that of the cúi-kent which he believes corresponds to the Kanyerú-ag-votoro (p. 151). Métraux adds that since Hoerhan does not indicate any class which would correspond to that of the pair of either moiety it is probable that such a group did not exist among the Aweikoma. He also graphically depicts the social structures of both tribes but his representation is virtually identical with that drawn by Nimuendajú.[13] His personal reinterpretation entails, however, a very different schema but for some unspecified reason does not provide it, so the depiction shown below is one that I have constructed in accordance

David Hicks

with Métraux's reordering of Hoerhan's data and is in fact the only logical one congruent with the import of his remarks.

Mê-vídn moiety (dots)
Cúi-kent class (circles with central dot)
Mê-to páa-pa class (spots)

Mê-cálêbn moiety (stripes)
Mê-cúi-ken class (circles)
Zôo-zí class (horizontal stripe over vertical ones)

Aweikoma social organization thus consists of the moieties Mê-vídn and Mê-cálêbn linked with four classes; cúi-kent, mê-cúi-ken, mê-to páa-pa, and zôo-zí whose respective body paintings are shown in the schema.

INTERPRETATION

One by-product of the task of analysing Aweikoma social structure is the simple collation of all the available published information on the relevant facts of the social organization. As a consequence of this activity alone it is possible to detect obvious contradictions between the several series of ethnographic data at our disposal and one can only regret that neither Métraux nor Henry attempted to relate their personal interpretations to those of the other.[14] The latter, as previously remarked, does not even mention the existence of his earlier paper in the subsequent monograph, though both publications adduce evidence which provides the basis for two different structural conceptions of this society.

We are therefore left with a confused compound of factual knowledge as well as four distinctive models of the social structure; dyadic, triadic, quinary, and senary. An essential step at this point is thus to determine if possible just how many social groups there are, their names, and the pattern of their body paintings.

In comparing the respective sets of group names provided by Hoerhan and Henry a phonetic similarity can be discerned between some names.

Hoerhan	Henry
Crên-ndô	Klendó
Zêit-tsch-*cá-i-lê*	Kainlé
mê-vídn	mêvídn
mê-*cálêbn*	kalébm
mê-*cúi-ken*	kuikên

Apart from the prefix 'mê-' reported by Hoerhan, the last three names on both lists are virtually identical and except for his use of 'r' employed instead of 'l' there is also agreement on the form of the first name. The second occasions a temporary doubt but the '-cá-i-lê' suffix given by Hoerhan is similar to Henry's 'Kainlé' and the 'Zêit-tscha-' part of the former's term may be some kind of personal prefix added to the group name in the case of certain individuals.[15] In each instance the designs of the respective groups are, however, the same and it would appear likely that both sets are structurally identical.

With this initial factual agreement between the two authorities established, we can compare our other series of data, reject what is inconsistent or illogical, and conflate the rest.

According to Henry's description there are three culture-heroes, Wanyekí, Klendó, and Kainlé, who are each symbolically associated with an eponymous group. Hoerhan's equivalent names are Uvanhêcü, Crên-ndô, and Zêit-tsch-cá-i-lê but for both authorities the first hero's group is denoted by spots, the second by stripes, and the third by rings.

Whereas in Henry's account the name of the group is that of the hero, Hoerhan's observations enable Nimuendajú to remark that '. . . the true clan names seem [sic] to be mê-vídn, mê-cálêbn, and mê-cúi-ken' (p. 83), denotations which in Henry's view describe only the pattern of design worn by group members. Hoerhan himself, to judge by his apparent hesitancy in the above extract, is not completely certain on this matter and for this reason Henry's data in this respect at least would seem the more reliable.

Henry's term *kôika hë* and Hoerhan's *caïcá* obviously refer to the same thing, i.e. collections of people denoted by the preceding name, but only the latter records the indigenous generic term for the social group. This is *uváin hodn*.

Although Hoerhan's list of names lacks that of the Wanyekí, a group to which pertains a dot design described by the Aweikoma as mê-vídn, these latter two informational points suggest that the Wanyekí and Uvanhêcü (or mê-vídn) groups are one and the same and this possibility is substantiated by the fact that in Henry's text the third culture-hero is Wanyekí whereas in Hoerhan's account it is Uvanhêcü. Nevertheless, their names are undeniably different and unfortunately nothing in the Aweikoma literature sheds light on this apparent inconsistency.[15]

Only two more groups are mentioned by Henry and neither is named, though a term describing the objective character of their respective designs is provided. These groups are the kaktêng kŭ kalébm, whose painting consists of a horizontal stripe over the vertical ones thus corresponding pictorially to Hoerhan's zôo-zí, and the kanêm, whose design is a spot and which is thus analogous to the latter's mê-to páa-pa.

Hoerhan describes a sixth group, the cúi-kent, whose design consists of circles with a central dot. Our other authority omits any reference to such a group in his book, but in 1936 described the social organization as comprising six groups, not just five, and on page 177 of his monograph remarks that in about 1927 a certain number of persons added the circle design to their other paintings. Presumably, therefore, those wearing dots ringed them with circles so that in design at any rate these could be regarded as equivalent to the cúi-kent people.

Apart from this sixth group, then, we have two whose designs are identically described by both authorities but the names of which are quite different. As in the case of the named groups, the published ethnography does not help in the elucidation of this problem but it may be that a group is known by more than one name.[15] There can be, however, no mistaking the coincidence of design and this equivalence induces me to postulate that the zôo-zí are Henry's kaktêng ku̧ kalébm and the mê-to páa-pa are the kanêm. Finally, the unambiguity attending Hoerhan's report of the existence of a group called the cúi-kent contrasts so favourably with Henry's self-contradictory evidence that in this matter greater confidence is more reliably invested in the former's assertion.

There would therefore appear to be six social groups among the Aweikoma. These are:

Wanyekí or Uvanhêcü or mê-vídn (dots)
Klendó or Crên-ndô or mê-cálêbn (stripes)
Kainlé or Zêit-tsch-cá-i-lê or mê-cúi-ken or kuikên (circles)
kaktêng ku̧ kalébm or zôo-zí (horizontal stripe over vertical ones)
kanêm or mê-to páa-pa (spots)
cúi-kent (circles with a central dot)

This conclusion leads to the central question concerning the mode of relation articulating these groups, and the answer provides the key to apprehending the dominant structural principle regulating this aspect of Aweikoma social order.

According to the respective analyses of Hoerhan and Métraux, some of the groups are on a different structural level from that of the rest; either three (Hoerhan) or two (Métraux) are major segments of the society and the others are minor inclusions within them. Henry, contrarily, maintains that each group is of the same structural order but if he is correct in this assumption then it is difficult to elicit any ordering principle integrating them.

Three pieces of evidence favour the assignation of certain groups to a distinctive and superior structural level. First, Henry provides only three named groups so that nominally at least these groups differ from the anonymous ones.[16] Second, only these three have the suffixes *kôika hë* since no such designation is attached to the ethnographer's other two and, finally, only these three groups are each ritually and mythologically linked with an eponymous hero.

Métraux's explicit (and Nimuendajú's implied) characterization of the structure of Aweikoma society as radically dyadic is, however, surely fallacious and both authorities reach this inference only by manipulating the social groups of the Aweikoma in such a manner as to fabricate a structural pattern congruent with that of Kaingang social structure. This adjustment is made on the basis of an alleged similarity in body-painting design between certain groups of the Aweikoma and analogous ones among the Kaingang and no plausible justification for this equation is given, though it is clear that for unstated reasons both authorities assume *a priori* that the two tribes must have identical forms of social structure and that as between the two societies the relation linking the groups as emblematic units and as structural entities must be homologous. Hoerhan's data are more comprehensively reorganized by Métraux than by Nimuendajú, who was evidentally more concerned with recording the information, and a criticism of the dyadic model must necessarily be directed at Métraux's analysis.

The mê-vídn and mê-cálêbn social groups own dots and stripes respectively, as do the Kanyerú and Kamé moieties of the other tribe; thus Métraux structurally equates the mê-vídn with the Kanyerú and the mê-cálêbn with the Kamé. Hoerhan remarks that the third major segment of Aweikoma society, the mê-cúi-ken which owns circles, is of the same structural order as the mê-vídn and mê-cálêbn, but as the Kaingang votoro class also has circles as its design and Kaingang society is a moiety system, Métraux demotes in a structural sense the mê-cúi-ken to a segmentary level logically equivalent to that of the votoro.

Since the cúi-kent subgroup with its central dot in each circle seems nicely to correspond to the Kanyerú-ag-votoro class, the mê-cúi-ken can only fit into that vacant structural slot in the hypothetical Aweikoma social structure opposite that occupied in the Kaingang system by the

Kamé-ag-votoro; hence the gap in the schematic depiction of both authors, but even in so far as the matter of design is concerned no analogy can be established for the painting of the Kamé-ag-votoro is not circles, as is that of the mê-cúi-ken, but circles and stripes!

There is not the slightest empirical or logical justification for managing the Aweikoma facts in this cavalier fashion and one is not entitled to make the *a priori* assumption that the Aweikoma social structure is the same as that of the Kaingang. The evidence, in fact, suggests otherwise and, while as a matter of comparative cultural interest the design similarity between the two tribes deserves attention, there is absolutely no reason to assume that a group owning one kind of design in Aweikoma society occupies the same structural place as one having the same design in the other society. Métraux therefore errs in altering the structural character of the major segment, that is the mê-cúi-ken, simply on the grounds that its circular designs correspond to those of a minor segment of Kaingang society. He seeks to support this rearrangement by claiming that a triadically ordered Aweikoma society would be unique in Brazil but this can hardly be regarded as serious justification for blandly reshaping the admirably clear data provided by an experienced observer of the Aweikoma.

One is thus left with Hoerhan's original triadic model and on the evidence of the published material there seems no reason whatever to doubt his rendering of the social facts. The detailed form of the triad is, however, open to query and in my view the ethnographic data can be more effectively redeployed so as to construct a model of Aweikoma society which explains a wider range of social and symbolic fact than that posited by the ethnographer.

In the latter's interpretation there are three 'major clans', social segments I shall henceforth label 'groups', and each has two different kinds of name. One is that of an eponymous hero and the other is a denotation describing the objective pattern of the design. Each group is said to include within itself a subgroup which is also named; this subgroup Hoerhan terms 'subclan'.

But if a group is internally divided then logically it must consist of at least *two* subgroups, not merely one as Hoerhan implies. In this society only one of these subgroups is named and has a design pertaining to it. While it could be claimed as a matter of principle that a series of unnamed subgroups without designs is conceivable, within the Aweikoma structural framework the presence of a plethora of names and designs featured in the social organization and their evident social and symbolic importance makes it scarcely credible that subgroups of a structural significance at least as great as that of the three named and pictorially represented subgroups should be anonymous and lack paintings.

Since Hoerhan describes three triads each consisting of one group with two names and a design, a subgroup with one name and a design, and implies the existence of one subgroup with neither name nor design, there is logical space enough here for a more effective recasting of the data and on the basis of the existing information I would propound the following model.

One of the three groups is Wanyekí (Uvanhêcü) which is divided into a subgroup called mê-vídn owning dots and another called kanêm (mê-to páa-pa) which owns spots. The second is that of Klendó which is bifurcated into the subgroup called kalébm (mê-cálêbn), which has stripes, and a second called kaktêng kų kalébm (zôo-zí), which owns the design with a horizontal stripe over vertical ones. The third group in Aweikoma society is that of Kainlé (Zêit-tsch-cá-i-lê), which is divided into the subgroups of kuikên (mê-cúi-ken) owning circles, and cúi-kent owning circles with a central dot.

The groups each have a name, which is that of an eponymous hero, but no *group* owns a specific body painting. A structural model of this kind can be schematically portrayed thus:[17]

Group and Eponym	Subgroup	Body-painting Design
Wanyekí	{ mêvídn	dots
	kanêm	spots
Klendó	{ kalébm	stripes
	kaktêng kų kalébm	horizontal stripe over vertical ones
Kainlé	{ kuikên	circles
	cúi-kent	circles with a central dot

The essential form of Aweikoma social structure having been determined, the next task is to decide the social and symbolic properties of the groups and subgroups. Henry (p. 176, passim) indicates that they are not lineally ordered but he notes that in native theory, though not in practice, they are exogamous. Hoerhan describes the groups as both patrilineal and exogamous but confides no analogous information on

the subgroups (Nimuendajú 1946: 83). The problem is therefore to
determine which of the two group characterizations is more likely to be
correct.

Neither Hoerhan nor Henry suggests that members of a group believe
themselves descended from one of the three culture-heroes and even
Hoerhan remarks that the members of a group only 'claim kinship' with
a hero (Nimuendajú 1946: 83). But Henry does not go even so far as
stating this and the cognatic relationship terminology he details so
admirably is consistent with his alineal interpretation (pp. 177–9). The
present evidence, then, points to the operation of exogamous but alineal
groups in Aweikoma society.

It is evident, according to his comments already presented, that Henry
considers the groups to be unimportant in Aweikoma society in contrast
to Hoerhan who, judging from his elaboration, believed them to be
significant enough to justify communicating the details of their structure
to the leading South Americanist of the day. It may be, of course, that
social forms had so altered by 1932 that the former ethnographer
properly stresses their insignificance but one wonders whether by
emphasizing the apparent lack of structural patterns in this society
Henry did not unconsciously overlook formal relations detrimental to
his interpretation of the nature of this society. Thus, after remarking
that informants told him that there is an association between the social
groups and particular aspects of the death ritual, the ethnographer
cannot resist doubting the validity of this information though he gives
no reason for so doing.

If the groups are exogamous they must to some extent regulate
marriage but their prime importance indubitably relates to symbolism.
The Aweikoma claim that the groups are associated with certain features
of the death ritual and no evidence that Henry provides contradicts this
claim. The text of *Jungle People* further contains enough material to
demonstrate that each group is the focus of a series of symbolic referents
but no systematic attempt is made by its author to elicit a pattern,
consistent and pervasive, in Aweikoma idealogy. He tantalizingly alludes
to the 'confused origin myths' that link men with animals and plants
but, probably because these are 'obviously fossilized' (!), does not bother
to record them (p. 91). Still, by collating what material he and Hoerhan
provide, one can glean some idea of the Aweikoma symbolic order.

Hoerhan, it will be recalled, says that the three culture-heroes created
the various animals which have skin markings corresponding to the

body paintings of each group. Thus Wanyekí is associated with spotted animals, Klendó with striped ones, and Kainlé with animals having circular markings.

Henry (p. 91) remarks that the jaguar and tapir are Wanyekí's *mang*[18] because he made them in the very beginning when the first people emerged out of the shoreless sea to the east and over the 'hard' mountains to the west. The objects pertaining to a group are omens of death in certain situations for its members, and when a Wanyekí person is about to die the tapirs are thin (p. 92). Wanyekí individuals came over the 'hard' mountains and thus before a person from this group dies the rivers dry up; after the death they rise considerably (p. 93). When the period of ritual isolation is concluded, a widowed Wanyekí person must abstain from cooked food for a much longer time than a Klendó individual and the former also has to keep his body paintings on for a much longer period afterwards (p. 185). During the baby-blackening ritual, members of this group imitate the cries of a species of small hawk while Kainlé persons utter a different kind of cry (p. 197).

Bees belong to the Klendó group and when a member of this group is going to die there is no honey available, though this insect can be seen (p. 92). The oblique and frustrating references to 'origin' myths indicate that they must contain a wealth of symbolic matter which would broaden the factual base of any analysis of Aweikoma classificatory thought. Thus we are informed that 'There is a story in an origin myth of one of the line people [sc. Klendó] who swam about in the water so much that he became a capavary, so that now the line people do not eat capavary; if they were to do so it would be like eating their own people' (p. 92). The Klendó are symbolically associated with water. They are thought to have come out of the shoreless sea, and rain and swollen rivers are death auguries for them (pp. 92–3).

The Kainlé group is associated with the pine-tree so that there are no pine-cones about when a member of this group is about to die and the deceased is cremated in a dry pine-tree (pp. 91–2).

This is the total information available on the symbolic aspects of the three social groups. Of interest is the fact that nowhere does the ethnographer depart from this triadic mode of symbolic description despite his ascribing five, not three, groups of identical structural order to Aweikoma society. The two nameless ones, however, appear to be excluded from the symbolic classification and their absence, in my opinion, confirms the basic trinomial character of Aweikoma social structure, as do two remarks by Henry which further serve to substantiate my claim that each group is itself dyadically formed.

Henry remarks that when a man returns from his ritual isolation he is given food by a woman of the *opposite* 'mark' (p. 185). This is only one of a series of ritual reversals which occur after the isolation, but the ethnographer's employment of the term 'opposite' in this context is both curious and revealing, for nowhere else in his book does he either state or infer that any 'mark', i.e. social group or subgroup, has its opposite. But if this is indeed systematically the case, each group or subgroup has an opposite and since the social structure is almost certainly triadic rather than dyadic a weighty item of support is added to my inference that each group is composed of two subgroups.

On page 91 of the monograph Henry, after recording that the Awei-koma say that the pine-tree is the exclusive property of the Kainlé, notes that this association disaccords with the statement of an origin myth and adds 'it is impossible to determine why the pine tree might not just as well be the property of the dot [*sc.* Wanyekí or mêvídn] or disc [*sc.* kanêm] people'. Now, these two subgroups, i.e. mêvídn and kanêm, are precisely those which I would subsume into the Wanyekí group, and if there were no formal property in common and a structural relation linking them why does Henry in this symbolic context classify both together? At no other place in his book does he even hint that they are somehow related and, if they constitute a pair, what of the other two pairs? Unhappily, on this score the ethnographer is typically silent and even the above data are for the most part incidental illustrative material for a psychologically orientated approach to the study of the Duque de Caxias community.

CONCLUSION

The mode of articulation of the Aweikoma social groups is thus triadic. This conclusion has at least three interesting consequences. First, though the Aweikoma tribe is conventionally classed as a representative of the Gê-speaking peoples in this structural respect they appear to be in a singular position, since while triadic arrangements may be featured in some Gê societies such as the Akwĕ-Shavante (cf. Maybury-Lewis 1967: 75), in each case the *radical* principle of order regulating the social forms is not triadic. Typically, in fact, it seems to be dyadic. A second entailment is that a structural incongruence between the triadic social order and the dyadic symbolic order can be detected.[19] The final effect of this conclusion is to demonstrate yet again that the social order of Aweikoma society is fundamentally different from that of the dyadic Kaingang and constitutes further justification for distinguishing them.

NOTES

1. The first draft of this essay formed part of the Bachelor of Letters dissertation which I submitted to the University of Oxford in 1964 for examination by, as it eventually happened, Professor E. E. Evans-Pritchard and Mr Francis Huxley, both of whom I wish to thank for their useful comments on that earlier analysis. My supervisor at the time was Dr Rodney Needham, who typically devoted detailed attention to my research problems and to him especially go my thanks. The award of a State University of New York Faculty Fellowship for the summer of 1969 enabled me to rewrite the present study with no financial preoccupations, and to the Research Foundation of that institution I express my grateful thanks.

2. *Vide* Maybury-Lewis (1967: vii–ix).

3. It would be irrelevant to delve into the semantic differences between the notions of 'social structure' and 'social organization' here, and all that matters for the purpose of the present essay is that I apply the first term to denote the more abstract model while the latter refers to a model at the level of empirical reality. The difference is more one of degree than kind.

4. The leading Aweikoma authority, Jules Henry, applies the term 'extended family' to denote this social unit but I prefer that of 'subtribe' for reasons which it is not necessary to specify here.

5. Henry himself makes this mistake and eschews the name 'Aweikoma'. In his book the Duque de Caxias community are 'Kaingang'. *Vide* Hicks (1965, 1966a, and 1969).

6. Under the name 'Blumensohn'.

7. All page references to Henry unless otherwise described refer to *Jungle People* and to the 1964 edition only.

8. In his monograph the ethnographer gives no reason for dropping one of the six groups mentioned in the 1936 note and in fact makes no reference whatever to his earlier publication.

9. A spot is a mark I take to be larger than a dot.

10. A member of the Aweikoma community.

11. Nimuendajú's 'Botocudo' are my 'Aweikoma' and his 'votõ'ro' are my 'votoro'; despite certain obvious errors of transcription in this extract, Nimuendajú's own orthography is used. The letter 'B' = Botocudo and 'K' = Kaingang.

12. His depiction is vague and unsatisfactory even according to the information he himself records. Thus the broad design categories 'rings' and 'patches' each include two subgroups whose emblems must, by the logic of the system, differ from each other's and a gap is left in the Aweikoma set of subgroups opposite that of the Kaingang Kamé-ag-votoro, which is clearly where the mê-cúi-ken would fit, but Nimuendajú fails to complete his diagram. The italics in my transcription of his schema are my own. They are added for the sake of clarity.

13. The only differences are minor expository ones, e.g. continuing Nimuendajú's equation signs (=) down through the line of subgroups, i.e. what Métraux terms 'classes'.

14. Henry certainly had the opportunity to do so in the second edition of his monograph but instead preferred to defend the basic theoretical approach of the first edition.

15. The multiplicity of names for a group in a culturally related tribe, the Shavante, is attested by Maybury-Lewis (1967: 170). This phenomenon may also occur among the Aweikoma and might explain the nominal inconsistency which is one of the puzzles of the published ethnography.

16. The names Wanyekí, Klendó, and Kainlé are, it will be recalled, Henry's 'basic ones'.

17. For simplicity of exposition it is best to select one or other of the nominal sets and orthographic versions. Unless there is a special reason for departing from Henry's system of nomenclature, further reference in this essay will be to his names and orthographic mode. When, therefore, Hoerhan, Ninuendajú, or Métraux's data or models are commented upon it is to be understood that, whereas in their original texts Hoerhan's own names and orthography were used, I am employing those of Henry. There is, however, no essential reason why Hoerhan's system could not have been adopted and, indeed, as can be seen in the representation, one of his subgroup names (that of cúi-kent) has to be exploited because Henry gives no corresponding name. But since later reference is made to symbolic motifs and referents almost all of which are located in Henry's text it is more generally consistent to follow his rendering with regard to the social groupings.

18. A possessive form applied to animals which are owned.

19. The operation of the principle of complementary opposition in Aweikoma symbolism is analysed in my 1966b essay.

REFERENCES

HENRY, JULES 1936 A Preliminary Sketch of the Kinship and Social Organization of the Botocudo Indians. *Boletim do Museu Nacional, Antropologia* (Rio de Janeiro) **12**: 49–58. [Published under the name 'J. H. Blumensohn'.]

— 1941 *Jungle People: a Kaingáng Tribe of the Highlands of Brazil*. New York: J. J. Augustin. Second edition New York: Knopf and Random House, 1964.

HICKS, DAVID 1965 *A Comparative Study of the Kaingang and Aweikoma of Southern Brazil*. Unpublished B.Litt. thesis, University of Oxford.

— 1966a The Kaingang and the Aweikoma: a cultural contrast. *Anthropos* **61**: 839–846.

— 1966b A Structural Analysis of Aweikoma Symbolism. *Ethnos* **31**: 96–111.

— 1969 A Comparative Analysis of the Kaingang and Aweikoma Relationship Terminologies. MS.

MÉTRAUX, ALFRED 1947 Social Organisation of the Kaingang and Aweikoma According to C. Nimuendajú's Unpublished Data. *American Anthropologist* **49**: 148–51.

MAYBURY-LEWIS, DAVID 1967 *Akwě-Shavante Society*. Oxford: Clarendon Press.

NIMUENDAJU, CURT 1946 *The Eastern Timbira*. Berkeley and Los Angeles: University of California Press.

Rapports de symétrie entre rites et mythes de peuples voisins

CLAUDE LÉVI-STRAUSS

La place unique qu'occupe l'œuvre d'Evans-Pritchard dans la littérature ethnologique provient, me semble-t-il, de l'harmonie qui y règne entre les deux tendances principales de nos recherches. Le goût bien connu de notre collègue pour l'histoire ne l'a jamais détourné des analyses formelles. Personne, sans doute, n'a su dessiner avec autant de sobriété et d'élégance les contours essentiels d'un système de croyances et de pratiques, exposer son ossature et faire jouer le mécanisme de ses articulations. Mais, en même temps, Evans-Pritchard reste toujours attentif aux cheminements arbitraires qu'empruntèrent les événements pour façonner la physionomie propre d'une société, et lui donner un caractère original à chaque étape de son devenir. Nulle méthode, mieux que la sienne, n'est propre à démentir la fausse affirmation selon laquelle on ne saurait approfondir les structures sans sacrifier l'histoire. Chez lui au moins, la rencontre d'une vaste érudition, d'un sens aigu des valeurs humaines, d'une extrême finesse psychologique et d'un incomparable art d'écrire, a permis que se conjuguent au service d'une même entreprise les deux courants qui, depuis l'origine, ont trop souvent tiré la pensée ethnologique dans des directions opposées.

Aussi m'a-t-il paru convenable de choisir, pour cet hommage, un thème manifeste la solidarité de l'histoire et de la structure, et qui éclaire la manière dont elles s'influencent mutuellement. Deux tribus des Plaines centrales de l'Amérique du Nord se prêtent fort bien à cette tentative. En effet, les progrès récents de l'archéologie ont apporté beaucoup d'informations sur leur passé, en même temps que, grâce aux deux admirables volumes de A. W. Bowers complétant des observations plus anciennes, nous disposons aujourd'hui d'analyses détaillées concernant leurs mythes, leurs rites et le cycle de leurs cérémonies.

Au début du 18e siècle, quand les Blancs arrivèrent sur le Haut-Missouri, les tribus dites 'villageoises', établies dans les vallées qui traversent les Plaines, partageaient une culture commune. Les Arikara de langue caddo, les Mandan et les Hidatsa de langue sioux, occupaient des territoires contigus correspondant aux Etats actuels du *South* et du *North Dakota*. Pendant l'été, ils vivaient dans des cabanes recouvertes de mottes de gazon, groupées en villages sur les terrasses surplombant les rivières. Ils cultivaient des champs en contrebas et, pendant que mûrissaient les récoltes, ils chassaient le bison dans les Plaines. A l'approche de l'hiver, ils se transportaient dans des villages mieux abrités au fond des vallées boisées. Mais cet état de choses ne remontait pas à une époque très ancienne. Nous laisserons de côté les Arikara, venus de sud vers le début du 18e siècle. En dépit de leur appartenance à une même famille linguistique, les Mandan et les Hidatsa ne constituaient pas non plus des groupes homogènes. Un très ancien peuplement mandan, originaire des régions à l'est et au sud, a sans doute occupé de façon continue la vallée moyenne du Missouri depuis au moins le 7e ou le 8e siècle, soit un millénaire avant le début de la période historique. D'autres groupes arrivèrent plus tard et remplacèrent les cabanes à demi enterrées et de plan rectangulaire par les constructions arrondies qui furent ensuite de règle. En ce qui concerne les Hidatsa, les choses semblent encore plus complexes. Un groupe venu du nord-est, les Awatixa, atteignit le Missouri vers le 15e ou 16e siècle, et vécut près des Mandan dont il emprunta le genre de vie et les croyances. Deux autres groupes quittèrent à leur tour les régions boisées à l'ouest des grands Lacs, au début du 18e siècle, pour s'établir dans les Plaines. Comme les Awatixa, les Awaxawi étaient d'anciens agriculteurs, mais les Hidatsa proprement dits vivaient surtout de chasse et de collecte, même à l'époque historique où ces différences frappèrent les premiers voyageurs. Les traditions des Mandan et des Hidatsa font état de ces origines diverses. Celles des Hidatsa relatent comment les deux groupes septentrionaux se scindèrent et donnèrent naissance aux Crow, qui s'établirent plus à l'ouest. Des légendes mandan préservent le souvenir de migrations successives et de l'arrivée, sur la rive orientale de Missouri, du plus ancien groupe hidatsa. La pénétration européenne, suivie d' épidémies qui firent des ravages à la fin du 18e et au début du 19e siècle, contraignit une population décimée à déplacer plusieurs fois ses villages. Il fallut que les tribus changeassent leurs rapports dans le sens d'une solidarité encore plus grande. Ces bouleversements s'achevèrent quand les autorités regroupèrent les derniers survivants dans la réserve de Fort Berthold. En 1929–1933 cependant, période durant laquelle

Bowers fit ses enquêtes, les vieux informateurs Mandan et Hidatsa différaient encore de manière substantielle selon leur groupe ou village d'origine: les mythes, les traditions légendaires, les règles de transmission des charges et offices n'étaient pas les mêmes. Et pourtant, en dépit de ces divergences qui concordent avec l'archéologie pour attester l'influence toujours active d'un passé historique très complexe et lesté de facteurs hétérogènes, tout se passe comme si, sur le plan des croyances et des pratiques, les Mandan et les Hidatsa avaient réussi à organiser leurs différences en système. On croirait presque que chaque tribu, pour ce qui la concerne et sans ignorer l'effort correspondant de l'autre, s'est appliquée à préserver et à cultiver les oppositions, et à combiner des forces antagonistes pour former un ensemble équilibré. C'est ce que nous voudrions à présent montrer.

On a vu que les tribus villageoises vivaient sous le régime d'une double économie saisonnière. Ce n'est pas assez dire, car la période estivale offrait elle-même deux aspects: d'une part celui des travaux agricoles, dans les bas-fonds abrités au pied des villages; et d'autre part, quand le maïs avait atteint la hauteur du genou, la chasse nomade qui conduisait pendant un mois la population loin dans les plaines, à la poursuite des troupeaux de bisons. Si les villages d'été, entourés de remparts et de palissades, étaient pratiquement inexpugnables, les expéditions de chasse ressemblaient à celles pour la guerre et parfois en offraient l'occasion; car il arrivait que les chasseurs se heurtassent à des troupes ennemies. Ainsi donc, des caractères antithétiques marquaient les travaux de l'été: vie sédentaire dans les villages protégés, et courses nomades dans des territoires exposés; agriculture d'une part, chasse et guerre d'autre part, ces deux dernières intimement associées par contiguïté spatiale et par affinité morale, puisqu'il s'agit de types d'activité violente, grosses de dangers et s'accompagnant de sang versé, et qui, de ce point de vue, diffèrent surtout en degré.

Or, ce système, qui met en jeu des oppositions complexes, s'oppose à son tour, et en totalité, à l'économie hivernale. On ne sortait guère des villages d'hiver où les provisions de vivres accumulées ne suffisaient pas pour protéger la population de la famine. Tout l'espoir reposait alors sur une recrudescence du froid et des tempêtes, qui chasseraient les bisons des plaines et leur feraient chercher refuge au voisinage des villages d'hiver, dans les vallées protégées où subsistaient des pâturages non encore recouverts par la neige. Quand on signalait l'approche des troupeaux, il fallait qu'un silence absolu régnât et les corps de police y veillaient. Les gens se cloîtraient avec leurs chiens dans les cabanes, ils s'abstenaient de couper du bois, ils éteignaient les foyers. Un chasseur trop empressé, une ménagère négligente, un enfant riant ou criant, eussent été sévèrement châtiés. Même si quelque bête s'aventurait dans le village et frôlait les habitations, les Indiens affamés n'avaient pas le droit de l'abattre de peur d'effrayer le gros du troupeau. Par conséquent, des genres de vie contrastés, que l'économie estivale juxtaposait sans les confondre, acquerraient pendant l'hiver une unité synthétique: on dépendait de la chasse comme en été, mais cette chasse hivernale s'opposait à l'autre puisqu'elle était sédentaire, non nomade, et que, sous ce rapport, elle s'apparentait plutôt à l'agriculture, laquelle s'opposait à la chasse pendant la période d'été. Ce n'est pas tout: la chasse d'été éloignait les hommes du village et les conduisait loin vers l'ouest, à la poursuite des bisons. En hiver, tous ces rapports s'inversaient Au lieu que les Indiens s'écartent des vallées et s'aventurent dans les plaines, le gibier s'écartait des plaines et s'enfonçaient dans les vallées. Au lieu que la chasse attire les Indiens hors des villages, elle se déroulait parfois en plein village, sinon tout près, quand le gibier s'approchait. Et, puisque la chasse s'apparentait à la guerre, tout se passait en hiver comme s'il eût fallu, pour ne pas périr de faim, que le village s'ouvrit tout grand aux bisons que la pensée indigène compare à des ennemis en été, mais que l'hiver transforme en alliés. Nous limitant pour le moment aux deux types de chasse, il ne paraît pas forcé de dire qu'elles s'opposent à la façon de ce qu'on pourrait appeler une 'exo-chasse' pour l'été, une 'endo-chasse' pour l'hiver.

Considérons d'abord les mythes et les rites de la chasse d'été. A la différence de leurs voisins Hidatsa et des autres tribus des Plaines, les Mandan ne célébraient pas en été la danse du soleil (*Sun Dance*). A la place, ils avaient une cérémonie complexe, s'étendant sur plusieurs jours, qu'ils appelaient *okipa* ou 'imitation'. Cette cérémonie, dont le mythe fondateur était à peu de choses près le même que celui des travaux agricoles, remplissait une double fonction: d'une part, commémorer des évènements mythiques, d'autre part stimuler la fécondité des bisons. Elle offrait donc un caractère syncrétique et son influence devait s'exercer pendant plusieurs mois: aussi longtemps que dure la période de gestation. Bien qu'elle eût toujours lieu au cœur de la saison chaude, l'*okipa* n'avait pas de lien électif avec la chasse estivale, mais plutôt avec la chasse en général, aussi bien d'hiver que d'été.

En revanche, le rituel de la 'Petite Buse' (*Small Hawk*) servait soit pour la guerre à n'importe quel moment de l'année, soit pour la chasse, mais alors seulement de juin à août. Le mythe fondateur (Beckwith 1938: 63–76; Bowers 1950: 270–81) raconte qu'une vierge farouche nommée Soie-de-Maïs (*Corn-Silk*), offensée par ses parents qui lui reprochaient de rester célibataire, partit au bout du monde pour épouser un ogre. Elle réussit à triompher des épreuves qu'il lui imposa et à le rendre docile. Mais l'ogre retrouva sa nature première et l'abandonna avec son fils dont, après qu'il eût grandi, elle s'éprit. Le jeune homme repoussa les avances incestueuses de sa mère. Il s'appelait Chasse-de-haut (*Look-Down-To-Hunt*) et était un maître de la chasse, car son père lui avait transmis sa nature d'oiseau de proie.

A cette époque, deux femmes s'introduisirent dans sa vie. L'une était brune, venait du nord et apportait de la viande séchée; elle s'appelait la Bisonne. L'autre, nommée Soie-de-Maïs comme la mère du héros, était blonde, venait du sud et apportait des boulettes de farine de maïs. Il les épousa, mais bien que Soie-de-Maïs fut patiente et généreuse, la jalousie et la susceptibilité de la Bisonne compromirent l'harmonie du ménage. Les deux femmes se querellèrent au sujet des services que chacune rendait aux humains. Vexée, la Bisonne partit avec son jeune fils.

Soie-de-Maïs persuada son mari d'aller à la recherche de la femme disparue. Elle était de force à supporter son absence, lui resterait fidèle et le protégerait de loin. Le héros parvint enfin chez ses beaux-parents les bisons, qui s'ingénièrent à provoquer sa perte. Mais il surmonta les épreuves et obtint des bisons la promesse que, dorénavant, ils serviraient de nourriture aux humains. La famine régnait au village quand il y revint, car le gibier manquait et la sécheresse menaçait les récoltes. Le héros ramena les bisons nourriciers et les pluies fertilisantes.

Il est à peine besoin d'interpréter ce mythe, tant il se montre explicite sur tous les points. Dès le début, l'héroïne Soie-de-Maïs se charge de définir les références sociologiques, car sa conduite met en corrélation et en opposition deux types extrêmes de mariage: l'un exogame, avec un ogre qui vit au bout du monde; l'autre endogame, avec son propre fils. Mais elle-même incarne l'agriculture, comme l'indiquent à la fois le nom qu'elle porte et la fonction avouée de son homonyme, tandis que son mari, puis son fils, sont des maîtres de la chasse. Par conséquent, le mariage exogame eût exporté l'agriculture en dehors du village, l'union endogame eût importé la chasse au dedans. Ni l'une ni l'autre éventualité

165

n'est concevable, comme le prouvent les humeurs incompatibles des deux épouses qui personnifient ces formes d'activité économique. Pour suivre la femme Bisonne, il faut délaisser la femme Maïs. Mais si la première se montre exigeante et jalouse, et fait du succès à la guerre la condition *sine qua non* du succès à la chasse, par sa tolérance et sa générosité l'autre garantit que la chasse réussie apportera les récoltes abondantes, en quelque sorte, par dessus le marché. Et c'est bien là ce qui se produisait dans la pratique : dès que le maïs était haut, les Indiens abandonnaient leurs champs et leurs villages pour mener une vie nomade consacrée à la chasse. Pendant leur absence, les plantes achevaient de croître ; au retour, il n'y avait plus qu'à récolter. Le mythe superpose donc des termes groupés par paires, dont il affirme l'homologie, bien qu'elles se situent sur des plans différents qui vont depuis les formes d'activité techno-économique jusqu'à la morale domestique, en passant par les règles de la vie sociale : l'agriculture implique la chasse comme la chasse implique la guerre ; du point de vue économique, l'agriculture est comme l'endogamie du point de vue sociologique, puisque l'une et l'autre s'inscrivent dans les limites du village ; en revanche, la chasse et l'exogamie regardent vers le dehors. Enfin, la constance et l'infidélité conjugales (dont le mythe prétend expliquer l'origine, cf. Bowers 1950, p. 281 : 'This was also the beginning of the custom of a man parting with his wife and child and thinking little about it') sont entre elles dans le même rapport que l'endogamie et l'exogamie, ou que l'agriculture d'un côté, la chasse et la guerre de l'autre.

Après la problématique de la chasse d'été, considérons maintenant celle de la chasse d'hiver. La cérémonie du Bâton rouge (*Red Stick*) servait, de décembre à mars, pour attirer les bisons près des villages. On sait qu'elle consistait essentiellement dans une cession, par les jeunes hommes, de leurs épouses, nues sous un manteau de fourrure, à des anciens qui incarnaient les bisons. Au cours du coït cérémoniel qui suivait de façon réelle ou symbolique, les aînés transmettaient aux cadets leurs pouvoirs surnaturels par l'intermédiaire des femmes, et leur procuraient ainsi le succès à la chasse et à la guerre. Les Mandan et les Hidatsa célébraient ce rite de la même façon.

En revanche, les mythes fondateurs différaient d'une tribu à l'autre, car chacun réservait le rôle principal à une seule des deux femmes associées par le mythe fondateur du rituel d'été, en qualité d'épouses du héros. Et, comme on pouvait s'y attendre à cause des caractères contrastés de la chasse estivale et de la chasse hivernale, les fonctions sociologiques des femmes s'inversaient en passant de l'une à l'autre. Dans le mythe mandan du Bâton rouge, Soie-de-Maïs n'est plus qu'une fille capricieuse et excentrique; dans le mythe homologue hidatsa, la Bisonne se change en héroïne nationale.

Ce n'est pas tout. Car, si le mythe mandan du Bâton rouge (Bowers 1950: 319–23) débute, comme celui de la Petite Buse, par l'histoire de la vierge rebelle au mariage et qui tombe au pouvoir d'un ogre, il continue de façon différente: l'héroïne échappe à son ravisseur; sur le chemin du retour, elle adopte une mignonne petite fille (*First Pretty Woman*) qu'elle ramène au village. Le bébé se révèle être une ogresse, personnification de la famine, qui dévore tous les habitants. Des bisons secourables la dénoncent, on la fait périr sur un bûcher. Désormais, quand la famine menacera le village pendant l'hiver, les bisons viendront s'offrir comme nourriture, en échange des femmes qu'on leur aura livrées.

Dans ce mythe, par conséquent, Soie-de-Maïs importe la famine au village. Or, les versions hidatsa (Bowers 1965: 452–4) inversent tout le système: elles remplacent Soie-de-Maïs, exportée hors du village, par la Bisonne, établie au dedans. Au lieu que Soie-de-Maïs, héroïne téméraire, rapporte la famine de son voyage lointain, la Bisonne, héroïne avisée, importe les bisons d'hiver, moyen d'échapper à la famine pour les Indiens devenus ses concitoyens.

Dans le mythe fondateur du rituel mandan de la chasse d'été, le héros réussit à rejoindre sa femme Bisonne et à échapper aux persécutions de ses beaux-parents, grâce à la complicité de son jeune fils qui se montre donc le contraire d'un ogre. Fille adoptive au lieu de fils légitime, et qui manifeste l'absence meurtrière des bisons, cause de la famine (au lieu de neutraliser leur présence meurtrière, puisque à ce stade, les bisons se conduisent comme des ennemis), la belle enfant du mythe mandan de la chasse d'hiver inverse le personnage du jeune bison secourable, dans celui de la chasse d'été. Or, un troisième renversement affecte le même personnage dans un autre rite de la chasse d'hiver, celui de la Bisonne blanche (*White Buffalo Cow*), célébré de décembre à mars par une confrérie féminine. En effet, le mythe fondateur (Bowers 1950: 325–6) relate la capture de deux enfants bisons dont on réussit à garder l'un au village, contraignant ainsi les bisonnes à venir le visiter chaque hiver et à rapprocher du même coup les troupeaux. Cette fillette, cause passive de l'abondance de bisons, est donc contradictoire avec la petite ogresse qui manifeste activement leur absence comme incarnation de la famine, et dont le fils bison, qui frustre les projets cannibales de sa famille, est le contraire.

Si l'on se place à un point de vue formel, on aperçoit d'autres relations entre les mythes et les rites selon qu'ils concernent la chasse d'hiver ou d'été. A la fois quant au mythe et quant au rite, le cycle de la Bisonne blanche était commun aux Mandan et aux Hidatsa, ceux-ci l'ayant, croit-on, acquis de ceux-là (Bowers 1965: 205). On ne saurait en dire autant du cycle du Bâton rouge, commun seulement quant au rite, mais dont on a vu que les mythes fondateurs diffèrent pour chaque tribu au point qu'ils offrent l'un de l'autre une image inversée. La même relation prévaut entre les cycles du Bâton rouge et de la Bisonne blanche, mais cette fois sur le plan du rituel dont des femmes jeunes et désirables fournissaient la matière dans un cas, tandis que, vieilles et ayant passé l'âge de la ménopause, elles étaient les agents dans l'autre cas. Il y a plus: quand on compare la disposition des officiants dans la cabane cérémonielle à l'occasion de chaque rite (Bowers 1950: 317, 327), on relève plusieurs contrastes. Les participants au rite de la Bisonne blanche étaient de sexe féminin, ceux du Bâton rouge incluaient des hommes et des femmes. A cette opposition bi-sexuée correspondait, dans l'autre rite, une division des membres du groupe mono-sexué en prêtresses et assistantes, celles-ci passives, celles-là actives. Dans les deux cas, le propriétaire de la cabane et sa femme jouaient un rôle, mais la place qui leur était assignée se trouvait dans le cercle des officiants, ou en dehors. Résumons tous ces aspects: la cérémonie hivernale de la Bisonne blanche était commune aux Mandan et aux Hidatsa, à la fois quant au rite et quant au mythe. L'autre cérémonie majeure pour la chasse hivernale, celle du Bâton rouge, était commune quant au rite et différente quant aux mythes. Enfin, sur le plan du rituel, les deux grandes cérémonies hivernales se reflétaient à l'envers.

Les Hidatsa connaissaient des variantes faibles du mythe de la Petite Buse (cf. Beckwith 1938: 77–78), dont on se souvient qu'il concerne la chasse d'été, mais, semble-t-il, sans célébrer le rite correspondant. Pour compléter le système des rapports entre les mythes et les rites des deux tribus, il faudrait donc trouver chez les Hidatsa un équivalent, ou un substitut des rites pour la chasse d'été.

Les rites de chasse des Hidatsa se rattachent à une mythologie des buttes, éminences de terrain qui s'élèvent çà et là au dessus des Plaines.

L'une d'elles abritait deux Esprits tutélaires : Hirondelle (*Swallow*) et Buse (*Hawk*), qui procuraient une bonne chasse aux Indiens malheureux (Beckwith 1938: 234–8; Bowers 1965: 433–6). Or, le héros mandan du mythe de la chasse d'été est une buse, et il éprouve pour les buttes une prédilection : '. . . during his leisure, he would sit on a pile of rocks on the hill back of the village' (Bowers 1950: 275). Comme le protégé des oiseaux tutélaires selon le mythe hidatsa, il dédaigne aussi le village d'hiver et préfère camper avec les siens à la tête des vallées. Enfin, les Hidatsa rapportaient toutes ces croyances à la chasse d'été (Bowers 1965: 436–7).

On dispose donc d'indications convergentes qui suggèrent que ces rites, dits du Nom de la Terre (*Earthnaming*), correspondaient chez les Hidatsa à ceux de la Petite Buse des Mandan. Cependant, selon les Hidatsa, le maître des buttes était un hibou, personnage qui donne son nom à un des rites mandan de la chasse d'hiver : le Hibou des neiges (*Snow Owl*). Par conséquent, tout se passe comme si ce dernier rite, réservé à la chasse d'hiver par les Mandan, se transformait pour les Hidatsa en rite d'été.

Dans ces conditions, il paraît significatif que les Mandan associent le Hibou des neiges, non pas aux buttes qui s'élèvent au dessus du niveau du sol, mais à une vallée symbolique : la fosse-piège oú se cache le chasseur d'aigles. En effet, le héros du mythe fut emprisonné dans une semblable fosse par un rocher éboulé; et c'est en cheminant en dessous du sol qu'il parvint chez le hibou (Beckwith 1938: 149; Bowers 1950: 286). Ce héros s'appelait Loup noir. Or, si les Mandan célébraient les rites du Hibou des neiges pour la chasse d'hiver entre décembre et mars, c'est-à-dire pendant les mois les plus froids, les Hidatsa célébraient les rites en l'honneur des Loups tutélaires seulement pendant les mois les plus chauds (Bowers 1965: 418). L'inversion de l'hiver et de l'été se confirme par ce biais.

Nous avons remarqué que la chasse d'été et la guerre offrent une double analogie, à la fois sous l'angle de la ressemblance et de la contiguité : '. . . when on the buffalo hunt there were instances of death of Indians from enemies or from injuries inflicted by the buffaloes' (Bowers 1950: 277). Cette affinité explique que les Mandan et les Hidatsa conçoivent la guerre elle-même comme une chasse cannibale, oú les hommes deviennent un gibier pour le Soleil et ses sœurs, ogres célestes qui se repaissent des cadavres abandonnés. Puisque les mythes fondateurs de la chasse d'hiver offrent des caractères inverses pour chaque tribu, et puisque la chasse d'hiver est elle-même l'inverse de la chasse d'été, il résulte que des inversions symétriques doivent apparaître, d'une part entre les mythes mandan et hidatsa relatifs au Peuple d'en haut, d'autre part entre les mythes de guerre d'un groupe et ceux qui se rapportent à la chasse d'hiver dans l'autre groupe.

Commençons par ce second point. Sans qu'il soit nécessaire d'entrer dans le détail de mythes longs et compliqués, un rapprochement s'impose au premier coup d'œil entre le mythe du Peuple d'en haut des Mandan, qui fonde les rites de guerre, et le mythe du Bâton rouge des Hidatsa, qui fonde les rites de la chasse hivernale. Tous deux ont trait à une dispute des frères Soleil et Lune, au sujet soit d'une femme cheyenne et cannibale, *qui mange* les humains, soit d'une femme bisonne, donc représentant une espèce *que mangent* les humains. Chaque fois aussi, les mythes rendent compte de l'origine des jeux de hasard (conçus par les Indiens comme une sorte de guerre), et de la guerre elle-même avec son objectif suprême: la chasse aux têtes (comparer: Bowers 1950: 299–302; 1965: 452–4).

La relation parallèle entre les mythes alternes peut être mise en évidence de deux façons. Indirectement d'abord: comme le mythe hidatsa du Peuple d'en haut, le mythe hidatsa du Bâton rouge relate un conflit entre les cannibales célestes et les humains, où prennent leur origine les jeux de hasard, la guerre et les rites guerriers. Cette armature identique n'exclut pas des différences sur lesquelles nous reviendrons plus loin. Pour le moment, il suffira de rappeler que le mythe mandan du Bâton rouge inverse le mythe hidatsa fondateur du même rituel et, par voie de conséquence, le mythe hidatsa du Peuple d'en haut qui a même armature que lui. Cette inversion se vérifie aussi directement: dans le mythe hidatsa du Peuple d'en haut, il est question d'un nourrisson céleste qui renaît comme fils légitime à une Indienne, et qui devient responsable de la déroute des Hidatsa devant les ennemis qu'ils ont attaqués. Ce que le mythe dit ici en 'clé de guerre' – si l'on nous passe l'expression – équivaut à ce que le mythe mandan du Bâton rouge exprime en 'clé de chasse': là, en effet, un nourrisson terrestre, du sexe féminin, adopté par une Indienne, se révèle être un ogre qui dévore les Mandan et symbolise la famine d'hiver, résultant du fait que les bisons n'envahissent pas les villages ou leurs abords.

Où en sommes-nous? Nous avons constaté que les rites de chasse des Mandan et des Hidatsa formaient, chacuns de leur côté, un système; ensuite, que ces deux systèmes offraient l'un de l'autre une image symétrique, de sorte que le réseau de leurs relations réciproques peut se représenter comme suit (*Figure 1*):

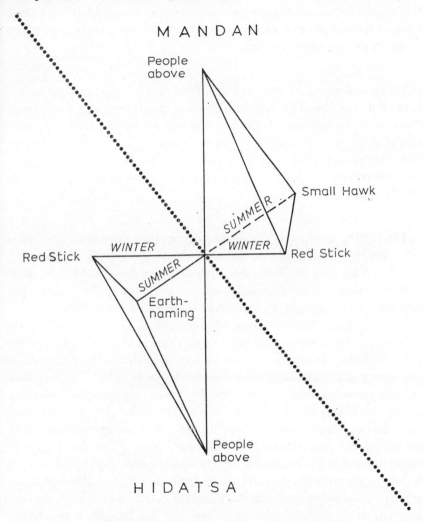

MANDAN

People above

Small Hawk

SUMMER

WINTER   WINTER

Red Stick   Red Stick

SUMMER

Earth-naming

People above

HIDATSA

Pour chaque tribu, les principaux mythes de chasse occupent les sommets d'un tétraèdre. D'une tribu à l'autre, ils se répondent aux sommets opposés. Ainsi, des relations symétriques unissent deux à deux les mythes du Peuple d'en haut (inclus au titre de chasseurs cannibales); ceux du Bâton rouge, qui est partout un rite d'hiver; celui du Nom de la Terre et celui de la Petite Buse qui, pour les Hidatsa et les Mandan respectivement, appartiennent à l'été. Mais le schéma appelle d'autres remarques.

1. Les deux axes perpendiculaires qui se coupent au centre de la figure correspondent respectivement à l'hiver et à l'été. Aux deux extrémités de l'axe de l'hiver, on trouve les rites du Bâton rouge, identiques dans les deux tribus mais qui, en raison de l'inversion des mythes fondateurs, occupent des sommets opposés.

2. De même, aux deux extrémités de l'axe de l'été, on trouve le mythe de la Petite Buse pour les Mandan, du Nom de la Terre pour les Hidatsa. Nous avons vu que ces rites se correspondent sous plusieurs rapports: dualité de héros (Hirondelle et Buse) ou d'héroïnes (Soie-de-Maïs et Bisonne); présence ici et là d'un héros nommé Buse, qui a une prédilection pour les éminences de terrain; enfin, association des deux rites avec la chasse d'été.

3. Les mythes du Peuple d'en haut occupent les extrémités d'un troisième axe, perpendiculaire aux deux autres en leur point d'intersection. En effet, si les rites du Bâton rouge, de la Petite Buse et du Nom de la Terre offraient un caractère saisonnier et périodique, il n'en était pas de même pour ceux du Peuple d'en Haut qu'on pouvait célébrer de janvier à janvier (Bowers 1950: 108; 1965: 326), c'est-à-dire de façon apériodique, à n'importe quel moment de l'année. Que, chez les Mandan et les Hidatsa, ces mythes soient en opposition diamétrale ressort de plusieurs traits: dans la version mandan (Bowers 1950: 229–302) deux femmes terrestres, qui ne sont pas des sœurs, montent au ciel pour devenir les alliées par mariage de frères célestes. L'une, qui appartient à la tribu des Mandan, se disjoint d'un ogre: le Soleil, grâce à un cordon qui lui permet de redescendre jusqu'à son village. Pour se venger, le Soleil place son fils légitime à la tête des ennemis des Mandan, et il déclare la guerre à ces derniers. Dans la version hidatsa (Bowers 1965: 327–9) tout se passe exactement à l'envers: deux frères célestes descendent sur terre pour se faire concevoir par des humaines et renaître comme des petits enfants. La sœur du Soleil, qui est une ogresse, se conjoint un personnage terrestre grâce à un cordon. Elle fait de lui son fils adoptif et le place à la tête des ennemis des Hidatsa. En conséquence de quoi la guerre, déclarée par ceux-ci risque de tourner à leur désavantage. Dans une version, la Lune et les oiseaux-tonnerre combattent aux côtés des Mandan et leur donnent la victoire; le fils de la Lune, devenu chef des Mandan, aime à s'asseoir au sommet des buttes. Dans

l'autre version, les héros Hirondelle et Buse, que nous savons être des maîtres des buttes, retournent la bataille au profit des Hidatsa.

4. Il résulte de ce qui précède que, chez les Hidatsa, un lien direct existe entre le mythe du Peuple d'en haut, fondateur des rites de guerre, et celui du Nom de la Terre, fondateur des rites de la chasse d'été. Les Esprits tutélaires sont les mêmes ici et là. Les informateurs hidatsa précisent que les évènements rapportés dans le mythe du Peuple d'en haut se situent au début d'une histoire dont le mythe du Nom de la Terre raconte la suite. D'autre part, un lien direct existe aussi entre les mythes hidatsa du Bâton rouge et du Peuple d'en haut: ils traitent pareillement d'une visite de frères célestes chez les humains, aux fins de conception dans un cas (puisque les astres renaissent sous forme d'Indiens), de copulation dans l'autre (le but de la visite étant alors de devenir les amants, et non les enfants des Indiennes). Une guerre s'ensuit, mais subie par les Hidatsa au lieu de provoquée par eux, et où le Soleil, non sa sœur, combat avec les ennemis.

5. On observe entre les mythes mandan des connexions du même type. Dans le mythe du Peuple d'en haut et dans celui du Bâton rouge, une héroïne qui est aussi une concitoyenne, nommée chaque fois Soie-de-Maïs, partie pour épouser un ogre qui habite au bout du monde soit très haut (axe vertical), soit très loin (axe horizontal), ou bien enlève son fils légitime pour éviter qu'il ne devienne un cannibale (Bowers 1950: 300-1) ou bien adopte une fillette malgré que celle-ci soit une cannibale (ibid.: 321). Soie-de-Maïs est aussi l'héroïne du mythe de la Petite Buse où elle fait paire, en qualité de végétarienne, avec la Bisonne carnivore, fille et sœur de cannibales. Dans le mythe du Peuple d'en haut, elle fait paire avec une femme cannibale, et dont les frères ont les mêmes appétits. Les bisons du premier mythe inversent la chasse en guerre, les cannibales du second inversent la guerre en chasse, puisque les ennemis sont mangés (ibid.: 301).

Notre schéma offre deux caractères remarquables: d'une part, l'extrême symétrie de l'ensemble; d'autre part, la fragilité du lien unissant les deux sous-systèmes, qui ne semblent tenir l'un à l'autre que par un fil. Mais, en fait, il résulte de nos remarques antérieures qu'un accrochage solide s'effectue d'autres façons.

En premier lieu, l'axe hivernal est doublé sur toute sa longueur par le

173

cycle de la Bisonne blanche, intégralement commun aux Mandan et aux Hidatsa, à la fois quant au mythe et quant au rite (cf. plus haut, p. 168).

A cette liaison statique s'ajoute une autre, dynamique. Car le cycle du Hibou des neiges, présent dans les deux tribus, y remplit une fonction alternativement hivernale et estivale, liée tantôt aux vallées, tantôt aux buttes. Si donc le cycle de la Bisonne blanche ignore l'opposition des deux sous-systèmes et renforce ainsi leur solidarité, le cycle du Hibou des neiges rend leur symétrie manifeste et joue le même rôle, bien que par des voies différentes.

A l'appui de cette interprétation, on fera valoir que, sur le plan formel, les deux cycles se trouvent en nette opposition. De tous les rites de chasse, celui de la Bisonne blanche offre le caractère périodique le plus accentué. On n'avait pas le droit d'en parler hors saison, de crainte – même au mois d'août – que les froids ne surviennent et détruisent les jardins; la célébration ne pouvait avoir lieu qu'au solstice d'hiver, pendant les jours les plus courts de l'année (Bowers 1950: 324–7; 1965: 206). De plus, le rite avait un but unique: rendre l'hiver rigoureux pour chasser les bisons à proximité des villages. En revanche, les rites du Hibou des neiges offraient un caractère éclectique: ils servaient pour la chasse l'hiver, pour les pluies au printemps et en été, et pour la guerre à n'importe quel moment de l'année (Bowers 1950: 108). Les rites de la Bisonne blanche excluaient toute autre forme d'activité, ils n'étaient compatibles avec rien. Ceux du Hibou des neiges étaient, au contraire, compatibles avec tout (Bowers 1950: 282; 1965: 433–4).

Il semble donc que les rites qu'on pourrait appeler 'blancs' (Bisonne *blanche*, Hibou des *neiges*) opéraient un double verrouillage, passif et actif, des rites 'rouges' (Bâton *rouge*) dont les mythes fondateurs rendent la liaison précaire à cause de leurs caractères divergents. On notera à ce sujet qu'une des versions du mythe hidatsa du Bâton rouge précise que les bisons tutélaires employaient cette couleur pour les peintures corporelles, à l'exclusion du blanc ou du noir (Bowers 1965: 452), ce qui suggère que l'opposition des rites par la couleur était pertinente.

On se souvient qu'une prédilection du ou des héros pour les buttes servait de trait d'union entre le mythe mandan du Peuple d'en haut et le mythe hidatsa du Nom de la terre. En effet, les buttes, qui dominent la plaine, constituent un symbole approprié de la médiation entre le ciel et le monde chthonien. Mais, pour que le système global soit cohérent, il faut alors qu'une liaison du même type apparaisse entre les mythes qui occupent les positions symétriques dans le schéma, soit ceux du Peuple d'en haut pour les Hidatsa, et de la Petite Buse pour les Mandan. Cette conséquence hypothétique se vérifie intégralement grâce à un détail du second mythe : pour échapper aux attaques de l'ogre céleste (c'est un oiseau) qu'elle prétend apprivoiser et épouser, l'héroïne aidée par des animaux chthoniens, les taupes, s'allonge dans une tranchée pour que son corps soit de niveau avec le sol et n'offre pas de prise aux serres du rapace. Autrement dit, elle reconstitue un équivalent approximatif de la fosse-piège du chasseur d'aigles, où nous avons reconnu un symbole de la vallée, elle-même en opposition avec la butte.

Par conséquent, dans un cas, les buttes jouent le rôle de médiateur positif entre le haut et le bas, dans l'autre cas un vallonnement, inverse des buttes, joue le rôle de médiateur négatif. On peut donc suivre une triple transformation, depuis le plan imaginaire jusqu'au plan empirique en passant par le plan symbolique :

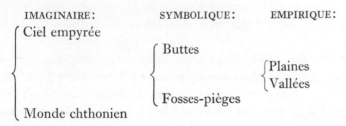

La seconde preuve de la cohérence du système serait à trouver dans le code éthique. Nous avons noté à plusieurs reprises que les mythes opposent tout à la fois des formes d'activité économique, des types de rapports sociaux et politiques, et des conduites qui relèvent de la morale domestique. Le mythe de la Petite Buse explique l'origine de l'inconstance (Bowers 1950 : 281) ; en revanche, celui du Hibou des neiges explique l'origine de la jalousie (ibid. : 294). Le rite de la Bisonne blanche était neutre, puisque les femmes qui le célébraient avaient passé la ménopause ; les mythes du Bâton rouge persuadaient les hommes de de dominer leur jalousie quand ils livraient leurs jeunes épouses aux anciens. Reste le mythe hidatsa du Nom de la Terre, qui devrait offrir lui aussi une connotation morale.

Cela étant posé de manière hypothético-déductive, que dit ce mythe ? Il raconte l'histoire (Bowers 1965 : 434–5) d'un étranger adopté, qui risque sa vie pour libérer ses 'sœurs' ravies par les siens aux Hidatsa : éloge de la fidélité fraternelle, donc, qui transcende à la fois le plan de la vie sexuelle et celui des frontières tribales, à l'opposé du mythe de la Petite Buse qui excuse l'infidélité sexuelle aussi pratiquée en dehors des frontières tribales, tandis que l'infidélité sexuelle, que préconisent les mythes du Bâton rouge, s'exerce dans limites del a tribu et même du village.

Jusqu'à quel point les Mandan et les Hidatsa étaient-ils conscients de ces rapports complexes de corrélation et d'opposition, de symétrie et d'antisymétrie entre leurs mythes respectifs? Pour tenter, en guise de conclusion, de répondre à cette question, il faut d'abord souligner que la mythologie des deux peuples offrait, en plus des différences que nous avons relevées, toutes sortes de points communs. Ils connaissaient les mythes les uns des autres et savaient les raconter dans les mêmes termes ou dans des termes voisins. On ne saurait donc nous objecter l'existence ici et là de récits presque identiques: nous avons seulement voulu montrer que dans un patrimoine devenu commun, chaque tribu avait tendance à choisir des variantes opposées ou complémentaires, quand il s'agissait de fonder des rites semblables ou remplissant la même fonction.

A l'origine des différences introduites dans les systèmes mythiques, il y a donc des ressemblances acceptées sur le plan des rites, lesquels enclenchent, si l'on peut dire, les formes d'activité technique et économique sur l'idéologie. Les rites des Mandan et des Hidatsa se ressemblent parce que, en arrivant sur le Missouri, ceux-ci les ont empruntés à ceux-là en même temps qu'un genre de vie dont ces rites aidaient à circonvenir les problèmes et à voiler les contradictions. En un sens, donc, la manière dont les mythes fondateurs des rituels s'opposent d'une tribu à l'autre comme des espèces au sein d'un genre, reflète la double évidence d'une origine historique distincte pour chaque tribu soucieuse de préserver son individualité, et d'une pratique que cette histoire même a conduit les deux peuples à partager.

Mais n'est-il pas toujours vrai, même chez nous, que le bon voisinage exige des partenaires qu'ils deviennent pareils jusqu'à un certain point en restant différents? La philosophie indigène avait conscience de cette nécessité dialectique, bien qu'elle la formulât en termes d'histoire plutôt que de structure. Les Mandan appelaient *Minnetaree*, mot qui signifie dans leur langue 'ils ont traversé la rivière', le plus ancien groupe Hidatsa venu du nord-est, qui arriva sur le Missouri à la fin des temps préhistoriques et qui apprit la culture du maïs auprès d'eux. Mais, selon leurs propres traditions, les Mandan ne souhaitèrent pas que cette cohabitation se prolongeât, et ils exposèrent à leurs hôtes leur point de vue dans ces termes:

'It would be better if you went upstream and built your own village, for our customs are somewhat different from yours. Not knowing each other's ways the young men might have differences and there would be wars. Do not go too far away for people who live far apart are like strangers and wars break out between them. Travel north only until you cannot see the smoke from our lodges and there build your village. Then we will be close enough to be friends and not far enough away to be enemies' (Maximilien 1843: 368; Bowers 1965: 15).

Cette haute leçon de philosophie politique, répétée presque dans les mêmes termes à un siècle d'intervalle, définit en termes de géographie et d'histoire la configuration structurale qui devait résulter de sa mise en pratique, et que notre analyse rétrospective a simplement retrouvée. Aux êtres qu'elle unit tout en les opposant, la symétrie n'offre-t-elle pas le moyen le plus élégant et le plus simple de s'apparaître semblables et différents, proches et lointains, amis bien qu'ennemis d'une certaine façon, et ennemis tout en demeurant des amis? Notre propre image, contemplée dans un miroir, nous semble si prochaine que nous pouvons la toucher du doigt. Et pourtant, rien n'est aussi loin de nous que cet autre nous-même, car un corps imité jusqu'aux moindres détails les reflète tous à l'envers, et deux formes qui se reconnaissent l'une dans l'autre gardent chacune l'orientation première, que le sort lui a assignée. En fin de compte, si les coutumes de peuples voisins manifestent des rapports de symétrie, il n'en faut pas chercher la cause dans quelque loi mystérieuse de la nature ou de l'esprit. Cette perfection géométrique résume au mode présent des efforts plus ou moins conscients mais innombrables, accumulés par l'histoire et qui visent tous le même but: atteindre un seuil, sans doute le plus profitable aux sociétés humaines, où s'instaure un juste équilibre entre leur unité et leur diversité; et qui maintienne la balance égale entre la communication, favorable aux illuminations réciproques, et l'absence de communication elle aussi fertile, puisque les fleurs fragiles de la différence ont besoin de pénombre pour subsister.

Claude Lévi-Strauss

BIBLIOGRAPHIE

BECKWITH M. W. 1938 Mandan-Hidatsa Myths and Ceremonies. New York: *Memoirs of the American Folk-Lore Society*, **32**.

BOWERS, A. W. 1950 *Mandan Social and Ceremonial Organization*. Chicago: University of Chicago Press.

1965 Hidatsa Social and Ceremonial Organization. Washington: *Smithsonian Institution, Bureau of American Ethnology, Bulletin 194*.

MAXIMILIAN, PRINCE OF WIED 1843 *Travels in the Interior of North America* (transl. by H. E. Lloyd). London.

Prophets and Rainmakers

The Agents of Social Change among the Lugbara

JOHN MIDDLETON

INTRODUCTION

Some of the more important figures in Lugbara society, both in the past and today, are certain ritual functionaries, of which there are a considerable number. These are prophets, diviners, sacrificing elders, and rainmakers. All seem at first sight to have different roles, and this is true; but it is clear that they are also complementary. The point of this paper is that they are necessarily so, in the sense that by this complementarity the Lugbara are able to deal with one of the difficulties facing ritual leaders who play innovative roles: the old Weberian problem of the routinization of charismatic authority. Weber saw the problem as essentially one of individuals, whereas I see it as one of societies; but it is the same. In addition, the roles of these ritual functionaries help us to understand something of the relationship between a particular social structure, on the one hand, and the constellation of related ritual powers and representations of that structure in ideology, on the other.

As a basis for the discussion of this problem, I wish to describe the histories of two spirit cults among the Lugbara of Uganda.[1] One, known as Yakan, appeared about 1890; the other, known as Balokole, appeared a few years before the Second World War. Both exist today but in forms very different from those they possessed during their heydays. Both started elsewhere, but in Lugbara have had similar developments, the phases in their histories being related to changes in the basic structures of power and authority in Lugbara society.

The Lugbara of northwestern Uganda and northeastern Congo are a Sudanic-speaking agricultural people. They are related to other groups to their northwest, of which the best-known are the Azande and the Mangbetu. The Lugbara live on a high open plateau and number some 240,000 people living at a density of up to 250 persons per square mile.

Their social organization is based upon a segmentary lineage system, in which the principal holders of authority are at the very lowest levels of segmentation, that of a three- or four-generation patrilineal lineage. The largest indigenous political units are the approximately sixty subtribes, each averaging about four thousand people, and each with a rainmaker who has ritual and some rudimentary political authority. There are also influential men, known as 'men whose names are known', who exercise occasional political authority. Today there are also government-appointed chiefs, originally the creations of the British and Belgian colonial powers.[2]

THE YAKAN CULT

The Yakan cult has had several phases. The southern Sudan was the scene of slave- and ivory-raiding by the Arabs throughout the nineteenth century. Most of the small tribes of the region were severely affected, although the Lugbara, on the southern limits of the area, escaped most of the damage suffered by their neighbours. Besides the slavers, there were other events in the region that seriously affected the smaller groups. One was the rise of the Azande and Mangbetu states to the west, which conquered and absorbed many of their lesser neighbours. The second was the rise among the Arab peoples to the north of the Mahdi, the Messiah, who set up a theocracy in Khartoum in 1885. The third was the appearance of Europeans, most of whom formed the administrative staff of the Egyptian Sudan. After the rise of the Mahdi they withdrew, but some were in the area in the last years of the nineteenth century; the best-known was Emin Pasha. The last event was the outbreak of epidemics, rinderpest among cattle and cerebrospinal meningitis among humans. These epidemics upset the balance between men and their cattle, and also between the distribution of men and the availability of land, suddenly making some men and lineages relatively poor and weak. These several disasters, particularly the epidemics and the Europeans, were causally related by the Lugbara, who saw them both as manifestations of Divine Spirit.

In 1883 the Dinka revolted against the Egyptian administration; also about the same time many of the small tribes of the region joined together in the Nebeli cult to protect themselves against the Azande. Both the Dinka and the others were led by prophets of cults of which the central part was the mass drinking of magic or sacred water. About 1891 some important Lugbara 'men whose names are known' from the area nearest Wadelai, Emin Pasha's fort on the Nile, crossed Lugbaraland and went to the Kakwa, a Nilo-Hamitic-speaking group to their immediate north, and there obtained magic water from a man called Rembe. They returned with it and dispensed it to other Lugbara and with its help defeated some of the patrols of Emin's Sudanese troops from Wadelai.

In 1900 the Belgians set up a post in Lugbaraland, then part of the Lado Enclave. They created chiefs, which, like other colonial powers, they considered essential for orderly government, by asking the Lugbara to put forward their important men. The dispensers of magic water came forward. They had, after all, used the water to defeat European- and Arab-led troops and knew how to deal with these strangers. They were made chiefs and became rich and powerful. They were almost all related to one another by kinship and came to form a rudimentary political elite. The Belgians left the area in 1907, and although nominally it became part of the Sudan there was a virtually unadministered interregnum until 1914, when it became part of Uganda. This period, about which little is known in detail, was one of uninterrupted and uncontrolled ivory-poaching by Arab and European adventurers, who treated the local population in as brutal a manner as they could. Lugbara say that at this time there was much more local feuding and warfare than ever before, especially between very small local groups.

In 1914 the area became part of Uganda. The British administrator reappointed most of the chiefs of the Belgians, and introduced taxation and recruitment for the army. There were further outbreaks of cerebrospinal meningitis, smallpox, and later also Spanish influenza. The Lugbara, again believing that the reappearance of Europeans and these epidemics were interconnected, turned once more to magic water. On this occasion, Rembe, the Kakwa prophet, was invited to enter Lugbaraland; he travelled about the northern part of the country setting up lodges at which he dispensed water. He had an assistant named Yondu. Rembe was captured and sent to Yei, in the Sudan, where he was hanged, probably in 1917. Yondu continued to organize the movement, and it culminated in a rising in 1919, after which it died down.[3]

Two factors are significant in this second phase. The first comprises the aims of the cult. These were to remove epidemics and Europeans and to bring peace. Rembe told his followers to accept the Europeans without argument, since his water would later send them away in any case. To drink the water would remove sickness, bring everlasting life,

John Middleton

bring back the ancestors and the cattle lost in the epidemics, and would also bring rifles to drive out Europeans if this had later to be done; any man who drank the water would be immune to bullets. The cult was known at this time as *Dede*, the Lugbara word for grandmother, since it protected its members as does a grandmother. The power of the water came from Rembe's pool, in which there was a snake-like creature, half man and half monitor-lizard. And Rembe was thought to gain his mystical powers from Divine Spirit. Today it is maintained that Rembe never died and one day will return. His behaviour has been described to me by many eye-witnesses: he went into trance and then divined using a gourd, he had the attributes of a mythical personage, such as being able to travel over great distances in a few moments and of escaping from chains when imprisoned. He is given certain feminine attributes in appearance, did not sleep with women, and had no children. He was a prophet and a medium for Divine power; through him this power could become manifest to men (Middleton 1968, 1969a).

The other factor that was significant is that of the organization of the movement. The adherents were divided into three ranks. First were the *opi* or chiefs,[4] who received water from Rembe himself. Next were the dispensers who received water from the chiefs. And last were the ordinary cultmembers. In most parts of northern Lugbaraland, where the movement was strongest, membership was virtually universal, there being a good deal of terrorism to enforce this. Both men and women joined; informants stated that when they encamped in the bush, danced, and drank the water, they later had sexual intercourse irrespective of clan or lineage affiliation. Old and young were also regarded as equal in rank. That is to say, the three principles of traditional social organization, descent, sex, and age or generation, were all treated as irrelevant. In addition, of course, the promise to bring back the dead ancestors implied the destruction of the cult of the dead, which was at the basis of the Lugbara system of social sanctions.

The cult died out in that particular form after 1919, for several reasons. One was the hanging of its prophet and the deportation and imprisonment of its leaders, the *opi* or chiefs. Another was that the aspirations to freedom from the authority of the senior men on the part of the younger men and women were satisfied in other ways, especially by labour migration. This assumed an economically and socially important role in the following years, with the development of southern Uganda and an increasing demand for labour and the opportunity to acquire cash for labour. In addition, they were slowly to develop markets for some of the local crops such as sesame and groundnuts, and later tobacco. Young men could increasingly become economically independent of their senior lineage members.[5]

I may summarize some of the things that happened to the Lugbara with the development of this cult between 1890 and 1920. They found that their traditional organization and defences against the outside world had proved to be inadequate to the threats and events that endangered their way of life. There had been the appearance of the various disasters which upset much of the demographic and economic balance of the traditional society. At first they tried to counter these events by traditional means – mainly by the offer of prayers to Divine Spirit by the rainmakers. These proved ineffectual. At the same time this was also a period in which land was becoming short. The Lugbara had formerly been moving slowly to their southeast; there was only sporadic and occasional land shortage, a stretch of land being exploited and local groups then moving on. After the advent of colonial administration the boundaries between subclan territories were fixed by administrative decree, and there developed an increasing disparity between the carrying capacity of the land and the actual distribution of the population.[6] This, of course, had always happened on a small scale; it was dealt with by lineage and subclan movement, and the disputes and tensions engendered were dealt with by the elders of family clusters who used the religious sanctions of the cult of the dead for this purpose.[7] The Lugbara cult of the dead is centred upon the exercise of authority by elders over their juniors; if this authority becomes difficult to exercise effectively, as it does in a period of land shortage (since the tensions engendered by land shortage cannot in fact be settled by the elders, despite their efforts), then the elders find themselves in the position of having continually to exercise more and more repressive authority, and finally the junior men rebel against it.

In the new cult organization the authority of elders and ancestors was quite specifically ignored and a new system of authority, based upon that of the prophet and the chiefs of the cult, set up in its place by the younger men and women. The changing relationship of senior and junior men and women, especially men, was clearly a factor of central importance. One aspect was the sense of resentment by juniors against their seniors for refusing to let them have as much land as they wanted and for continual invocation of the dead against them. I was told by informants who remembered this phase of the cult that this was taken by the younger men as a sign of witchcraft and as unjustified abuse of their authority on the part of the elders.

The Lugbara have a view of their society as being essentially unchanging. It has a basic structure of relations of power and authority, between living and dead, men and women, old and young; these relations are conceived in terms of a framework of clans and lineages. They are seen as ideally unchanging, but of course they do change, continually if slowly; occasionally they may change very rapidly at times of stress, usually caused by some kind of external intervention. In order to accommodate rapid change with the notion of an unchanging structure, Lugbara bring in the concept of Divine Spirit which created the world, can destroy it, and can change its form. Society, or the field of socially ordered relations based upon the recognition of proper authority, is conceived as being set inside a chaos of uncontrollable and unpredictable power associated with Spirit. Since Spirit, although omnipotent and timeless, is not a person, it gives its power to certain living intermediaries who can express it to living men and also express their responses and wishes to Spirit in return. At times of real crisis Spirit may even send persons with direct manifestations of its powers. Such a man was the prophet Rembe, a non-Lugbara (and so from outside the society) who is today, at any rate, thought to be everlasting and extremely powerful and who may one day return to the Lugbara if they need him to cope with other disasters of the order of the coming of the Europeans and epidemics.[8]

I come now to the later phases of the movement. The third occurred between about 1920 and about 1930 (perhaps rather later), and the fourth was still in being at the time of my stay in Lugbaraland. Yakan is no longer a cult, and the name Dede given to it earlier is no longer found; the aspect of protection from Europeans is no longer significant.

The third phase was that during which the leaders of the cult tried to keep their new authority but failed to do so in the face of the demands of their juniors. The important men of the movement, those who were given water by Rembe or Yondu, were given a stick of a particular wood on which was carved a monitor-lizard, the cult emblem. Possession of these sticks gave prestige and the right to certain first-fruits by the members of their holders' major lineages. Their owners regarded themselves as 'brothers'. The organization was controlled in each subclan by the rainmaker, who in this role was known as the *opi* of the stick-holders:

he controlled times of planting and harvesting. This phase was marked by a partial return to traditional lineage values and the traditional authority of the rainmakers. Today the owners of these sticks are very old men, and the power they once enjoyed through possession of them has become very slight, although the possessor of a stick enjoys considerable prestige. I found that it was typically they who spend the days talking with the rainmakers.

The fourth phase of the movement is found today. It is not of great importance. Yakan is the name used for one of several rather similar spirits. It is said to be invisible and to gain its power from Divine Spirit. It 'comes in the wind' and 'seizes' people who are then possessed by it in the form of trembling and speaking with strange words. It is said that the victim is seized because he has wandered away from the compounds and cultivated fields, the places of men and the ancestors, into the uncultivated bushland which is found along most of the larger streams and on the slopes of the mountains, empty places considered to be the domain of Divine Spirit in its immanent aspect. The victim has failed to recognize accepted cosmic and social boundaries between the realm of men, the ancestors, and ordered authority, on the one hand, and of Divine Spirit, other spirits, wild animals, disorder and unregulated power, on the other. The people who are possessed are treated by diviners, whose power also comes from Divine Spirit and who use techniques introduced by Rembe himself.[9]

Those possessed tend to be young to middle-aged married men who are considered by their elders to be disobedient or generally rather unworthy members of their lineages. The relationship between the generations is always difficult, and in a rapidly changing society like that of the Lugbara today it is a relationship that undergoes continual change and stress. This is both because of maturation and change in status of younger men, and because of the opportunities presented to them today to acquire their own wealth and prestige outside the lineage system. They do this by working as labour migrants or by growing cash crops on the borders of Lugbaraland. But they find on their return home that the traditional authority of the lineage elders is still there and they are firmly kept in their place by them. After their period of labour migration, possession by Yakan is a way of demonstrating their independence, by showing that they have been singled out by a spirit, as distinct from the lineage ancestors. They cannot be treated by their elders (as they would if seized by ancestrally sent sickness) and they are mystically set apart from them. A man so possessed builds a special shrine of his own to Yakan and acquires a certain amount of prestige from doing so.[10] In addition, of course, he shows his independence in this manner without discarding traditional Lugbara religious beliefs. Other ways of doing so are merely to move away to settle with a matrilateral or affinal kinsman or to become a permanent and 'lost' labour migrant. But these means have serious disadvantages, since a man is likely thereby to lose rights in lineage land and property. Yet another way is to become a Christian or a Muslim, but to do so requires at least a smattering of education. To become an adherant of Yakan is rather the solution of an illiterate and traditionally minded man.

Occasionally there are epidemics of possession by Yakan. I do not know whether there is a sociological reason for them, but it is significant that the rainmakers then make offerings to Divine Spirit on behalf of the entire subclan, rather than leaving the matter to diviners.

THE CULT OF BALOKOLE

The other movement I wish to describe is a much more recent one, which entered the country only a few years ago. It is called Balokole. The word comes from the LuGanda word *Abalokole* ('The Saved Ones'), the adherents of independent Protestant sects in southern Uganda and Ruanda which have, or have had, connexions with the Moral Rearmament movement. The spirit itself, known by Lugbara as Balokole, is said by them to have entered their country about 1929, at the time when the Baganda Joswa Mugema and Malaki Musajjakawa were deported to Lugbaraland for seditious activities associated with the so-called Society of the One Almighty God, or *Abamalaki*, whose members prohibited the use of European medicines.[11] These men gained a small following among Lugbara Christians. During the late 1940s Lugbaraland was visited by many Baganda evangelists who tried to convert them to the tenets of the Moral Rearmament movement – not that the Moral Rearmament movement and the *Abamalaki* were the same movement, but many of the local personnel were the same. Their Lugbara converts compared them to Rembe, saying that they were prophets coming at a time of trouble sent by Divine Spirit. The effect upon Lugbara Christians, especially Protestants, was considerable. At the time of my stay there were small cells of the Moral Rearmament among the adherents of the Africa Inland Mission and ideas about them had spread out among the mass of the people. There were two movements, the original one with a considerable degree of organization, and the more recent and more widespread one, without such organization.

The former consisted of 'proper' Balokole converts, who regarded themselves as staunch Christians and were generally so regarded by other Christians who remained more orthodox members of the mission church. The behaviour of these adherents originally included public confession of their own sins, and the public accusation of sin against non-members who were prominent in the mission organization and especially against European pastors and their families;[12] later I was told that it came to include speaking with tongues, and forms of possession and divination while in trance; some adherents were said to wish to share property and wives; an important activity was the destruction of shrines, referred to as the things of *Shetani*, the Swahili word for Satan.[13] At least 70 per cent of the adherents of this movement in 1950 were members of the families of evangelists and teachers. Most were Protestant; all were literate; about a quarter were women. They showed by membership of the movement that they wished to be the members of a new Christian elite but that they wished to deny the contemporary authority structure of the Christian community and thereby to remove themselves from the existing system of government and mission power and authority. Here it is pertinent to note that almost all positions of political power were at that time held by Christian-educated men (and by a handful of Muslims) (Middleton 1956, 1965).

This formal movement began to weaken a year or two later, and was soon in disarray. There were several reasons. One was the imprisonment of some of the Lugbara leaders for libel and public disturbance; another was the deportation from the district of most of the non-Lugbara leaders; a third was the introduction of election to government offices by ballot, which broke much of the power formerly held by the older Christian chiefs and other officials; a fourth was a dislike among the wealthier adherents of sharing property with poorer members.

At the same time some of the beliefs of the movement spread out among the general illiterate and near-illiterate members of the population. Many people, mainly numbers of young and middle-aged women, began to call themselves 'the people of Balokole' and to undergo forms of seizure and possession. Their main belief was in a spirit thought to be closely associated with the power of the Baganda, who were feared as would-be colonialists throughout northern Uganda; but its Ganda origin was soon forgotten and Balokole came to be regarded as a refraction or emissary of Spirit. The spirit itself was said to 'come in the wind', like Divine Spirit and Yakan, and to seize individuals with trembling and speaking with tongues. At first the people so seized were almost all Christians, and later the majority were at least related to Christians. The diviners called at first to find out the mystical cause of this apparent sickness stated that the spirit concerned was Balokole, whose power came from Divine Spirit (*Adroa*) through the intermediary form of the Christian God, for whom the missionaries use the Swahili word *Mungu*. The victim, when treated by a diviner, set up a small shrine called Balokole, at which offerings were made as in the case of the present-day Yakan shrines. The offerings were of milk and grain, the proper oblation for Spirit, and not blood and meat, the oblation for the dead.

These people began to form themselves into loose groups, and the Balokole shrines increased in importance and number. Such people were despised by the Balokole converts proper, based on the mission stations. But ordinary Lugbara, who regarded the proper converts as arrogant and dangerous, pointed out that these too went into trances and spoke with tongues at their church meetings. Over three-quarters of the people seized were women, although all the leaders whom I met were men in middle age. The organization of the movement was simple in the extreme. The women met regularly, but particularly on the Christian Sabbath, near the homesteads of leaders. They met in the bushland outside the settlements, the domain of Spirit, where the leaders often erected large Balokole shrines. Many that I saw were placed near large rock-pools, and water from them was used for lustration. They did not build churches or meeting halls. Each cluster or cell consisted of perhaps ten to twenty women, sometimes with a few young men attached, and there was in most areas one such group every few miles. The leaders were all ex-evangelists or mission helpers, so that each group was itself in opposition, both ideologically and historically, to one or other small mission outpost. Except for the leaders, ranking was not important, but members vied for prestige by showing how deeply possessed they were, as measured by the extravagance of their behaviour. However, the leaders could always beat them at this. The leaders took on some of the attributes of prophets; they wore eccentric clothing and ornaments, and usually abstained from sexual relations on the night preceding the Sabbath. Women did not wear uniforms or special adornment, although it was usual to wear a small crucifix and at least to cover their nakedness by pieces of cloth. Many women wore their hair long and unkempt, often braided with small coins. Most could read the Bible a little, and even if illiterate would claim to be able to do so if the spirit moved them. There was no sharing of property for the simple reason that as women they had little property to share.

There was little linkage of cells to one another, although some formal visiting and tea-drinking took place. The members saw themselves as chosen people, and did not seek ties elsewhere. They scorned the Balokole proper for their having ties with other Moral Rearmament units. Although there was no formal initiation, the leaders usually tried to cleanse the new adherents of any possible taint of sorcery, traditionally associated with women (Middleton 1963b), by lustration. Many of the leaders had contact with and support from rainmakers; these unlikely allies regarded themselves as having common cause against ordinary Christians and against sorcerers.

The overt aim of the Balokole people was to cleanse and re-form society. I was told that since the troubles of society are due to the overbearing exercise of authority of older men and the arrogant and selfish behaviour of younger men, it was clearly the responsibility of the women to carry out this task. They needed spiritual leaders who had direct contact with God (both the Christian God and the Lugbara Divine Spirit), but these were merely asexual vehicles for divine power rather than 'men' as such. The women's contact with Spirit was mediated through the spirit Balokole. Much discussion at Balokole meetings was devoted to the Lugbara myths of creation, in which several categories of women feature, and the role of women in society was analysed: the rainmakers were called in as experts on Lugbara myth. In addition, the Lugbara myths were compared to those of the Old Testament. The other main topics of discussion were education and whether women should adopt clothing (and, if so, whether European, Ganda, or Congolese styles).

COMPARISON OF THE TWO MOVEMENTS

There are both certain differences and certain similarities between the two movements that merit some discussion. Membership in the Yakan cult was in most of the region universal; that in the 'people of Balokole' was limited to women and very few of the younger men. The Christian cult provided a social function that has also been provided by other institutions, each having an appeal to a different sector of the population. Let us look at this situation from a different viewpoint.

Traditionally Lugbara society had little if any significant differences in wealth, standard of living, prestige, or rank. It was not a totally egalitarian society in the sense of its having as many differences in statuses as there were would-be holders of them; but there was certainly a lack of recognition of marked differences. What differences there were were mainly those in statuses ascribed by birth, sex, age, and generation. The only examples of formal status-achievement were diviners and 'men whose names are known'.

I have mentioned that one of the reasons – perhaps the main reason – for the ultimate failure of the Yakan cult in the early 1920s was the development of labour migration and cash-crop growing, by which young men could shake off much of the control by their seniors. Thirty years later the general socio-economic situation has changed a good deal (Middleton 1971). The significant factors in this context are several. First has been the increase in labour migration, by which young and middle-aged men go to southern Uganda as migrants; there they form various kinds of tribal association; on their return they continue ex-migrants' associations; they now have some money of their own and a different experience of the total Uganda social system; they conceive and measure the acquisition of higher status by this experience and by wealth in money instead of the traditional livestock (Middleton 1970). Second has been the growth of cash crops, especially of tobacco. This has become more and more the domain of the younger men, who may move into the marginal land on the borders of Lugbaraland to grow their crops; also younger women may grow tobacco, although most do so at home and not in these border settlements. There has developed a category of younger men who see themselves as at odds with their seniors, and so with the traditional Lugbara way of life. They are, as it were, at the margin of the widespread category of young people in a newly affluent society who are aware of their inability to achieve the affluence and power that they are encouraged to seek and which are so obvious in the society at large. They become the 'juvenile delinquents' of their society. These Lugbara men have much of this quality. They see that although Lugbara society in its traditional dimensions is still poor and without marked affluence and differentiation of statuses, it is now part of the wider national system in which it is possible to acquire wealth and power. Their reaction is to join associations, to possess the trappings of Western influence (clothing, gin, Coca-Cola, and so on) to show that they have the experience of the 'New Society'. They are the modern descendants of the young men who joined the earlier Yakan cult, but their behaviour is in secular terms.

But what are the reactions of the other categories in Lugbara society? These are the older men, and the women of all ages. The senior men regard their juniors in what might be called delinquent terms, and retain as strongly as they can their traditional ideologies and practices. The women, however, do not do this, since they are always on the fringe of the traditional ritual system; they are said to be 'evil' and so on (Middleton 1968). Women cannot obtain money and the 'new' experience by working as labour migrants, although they can, and to some extent do, gain money and independence by growing tobacco; nor do they accept the ambitions, hopes, and fears of the senior men, under whose authority they must none the less remain. If they can break away, then they do so. There is said by all Lugbara to be a noticeable increase in recent years of the numbers of 'free' or divorced young women and of sexually promiscuous unmarried women (postponement of the age of marriage has something to do with this, of course). They can break away in sexual terms from the authority of their guardians. They can do so ideologically as well by turning to religious cults.

When they do this they do not turn to the ancestors and ghosts but directly to Spirit, and in particular to that aspect of Spirit associated with the 'new' experience and money, the Christian God and His angels and saints. They could do this by joining the Christian missions, and some of them do so. But this means accepting much of the secular authority of the missionaries and evangelists and so leaving that of their fathers and husbands, who try to prevent this. It is also expensive, as they must at least buy clothes; and they are not allowed to grow tobacco by the mission authorities. So they turn instead to prophetic movements, under the authority of Divine Spirit who at times speaks to them directly without the intervention of human authority; the fact that the power of Balokole was originally associated with the Baganda is also significant – Buganda is the wealthiest and most 'advanced' part of Uganda. They are also under the sporadic authority of prophets and evangelists who are ideologically removed from the everyday system of rank and authority in the ways I have mentioned – asexuality, eccentric and bizarre clothing and behaviour, and so on. Just as the older men see the young men as secular deviants and delinquents, so do the senior and more orthodox

Christians see the 'people of Balokole' as ritual deviants and delinquents. The old men themselves are uncertain about the women. They may have strange religious notions, but they still accept the authority of fathers and husbands in everyday matters and their cult activities do not disturb the traditional worship of the dead in any way. Also many of the rainmakers seem to support the Balokole leaders.

I am suggesting that these two religious movements among the Lugbara have been ways by which resentment felt by newly evolving categories of persons against traditional authority and their aspirations in new economic and social situations have been expressed and formulated. The resentment would seem always to be present, as part of the general relationship between seniors and juniors, the latter always socially maturing and demanding greater personal independence and authority at the expense of their elders. At certain times, however, events occur which accentuate this feeling on the part of the juniors. One was when Lugbara elders felt that they had to emphasize their authority in the face of increasing land pressure and the consequent increasing number of disputes over its allocation. Another was after the Second World War, when the rewards of independent economic enterprise became suddenly more marked than before, for both men and women; it is possible also that the effects of military experience by men recruited into the army were relevant here. In short, these two periods were marked by junior men and women becoming intensely aware of a wish for independence from their elders.

In the realm of belief, traditional ancestral power was supplanted by divinely inspired prophets or evangelistic leaders. When the Lugbara have tried to change their society they have not tried to bring back the 'traditional' past as they remember it, but rather to revert to a pristine, primordial state of innocence, in which there is no authority of one man over another, nor of man over woman. The leaders of the original Yakan cult tried to do this, as I have shown. Lacking any model of society except that of their own experience, they tried to re-form society as myth told them it was after the time of creation. This could only be done by acting in ways contrary to their present cultural behaviour. The Utopia of the future is the same as the Eden of the past. This is, of course, a widespread feature of all such movements, and I need say no more about it except that it seems always to be doomed to failure. The situation at the time of the appearance of the first Balokole was somewhat different, in that people had a wider experience of the world than they had had in 1914. Whereas in the Yakan cult the change was seen as one of abolishing statuses defined by birth, sex, age, and generation, in the Balokole movement new status was defined in addition by new experience. None the less, the ideal statuses in each movement have been similar: they have been those of asocial, primordial, 'natural' persons recognizing only pan-human obligations. In this context a man can lose his existing status in only three ways: by dying, literally; by dying metaphorically and being reborn after purification; or by leaving his society altogether and either joining another one or becoming a hermit. Many Lugbara have chosen to join other societies, by becoming 'lost' labour migrants, but I need not discuss this here. With regard to the other means, death and purification of this radical kind is the consequence, in Lugbara thought, of the activity of the Creator Spirit. According to their myth, Spirit created the world and peopled it with asocial human beings innocent of the values of kinship and society at large. These values came into being as the work of the Hero-ancestors (Middleton 1960a, 1965). So that the intentions of the cult-adherents fall into two phases: the re-creation of a world peopled by innocent, reborn, purified human beings; and the formation of a new kind of society, founded on natural justice and equality, under the guidance of prophets and others who play roles equivalent to those of the Hero-ancestors of myth, and who are given some of the attributes of the Heroes and the rainmakers.

Now in both cases the adherents have tried to achieve the first aim and have thought for a time that they have succeeded. They have managed temporarily to overthrow traditional social relationships and to subsitute new ones (although the Balokole women have found it difficult to get very far in this respect). They have tried to purify their land of sorcery. They have seen themselves as a chosen people of Utopia. But they have not been able to achieve the second aim. This has been due to several factors. One is that the notion of an egalitarian Utopian society seems not to work in practice. Another has been that the traditional lineage system of the Lugbara seems to be the most suitable form of organization in the actual historical and ecological situation. Marked changes in these spheres could lead to a new form of social organization, but so far this has not happened.[14] A third factor has been the satisfaction of the aspirations of adherents by other means, by opportunities presented by labour migration, by increase in social mobility, and the like. This applies more to the younger men than to the women; and it is significant that the Balokole adherents refer to the younger men who do not join them, despite having some literary and Christian education, as being apostates and renegades who prefer to walk around in dark glasses drinking gin than turn to God. The final reason is the absorption of these movements into the traditional religious system – I discuss this below.

It may be that there is yet another phase in the development of these movements. As I have said, one aspect of the later phases is the association of the original 'external' power (epidemics, Europeans, Baganda, and so on) with Divine Spirit, which removes it from human control and responsibility: both Yakan and Balokole have become refractions of Divine Spirit, as 'spirits in the wind'. There are other such spirits in Lugbara. One, for example, is that known as Mmua ('secret'), a spirit that is said to bring pneumonia and other chest complaints to those whom it seizes. But Mmua is not merely a 'spirit in the wind'. It is said to 'dwell' in the far northwest of the country and in the lands of the Logo and Azande to the northwest of Lugbaraland. There it is said to be associated with a clan of the same name, and it is controllable by the clan rainmaker. In fact there is no such clan, but Lugbara say that there is. In southern Lugbara, where the influence of Yakan in its early phases was slight, I have heard people say that there is a clan called Yakan that has its home somewhere near the Kakwa border – the northern border of Lugbaraland; and the prophet Rembe was a Kakwa. In other words, a last phase of these movements may be the attribution of this external power to a supposed clan-group. A clan is, in Lugbara thought, an everlasting and unchanging social group, founded by a son of one of the two Hero-ancestors. So that the attribution of a spirit to a clan implies both that the power is now a permanent part of the powers that control the well-being of the Lugbara and that it has been such a power since the beginning of society; it has merely been hidden from ordinary knowledge. This process – the power being seen first as basis for the authority of an 'external' prophet associated with a reversion to a primordial asociality; then as a refraction of Divine Spirit; then, finally, associated with a social group – parallels the process of development of the power of the individual human soul in Lugbara thought – it is first the responsible element of a living man, then at his death it goes to dwell with Divine Spirit in the sky during a period of asociality in the homestead and lineage, and finally it is brought back by a diviner and associated with a shrine in the lineage compound of the dead man

(Middleton 1960a: ch. 4). In this way the Lugbara can control this potentially dangerous power, and they may do much the same with the far more dangerous powers originally associated with external forces – perhaps the Azande expansion in the case of Mmua; the Arabs, Europeans, and perhaps the Kakwa (who were sometimes in league with the Arab slavers) in the case of Yakan; and the Baganda in the case of Balokole.

RAINMAKERS AND THE ACCOMMODATION OF CHANGE

I have tried to show that the prophets and evangelists, whom we may class together as innovators, act to accommodate the changing aspirations and demands of newly developing and newly important categories of persons at times when the society is undergoing radical social change. Once this has been done, however, there remains the need to incorporate the achieved statuses, to which the members of the new categories had aspired and which in some cases they have achieved, into the traditionally accepted total structure of the society. There is also the need to construct the full constellation of these statuses on the ritual or spiritual level: the attainment and retention of any social status places the holder of it in a mystical relationship with a spiritual power associated with it and in some ways controlling and sanctioning its well-being and continuation and the behaviour of the holder.

I turn here to a consideration of another ritual functionary, the rainmaker, *opi-ezo* (chief of rain). I shall discuss rainmakers under four headings – who they are; what they do; how Lugbara conceive of them and their powers; and how they are related to the ritual innovators I have mentioned.

There is one rainmaker in every subclan, of which there are about sixty in the entire society. Rainmakers are the most important figures in traditional Lugbara society, both in ritual and in political terms. The rainmaker is the senior member of the senior descent line in the subclan – thus he is the most direct descendant of the clan-founder. The power of controlling the rain is said to have been given by Divine Spirit direct to the two Hero-ancestors, who transmitted it to their sons, the founders of the sixty or so clans. The power is inherited by the person who is the most closely related to the former rainmaker in the following generation. The importance of the directness of the link may be seen from the fact that if there is no son by the rainmaker's senior wife (or if his sons are dead), the power can pass to the son of the rainmaker's eldest full-sister, who is seen as more closely related in a spiritual sense than a junior son or brother's son. My evidence is lacking on this point, but in fact I doubt whether this ever applies unless the sister is also the first-born and so older than her rainmaker-brother – such a woman is anomalous in terms of mystical succession.

The rainmaker has a raingrove, into which only rainmakers may enter: he has there a rainpot in which are rainstones. By the manipulation of the stones (of quartz, and known as male and female) he can cause rain to fall, to cease, or not fall at all. He could formerly offer a human being to Divine Spirit to ask for rain (the only example of human sacrifice in Lugbara); today he offers a sheep instead. He can stop epidemics such as cerebrospinal meningitis by offering a sheep to Divine Spirit – the sheep is led around the subclan boundary and then driven across water up to the hills, where it becomes associated with Spirit and causes rain (which brings meningitis to a temporary end). He can pray to Divine Spirit in cases of cattle epidemic or famine; he can do the same in cases of frequent barrenness of the wives of the subclan. He could in the past stop feuds (within the subclan), and by acting conjointly with other rainmakers could stop warfare (between subclans); rainmakers do this by their powers of cursing the men concerned with sterility and their wives and cattle with barrenness. He could provide a sanctuary to a homicide or certain other sinners. In brief, his power is concerned essentially with fertility of land, women, and livestock and with stopping homicide and death. He is not concerned with sacrifices to the dead, the concern of lineage elders; thus he is not concerned with lineage and sectional squabbles and segmentation, nor with the dead. He is concerned with Divine Spirit and with the factors that ensure the perpetuity of the subclan as a single entity.

I have said earlier that the Lugbara see their world as divided into the sphere of order and authority, on the one hand, and on the other, beyond or outside this sphere, the realm of chaos, disorder, uncertainty, and powers uncontrollable and unpredictable by ordinary men who reside in the sphere of order. Certain people – prophets, diviners, and sacrificing elders – step outside the sphere of order while practising and then return into it afterwards. All are given symbolic asexual characteristics (Middleton 1968). This sphere of the 'outside' has another important feature: it has no time, in the sense of the structural time of everyday ordered life – that of the passing of the generations, seasons, months, and days. It is a sphere of timelessness, or, perhaps more accurately, a sphere of presocial, asocial, and amoral time. The Lugbara state quite explicitly that the rainmakers are associated with this timelessness or presocial time, that their activities (to do with curing non-fertility and preventing death) are like those of the earliest personages of myth, who existed before Lugbara society was formed and who knew no kinship, no marriage, no feud or law, no legitimacy of sexual relations, and, it is sometimes said, no death.

A rainmaker is not buried as are ordinary people. The corpses of ordinary people are placed in the grave where they are insulted and cursed; they are covered with earth to the beating of drums and singing of death songs and dances. The rainmaker is placed in his grave at night-time, in complete silence; he is not insulted or cursed. At death he becomes a leopard (a beast associated with the bushland and with rain). The cursing and insulting of an ordinary corpse desocializes and de-humanizes him, so that he becomes meaningless, nothing, primeval matter. But a rainmaker is insulted at his initiation (when he first inherits his powers) by neighbouring rainmakers from related subclans. We might say that a rainmaker is in a sense socially dead, although not physically so.

Finally, there is the link in Lugbara thought between timelessness and absolute 'truth' (*a'da*). Elders, diviners, and prophets all are said to speak 'words of truth' when formally practising ritually and when hedged with certain taboos that remove them from the ordinary world of social relations and time. Rainmakers, however, are said always to speak the truth. The notion here is that in ordinary situations men do not think or speak the absolute truth – they are ignorant of it and can see their society only in sectional terms (i.e. in terms to do with lineage relations and processes of segmentation, relations associated with structural or social time only). Rainmakers, on the other hand, know the absolute truth; they are concerned with the eternal perpetuity of their subclans and Lugbara society, without reference to the petty disturb-ances and stresses within these groups. They are representations of Lugbara subclans, the unchanging segments of the total society, and, being 'brothers', they are in all also a representation of the total society. In this way they are said to be 'like' or 'together with' the Hero-ancestors of myth, in some ways everlastingly 'true' and outside the ordinary vicissitudes of change, growth, and death.

Elders sacrifice to the dead – they are concerned only with the everyday reorganizing of lineage relations and with recognizing small repetitive changes in lineage authority. They are not concerned with any radical changes, with innovations in social structure. On the other hand, the prophets and rainmakers are not concerned with repetitive lineage change; but they deal, each in their own different ways, with the more basic changes in subclan and tribal structure. Prophets are concerned with innovation at this level, but rainmakers are not; even at the time of Yakan, the rainmakers withdrew and allowed the prophets to gain what was in traditional Lugbara terms immense power. Prophets are men who have essentially temporary contact with external Divine power, with timelessness and absolute truth. But their contact is only temporary, and the powers they have are not intrinsic or inherent to them: they have to use water as a mystical vehicle for this Divine power which they would seem really not to understand or to control, and when they speak in tongues they never claim actually to comprehend what they say, as they are only the mouthpieces for the words of Divine Spirit.

But rainmakers are in permanent – perhaps everlasting – contact with Divinity: they know the absolute truth. Structurally, they take over control and knowledge of this spiritual power associated with the new statuses and relationship that have been the object of innovation by the prophet. In this they act in what I suspect to be a somewhat unconscious cooperation with the other ritual specialists, the diviners. If a man is possessed today by Yakan, he is treated by a diviner; but if there is an epidemic of sicknesses associated with trembling (and so with Yakan, as well as other spirits), the rainmaker takes over by praying to Spirit and offering a sheep. The rainmakers are regarded as the leaders or chiefs (*opi*) of the old men who still possess Yakan sticks. The same applies to the spirit Mmua, and to other spirits that send trembling. Theologically, of course, these various spirits are refractions or emissaries of Spirit, so that rainmakers and diviners compose an earthly representation of the Spiritual hierarchy.

With regard to Balokole, there has not yet been time for much of this process to develop; the rainmakers have not yet had time to routinize the spirit-power involved, although they are involved in the movement, as I have mentioned. Yet I have heard it said that Balokole is 'like' Yakan. The adherents of Balokole have themselves told me that the rainmakers are 'like the rainmakers of long ago' and they surmise (as far as I know incorrectly) that 'elsewhere, far away' the rainmakers 'know the words of Balokole': the process is beginning. I suggest that this is one means of routinizing charismatic authority. There are two comments on this statement: The first is that in the cases I have mentioned the prophets would appear to have been themselves unsuccessful partly due to the changing statuses and aspirations of their followers, partly due to circumstances in their own careers. But although the prophets 'failed' in this way, they and the rainmakers succeeded in others: the Society was enabled to continue without any real harm, and the dangerous 'outside' powers were contained, transformed, and absorbed. They were the responses by a weakly organized society to ecological disaster and change due to external impact, and it was successful as a response.

The second is that the form and means of such incorporation of outside power might be expected to have very different emphases in a society with, say, a king who was himself at the centre of the ritual system. Presumably he would himself play the role of the Lugbara rainmakers, or it would be played by a royal or court priest. But the Lugbara pattern might be expected in stateless societies of this kind.

NOTES

1. I carried out field research among the Lugbara from 1949 until 1952 with assistance from the Worshipful Company of Goldsmiths and the Colonial Social Science Research Council, London; the initial writing up of field material was made possible by help from the Wenner-Gren Foundation for Anthropological Research, Inc., New York. This paper was originally read at the 1965 meeting of the American Anthropological Association at Denver, Colorado. Some of the data in it were previously published in Middleton (1963a), which includes bibliographical references to the historical events mentioned; I am grateful to the editor of the *Journal of the Royal Anthropological Institute* for permission to republish material from that article.
2. Accounts of Lugbara social and administrative organizations are in Middleton (1956, 1958, 1960b, and 1965).
3. See Middleton (1963a) and Driberg (1931) for detailed accounts of these events.
4. *Opi* is a traditional Lugbara word, used to refer to rainmakers and 'men whose names are known'; it is also used for present-day government chiefs.

John Middleton

5. See Middleton (1962) for an account of the introduction and effects of a cash economy.
6. See Middleton and Greenland (1954) for an account of the changing systems of land tenure and the effects of land shortage.
7. See Middleton (1960a, especially chapter IV) for an account of ancestrally sent sickness and its relationship to intergenerational conflict.
8. See Middleton (1960a, chapter V; and 1968) for accounts of Lugbara cosmological beliefs.
9. See Middleton (1969b) for an account of Lugbara diviners.
10. Middleton (1963a) has a fuller account of Yakan today.
11. See Welbourn (1961) for an account of this movement in southern Uganda.
12. The accusations of which I heard were all totally unfounded. I regret that I was unable to collect information about the psychological condition of the individuals whom I witnessed making the accusations.
13. This had formerly been an activity strongly supported by some members of the Roman Catholic mission in the area. It ceased after a party of shrine-destroyers had been struck by lightning, which was taken by Lugbara as a sign of divine disapproval.
14. The recent introduction of coffee, a permanent and valuable cash crop, could alter the pattern of land-holding. The introduction of industrial employment in the area would also have marked consequences in this regard.

REFERENCES

DRIBERG, J. H. 1931 Yakan. *Journal of the Royal Anthropological Institute* **61**: 413–20.
MIDDLETON, J. 1956 The Roles of Chiefs and Headmen in Lugbara. *Journal of African Administration* **8** (1): 32–8.
— 1958 The Political System of the Lugbara of the Nile-Congo Divide. Pp. 203–29 in Middleton, J., and D. Tait (eds.), *Tribes without Rulers*. London: Routledge and Kegan Paul.
— 1960a *Lugbara Religion: Ritual and Authority among an East African People*. London: Oxford University Press.
— 1960b The Lugbara. Pp. 326–43 in Richards, A. I. (ed.), *East African Chiefs*. London: Faber and Faber.
— 1962 Trade and Markets among the Lugbara of Uganda. Pp. 561–78 in Bohannan, P., and G. Dalton (eds.), *Markets in Africa*. Evanston: Northwestern University Press.

MIDDLETON, J. 1963a The Yakan or Allah Water Cult among the Lugbara. *Journal of the Royal Anthropological Institute* **93**: 80–108.

— 1963b Witchcraft and Sorcery in Lugbara. Pp. 257–75 in Middleton, J., and E. Winter (eds.), *Witchcraft and Sorcery in East Africa*. London: Routledge and Kegan Paul.

— 1965 *The Lugbara of Uganda*. New York: Holt, Rinehart and Winston.

— 1968 Some Categories of Dual Classification among the Lugbara of Uganda. *History of Religions* **7** (3): 187–208.

— 1969a Spirit Possession among the Lugbara. Pp. 210–31 in Beattie, J., and J. Middleton (eds.), *Spirit Mediumship and Society in Africa*. London: Routledge and Kegan Paul.

— 1969b Oracles and Divination among the Lugbara. Pp. 261–78 in Douglas, M., and P. Kaberry (eds.), *Man in Africa*. London: Tavistock Publications.

— 1970 Political Incorporation among the Lugbara. Pp. 55–70 in Cohen, R., and J. Middleton (eds.), *From Tribe to Nation in Africa*. Scranton: Chandler.

— 1971 Some effects of Colonial Rule among the Lugbara of Uganda. Pp. 6–48 in Turner, V. (ed.), *Profiles of Change*. London: Cambridge University Press.

MIDDLETON, J., and D. GREENLAND 1954 Land and Population in West Nile District, Uganda. *Geographical Journal.* **120**: 446–57.

STIGAND, C. H. 1923 *Equatoria: the Lado Enclave*. London: Constable.

WELBOURN, F. B. 1961 *East African Rebels: a Study of Some Independent Churches*. London: SCM Press.

Penan Friendship-names

RODNEY NEEDHAM

Professor Evans-Pritchard has recently declared that he would perhaps regard himself 'first as an ethnographer and secondly as a social anthropologist' (1965: 34), and certainly it is by his ethnographical accomplishments, in the first place, that he has secured an enduring pre-eminence among practitioners of social anthropology. It is appropriate, therefore, that the present paper written in his honour should be offered as a contribution to ethnographical knowledge.

The account which follows is a straightforward description of a type of name used in the interior of Borneo. The usage has not previously been reported from that island, and it appears not to be practised by peoples elsewhere. It thus possesses, in addition to its intrinsic interest, some minor importance as an apparently singular custom.[1]

I

The Penan are a population of middle Borneo, numbering in all about 2650 individuals and dispersed in approximately 70 groups over an area of roughly 2500 square miles. They are traditionally, and for the most part still remain in fact, forest nomads, but a number of groups have left the forest and have settled in fixed habitations where they depend on agriculture for their subsistence. In the literature they have usually been known as 'Punan', and have thence been confused with the culturally quite distinct nomadic Punan and with the settled Punan Ba (Needham 1954b; 1954c; 1955); but the degree of identity which demarcates them does not constitute a cultural or political unity. The Penan speak two main and fairly contrasted dialects and are divided into two corresponding tribes, separated for the most part by the course of the Baram river, which have been designated Eastern Penan and Western Penan. The linguistic differences are accompanied by certain variations in the institutions which are common to both tribes.

The extreme locations of Penan groups are the headwaters of the

Limbang and the Kelabit plateau to the northeast, the headwaters of the Kayan river (in Kalimantan, Indonesian Borneo) to the east, the upper Rajang above Belaga to the southwest, and the China Sea coast to the west. This area is not only very large but it encloses some of the most accidented and hazardous terrain in Borneo, and communications within it are extremely slow and uncertain. Moreover, the dominant peoples in the area are the settled tribes, such as the Kenyah, Kayan, and Iban, who claim and to some extent exploit both the land in which the Penan live and the Penan themselves. It will be easily appreciated, therefore, that there is no corporate political organization of the Penan people. In fact, there is little recognition of common interest except between relatively close and directly related groups, and there are no occasions for cooperation between these. It is, in an extreme form, a segmentary society; and the isolation and self-sufficiency of its segments (the local and nomadic groups) are accentuated by an oppressive and formerly hostile social environment. There is, however, no system of descent or of affinal alliance such as might yet combine the groups into a larger frame of organization. The relationship terminology is non-lineal, kinship is reckoned cognatically (Needham 1966: 6–10), and the Penan marry by preference within the natal group. There is not, and there could not well be, any centralized ritual or economic organization or any other unifying means by which the Penan, or even one of the tribes, could be integrated. On the other hand, there is no conflict of interest between groups; they do not, for instance, claim exclusive rights in the territories over which they wander, and their highly infrequent contacts are marked by an evident sense of mutual concern (Needham, 1971).

Typically, then, Penan social life is restricted constantly and almost entirely to an informal grouping of close relatives numbering, at a mean figure, about thirty-two individuals of all ages. The members of such a group are ideally and consciously held together not by the constraint of coercive institutions but by a concerted commitment to certain moral values connected especially with their joint survival. These enjoin in the first place a strictly equal sharing of the staple foodstuffs, and in the nomadic groups this is most scrupulously carried out (Needham 1954e). There are no marked or ascribed differences of status, but instead there prevails an express tendency to informality, closeness, and cooperation. The members of a Penan group depend utterly upon one another; they know it, and they foster this recognition. This explicit sense of solidarity becomes attenuated as Penan settle and become im-

View to the north over the Apoh and Tutoh valleys

Penan territory, looking east over the Paong valley
(Kalulong massif left centre)

plicated in a wider society (Needham 1965), but it still persists as a characteristic value of the Penan. It is a solidarity not of group against group but, within the group, of individual with individual.

II

The Penan conceive a human being as consisting of three components: body, soul, and name. For the Eastern Penan (with whom this paper is chiefly concerned) these are respectively *usah*, *sahé*, and *ngaran*.

The body (*usah*) can be said to be merely the 'container' (*lusan*) of the soul, but it nevertheless distinguishes the individual and contributes to his identification. The word *usah* is in fact used, in one common context, where English uses 'soul': e.g. if one wishes to know how many people there are in another group, the question is phrased as how many bodies (*kura usah*) there are. It is also used as a classifier for persons, as in *duah usah lakéi*, two men. The body is linguistically identified with the person, so that if in a strange group one asks after someone who has been said to belong to it, the individual in question may identify himself by responding, *siteu, usah ké*, I'm here, in person (here, my body).

The body is occupied by the soul (*sahé*). Three manifestations of the soul are distinguished: *sahé bok*, soul of the hair (of the head); *sahé anak maten*, soul of the pupils of the eyes; and *sahé usah*, soul of the body. The Eastern Penan have no orthodox doctrine of the soul,[2] and reports differ on the question whether these are three separate souls or whether they are (as I take to be the preponderant view) three aspects of spiritual identity. Even by the former interpretation, however, the three types of *sahé* are not independent but live and die together, so that the *sahé* component of man may be considered as unitary.

The combination of body and soul, finally, is denoted by one or another name (*ngaran*). This is the most elaborately developed part of the constitution of the personality, and in order to understand how this is so we need first to take into account the definitive contrasts between body, soul, and name.

The body can undergo changes of state (such as normal fluctuations of strength and agility) and of form (especially cultural mutilations such as perforation of the glans, penis, and the ear), but in gross it is immutable; it can be moved by inner direction, but it is subject to the same physical conditions as any material object. The soul is similar to the body in that it can undergo changes of state, but it has no discernible form, and it is characteristically dissimilar in that it is volatile; through-out the life of the individual the soul has a persistent and individual character, but it possesses an extreme liberty of motion which is possible only to the immaterial. The body is temporal and mortal; the soul comes from God's eternal presence, conjoins impermanently with the body, and then returns to God. It is this uncertain conjunction of body and soul that is marked by a name. The name is a component of the per-sonality, for without a name there is no person, and the name by which an individual is known can affect his bodily and psychic state. But the name, unlike the body, is infinitely changeable; and, unlike the soul, it has no independent existence. The name is not a mere designation, but even to the extent that it is such it is not just a social convenience; it is the crucial identification of the individual, not only for men but also for the innumerable and unseen spiritual powers (*balēi*) to which men are always subject.

There is not only one kind of name, however, and an individual does not bear only a single name at a time. There are a number of types of name, and an individual can be designated by various combinations of these. The result, as Elshout has ruefully commented on the Kenyah system, is that to a European 'the entire nomenclature makes . . . the impression of an incomprehensible confusion' (1926: 156).[3] But the fact of the matter is that it is Penan social life that is largely incompre-hensible unless we first understand the nomenclature.

III

Certain principal forms of naming among the Penan have already been described elsewhere, and in order to comprehend the topic of the present paper it should be sufficient therefore to provide merely a summary catalogue.

Every Penan possesses a personal name, *ngaran usah* (name of the body), which is intended to be a personal, i.e. unique, designation. There is a practically innumerable variety of such names, and it is only adventitiously, and in groups out of any communication with each other, that two individuals will simultaneously have the same name. When, by travelling or at a trading-meeting, this is found to have happened (as with myself and Lidem of Long Buang), there is a special appellation, *adi'*, which is employed between the two concerned, but this is an extremely rare occurrence. In effect, then, each Penan is distinguished, among the living, by a personal name which is his and his alone. It is subject to change, however, if he falls ill or when certain relatives die, and an individual may hence bear a series of personal names in the course of his life. When he becomes the parent of a child he acquires also a teknonym, but this too is subject to change if that child or another of his children should die. Whether married or single, moreover, a Penan assumes another kind of name on the death of a relative; the Penan call this *ngaran lumo*, mourning-name, but I have found it ethnographically more convenient to describe it as a death-name (Needham 1954g). The death-name that is taken is determined by the relationship of the survivor to the deceased. Among unmarried siblings there is an alternation between personal name and death-name, occasioned by the successive births and deaths of brothers or sisters. For a married person there is a similar alternation, occasioned in this case by the births and deaths of children, between teknonym and death-name. Within a restricted set of close relatives, among the Western Penan, there is in addition yet a further usage involving death-names; when one member of the set dies the other members, who belong to two proximate genealogical levels, are terminologically put at a distance from each other by the reciprocal employment of death-names which are otherwise appropriate to grandparents and grandchildren (Needham 1954f). Finally, relationships outside the group are also nominally distinguished: deceased Penan are known for a period by special terms of reference which are not applied to the living (Needham 1954d); and non-Penan with whom traditionally a blood-pact is concluded, or with whom today there is a trading-agreement, are addressed by the reciprocal term *sebila*, translated as 'best friend' by Elshout (1926: 159) but not used between Penan friends (Needham 1954a).

Among all these appellations the chief forms of nomenclature are the personal name, teknonym, and death-name. These are systematically related, as indicated above, and the permutations of this basic system of names form the principal means for the designation of individuals. This is not to say, however, that the employment of the names is always rigorously systematic in practice. As among the Kenyah, not everybody addresses a man by his new name, and the declared rules for the application of the names are not strictly followed (cf. Elshout 1926: 156, 161, 168, 171); the Penan themselves sometimes hesitate or fall into confusion when certain name-changes are called for (Needham 1954g: 425); and, as is often the case with Penan customs, the nomenclature is subject

207

to variation by individual inclination. Nevertheless, these names are the standard and indispensable resources for the definition of the person among the Penan.[4]

Terminological systems of this kind can be correlated sociologically with a very small-scale form of segmentary organization, typified by Penan society (Needham 1959); and there is historical and comparative evidence that the death-names are intrinsically connected with the solidary relationships which constitute the Penan group and which for the Penan compose the paradigm of social existence (Needham 1965).

IV

The above may well seem an adequate enough repertory of designations, but there exists in Penan culture still one more type, the friendship-name. It is found in an elaborate form among the Eastern Penan; the Western Penan possess only a minimal development of the institution, and certain settled Penan have nothing of the kind.

A friendship-name is one that is used reciprocally and exclusively between two Penan individuals. It is assumed as a token of friendship, and commemorates an activity or an experience which the two have shared together. Although there are certain common forms, it can be concocted to match any circumstance, and it may be wholly invented. It has in addition a special construction which distinguishes it from other kinds of name.

Elshout reports nothing of the sort from the Kenyah around Long Nawang, and so far as I know the ethnographic literature contains no record of it among any other Bornean people. I have checked that it is not used by the Kenyah of Long San, on the upper Baram, and I was told by Kayan at Long Tebangan that their people had no such custom. As will be seen, however, friendship-names are such that they may very easily remain unknown to a foreign visitor, and since they are used by certain tribes in the area it is to be expected that specific inquiries may hereafter reveal their existence among others also. For example, a Long Kiput man, from the substantial longhouse complex at the confluence of the Baram and the Tutoh rivers, told me that the Long Kiput do have this usage. They call it *ngaran é'*, but my informant, though informed and intellectually alert, did not know what the qualifier *é'* could mean. Since the Long Kiput are classed locally among the Lepo Pu'un, i.e. original settlers,[5] the likelihood is that other longhouse groups on the Baram and its lower tributaries may also employ friendship-names.

As far as the Penan are concerned, I first discovered the usage at Long Buang, on the Apoh river, and later confirmed that it was practised by a nomadic group of Eastern Penan with whom I travelled on the western slopes of Mt Kalulong and then by distant groups around the extreme headwaters of the Baram. As it is from the Penan of Long Buang that I have the fullest record of friendship-names, supported merely by examples and positive reports from other groups, we may best concentrate directly upon them. There are in addition certain features of their situation which excellently reveal the principles of the system.

The Penan of Long Buang live in a small longhouse of fourteen doors on the left bank of the middle Apoh, a tributary of the Tutoh (see map; cf. Needham 1964: 138–40). In 1951 they numbered eighty-five individuals. They are Eastern Penan, but some of them have been settled for a generation or more; they plant some rice, and they fell timber for sale downriver. Yet they still spend long periods away from the longhouse, hunting in the forest and working the wild sago which is the traditional Penan diet. Fifty-two members of the group are however more recent immigrants, most of them from nomadic groups in the Penipir, Melinau, Magoh, and Melana. Although the settlement is referred to as one house, and in arrangement and overall appearance gives a unitary impression, it actually consists of two separate buildings placed end to end along the river-bank; the lines of construction make a direct continuation, but between the two there is a gap of some five paces, spanned at the front by a bridge linking the two galleries.[6] In the main, one house is lived in by original settlers and the other by immigrants. The latter especially maintain a fairly frequent communication with the nomads, both at the government-supervised trading-meetings on the rivers and by travelling into the forest to find them. They use the house largely as a base and as a point of contact with riverine society and its goods; in effect, they still form part of traditional Penan society and they continue to follow Penan custom.[7] This communication is sustained, furthermore, by visits to the longhouse of parties of nomads. None were there during my short stay, but I was told that the Penan Iman (from an area just to the south of the junction of the Melinau with the Tutoh), under Labang, used to make repeated visits. They would stay for a few days, perhaps as many as ten, and then return to the forest because (in the conventional plaint) they could not stand the *pété*, the glare and direct

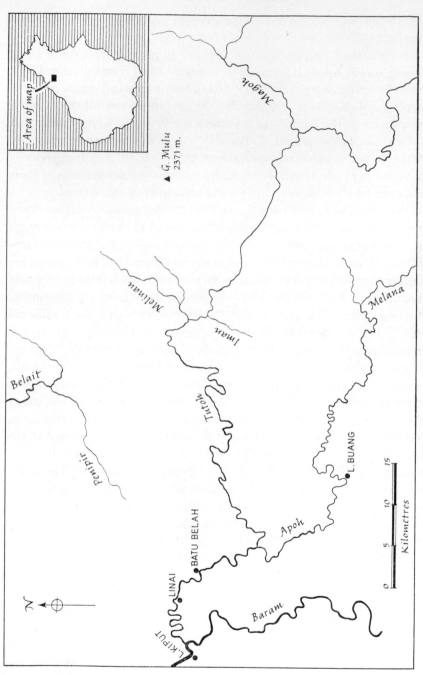

LONG BUANG SETTLEMENT AND ENVIRONS

heat of the sun. Long Buang is thus unusual in its composition, a feature which will nevertheless be seen to be instructive, but remains essentially Penan in culture.

At this point it is necessary to revert briefly to the topic of personal names and the circumstances of their use. In general, Penan of any status or condition can be referred to, in their absence, by their personal names, but there are two main classes of exceptions. The first is that of the dead, who should be referred to by special designations based on their relationship to the speaker (Western Penan) or the place where they died (Needham 1954d), and if their personal names were pronounced they would be offended and would retaliate with sickness or other misfortunes. But this ban is in force for only a limited period after a death, commonly some months but said usually to be a year; afterwards, the personal name of the deceased is easily mentioned, at least by those not closely related and inhibited by sentiment. The second class of exceptions is that composed of grandparents, parents, spouse, and affines. Their personal names may never be mentioned at all, and to do so could provoke an automatic spiritual punishment (*lemeto*): at worst, when a very senior person was in question, this could be death; otherwise, it might take the form of illness or accident or some embarrassing affliction such as involuntary defaecation in one's loincloth while in company. To mention the personal name of a coeval or a junior member of this class, viz. a spouse or a sibling-in-law, would not necessarily incur such a penalty, and an unintentional breach of the prohibition might then entail no more than an acute sense of shame. As for other people, they are usually referred to by their current styles, which for adults will typically be either a teknonym or a death-name; but when they are not present their personal names are quite readily employed if there is occasion to do so. If they are present, however, or within earshot, the names of most people should not be mentioned. Children's names can be uttered freely, whether or not they can hear, but they too are often known by death-names and is by these that they will then be referred to. The use of personal names is more strictly governed in the case of direct address, in which situation few other than small children will normally be called by their names. Close relatives of the same genealogical level and below, particularly siblings and close cousins (both classed as *padé*), can indeed be addressed by personal name, but more usually kinship terms, teknonyms, or death-names will be used instead. There are other exceptions, but these clearly involve taking a certain liberty, as when an old man or woman uses the personal name to a much younger one by way of intimate adjuration. The normal mode of address, if a personal appellation is used, is a teknonym or death-name. On the whole, therefore, personal names tend to be avoided, either from fear of mystical retribution or out of shame.

Penan say that they are 'ashamed' or 'shy' (*menya*) to pronounce the names of people who are somewhat distantly related or who belong to, or come from, another group. It is possible to use their personal names, in the sense that it is not forbidden by mystical sanction (*ngilin*) to do so, but one ought rather to employ a friendship-name once a relationship exists.[8] There is no obligation to use this kind of name, again in the sense that there would be no ill consequence if one did not do so, but all the same this is the customary appellation. The Penan of Long Buang distinguish a friendship-name as a *ngaran ai'*, an *ai'*-name, doubtless after the Long Kiput *ngaran é'*, for this designation is not used or recognized by the Eastern Penan in general, especially by those farther in the interior. As with the Long Kiput informant, however, I could not elicit any explanation of the word *ai'* except that it referred to this type of name. In a number of dialects in Sarawak *ai'* means 'sand' (Ray 1913: 143, 185), as it does among the Kenyah of the upper Baram (Douglas 1911: 109), but the friendship-name has nothing to do with sand. At Long Buang, to apply a friendship-name to someone is *maneu ai'*, to make *ai'*, but it is also described as *pebakéh*, which is the expression commonly used by other groups. In both Penan dialects, eastern and western, *pe-* is a transitive verbal prefix, and *bakéh* means 'friend' or 'companion,' so that the word can be rendered as to treat someone as a friend, to call someone friend, or, closest perhaps, to make friends. The obvious question is how exact or informative a translation it is to say that *bakéh* means 'friend'. The answer is to be found, to some extent at least, in the institution of friendship-names and in the relationships involved.

A friendship-name proper is composed of a prefix *ke-* and a word denoting some activity, thing, or state. The grammatical function of the prefix is difficult to define in isolation but may be described as attributive, i.e. it attributes to the person named a connexion of some kind with what is denoted. No other type of name incorporates this prefix, and it is not phonetically a feature of personal names.[9] I have referred to a friendship-name 'proper' because there are other forms of address which are used as friendship-names, and can actually be called *ngaran ai'*, but which have not this construction. One is the word *bakéh* itself, which can be used also to address a non-Penan; another is *sabai*, brother-in-law, but employed with this intention towards someone who is not a Penan and is not in fact so related; and a third is *adi'*, which is used between Penan who happen to have the same personal name. At Long Buang there is also a term *buki* which is prefixed to the personal name, e.g. Buki Avun, as a term of address and is used as a general *ngaran ai'*; it was said to have no other meaning than this use, and I do not know if it is used by other Penan groups. These names lack not only the distinctive prefix but also the descriptive component. Other names lacking both of these features can be made up, also, but the typical friendship-name is one constructed with the prefix, indicating its special significance, and the descriptive component.

The second part of the name commemorates the activity or experience which is made the occasion of contracting friendship. Some common examples are: Ketavang, from being lost (*tavang*) together;[10] Kepelep, from collecting wild rubber (*pelep*); Kejuhi', from shooting at birds (*juhi'*) with blowpipes; Kebabui, from tracking wild pig (*babui*); Kebasa', from falling into a deep part of a stream and getting all wet (*basa'*); Kesigup, from obtaining or sharing tobacco (*sigup*); Kena'o, from eating boiled sago (*na'o*); Kesuha', from sustaining a wound (*suha'*); Kebua, from finding or eating a great quantity of fruit (*bua*); Kebayuh, from returning empty-handed (*bayuh*) from the hunt; Kesigo, from eating a certain kind of fried sago (*sigo*); Ketorok, from killing or eating a *torok*, a species (probably *Chrysocoris eques*) of snake; Kemedok, from hunting *medok*, a certain species (*Macacus nemestrinus*) of monkey. Some such friendship-names are standard, and tend to recur in different groups, but there is a practically unlimited variety of names, which can be concocted to suit a similar variety of contingent circumstances which they commemorate. Words from other languages, even Malay, can also be incorporated.

Friendship-names can be assumed from early youth, i.e. as soon as a boy (or, less usually, a girl) begins to acquire some adult independence and identity, and whenever a suitable occasion offers. They have no formal connexion with other signs of maturity such as adopting the penis-pin or wearing ornaments in the helix of the ear, and they do not depend on any particular status. They are employed, typically, between two individuals of the same sex, and of roughly the same age; I have been told that men do not employ friendship-names with women, but in practice they sometimes do. The individuals concerned adopt the name, usually, because they are not initially at ease with each other; but it can also be taken by a pair of close friends in order simply to confirm and signify their friendship, in which case the name is said to be assumed 'for fun' (*seminga'*) or because they feel content (*jian kenin*) in each other's company. In the more normal case, however, the parties are in what the Penan themselves call a 'distant' (*ju*) relationship which is marked by some tension. It is this consciousness of social distance which is referred to when the Penan say that they use friendship-names because they are 'ashamed'. Although they can state the conditions in which the names are employed, and the sorts of persons with whom friendship is contracted, they do not (in my experience) have a conventional reason for the sense of unease; not unexpectedly, they state merely that they are ashamed because it is their custom (*ade'*). In practice, the line of application is that between close relatives (*panak*) and Penan whose relationship is remote or unknown. Thus Avun, of Long Buang, explained that he had no friendship-name with Jating, his father's brother's son: 'We grew up together and are not ashamed.' By contrast, he said of a certain affine that he had made friendship with him 'because if there were a divorce we would not be related'. The line between comradeship and unease is not firmly defined, and a friendship-name may be used neither for fun nor yet out of shame; e.g. Pé' comfortably declared that she was not ashamed to use the personal name of Akem, a very distantly related aunt (*vé*), but that she was nevertheless reluctant (*leko*) to do so and therefore had a friendship-name with her. Unrelated individuals, with whom friendship-names are typically employed, are referred to as *irah jah*, which may be most precisely translated as people (*irah*) who are 'other' (*jah*). Such individuals may be met at the trading-meetings, which are held only about three times a year, or by travelling in the forest. When a Penan thus encounters a strange group he will contract friendship-names, the Penan say, with 'everybody', which in fact means with all those to whom the relationship is appropriate. The assertion is more understandable, also, in the light of the fact that the membership of another group is normally reported as the number of adult men in it; so if one asks how many individuals (*kura usah*, how many bodies) there are in a certain group, the number and the names given in reply will in the first instance relate only to men.

A strange group, incidentally, is paradigmatically another group of the same tribe, and friendship-names are not used between Eastern

Penan and Western Penan. Until recent years all of the nomadic groups in the one tribe were physically separated from all of those in the other by the broad stretch of the Baram river, the largest in the area; the Eastern Penan have been given this ethnographical designation because their habitat lies to the east of the Baram, and the Western Penan because theirs lies to the west. In the few contacts between Eastern Penan and Western Penan at which I have been present (at trading-meetings on the Baram, and once when Western Penan guided me to an Eastern group which had been transported across the river in order to exploit the forest around the Kalulong massif) the relations between them were not in fact markedly amical; the Eastern Penan were shy and self-effacing, as they are in the presence of longhouse tribes such as the Kenyah, while the Western Penan treated them with the arrogance and barely concealed contempt with which they themselves are in turn regarded by the Kenyah. No friendship-names were contracted, to my knowledge, between even the Penan Kelamé and the Penan Akah, a western and an eastern group respectively which met on a number of occasions. It is true that some men at Long Buang address certain non-Penan individuals downriver, e.g. trading-partners at Batu Belah, by names which they describe as *ngaran ai'*, but these nevertheless are not traditional names with the *ke-* prefix. Strictly speaking, therefore, friendship-names are fitting only between members of the same Penan tribe, eastern or western, and in a relationship which is implicitly friendly and egalitarian.

The assumption of a friendship-name is informal and even casual, and it can take place quite soon in the relationship. I have never chanced to observe such an agreement between true Penan, but I think my own case is typical in these regards. One day I went with Usang, a young Long Buang man, to look at an *Antiaris toxicaria* tree, from the sap of which blowpipe-poison is made. He was probably a few years younger than myself, married but with no children. We had known each other casually for no more than a fortnight, and this was the first real contact that we had. He and I travelled together, with no companions, so the setting was right: there were just the two of us, and we were sharing a normal but distinctive enterprise. On the way back we were carrying on a desultory conversation as we walked, when without any previous reference to such a matter he said to me: 'You are new (*maréng*) among us, and we have been to look at the poison-tree together; we shall be Kemaréng.' This is an instructive example on a number of counts. I should explain that the people of Long Buang were greatly surprised, and very pleased, that I spoke Penan and that I lived with them as they did and on equal terms; although obviously not a true Penan, they said, I was just like a Penan. Of course, an ethnographer has to inure himself to flattery, but I had reason to take this as essentially sincere; the Eastern Penan are not given to dissimulation, Usang and I actually got on very well, and the relationship was moreover appropriate to the kind of name that was made up. If I had been regarded as a real foreigner (*va'é*), or as a member of a longhouse tribe (*lebo*), a *ngaran ai'* could have been assumed, but it would then have been a name without the prefix, i.e. one which while signifying a relationship let it be understood that this was not between Penan and had not the moral connotations of friendship. The fact that I was given the name of Kemaréng fitted my position as a member of one of the families (not that of Usang himself) in the group, as well as the declared attitude of the Penan towards me. The traditional form of the name also indicated, finally, that the manner and circumstances of its assumption were normal. The descriptive component itself, however, appears rather uncommon, for it refers to the condition of one of the parties only, not to a condition shared by both. Something else about this particular name is worth reporting, namely the grounds for choosing the descriptive component. The tree we had gone to see was a poison-tree, *kayeu tajem*, and one might therefore have expected that the name would refer to this fact, i.e. to an obvious feature (as was indicated by Usang himself) of the shared activity which occasioned the formal friendship. But Kekayeu, from *kayeu*, tree, would have been very unspecific; and Ketajem, from *tajem*, poison, would have been impossible as a friendship-name. The word *tajem* has, understandably enough, connotations of death for the Penan, and it can indeed be employed as a euphemism for *matai*, dead; so Usang and I could not have assumed so inauspicious, if not positively dangerous, a name as Ketajem, for a name affects one's fate.

Friendship is also signified by an exchange of gifts, most commonly pinches of tobacco or clutches of blowpipe-darts (which are easily made by the score), but such gifts are not peculiar to this relationship. More important is the consequent right to make demands for more substantial prestations, of a scale appropriate to a recognized moral commitment between Penan and which may not be refused once such a connexion is admitted. All Penan habitually make small presents to one another, gifts which as elsewhere are regarded as symbols of social communication, and they define a moral obligation among Penan as one which entails sharing; but these exchanges obtain only within the group or with members of other groups towards whom there are explicit duties owed as individuals. The formal friendship marked by a friendship-name creates a moral claim of this special kind. This relationship holds only between the two individuals concerned, and does not entail a wider connexion between families or groups.

Any individual may accumulate tens and even hundreds of friendship-names. I was assured that this led to no difficulty; and in fact it is rather like knowing the names of members of a college or a battalion, only in every case the name applied to another individual is also one's own name. Although each name is used reciprocally and exclusively by the two individuals whose friendship it marks,[11] it is not secret or otherwise concealed. On the other hand, there is no point at all in knowing the friendship-names of someone else, and there would be just as little in attempting to address another by a name not shared with him. Reasonably, therefore, to pronounce a friendship-name is subject to no penalty, either mystical or social, and people talking in company can hear and uninhibitedly speak of one another's names. The latter situation is artificial, of course, and brought about only when an ethnographer is asking questions. Normally, a man will not know the friendship-names of another; e.g. Avun, of Long Buang, was friends with Abu, with whom he had been acquainted for years, but he knew only one of his friendship-names with other men.

This fact introduces a linguistic detail of some interest. The Penan say that they 'enter' (*masek*) a death-name, when they are first in the condition to be addressed by one (Needham 1954g: 418; 1959: 73n.), but I have not heard them use this verb in connexion with friendship-names. Indeed, from the common use of the expressions *maneu ai'* and *pebakéh* I should tend rather to conclude that the adoption of friendship-names is conventionally described by phrases which significantly separate them from death-names. A death-name is 'entered', I think, because it is a public status; a friendship-name is not, because it is a private relationship.[12] Also, a friendship-name, unlike other kinds of name, is not abandoned or changed; it is not discarded when the friendship has become firmly established, even after years, and it is not replaced by any other. Naturally, there is no death-name specific to this friendship, and the name lapses with the demise of the partner. Short of this terminal extinction, as a matter of fact, a friendship-name is the most stable name that a Penan can have.

V

The following are examples of friendship-names as employed by seven men and three women at Long Buang. For each individual the personal name of the partner is given first, then the friendship-name; this is provided with an explanation of the descriptive component (when I know it) or other form, and is followed by an indication of the relationship, or more usually the lack of relationship, between the partners.

1. Avun Julong (son of original settler at Long Buang):

Bengayan: Ketavang < *tavang*, to be lost; son of an immigrant from Batu Balah.

Abu: Kebasa' < *basa'*, wet; from falling into a river; son of immigrant from nomadic group (Penan Melinau).

Upai: Kepadan; from travelling on the hunt together and enduring the same fortunes (this last being given as the meaning of *padan*); son of immigrant from Penan Melinau.

Paren: Kemalu < *malu* (Malay), bashful; from sitting shyly together as youths, away from others; son of immigrant from Penan Melinau.

Apon: Keluding < *luding* (Malay *runding*; cf. Needham 1958), calculation; from an uncalculating (*sic*) sentiment of friendship; son of immigrant from Penan Melinau.

Jin: Kejamin < *jam*, to know, understand; from teaching each other; brother of Apon.

Beluluk: Akéh < *bakéh*, friend; from getting on well (*kenin kua'*) together, in full agreement; father's mother's brother's son; child of immigrant from Penan Melinau.

Ali': Kejara' < *jara'*, explained as suffering or misery; from spending a miserable night in the forest together when hunting, wet and cold, with nothing warm to put on, no fire or food, and plagued by mosquitoes; son of immigrant from Penan Melinau.

Gepi: Kesama < *sama* (Malay), identical; from being the same kind of person, 'no differences'; immigrant from Penan Melinau.

Tingang Sunen: Ketuvah < *tuvah*, a plant (*Derris elliptica*) the root of which is used to stupefy fish; from catching fish together by this means; immigrant from Penan Melinau.

Imang: Kesayang < *sayang* (Malay), regret, sorrow, pity; from suffering a disappointment; son of Batu Belah immigrant and Penan Melinau woman.

Lawai: Kesian < *kasehan* (Malay), kindness, pity;[13] [no occasion recorded]; son of Batu Belah immigrant and Penan Pelutan woman.

Penan Friendship-names

Bangang: Kelamui < *lamui*, explained as to receive nothing; from begging, and then offering to buy, a large knife (*po'é*; usually known in the ethnographical literature on Borneo by the Malay term *parang*) from some Kelabit, who refused to part with it; immigrant from Penan Magoh.

Bugak: Kevayan < *vayan*, a fruit; from finding that this fruit had not ripened when they went to pluck it; half-brother of Beluluk by a Penan Magoh woman.

Bekakong: Kelamui < *lamui*; [occasion not recorded]; immigrant from Penan Melinau.

Lidem: Bakéh < *bakéh*, friend; from holding long friendly conversations about Penan culture, yet 'ashamed' to pronounce personal name; ethnographer.[14]

Konoh: Padé < *padé*, sibling, cousin; [no occasion recorded], for fun, by amusing contrast with the normal use of *padé* as a term of address, when it connotes distance; daughter of immigrant from nomadic Penan in the Belait.

Akem: Jarih < *jarih*, sorrow, regret (*darih* is the common form among other Eastern Penan); [occasion not recorded]; woman, immigrant from Penan Melinau.

Ayu: Buki < *buki* (see above, § IV); [occasion not recorded]; woman, immigrant from Penan Melinau.

2. Layang Sota' (son of early settler):

Ana: Ketusah < *tusah*, difficult; from encountering many difficulties when hunting; brother ('we endured those hardships together and liked to take the name').

Gepi: Kebayuh < *bayuh*, empty-handed; from being unsuccessful in hunting; wife's brother ('ashamed').

Lawai: Ketuvah < *tuvah*; from fishing with derris-root; son of Batu Belah immigrant and Penan Pelutan woman.

Bugak: Ketavé < *tavé*, a kind of fish; from spearing a great many of this fish; mother's brother's son.

Beluluk: Nyak[15] < *nyak*, fat; from killing many pigs and rendering down a lot of fat; brother of Bugak.

Agu': Kepasang < *pasang* (Malay), pair; from the fact that each got a pig when they went hunting together; immigrant from Penan Melana.

Imang: Keburak < *burak*, rice-beer; from getting drunk together; brother of Lawai.

Ayan: Kesigo < *sigo*, sago-flour fried in lard; from eating a lot of this delicacy together; 'Penan Kenyah,' from further in the interior than those groups in the vicinity of the Apoh and Tutoh rivers.

Bengayan: Kejato < *jato* (? < Malay *jatoh*, to fall accidentally); from failing in a number of enterprises; brother to Lawai.

Rodney Needham

3. Ayan (immigrant from nomadic 'Penan Kenyah'):

Apon: Ketavang < *tavang*; from being lost in the forest; son of immigrant from Penan Penipir.

Upai: Kela'au < *la'au*, hungry; from being long without food in the forest; brother of Apon.

Usa: Bakéh < *bakéh*, friend; 'just for fun'; brother of Apon.

Lawai: Kepagung < *pagung*, a kind of fruit; from eating masses of this fruit; immigrant from Batu Belah.

Gepi: Ketusah < *tusah*, hard, difficult; from enduring hardships together in the forest; immigrant from different nomadic group (Penan Melinau).

Layang: Kesigo < *sigo*, fried sago; from eating this together; son of early settler.

Jalong: Kepasan < *pasan*, market (< Malay *pasar*; cf. Needham 1958: 173); from going down the Baram as far as Marudi, a large commercial centre; brother of Lawai.

Bekakong: Kemerem < *merem*, night; from travelling in the dark;[16] Penan Melinau.

4. Tingang Kawi' (early settler; Batu Belah father, Penan Melinau mother):

Ayan: Ketorok < *torok*, a kind of snake; from an unusual incident with such a snake encountered in the forest; 'Penan Kenyah' (but 'not ashamed').

Imang: Kelamui < *lamui*; from incurring a disappointment together; brother ('not ashamed').

Tingang Sunen: Adi'; because they bear the same personal name; immigrant from Penan Melinau.

Bekakong: Kesigo < *sigo*, fried sago; from eating this together; immigrant from Penan Melinau (but 'not ashamed').

Uning: Kesieng < *sieng*, food (e.g., fruit, monkey) of mysterious origin or nature; from eating *sieng* when young; wife's brother ('ashamed').

5. Abu Tingang (son of Tingang Sunen):

Upai: Kemerem < *merem*, night; from travelling in the dark; married to father's former wife.

6. Usang (brother of Avun):

No names recorded, but friends with the following: Abu, Apon, Imang, Jin, Lawai, Upai (see above, under Avun); Béng, brother of Apon; Jalong, brother of Lawai; Gi', immigrant from Penan Melinau; Lipang, son of Jalong; Beluluk (cf. under Avun), wife's father ('ashamed'). Lidem: Kemaréng, ethnographer.

7. Bang (brother of Avun and Usang):

No names recorded, but friends with the following: Abu, Beluluk, Imang, Jin (cf. above); Au, half-brother of Abu; Ayu.

8. Alui (mother of Avun, Bang, and Usang; immigrant from Penan Magoh):

    Iring: Kematen < *maten*, eye; [occasion not recorded]; immigrant from different nomadic group (Penan Melinau), wife of Jalong's brother Usa.

    Yang: Diang [meaning unknown; occasion not recorded]; brother's wife.

9. Pé' (wife of Avun; immigrant from Penan Melinau):

    Akem: Lebu (? < *lebu*, toggle on waist-cord of *parang*); [occasion not recorded]; immigrant from Penan Melinau; 'reluctant' (*leko*) to use personal name because she is a recent arrival, but 'not ashamed'.

    Upi': Kematen; immigrant from Penan Melinau, half-sister of Gepi.

10. Ayu (sister of Akem; immigrant from Penan Melinau):

    No names recorded, but claims friendship (*ai'*) with the following: Alui, Penan Magoh; Jating, Penan Melinau; Maya, Penan Melana; Mujan, daughter of Lawai (cf. above, under Avun); Sekuti', Penan Melana; Avun, Bang, Imang, Lipang, Usang (see above). [First five are women.]

VI

Certain general principles can be extracted from this evidence, even if there must remain a number of questions, both of principle and of fact, which cannot be answered by this investigation.[17]

1. The reciprocal employment of the friendship-name happens to be demonstrated by the separate reports of Layang and Ayan, each of whom gives Kesigo as the name for the other.

2. A particular friendship-name can be used by more than one pair of individuals in the same group and at the same time, e.g.:

    Ketavang: Avun and Bengayan; Ayan and Apon
    Ketuvah: Avun and Tingang Sunen; Layang and Lawai
    Kelamui: Avun and Bangang; Tingang Kawi' and Imang
    Kesigo: Layang and Ayan; Tingang Kawi' and Bekakong
    Ketusah: Layang and Ana; Ayan and Gepi
    Kemerem: Ayan and Bekakong; Abu and Upai
    Kematen: Alui and Iring; Pé' and Upi'.

3. The same name can be used simultaneously with more than one partner; e.g. Avun is Kelamui with both Bangang and Bekakong.

4. Men can have friendship-names with women, though apparently not many, and not all do so; e.g. Ayan expressly stated that he had no friendship-names at all with women. Here, at any rate, there are only

seven instances, viz.: Avun and Konoh, Avun and Akem, Avun and Ayu, Bang and Ayu, Imang and Ayu, Usang and Ayu, Lipang and Ayu.[18] In all these cases the partners are married to others; and I have been told elsewhere that bachelors do not have friendship-names with (unmarried) women, even with their mistresses.

An obvious feature of some of the cases above is that where the actual names are known (viz. Avun's female partners) the friendship-names have no *ke-* prefix. This is made quite certain by my note of the friendship-name between Avun and Konoh. After relating a list of prefixed names which he employed with men, Avun gave me the name Padé for Konoh; I automatically began to write it as 'Kepadé,' pronouncing it as I did so, but Avun corrected me and had me delete the prefix. I later asked Alui whether this was because women should not have friendship-names with the prefix, but this she denied. Nevertheless, it seems significant that in these cases the women were distinguished from men in this way. Moreover, whereas women can evidently employ prefixed names with other women, it may mean something that no friendship-name of this kind was recorded between a woman and a man.

5. The kinds of connexion between the partners are especially difficult to comment on, for the relationships within Long Buang are so complicated and intertwined that an article longer than this would be needed to describe them.

The chief cause of confusion is the frequency of divorce and remarriage; e.g. Gepi has had six wives in succession, Bangang has had five, Layang has had four, Ayan has had three, and Sekuti' has had seven husbands. When the half-siblings issued from such marriages themselves marry and divorce, the net of relationships becomes yet more tangled. In addition to these factors there is an expectable multiplicity of statuses; in a group of cognates, marrying by preference among themselves and in any genealogical level, any two individuals may be related in a variety of ways, occupying different respective statuses according to how the connexion is traced (Needham 1966). It is not possible, therefore, to define an individual's status with finality, or to determine an absolute or even preponderant relationship with another. Even when a genealogical connexion is recorded in my notes, therefore, or can be reconstructed, there is no immediate assurance that this is the relationship which counts in the explanation of the friendship-name. Thus there are two cases of friendship with the mother's brother's son (Layang with Bugak and Beluluk), but without further investigation into the circumstances of each case one cannot tell whether this is a close or a distant relationship in the eyes of those concerned, or whether there are not additional relationships which introduce other factors and might better define the connexion that is marked by the name.

In other cases, however, the connexion is tolerably clear, e.g. there are two instances (Layang and Ana; Tingang Kawi' and Imang) in which the partners are brothers. These illustrate one of the polar types of relationship which may be marked by a friendship-name, i.e. one of full and trusting friendship which the partners simply confirm by the only kind of formal designation which is available to them for this purpose. The opposite pole, that of avoidance, is equally clearly illustrated by those instances in which the partners are affines: two with the wife's brother, one with the wife's father, one with the father's wife's husband, and one with the brother's wife.

For the rest, the great majority of the friendships are between individuals who are either distantly related or are not related at all. It is a specially instructive feature of the Long Buang community, in this connexion, that such a clear line can be drawn between the earlier settlers and the immigrants from surrounding nomadic groups. In some cases relationship is indeed claimed between settlers and nomads, but the genealogical connexions offered as demonstration are nearly always exceedingly tenuous and inferential, so that they serve merely to emphasize the distance.

6. One would expect, in Penan society, a special stress on relative age in the employment of this nomenclature (cf. Needham 1966). In fact, I was explicitly told, on more than one occasion, that friendship-names were adopted only with people of roughly the same age. But this is not wholly the case. For example, Avun is considerably younger than Layang, by perhaps a generation, yet these two men have six friends (Bengayan, Beluluk, Gepi, Imang, Lawai, Bugak) in common. Even more clearly, Usang has contracted friendship with Jalong and also with Lipang, Jalong's son. Similarly, Usang has a friendship-name with Beluluk, his wife's father. Also, Alui told me that a friendship-name could well be adopted with a much younger person, only the latter had to be adult enough ('he has to know how to hunt') to enter a serious relationship; e.g. Lipang, who was already married, could contract friendship

with his far younger classificatory nephew (*ahong*), Tua, when the boy was bigger. Nevertheless, it does seem to be generally the case that friendship-names are employed between individuals of similar ages.[19]

VII

Later inquiries made of nomadic groups of Eastern Penan further in the interior confirmed the use of friendship-names as a standard custom among them also.

The first special check, after the discovery of the institution at Long Buang, was carried out in a group of Penan Akah, under Jengilan, who were then wandering in the area at the headwaters of the Paong river, to the west of the Kalulong massif.[20] They did not recognize the phrase *maneu ai'*, or the term *ngaran ai'*, but they readily understood *pebakéh* and explained that friendship-names (for which I could elicit no word, though the examples I gave were at once familiar to them) were a joking form of speech (*ha' seminga'*). They said at first that the names were used only with affines, but it turned out that they were used with distant cognates as well and with strangers (*irah jah*); they were not used with close relatives (*irah déhé*), particularly with direct descendants, or, at the other extreme, with members of the settled tribes (*lebo*) such as the Kenyah. Thus Belengan was Kena'o (<*na'o*, boiled sago) with Kuyang, his wife's brother, a member of the same group; and he was Kepayau (<*payau*, sambar deer, *Cervus unicolor*) with Gung, a distantly related nephew. The names used were of the common forms; e.g. Kebabui (<*babui*, wild pig), Kebua (<*bua*, fruit), Kemedok (<*medok*, macaque), Ketorok (<*torok*, a snake), Kesigo (<*sigo*, fried sago), etc. Kebayuh (<*bayuh*, empty-handed) was recognized,[21] but not Ketusah. Women were said at first to have no such names, and to address each other simply as *bakéh*, friend; but it was later conceded that they could after all use friendship-names, though only a few because, significantly, 'they do not hunt'. Thus Purai, the daughter of Jengilan, had two: she was Keli'eu (<*li'eu*, slow; 'because we travelled together very slowly') with her cousin Nok, whose father was distantly related and whose mother was a stranger from the headwaters of the Tutoh; and she was Kebayuh ('because we went fishing and got nothing') with her distant cousin (father's father's sister's son's daughter) Jalan.

These forms and principles were later checked among other nomadic groups, such as the Penan Sela'an, near the upper reaches of the Baram.

The institution was readily recognized, once examples were given, and the explanation commonly volunteered was that friendship-names were used only in play (*seminga' awah*).[22]

VIII

The Western Penan do not employ a proliferation of friendship-names of this kind. They have instead only the one name Kelieng, to which none was able to give any meaning.[23] It can be used between affines, but not with cognates. As with the Eastern Penan names, it is used only between Penan, and between individuals of the same sex and of similar ages. This minimal extent of the institution was established among the Penan Kelamé and was confirmed among the Penan Sila' and the Penan Lua. I was repeatedly told that there were no names other than Kelieng.

The Penan Buk, settled near the Tinjar, and the Penan Bakong, settled above Beluru, do not employ any kind of friendship-name.

NOTES

1. The research on which this paper is based was carried out in Sarawak in 1951–2 and 1958. An outline of friendship-names has previously formed part of an unpublished doctoral thesis, 'The Social Organization of the Penan' (Needham 1953; cf. 1965: 59), for which, as a matter of present interest, Professor Evans-Pritchard acted as senior examiner.

   I am grateful to the following for their kindness in reading and commenting on this paper: Dr J. K. Campbell, Professor Raymond Firth, Dr F. Korn, and Dr E. R. Leach.

2. Penan ideology is not in any case peculiar to them, but is in its main features held in common with certain settled groups commonly called Kenyah, and also with other longhouse groups of middle Borneo. The best account of Kenyah mystical notions is that by Elshout (1923).

3. The Kenyah names, described by Elshout (1926: 156–80), are essentially identical with those of the Penan, though they are in some respects more elaborately developed. There are grounds, indeed, for considering the Penan system as a rather impaired version of the Kenyah. Elshout's account, at any rate, is by far the fullest description of the naming usages of any Bornean society, only he does not explain what are the systematic connexions among the types of names that he so well lists. In this regard

it is the Penan customs which can throw light on the more complicated institutions of the Kenyah.

4. C. Lévi-Strauss, in *La Pensée sauvage*, has paid special attention to Penan nomenclature (1962: 253–63; cf. English trans., 1966: 191–9), but not, unfortunately, to any convincing effect. It is true that he complains of 'many obscurities' in the ethnographical description, but since he does not make plain what precisely he finds unclear it is difficult to see what information he thinks is lacking. The system itself is certainly hard to grasp (as he shows by his account of it), but that is not the same thing as a defective report by an ethnographer.

A worse fault, however, is to be found in Lévi-Strauss's own analysis, in that in certain respects, upon which his 'structural' interpretation depends, he gets the printed facts crucially and tendentiously wrong. For instance, he writes that after the birth of a child it is 'forbidden' (*interdit*) to call Penan parents by their personal names (1962: 257; cf. 263), whereas the source reports, without the slightest imputable obscurity, that the teknonym may be used 'prefixed to the personal name' (Needham 1954g: 417, 420). Similarly, he writes that a survivor 'loses' (*perd*) his personal name when he assumes a death-name (1962: 263), whereas the source clearly states that although it is common for the bereaved to change his personal name (and even then only when certain relatives die), 'there is no obligation' to do so, and that it rests with the individual whether he does so or not (Needham 1954: 425). As for the extraordinary asseveration that Penan who have begotten a child are 'dead' (1962: 258), a simple ethnographer can only respond with bewilderment that the theoretician has lost all touch with the reality of the situation – but since Lévi-Strauss contradicts the ethnography on another point of interpretation, while attributing to the Penan themselves ideas which they happen not to express (1962: 263n.) or, to the best of my knowledge, conceive, it can scarcely be expected that such an unstructural objection will register.

5. Kenyah *lepò*, settlement (Elshout 1923: 11); *pòòn*, origin (Elshout 1926: 185). Other Lepo Pu'un groups were given to me as: Narom, Berawan, Long Patah, and Peliit. These are all said to have come from the Kayan river and down the Baram.

6. This is a standard means employed by longhouse communities in Borneo in order to signify distinctions of origin.

7. Mr Hamer, of the Borneo Evangelical Mission, told me seven years later that the longhouse nearly always appeared empty when he passed it. He had the impression that the Penan settled there were decreasing in numbers, and that they spent most of their time in the forest, where they had a main camp about half an hour's walk from Long Atip (upriver from

Long Buang, below the mouth of the Melana). It was his opinion that they were reverting to nomadic life.

8. Prior to that point a stranger will be addressed with *kei*, a term used towards parents-in-law and which is also a polite, if distant, mode of address used with strange Penan and also with certain other individuals (e.g. Bornean government officers who protect Penan interests at trading-meetings) of comparable moral status. It is further employed, instructively enough, as a term of admonition to children, when it serves to set them at a distance.

9. In fact, the only name I can recall or discover which resembles a friendship-name in this respect is Kɛwén, the personal name of a girl in Jengilan's group; and in this case the syllable *wén* is meaningless, so far as I know, which precludes a real similarity to a friendship-name and is, descriptive component.

10. It is often said of forest nomads that they are never lost, and the Penan sometimes claim it of themselves; but in unknown or difficult country even the Penan do sometimes lose their bearings and thus fail to meet a rendezvous or to get back to camp before nightfall.

11. That is, it marks an exclusive relationship between these individuals. As will be seen, the name itself can be used with more than one partner, but there are then two mutually exclusive relationships.

12. I have not mentioned teknonyms in this connexion because I do not recall that Penan say they 'enter' a teknonym, and I cannot be sure that idiomatically the phrase would be acceptable.

13. The initial *ka-* of the Malay word has been conveniently assimilated to the *ke-* prefix of a friendship-name. It should not be thought surprising that Malay words should sometimes be used in this way. Malay is the lingua franca of riverine society, and as the settled Penan become implicated in this wider culture so they tend to learn some Malay. In their traditional life, also, they normally learn something of the languages of other peoples, such as Iban or Kelabit, with whom they come into contact; and they then, moreover, readily adopt words from these languages into their own speech. On *kesian* in particular, incidentally, see also Needham (1964: 138).

14. It was in fact this appellation, applied by Avun to myself, which first led me to friendship-names. Had he not spontaneously called me 'Bakéh' and if I had not asked why he did so, I might easily not have discovered the institution.

15. Expressly reported so, with no prefix.

16. Penan are uneasy at travelling, or even leaving camp, in the dark because this is the time when malicious spirits (*ungap*, etc.; cf. Needham 1964: 143) are abroad. To travel at night is a memorable adventure

which they would never undertake unless they were forced to do so.

17. It is regrettable that I did not make a really intensive study of friendship-names, but perhaps I may explain some of the reasons that I was scarcely in a position to do so at Long Buang. I had been little more than five months among the Penan, on my first ethnographic expedition, when I visited there, and I had not the opportunity to return later. At that time I was in any case largely occupied with plotting the distribution of the Penan and with trying to establish distinctive features of Penan culture and social organization. I had, moreover, to make inquiries in an unrecorded language (the great majority of Penan had no Malay or any other common language to which I could resort in learning their own) and was confused by differences between Eastern Penan and Western Penan which I had not well grasped. Also, of course, in my apprentice investigations, I did not realize what I had found or just how it should be analysed, which was the main reason that in subsequent inquiries among other groups I did scarcely more than check whether or not the custom was known.

18. I fear I have no idea, and cannot reconstruct one from my notebooks, why Ayu had this prominence among the examples I recorded.

19. I am sorry that I cannot provide figures to show this. The Penan do not reckon their ages, and at that time I had not realized the crucial importance of relative age in the organization of their affairs. I therefore did not even try to work out the probable ages of all the members of the group, and those individuals whose apparent ages I did note, or can now estimate, are not enough to constitute a proof.

20. To stress again the unobvious nature of friendship-names, and the consequent lack of significance in the fact that the ethnographical literature does not mention them, I may say that this was the first group of Penan that I ever knew, and one with which I formed a special connexion, yet before I had visited Long Buang I had no idea that they employed such names.

21. As an equivalent for *bayuh* they gave me *tolo*, a word of which I have no other record.

22. This phrase may give rise to the idea that what is in question is actually a joking relationship, but the Penan institution has little more than this verbal resemblance to what elsewhere is usually understood by such a relationship. There is no licensed familiarity or privileged aggression, nor any 'mutual ministration' (as Hocart well described it) of a formal or ritual nature, between the partners. There is indeed an express connexion between friendship-names and marriage, but they are most commonly found among people who are not affines, including close relatives (e.g. brothers) who could not possibly be related by marriage. The lack of

useful similarity may best be gauged by reference to what in my judgement is the best account of the joking relationship yet published, viz. Beidelman's paper on *utani* among the Kaguru (1966), which demonstrates by repeated contrast the extent to which Penan friendship-names lack the definitive features of a joking relationship.

23. The word *lieng* is used in Eastern Penan as a term of reference for a sibling-in-law after the death of the connecting spouse, but the equivalent for this term in the western dialect is *bieng*.

REFERENCES

BEIDELMAN, T. O. 1966 *Utani*: Some Kaguru Notions of Death, Sexuality, and Affinity. *Southwestern Journal of Anthropology* **20**: 354–80.

DOUGLAS, R. S. 1911 A Comparative Vocabulary of the Kayan, Kenyah and Kelabit Dialects. *Sarawak Museum Journal* **1**: 75–119.

ELSHOUT, JACOB MARINUS 1923 *Over de Geneeskunde der Kĕnja-Dajak in Centraal-Borneo in verband met hunnen Godsdienst.* Academisch Proefschrift, Universiteit van Amsterdam. Amsterdam: Müller.

— 1926 *De Kĕnja-Dajaks uit het Apo-Kajangebied: Bijdragen tot de Kennis van Centraal-Borneo.* The Hague: Nijhoff.

EVANS-PRITCHARD, E. E. 1965 *The Position of Women in Primitive Societies: and Other Essays in Social Anthropology.* London: Faber.

LÉVI-STRAUSS, CLAUDE 1962 *La Pensée sauvage.* Paris: Plon. (English ed., *The Savage Mind*, London: Weidenfeld and Nicolson, 1966.)

NEEDHAM, RODNEY 1953 The Social Organisation of the Penan. Unpublished D.Phil. thesis, University of Oxford.

— 1954a A Note on the Blood Pact in Borneo. *Man* **54**: 90–91, art. 129.

— 1954b Penan and Punan. *Journal of the Malayan Branch Royal Asiatic Society* **27**: 73–83.

— 1954c A Note on some Nomadic Punan. *Indonesië* **7**: 520–3.

— 1954d Reference to the Dead among the Penan. *Man* **54**: 10, art. 6.

— 1954e Siriono and Penan: A Test of Some Hypotheses. *Southwestern Journal of Anthropology* **10**: 228–32.

— 1954f A Penan Mourning-Usage. *Bijdragen tot de Taal-, Land- en Volkenkunde* **110**: 263–7.

— 1954g The System of Teknonyms and Death-Names among the Penan. *Southwestern Journal of Anthropology* **10**: 416–31.

— 1955 Punan Ba. *Journal of the Malayan Branch Royal Asiatic Society* **28**: 24–36.

— 1958 Notes on Baram Malay. *Journal of the Malayan Branch Royal Asiatic Society* **31**: 171–5.

NEEDHAM, RODNEY 1959 Mourning-Terms. *Bijdragen tot de Taal-, Land- en Volkenkunde* **115**: 58–89.

— 1964 Blood, Thunder, and Mockery of Animals. *Sociologus* **14**: 136–49. (Reprinted in John Middleton (ed.) *Myth and Cosmos*. Garden City, N.Y.: Natural History Press, 1967, pp. 271–85.)

— 1965 Death-Names and Solidarity in Penan Society. *Bijdragen tot de Taal-, Land- en Volkenkunde* **121**: 58–76.

— 1966 Age, Category, and Descent. *Bijdragen tot de Taal-, Land- en Volkenkunde* **120**: 1–35.

— 1971 Penan. In LeBar, Frank M. (ed.), *Ethnic Groups of Insular Southeast Asia*. New Haven, Conn.: Human Relations Area Files.

RAY, SIDNEY H. 1913 The Languages of Borneo. *Sarawak Museum Journal* **1** (4): 1–196.

On the Word 'Caste'

JULIAN PITT-RIVERS

Science requires precise words. If comparisons, the essence of science, are to be valid, we must be able to define unambiguously what we compare (cf. Cohen & Nagel 1964: 32–3; for a discussion of this point in the social sciences, cf. ibid.: 346). Essential properties must be distinguished from appearances, as the whole history of biology or chemistry shows, and a proposition regarding a class of phenomena must apply to all possible members of it. If the social sciences fail to attain the same kind of precision as the natural sciences, it is, apart from all other excuses offered for their imprecision, due to the fact that they face a difficulty that does not beset their more exact neighbours: not content to await the ethnographer to receive a name, the data of these 'inexact sciences' classify themselves according to their own whim and without regard for the convenience of the investigator or the problem of scientific taxonomy. The student is continually faced with a *fait accompli*. Whether he accepts this with good grace and sticks to the names which the people he studies have chosen to denote their experience or whether he rejects it in favour of a classification of his own devising, it remains true that his relationship to his object of study is different from that of the physical scientist, for he is dealing not merely with things, but with consciousness of things. His choice at any given point reflects the alternative between the subjective or objective view of human phenomena which he must somehow reconcile before his explanation can be counted valid.

After a long and confused struggle with this problem anthropology has reached the point today where the need is recognized at least to distinguish clearly between categories of thought at the level of ethnography – the names which the people studied give to the social phenomena of their own society – and the analytical concepts of the discipline. It has become evident that neither by itself is adequate: if the investigator chooses to accept the 'natives' view' of their own world as if it bore the credentials of science, he confines himself to a parochialism

231

which excludes all comparison, but if he rejects it and sets out to sum up their social system on the basis of his preconceived concepts, he corrupts his data. His real task is to re-order that which they order and discover behind their ordering a more abstract order that explains it. Yet in what terms can this 'higher order' be expressed? A certain penchant for verbal inventiveness has already earned anthropology the distrust of older disciplines that are content to call a spade a spade. But if it does not invent its own vocabulary then its task is doubled, for in borrowing from ordinary speech the terms it strives to make precise, it must first strip them of their everyday connotations based on the assumptions of the investigator's culture, redefine them in accordance with its general theories, and guard their semantic purity from then on against the encroachments of a spurious common sense. It is not surprising, then, that a whole generation of anthropologists sought to evade the predicament by borrowing the terms they lacked from the ethnography of some exotic region; these could, they thought, be used in analogy to define a universal category (cf. Evans-Pritchard 1965: 12).

Called to do service in that higher order, the customs of the Redskins or the Polynesians fulfilled their novel function for a time; at least they offered an escape from the straitjacket of our own culture, or so it appeared. But the procedure was questionable from the theoretical point of view: how could such terms serve at both levels and retain their unity? Like a hunters' trophies furnishing his home (antlers for a hatstand or hooves transformed as inkwells), they changed their meaning once they were put to new uses and it became doubtful whether they really applied any more to the institutions from which they originated. *Mana*, for example, was taken to represent a certain mode of magical thought, defined by its indifference to reason and its dependence upon the sentiments. Its worth as an analytical concept depended upon accepting the thesis that 'natives' react without using their brains, and once this was questioned it became doubtful whether even the Polynesians had 'mana' in the anthropological sense. Borrowed concepts proved a poor substitute for the tools of scientific reasoning. In the end moreover, the endeavour paid off badly, for inasmuch as these new words gained acceptance they were pilfered by neighbouring disciplines and endowed with connotations foreign to their anthropological sense. *Mana, tabu, fetish, totem, potlatch*[1] became the common currency of the intellectuals of the period and eventually of the journalists, so that the anthropologists found themselves, with their vocabulary corrupted, facing once more the problem of lexical purity, and facing it at a further disadvantage in that these words might no longer apply correctly even in the society that had provided them.

The problem is not merely to guard against the implications of popular usage when employing words as scientific terms. It is a question of determining the heuristic status of the words we use. To what extent are they able to carry an analytical load? The more immediately they are related to the observation of events, the less they are able to do so, since a factual description does not require that the defining characteristics of the terms used in it be specified: it is apparent what they denote to the members of the society that uses them. Yet how they may be applied elsewhere (and this must be possible if they are to be granted analytical status) is open to doubt, since equivalences between different cultures are not easily established. In order to do so it is necessary to resort to abstractions; the greater the difference between the cultures compared, the higher the level of abstraction that must be reached. Where there is no similarity at all, the ethnographic content is irrelevant, they can only be defined in terms of their structure. They no longer refer to that which is empirically recognizable but to properties which are revealed only by the application of a framework of analytical thought. Restricted to the ethnographical level, a term remains, as it were, embedded within the culture which gave it birth, but elevated to the status of a scientific concept, it falls victim to changes in fashion in anthropological theory – like *fetish, tabu, mana, totem, potlatch*, terms which have been returned today to the ethnographical level, soiled by the speculations of anthropologists who failed to perceive the real significance of the institutions to which they referred in the ethnography and elaborated false categories of analysis from them. To grasp the distinction between the two levels it is only necessary to imagine asking the informant questions framed in analytical terms or to quote the jokes, once popular in anthropological circles, concerning the educated African chief who, when consulted about tribal custom, reached for his volume of Rattray or Nadel.

Any word may be used, in fact, at any level within the hierarchy of abstractions. What is important is to respect the implications of giving it status at one level rather than another. When the same word is used simultaneously at different levels the door is open to confusion. In this regard the usage of the word 'caste' in Latin America provides an object lesson.

233

The strands of meaning that intertwine to give us the modern word *caste* can be traced with less certainty than is generally thought. 'Castas', Corominas (1961) tells us, 'is a word originating in the Iberian Peninsula and common to its three languages. Its source is uncertain, perhaps from the gothic KASTS, a group of animals or a brood of nestlings.' He goes on to express forceful doubts about the common theory which would derive the word from the Latin CASTUS, for the sense of chastity is not found in the earliest mentions of the word.

Until the sixteenth century it referred primarily to species of animal or plant and race or lineage of men. It was closely allied with the notion of procreation, from which Covarrubias derived the missing link with the idea of chastity '. . . . for the procreation of children it is better not to be abandoned in the venereal act for which reason the restrained and those who have little to do with women have much progeny' (1611).[2] From the notion of species, breed, or lineage it is understandable that the Portuguese should have applied it to the 'castes' which they encountered in India. However, by dividing the world between the Spanish and the Portuguese, the Pope also divided the applications of the word 'casta': the Spaniards found nothing in any way resembling the castes of India in the New World and in addition to using the word in what was the normal way at that period to designate animal species, they applied it in the human realm to lineages or clans. Indeed, the word is still used in this sense in many parts of Latin America. In the Andes it commonly refers to the patrilineage, while the totemic matrilineal clans of the Guajira are also called *castas* to this day. In both English and French[3] the distinction between tribe and caste became clear only in the nineteenth century.

The notion of purity of descent was not essential to the word originally, so that one even finds mention of 'the caste of mules', but in view of the preoccupation of the times, especially in Spain, with regard to lineage and purity of blood it is not surprising that *casta* became associated with these ideas, for pure breeding, notwithstanding the mules, was thought to be superior to cross-breeding, particularly in the human species among whom social status was derived from descent. However, the greatest elaboration of the term came in the Spanish empire in the seventeenth and eighteenth centuries when it signified above all, not the pure, but the impure, the half-breeds, that is to say, the very people who in endogamous India would be regarded as outside the system. The *castas* were people of mixed ancestry, and a pseudo-biological vocabulary was elaborated from popular zoology and the slang of the day to accord a distinct social identity to each combination of white, indian, or negro.[4] Inherited status was what counted, not actual colour, so that anyone who could claim one-eighth or less of non-white descent was classed as white and the status of white could in any case at one period even be purchased without regard for antecedents.

The imperial legislation attempted at various times to stabilize the system by discouraging and even forbidding intermarriage between certain *castas*, but without the least success (Rosenblat 1954, II: 147, 159, 166, 167). Meanwhile the word continued to be used in the senses simply of breeding or race and with the various figurative meanings which derived from them. Given that the concept of descent occupied an important place within the social structure of the empire, and even though there existed a certain rough stratification which derived from the opposition indian/Spanish (equivalent to primitive/civilized), it must nevertheless be stressed that the notion of breeding was never entirely coordinated with the other criteria of superiority or inferiority. The Indian nobility of the sixteenth century illustrated how the classification of rank could cross-cut that of race, and even after they disappeared from the scene and even though the tendency for ethnic status to be assimilated to class status has on the whole increased from age to age, breeding has never been an exact coordinate of social status, but rather an alternative dimension to it, qualifying the other ones.

Once the notion of descent had ceased after Independence to have any juridical value, the *castas* were no longer distinguished within the general category of *mestizos*. Today the word *casta* is used only in its figurative senses, save in the antique local usages already mentioned which persist to indicate a lineage or clan among those who are recognized as Indians. It does not refer to any social status. This is perhaps inevitable with the rise of modern industrial society which no longer ascribes any formal value to ancestry. Yet its demise at the ethnographical level was followed by its resurrection at the hands of the social scientists, who found their precedent nowhere in the hispanic tradition but rather in that of English sociological literature. But for the preponderance of this it might have remained simply what it was in the vernacular. But it is found now, as in English, indicating a certain type of social distinction and applying in particular to that which divides the population of Latin America into indian and hispanic. This sense is quite different from that of lineage or clan or the categories of breed which were distinguished in the imperial epoch or the hierarchized occupational groups of the Hindus. It refers to no collectivity of any sort, except in so far as the entire population can be divided into two castes; a superior one, which is hispanic, and an inferior one, which is indian.

This usage owed its entry into Latin America to an analogy with the distinction between coloured and white people in the United States[5] which in turn is owed to an analogy with the castes of India.[6] The re-appearance of the term in Spanish was therefore anything but a simple revival of a usage which had fallen out of fashion but rather the invasion of a territory where the term once existed on the ethnographical level by the same word which, thanks to its sojourn on the far side of the world, had 'made it' to analytical status and thereafter claimed the right to apply anywhere, even to the past where it confronts its defunct antecedents. This has occurred in historical studies of the imperial epoch or in nineteenth-century Yucatan where the 'Guerra de Castas' is commonly translated as 'The Caste War' (e.g. Reed 1964). It is difficult to say what exactly this expression is intended to convey in English; if it is not simply an anglicization of the Spanish name, it can be seen to depend on an analogy of the same type as that which beguiles the student who sets off for Polynesia hoping to find *mana* or for the north-west coast expecting 'a potlatch society'.

In order to assess the usage in the New World we must outline the development of the word in sociology, where *caste* evokes first and foremost the caste system of the Hindus. Here we know that the introduction of the term is owed to the Portuguese who found it appropriate to describe the hierarchy of endogamous groups of Indian society. The British simply took it over and anglicized it, giving it a particular value based on the contrast with British institutions.[7] Yet its denotation in sociology remains unclear to this day, for while some writers take the castes to be the *varna*, the four categories of caste (this is the common-place view), others refer to the *jati*, the effective endogamous groups, as castes; the former then refer to the *jati* as 'subcastes', while for the latter the subcastes are the divisions of the *jati*. The question is further complicated by the fact that, while both *varna* and *jati* are found throughout India, they do not always correspond exactly from one area to another. The status of the equivalent groups varies from place to place and even the system varies in its connotations. It is further complicated again by the presence of groups which are marginal to the system, notably the Muslims and Christians, whose religion denies its very fundament but who are nevertheless deeply influenced by the Brahminical tradition and who present comparable characteristics that have sufficed the ethnographers of India to retain the word in regard to them. Whether rightly or wrongly, it is not for me to say.[8]

I need not go in detail into the discussions of the definition of caste and of the range of its validity, except in so far as this is necessary to decide what possibilities are open to us. A debate has been going on for years between anthropologists on this subject.[9] It hinges on whether or not the word 'caste' can be used to refer to social systems other than that of the Hindus, that is to say, whether the concept which derives from the Indian system of social differentiation can also be used to denote other systems, and, in that case, which. The degree of extension which may be allowed the term is here the point at issue and this relates, of course, to the status of the definition given. At one extreme it is maintained that Hindu society is fundamentally different in nature from those found elsewhere and therefore caste is a purely Hindu phenomenon incommensurable with systems of social differentiation in other parts of the world. This view pays attention to the nature of the system in all its detail and chooses to regard each aspect as necessary to the definition whose intension is thus so full that its extension outside India is ruled out. Indian caste is a phenomenon *sui generis*. This is to refuse all abstraction and remain at the ethnographical level, at least with regard to the 'caste system'. At the other extreme India is regarded merely as one among other societies which recognize a high degree of hierarchical differentiation, and the word 'caste' can therefore be employed wherever there is, in the well-known words of Alfred Kroeber, 'an endogamous and hereditary subdivision of an ethnic unit occupying a position of superior or inferior rank or social esteem in comparison with other subdivisions' (Kroeber 1937). Kroeber regarded caste as a kind of class, a development from it, distinguished from other kinds of class in that its members are conscious of belonging to a recognized caste. This definition enables Kroeber to subsume under this term the common usages of the word which denote military and aristocratic castes. Indeed, he never made it clear exactly where he would have the line drawn; any stratified system is likely to be more or less consciously endogamous if it recognizes descent in both lines, and status within it will tend to be hereditary, since people normally attempt to ensure that they are succeeded by their children. Moreover, the great majority of peoples who

237

classify themselves hierarchically recognize the fact, and the society of the United States is somewhat exceptional in its reluctance to do so consciously. Kroeber's definition can be seen, therefore, to be anything but stringent.

The views of most authors who have written on the subject lie somewhere between these two extremes and they sometimes represent an attempt at compromise between them, as, for example, when caste is first of all defined by its cultural characteristics and a world-wide validity is then claimed for it. It is not realized that a definition of caste in ethnographic terms is useless for comparison (Leach 1960: 2), if the comparative dimension is withdrawn from consideration, the result is folklore; the place of science is taken by common sense (which would not be common if it were not ethnocentric). If the concept of caste is to be used in cross-cultural comparison, i.e. if it is to be a sociological category,[10] it must be abstracted from the detail of culture and repose on an analytical definition, not a stereotype (which is a description masquerading as a definition). Yet definitions of caste have tended to be stereotypical rather than analytic and have stressed resemblances of qualities rather than the existence of essential properties. Thus Berreman (1960: 120), though he seems aware of the difficulty, defined caste as:

'. . . *a hierarchy of endogamous divisions in which membership is hereditary and permanent.* Here hierarchy includes inequality both in status and in access to goods and services. Interdependence of the sub-divisions, restricted contacts among them, occupational specialization and/or a degree of cultural distinctiveness might be added as criteria, although they appear to be correlates rather than defining characteristics. This definition is perhaps best viewed as describing an ideal type at one end of a continuum along which systems of social stratification might be ranged. There can be little doubt that the systems in India and the southern United States would fall far toward the caste extreme of the continuum.'

He further supported the assimilation of the two by numerous resemblances: rigid rules of avoidances; contamination through contact; enforced deference; distinct dwelling area, occupation, place of worship, and cultural behaviour; powerful sanctions exercised by the superior caste who rationalize their status; great differences in power and privilege within, as well as between, castes; elaborate barriers of intercourse; low-caste dependence maintained by economic and physical sanctions;

resentment of their status by the lower caste. The essential similarity lies in the fact that 'the function of the rules in both cases is to maintain the caste system with institutionalized inequality as its fundamental feature'.

He thus defended the application of the term to the colour-bar in the Deep South, stressing the similarity of attitudes found, on the one hand, between high-caste people and untouchables in an Indian village and, on the other, those which whites and negroes adopt towards each other in the South. He suggested that the view which contrasted rather than assimilated the two fields (and therefore denied the utility of the word 'caste' in the United States) was based on a comparison of the Indian caste system as it is ideally described (rather than as it is) with the United States as it is known to be. It is undoubtedly true that many descriptions of Indian caste are based upon an ideal view of the system, and it is only relatively recently that detailed ethnographic descriptions have revealed the degree of discontent with which certain members of the lowest castes accept their lot and the manœuvres whereby certain low castes attempt to raise their status. Nevertheless, Berreman's assimilation of the two rests upon the comparison of both with *class* relations as they are in the ideal view of Northerners; neither in India nor in the South do the principles of American democracy apply. He assimilates the two on the basis of the fact that they both share the characteristics of any society in which there are *approved* social disparities, for these are enough to place it at that extreme of his continuum and permit it to be contrasted with the northern United States where such disparities are *disapproved*. This observation of similarities and differences is undoubtedly useful in a preliminary approach to a field of data, but a scientific definition is not constructed in this way. A random selection of resemblances must be placed in an ordered relationship and the degree to which a characteristic is present or absent (if this is part of the definition) must be susceptible to measurement. The traits indicative of this characteristic must not be selected arbitrarily. They must be related to it necessarily rather than accidentally.

Faced with the difficulty of constructing a coherent definition of caste, some authors have abandoned the search for 'diagnostic features' and have remained content with qualities to be estimated by the light of common sense, returning thus to the wisdom of Kroeber, whose final summing-up of the definition was 'a very rigid class system'; 'Castes are closed classes' (Kroeber 1948: 276). Such a definition makes it somewhat awkward to oppose the word to 'class', since it is already subsumed by it.

Long before the present debate commenced among the sociologists of India, the word 'caste' had been adopted by students of race relations in the United States. Robert Park was using it in the 1920s. He defined 'caste' as race relations within a single society: what were formerly racial elements became castes once they were merged together. Quoting Bouglé, he maintained that this was the essence and origin of caste in India. As such, caste relations between negroes and whites are to be contrasted with class relations which obtain among persons of the same colour. The difference between the two is not merely one of degree but of nature. It is to be noted that in regarding caste as race relations grown in, so to speak, Park differs from Kroeber, who sees them as class relations grown out into something more rigid through self-recognition. It is not easy to see how caste, if it is a matter of colour, could have been derived from class, but Kroeber was not apparently concerned with history in this instance, but rather with sociological classification. Both agreed, however, in applying the term to the colour-bar in the Southern States and in situating caste somewhere between class and race.

There was, no doubt, a need to define a type of relationship that differed from class relations and could be opposed to it, for while there are distinctions of class among both negroes and whites, relations between them are not of the same nature; their reciprocal attitudes respond to quite different criteria and enjoin quite different modes of conduct. Though the word used in an antique sense was already applied to the negroes even before the Civil War, its use by social scientists was inspired by the analogy with the Hindu system. It is not obvious why it was thought necessary to borrow from the ethnography of India to refer to an institution that already possessed its own vocabulary in the ethnography of the United States, except that it was considered by Park as belonging to the class of 'race relations within a single society' and in this it was similar to India, he thought. The popularity of the usage depended upon more than this, however: both 'colour' and 'race', the terms used in the United States, were felt to be unsuitable as theoretical concepts, for they both imply that the distinction has a foundation in objective fact, and the scholars who studied the question were bent on pointing out that this is not so, that the distinction has no scientific justification but rests upon prejudices which are 'undemocratic', unscientific, and iniquitous. Caste, on the other hand, was well known to be primitive, irrational, undemocratic, and devoid of scientific justification. Moreover it was believed that enlightenment would put an end to it as, in the view of all good liberals, it would put an end to discrimination.[11] It was therefore a most satisfactory term to contrast with class, which was recognized as a legitimate institution in its American form.[12] The profound reasons for adopting it were moral rather than heuristic. It was nevertheless critized also 'because of its connotations of invariability and accommodation' (Myrdal 1962: n. 2.1222) by those writers who feared that such a usage would tend to perpetuate the system.

The distinction between colour and class hinges on the notion of social mobility, for, whereas class can be changed, colour cannot. This is the essential analytical distinction as well as the basis of the moral objections to the colour-bar of those who called it caste: the status attached to it is 'hereditary and permanent' because genetically transmitted. Equality of opportunity is denied. But heredity and permanence, though they appear to be the same in India and the United States and therefore justifiably assimilable, do not in fact carry the same significance within each system and it is the characteristic of the systems that we are concerned to establish before we can assimilate them. In the Indian case it is the principle of *social descent* which determines the system (hence the recognized rule of endogamy, qualified or not by a rule of hypergamy or hypogamy); in the American case the determinant principle is *genetic transmission*, since colour is what counts and those who are physically able to 'pass' can do so – at the sacrifice of their familial ties. As Dumont (1967) has pointed out, hierarchy and stratification are not the same phenomenon.

Though endogamy has been stressed by almost all[13] those who wish to use the word caste to define the colour-bar it is questionable whether this criterion is satisfied in the United States. Endogamy, as anthropologists normally use the word, refers to the custom of giving daughters in marriage (i.e. forming marriage alliances) within the group, whatever the group may be. Where daughters are not given but decide their marriage for themselves without thereby creating any alliance between groups of kin, it can hardly be said that endogamy is practised, since the necessary condition for such a custom is lacking. The 'endogamy' of the two North American 'castes' is not a rule within a system of marriage which restricts the alliance to a given social group, but simply the prohibition among the whites against acquiring a spouse who is coloured. The writers who regard the bar to intermarriage between negroes and whites as endogamy, rather than as an aspect of segregation, are committing the error of classifying together two phenomena that resemble each other on the level of appearances but whose nature is profoundly different. Indeed, were one to admit the term endogamy at all in modern Western society it would surely apply to marriage within a residential or occupational *group*, not within a phenotypical category. Empirically it is true that a prohibition exists in India against marrying a person of another caste, or in the U.S. a person of another colour, and that the infringement gives rise in either case to reactions which are similar, yet the significance of this fact is sociologically nil, since it rests on a misclassification. (Its psychological significance is another matter.) For this reason I propose to name this error 'the Empiricist Fallacy', since it results from a premature appeal to the 'facts'.[14] All that glitters is not gold, we are taught, but social scientists often seem indifferent to the lesson and to assume the utility of any classification based on a common characteristic.

The point is this: social phenomena are not isolates that can be identified independently of the system of which they are a function. They cannot be classified by accidental resemblances, but only on the basis of their relations within the society; the marriage prohibition which seems so straightforward a 'fact' in both instances is on closer examination not so; its sociological nature is quite different in the two cases and the resemblance between them must be counted, as things stand at present, as contingent. Had we a general theory of marriage that covered both societies based on kinship and modern industrial society it might be possible to devise a category that would include both 'facts', but while we have not it can only lead to error to do so.

To return to the social system in which this prohibition occurs; in Hindu society the individual's place is determined by the kin-group into which he is born; this is part of a subcaste and caste in whose collective status he participates. In the United States his place is determined by his appearance, which is due to his physical, not his social heritage; his status is not within a hierarchically ordered structure of communities of known persons, but as an individual within a class (in the logical sense of the word) of persons identified by their physique. For this reason, while it is possible for the same caste to have a different status from one place to another, colour is everywhere the same throughout the country. Where there happens to be a statistical correlation between physical feature and caste status in India, even if it should be perfect, this is contingent to the definition of caste, just as where there happen to be communities composed of groups of kin among whom a man lives, it is not this that makes him a negro. In fact, this is frequently the case, but negroes are negroes in the United States 'because' they are coloured, not 'because' they were born and bred as such and their culture reflects the fact. Indeed, negro style of speech, mentality, values, etc. have all been identified, but that a man may abandon them does not mean that he will not still be classed as a negro, nor does the adoption of a negro style of speech stop the 'white negroes' being classed as white. You cannot—to quote the most humourless joke in the literature on the coloured problem – resign from the coloured race, nor it might be added from the white race, but you can be expelled from your caste and reintegrated into it. The determining criterion is social allegiance in one case, physical appearance in the other, and this implies that the first is a collective status, the second an individual status. This difference reflects two quite different types of society: one structured in corporate groups, the other the open society; the one organized throughout by the principle of caste, the other inspired by the concern with individual worth. This is the basis of the distinction, fundamental in the thought of Dumont (1966: 300–1), between *Homo Hierarchicus* and *Homo Aequalis*, Western man, whose yearning for equality derives from an individualistic conception of mankind. The existence of a phenotypical distinction, determining membership of one or other of the two so-called 'castes', partially parallel systems of social stratification which are prevented from fusing into one by this distinction, poses a problem for the operation of the mechanism of social mobility upon which the social system of the United States is founded and a challenge to their ideological charter. Myrdal was right to choose the word 'dilemma' as the title of his study and to stress that it was above all a dilemma for white society. Caste structured Indian society down to the modern age, but colour discrimination, the physiological residue of a dismounted structure, that of a servile society, persists in modern America, defining the condition under which the system of social mobility can operate: that traces of servile descent should not be displayed by the socially successful.

We have established that the absence of social mobility is the most significant factor in the definitions of caste put forward by those who wish to include the southern United States. Moreover, there is much to be said in favour of such a criterion, since structures that permit a modification of social status have necessarily a quite different dynamic from those that do not. Whether or not this fact is sufficient to outweigh the objections to such a broad definition would depend upon the use which is made of it.

But were we to adopt this criterion there are two difficulties which must be overcome: no social structure can remain entirely stable, since change is inevitable; demographic and economic factors intervene to change the relationships of groups and individuals. There is therefore no society in which there is absolutely no social mobility at all. The attempts to improve their status of certain castes in India through what Professor Srinivas has called sanskritization has been amply documented, though, in conformity with the distinction already made, it is collective rather than individual social mobility that is aimed at here. Indians recognize that they can only improve their status collectively, they cannot become self-made men. Are we, then, to include both types of social mobility for the purpose of our definition? If so, there may be no society where mobility is lacking. If not, the degree to which status is collective becomes crucial. And in either case how are we to measure social mobility in order to place caste in cross-cultural perspective? Is it a question of the *number* of persons (or families?) who are recognized as socially mobile? or the *degree* to which they are mobile? The son of the private who becomes a field-marshal or the son of the peasant who becomes president is so undoubtedly, but if the first only becomes sergeant-major or the second only becomes a car-salesman? The attempt to reduce all the social activities of a society to a single scale which would permit such relative evaluations is already problematic even before we attempt to establish cross-cultural equivalences. The same profession can be evaluated in very different ways from one place to another, and in any case its standing changes from one generation to another in the same place. We might devise a prestige scale for each society, accepting the evaluations of the members themselves (supposing that they all agreed). But having once accepted their evaluation of their own social system, how do we make it comparable with others which use different criteria? In a society where all believed that they were equal there would be no social mobility, but if in one society we justified the opinion that differentiation was less than in another, the possibility of social mobility would be less; for a little would suffice to take one from the bottom to the top of the social hierarchy. It appears not to have been noticed that there is something logically antithetical between the ideals of equality and social mobility; each presupposes the absence of the other. And then, again, is social mobility to be measured uniquely in an upward direction? What about the downwardly socially mobile? Do they not count? What about the *'famille noble retombée en paysannerie'*? The two do not necessarily go together; for every peasant who becomes ennobled there is not necessarily a nobleman who declines, even though a total ranking order is always theoretically conceivable.

In the case of the United States, an additional factor can be invoked which goes far towards explaining the ideal of the self-made man and the attachment of the sociologists to the criterion of social mobility; the social structure of the U.S. has been developed for the past 100 years on the assumption that the population was constantly expanded by the immigration of foreigners, almost entirely into the lowest economic class. The result of this is that adaptation to the norms of the society which received them almost automatically involved upward social mobility, since their place in the lowest rank in American society was taken by more recent immigrants. The point could not be more clearly made than by the inscription on the Statue of Liberty: '. . . Give us your *poor* . . .' (my italics). Had the immigrants been wealthy the system would not have worked. It is not surprising, then, that the United States should be the extreme example of the ideology, common in greater or lesser degree throughout the modern West, that regards it as a good thing for individuals to be accorded social status according to their deserts, and therefore places a positive value on social mobility. Only there was it possible theoretically for everyone to be upwardly mobile.

In view of the difficulties we face when we attempt to provide an objective measure of social mobility that may be applied cross-culturally (and the questions asked above must surely show the arbitrary decisions that are involved in the attempt), we must ask ourselves whether the broad definition of caste does not delineate a residual category that we might define from a more objective standpoint as: a caste system is any system of social differentiation not inspired by the ideology of the modern West. At any rate we shall see that it is hard to find a common set of criteria for the definition of caste that will encompass not only India and the southern United States but also Latin America.

It is often difficult to know what is intended when we encounter the word 'caste' in Latin America. In Spanish the word *casta* may refer either to breeding, to a caste in the colloquial sense, to the *castas* of the colonial period or it may mean caste as a sociological phenomenon. Yet even when it is written in English, one may wonder whether the author intends simply to anglicize the term at the ethnographical level in order to avoid repeating a foreign word or whether he has a more analytical purpose. In many cases, deliberately or not, he accepts the word in the widest sense and applies it to any marked social discrimination. In that case the *castas* would rightly be called 'castes', and so would the modern distinction between Indians and those who are not. We must therefore examine the grounds for choosing a more or less restricted definition of the word in the light of the Latin American scene.

To begin with, this widest usage covers and even expands the sum of the senses to be found in the dictionary and the colloquial habits of modern speech. Its range is so great that it cannot be said to have any exact intension at all and is therefore analytically useless for the same reason that other popular terms are analytically useless. It then makes little sense to say (Tumin 1952: vii):

> 'While the general outlines of caste systems are similar in some degree wherever they are found, it is also true that there are numerous and important differences among them. An understanding of these differences, as well as the similarities, is essential to a true knowledge of castes. *Sound and genuinely comparable* [my italics] materials from a number of different caste systems are therefore needed.'

To know what can be classified as a caste system and can therefore be genuinely comparable we must have a definition and since Professor Tumin gives none, but simply asserts that in this village of Guatemala 'a caste system flourishes', it is impossible to decide on logical grounds what utility might be derived from the comparison he envisages. He was accepting the fact on the authority of his teacher, Professor Gillin. More prudent authors who were struck by the degree of the social differentiation between the two elements of the population of Central America, have often nevertheless hedged their bets and spoken of 'caste-like' in order to describe it.

Even though Tumin maintained in a later publication that the division into 'castes' in eastern Guatemala, the site of his study, was more marked than in the west of the country (Tumin 1956: 174–5), it is evident that Kroeber's definition of caste, if it were applied with any rigour, would exclude this case, and *a fortiori* the rest of Central America. For one cannot call these categories closed where the population is largely of mixed descent and where as many informants of the superior element 'would let their daughter marry into the other group' as 'would disinherit a child who married out' (Tumin 1952: 239–40). That the difference in social status is very great between indians and ladinos, no one would question, but the only definitions of caste that would include this instance are those of Park (race relations within a single society) and of Berreman in his most recent opinion, but not his definition of 1960.

Park's definition depends upon the meaning given to 'race relations', but unless one is to accept his interpretation of Bouglé and classify the castes of India as races, Hindu society must be said to be *not* a caste system (which looks anomalous in view of the history of the term, as anomalous as discovering that the Kwakiutl were not a 'potlatch society'). Berreman's later definition covers it approximately,[15] but one wonders what stratified society it can be taken to exclude. Certainly not Great Britain nor the eastern United States even without considering the negroes.

The diversity of usage is great in Latin American studies. It may be ranged as follows:

1. Those who accept the point of view of Gillin and Tumin uncritically, e.g. Reed (1964), Rosenblat (1954), and Harris (1964: 37) (though he underlines the difference between the United States and Latin America).
2. Those who accept the usage while showing signs of discomfort, either evading responsibility for it by putting it in quotes (Wagley, in Heath & Adams 1965) or by using the word 'caste-like' to show that it may not *really* be caste though it appears similar (Wagley, etc.).
3. Those who concede the usage but prefer to use another word. Beals prefers 'plural cultures', at least for Mexico, though 'the term (caste) has some applicability in Peru' (Heath & Adams 1965: 350).
4. Those who would reject the word altogether, save at the ethnographical level (Colby & van den Berghe, Bourricaud 1962: 65, Mörner 1967: 53).

While some writers employ the word more or less colloquially, and unreflectingly, others give it an implied analytical load and, while using it in other contexts, refuse it as a translation of the word *casta* where this applies to the castas of the seventeenth and eighteenth centuries in Latin America. Thus Van den Berghe (1967) tells us that 'they could be more accurately described as estates rather than castes'. Aguirre Beltrán (1963: 76, 275) suggests that sociologically considered they constitute '*una intercasta, un grupo social desheredado*', marginal men between the caste of Spaniards and that of Indians. Kubler and Fernandes, on the other hand, find the usage legitimate both in colonial and modern times, where they maintain it to be similar.

If we compare the nature of the distinction between indians and hispanics in Latin America with that between colours in the United States, we can see that the features which have been given most attention in justifying the similarity of the latter to Indian caste are not those which might do so in the former case. Social mobility is anything but lacking. Indeed, its extent is very impressive by any standards, especially in Mexico. At the time of Independence the Indians composed 60 per cent of the total population and the other 'castas', including the Spaniards, amounted altogether to only 40 per cent. In 1570 they had amounted only to 1·3 per cent (Van den Berghe 1967: 47). Today the indians are no more than 15 per cent; the hispanics are 85 per cent. Disregarding immigration and the differential rates of reproduction which would favour this tendency only before the eighteenth century, these differences are in the main due to social mobility, that is to say, to the number of persons who in one generation or more have passed from indian to hispanic status. One might say that in 150 years nearly half the population has been socially mobile. Let those who claim to be able to measure social mobility cross-culturally find a country with a comparable record – other than the United States, whose structure, as I have explained, is based upon the premise of universal social mobility. One can point to whole regions of Mexico which in one period or another have decided to change their ethnic identity and have done so successfully. Moreover, the two most powerful rulers of Mexico in the past century were both credited with being born indians.

The other feature which is frequently alluded to in stressing the similarity between Hindu caste and that of the deep South is the notion of pollution involved in contact with the inferior element. Though indians are commonly considered dirty by hispanics, no one is polluted by physical or even sexual contact nor by commensality, nor, in so far as it is possible to abstract ethnic status from class status, can it be said that there is any bar on intermarriage. To marry an indian is a

248

mésalliance because indians are considered socially inferior, but cases of such intermarriage abound and are accepted. Indians are separated from hispanics neither by religion (both believe themselves to be Catholic) nor phenotype (though indians commonly look 'indian' they are no less indian if they don't), but only by culture and social allegiance. Hence one finds everywhere persons whose ethnic affiliation is uncertain since they are in transition from one status to the other. If one wished to call this distinction caste one might say that the castes of Latin American are socially mobile and non-endogamous, open and fluid rather than closed and rigid, devoid of the notion of pollution and giving rise to no segregation. But having said that what remains as the concept of caste?

None the less, it should not be forgotten that there is one resemblance between indians and the castes of India which goes back to the original meaning of the word as 'breed' or 'tribe': they are organized in communities which possess collective identity (for this reason their phenotype is not a criterion of status). Moreover, there are even parts of Latin America where the different breeds are arranged hierarchically, for example in Oaxaca, where the social superiority of the Zapotecs over the Mixe or the Huave is clearly recognized. There is therefore the possibility of devising a definition of caste which would be not so all-embracing as to be useless and would yet include both the indians and the Hindus – but North America would be excluded. However, it would face other difficulties, for if the indians might be called castes by this definition one could not call the hispanics so, for they are not organized according to the same principles. In so far as racial background has significance among them, it is as individuals, and therefore phenotype takes on an importance that it does not have for indians; it does not provide a basis for segregation, as in the United States, but merely an indicator of social status, as among the coloured population of North America. Hispanic society is an open society where status is individual and therefore one can see that, following the distinction made above, Latin America is divided into a hispanic half, which constitutes a modern national state, and a number of indian communities, which are structured in accordance with a different principle, culturally distinct and marginal to it. Indeed, the Mexican government has founded its policy regarding the indians on the need to 'integrate' them into the national society. One might therefore question whether in the terms of Park's definition of caste we may here speak of 'race relations within a single society', for except in a physical sense it is not one; indians are not part of the social system in the way the negroes of the United States are, so that if we accept the criterion of a caste society as a total social system they would be classed as outcastes from it rather than castes, like the Eta of Japan or the gipsies (cf. Dumont 1967: 271–2). To confuse the two is to commit the Empiricist Fallacy. But this in turn poses the question of the extent of a social system. For wherever the indians are found they make up the majority of the population of the region, if not of the country. If, therefore, they are regarded as *not* part of hispanic society, they must be considered not as outcastes, but as a social system apart. We must then conclude that in Latin America we have not two societies but two social systems combined and economically interdependent within a single physical society.

I have outlined the theoretical difficulties involved in different attempts to provide an analytical definition of caste. Indian caste, and race relations in North America or Latin America, all involve relations of super- and subordination, but that is where their common characteristics end. Their principles of operation are different in each case and if they give rise at times to similarities of conduct this is due to the psychological reactions of those who find themselves in a superior or inferior status. It is common psychology, not common social structure, that produces them. A comparison of social structures must be concerned with the *elements* of social structure: hierarchy, authority, power, sanctity, the division of labour, the definition and solidarity of groups, the transmission of property, the rules of descent, etc., not with approximations to a stereotype, that is to say, a particular conjunction of features which may frequently be associated in fact but have no demonstrated necessary relationship to one another. The sterility of taxonomies based on stereotypes is evident: they contain no analytical definitions but classify at the level of ethnography. The Empiricist Fallacy is a fallacy because it neglects the first *démarche* of abstraction required as a preliminary to classification.

Is it then possible to provide the word caste with an analytical definition? Dumont does so (p. 269) '. . . caste exists only where this characteristic (disjunction between status and power) is present and we would like to classify under another heading all societies, even those constituted of permanent and closed status groups, which do not possess it.' As a key to the nature of Indian society this criterion could not be bettered, but it does not provide a category for a taxonomy of social systems such as those who have attempted to expand the term would wish, for Dumont finds that this criterion is missing in fact outside India: Swat and even Ceylon (p. 273) are excluded for caste proved 'non-exportable'. He is left, therefore, with a class of which there is only one known member and, though this fact detracts in no way from the analysis itself, it means that comparisons can only be made outside the category, that is to say, with systems which are recognized as not being caste systems; the cross-cultural comparison of caste is not possible. Caste is synonymous with the Hindu social system within which power and status are divorced. It is *sui generis*.

My conclusion is this: if by way of analytical definitions we can find none that is acceptable between Dumont's, which applies only to India (and is therefore hardly useful for taxonomic purposes), and Berreman's, which applies to any traditional system of social differentiation (and is therefore equally useless for the opposite reason), we should perhaps abandon the hope of using *caste, rather than the functions of which it may be constituted*, for the purpose of cross-cultural comparison and let it rest content in a humble station at the ethnographical level where it may without contradiction – since no comparison is here demanded – be used to denote the castes of the Hindus in India (*varna* or *jati* according to the writer's choice) or in Latin America the clans of the Guajira or the lineages of the Andes, or, in the seventeenth and eighteenth centuries, the breeds which were recognized as social statuses, or in nineteenth-century Yucatan the Indian tribes, their white rulers, and their *mestizo* overseers, and so forth, but not attempt to use it in cross-cultural comparison where it leads only to confusion, for as its history shows it is in fact, like *mana* and *tabu*, a heuristic parvenu that 'arrived' at the analytical level only thanks to the Empiricist Fallacy.

In employing the vocabulary of a past age which approved of distinctions of status and despised 'social climbers' I do not wish to imply that I myself do so – save in the case of words. For words and people are not the same. Nevertheless I may still perhaps be forgiven for borrowing the analogy of hyman descent in order to represent the history of the word 'caste'. In the place of the founding ancestor we may put the gothic root referred to by Corominas (KASTS, meaning a herd or a brood of nestlings). This produced the Iberian *casta* and the antique English usage of *caste* which predates the English occupation of India and was usually spelt without the 'e' until it was gallicized in the eighteenth century. It appears likely that the word *cast* in the sense of 'throw' is of the same stock, descended from a brother of the founding ancestor; it is given as characteristically Scandinavian in origin by Skeat. There is nothing surprising in this suggestion since we have other examples of progeny being represented as a projection into the future: the Latin synonym of the verb 'to cast', *jactare*, gives both 'rejeton' (a child or descendant) in French (Littré, sense 3), and 'ahechadura' (a clutch or nestful of chicks) in Spanish (*Diccionario de la Lengua Española de la Real Academia*, 18th ed., Madrid, 1956: 506). Once the British arrived in India they adopted the Portuguese word *casta* for the *caste* system and this form finally returned to England and usurped the place of its cousin, the old English word *caste* which had the sense of 'race, stock or breed (of men)' (*OED*, 1933). The lexicographers, like hack genealogists, have validated the lineage of the usurper giving him a noble (i.e. Latin) antecedence via the Portuguese, and exotic associations with the Hindus. From this was born the sociologists' usage whose claims to status I have examined.

Human beings are everywhere classified by their origins, however these may be conceived; the hypothetical point, geographical, genealogical, or temporal from which they are projected – might I say 'cast'? – into the present determines their status in it. Hence the distinction between societies where status is ascribed and those where it is achieved requires some reformulation, for status is first of all ascribed in all societies and in all it is modifiable in some degree over time. Some accept modifications of status more willingly than others. Modern America claims to welcome them, which explains perhaps the choice of the positively valued word 'achieved'. But there is no such thing as status which is uniquely achieved, for every individual receives a status before he is capable of achieving anything. His culture determines the rules of ascription and also those according to which it can be modified. Such rules change, however, in response to the demands of the social structure. That the word meaning originally offspring and hence breed should have passed through such a series of transformations as the word caste shows us how wide is the range of possible interpretations that secure the transmission of status from one generation to the next.

The doctrine of purity of blood in Spain, though it had roots in the Christian notion of hereditary sin, was only elaborated in the social struggle between the 'old' and the 'new Christians' (Sicroff, 1960). While the Iberian peninsula was shared between three 'races', defined essentially by religion, the problem of purity was hardly posed. It only became a problem with the conversions, especially of Jews, to the Catholic faith and their accession to power in the burgeoning modern state of Renaissance times. This was the outcome of the transformation of a plural society which accepted its diversity into a singular one demanding ethnic unity. Logically indeed, breed can be seen as pure only in opposition to impure, i.e. 'tainted' by an extraneous element of descent, not to a different breed. *Casta* became a matter of purity only when the loyalty of members of the upper class could be impugned through the implications of their heterodox antecedence.

In Asia and America the social structures were entirely different from the Iberian Peninsula and the word *casta* found fresh applications in those lands. In the sense of descent group it fitted the caste system of India which also happened to entertain notions of purity and pollution, albeit very different ones from the Portuguese. In America the empire remained a plural society and the significant categories of breed were derived, not from the orthodoxy of ancestors, but from the percentage of them who belonged to one race or another. (At the top of the social hierarchy, moreover, the Spanish rulers invoked a different principle altogether – place of birth rather than purity of descent – to maintain their exclusiveness from the colonial-born *criollos*.)

Each age and land has visited its anxieties upon the word caste, which has passed down from Covarrubias to Tumin via the nineteenth-century administrators of the Indian Empire who aspired to become a 'ruling caste' and the American social scientists who reconciled their egalitarian ideals with the inequalities of status in their own country by stigmatizing the colour-bar as something barbarous and alien. Recognition that a word that in origin meant no more than offspring should have done so much heavy, if unrecognized, duty in the cause of one ideology or another should surely incline the anthropologist to prudence in the choice of his analytical vocabulary, especially when the transmission of status is at issue, for our deepest and least willingly admitted assumptions relate to that.

NOTES

1. For example, the Larousse *Dictionnaire de la Philosophie* asserts (translated into English) 'the notion of "potlatch society" is often evoked by sociologists to designate the primitive state of society where goods are exchanged directly and not through the intermediary of money'. At the

time of the first descriptions of the potlatch the Indians of the Northwest Coast were already using currency and the economic function of the potlatch was, not exchange, but the conversion of surplus (whale-oil, blankets, slaves) into prestige. The most important objects conveyed as reciprocal gifts were heraldic coppers which were also broken, burned, and thrown into the sea. Even in the field of kinship terminology, the utility of borrowed models has been questioned: do the Crow really have a 'Crow' terminology?

2. The adjective *casto* (fem. *casta*) meaning chaste, from the Latin *castus*, appears to be a homonym, which Covarrubias was attempting to put forward as the etymology of the word *casta*.

3. For a discussion of the terms, see Lévi-Strauss (1966, Ch. IV).

4. Cf. Van den Berghe (1967: 58), see also Mörner (1967).

5. I have discussed this analogy in detail elsewhere (Pitt-Rivers 1967).

6. It appears to have been the fate of the New World to become confused with India, not only in the attribution of identity to its inhabitants, but in the analysis of their social structure: the sociologists of the twentieth century repeat the error of Columbus.

7. According to Corominas (1961), the word existed previously in English from the same root and in the same sense as *casta*. It has, however, been supplanted by the Indian usage, and the *Oxford English Dictionary* gives the Portuguese as the etymology of the word.

8. Cf. Leach (1960: 1–2); Barth (1960); and a critique of this in Dumont (1966: 263–5).

9. Most recently in the pages of *Contributions to Indian Sociology*.

10. The necessary condition for an adequate definition for cross-cultural comparison is that it should be given its intension in terms of structure, not culture.

11. Dollard (1949): 'I believe that Americans instinctively hate the caste system and will not too long abide it.' Cf. also Myrdal (1962: 667–9 and n. 1223).

12. American liberals have usually shown a certain ambivalence towards the question of class distinction, which is also subject to the accusation of being undemocratic. But it was above all a rigid class system such as was believed to exist in Europe that was subject to this accusation, not the fluid system of the U.S., which offered equality of opportunity to every immigrant (it was believed). The ideal of the self-made man and the supposedly high degree of social mobility purified the American class system of the moral taint of inegalitarianism. Indeed, without some stratification, there could be no social mobility; the self-made man could not exist if there were nowhere to make it to.

13. Berreman in fact drops this from a later definition (in press), in favour of

the criterion of ascription by birth: '. . . a common means of guaranteeing this status is by prescribing endogamous marriage in the caste, and assigning the child the caste affiliation of its parents. But this method is by no means universal even in India, for caste, like kin-group affiliation, can be assigned unilineally or according to other, more complex, rules based on birth.' It can be seen, then, that his objections to making endogamy an essential criterion for the definition of caste are not at all the same as my reasons for questioning whether it is met in the United States.

14. Reference is intended not to empiricism in the philosophical sense but to the general sense of the word empirical—'that is guided by mere experience, without knowledge of principles' (*OED*).

15. 'A caste system occurs where a society is made up of birth-ascribed groups which are hierarchically ordered and culturally distinct. The hierarchy entails differential evaluation, rewards and association' (Berreman 1966: 4).

REFERENCES

AGUIRRE BELTRAN, GONZALO 1963 *Medecina y Magia*. Mexico: I.N.I.
— 1967 *Regiones de Refugio*. Mexico: I.N.I.

BARTH, FREDRIK 1960 The System of Social Stratification in Swat, North Pakistan. In Leach, E. R. (ed.), *Aspects of Caste in South India, Ceylon and Northwest Pakistan*. Cambridge Papers in Social Anthropology No. 2. Cambridge: Cambridge University Press.

BERREMAN, G. D. 1960 Caste in India and the U.S. *American Journal of Sociology* **66**: 120.
— in press Stratification, Pluralism and Interaction, A Comparative Analysis of Caste.

BOURRICAUD, FRANCOIS 1962 *Changements à Puno: Etudes de Sociologie Andine*. Paris: Institut des Hautes Etudes de l'Amérique Latine.

COHEN, MORRIS, & NAGEL, ERNEST 1964 (reprinted) *An Introduction to Logic and Scientific Method*. London.

COLBY, B. & P. VAN DEN BERGHE 1961 Ethnic Relations in Southeastern Mexico. *American Anthropologist* **63** (4): 772–92.

COROMINAS, JOHN 1961 *Breve diccionario etimológico de la lengua castellana*. Madrid: Gredos.

COVARRUBIAS HOROZCO, SEBASTIAN DE 1611 *Tesoro de la lengua castellana o española*. Madrid.

DOLLARD, JOHN 1949 *Caste and Class in a Southern Town*. New York: Harper. 3rd edn, New York: Doubleday (Anchor), 1957.

DUMONT, LOUIS 1966 *Homo Hierarchicus; essai sur le système des castes* Paris: Gallimard.

EVANS-PRITCHARD, E. E. 1965 *Theories of Primitive Religion*. Oxford: Clarendon Press.

FERNANDES, FLORESTAN 1967 The Weight of the Past. *Daedalus* (Spring).

HARRIS, MARVIN 1964 *Patterns of Race in the Americas*. New York: Walker.

HEATH, D. B. & R. N. ADAMS (eds.) 1965 *Contemporary Cultures and Societies of Latin America: a Reader in the Social Anthropology of Middle and South America and the Caribbean*. New York: Random House.

KROEBER, A. L. 1948 *Anthropology*. 2nd ed. New York: Harcourt Brace.

— 1937 Caste. *Encyclopaedia of the Social Sciences*. New York: Macmillan.

KUBLER, GEORGE A. 1952 *The Indian Caste of Peru, 1795–1940: A population study based upon tax records and census reports*. Washington: Smithsonian Institution.

Larousse *Dictionnaire de la Philosophie* 1964 Paris.

LEACH, E. R. 1960 Introduction: What Should We mean by Caste? In Leach, E. R. (ed.), *Aspects of Caste in South India, Ceylon, and Northwest Pakistan*. Cambridge Papers in Social Anthropology, No. 2. Cambridge.

LÉVI-STRAUSS, C. 1966 *The Savage Mind*. London: Chicago: University of Chicago Press.

MÖRNER, MAGNUS 1967 *Race Mixture in the History of Latin America*. Boston: Little, Brown.

MYRDAL, GUNNAR 1962 *An American Dilemma: The Negro Problem and Modern Democracy*. New York: Harper.

PITT-RIVERS, JULIAN 1967 Race, Color and Class in Central America and the Andes. *Daedalus* (Spring).

REED, NELSON 1964 *The Caste War of Yucatan*. Stanford: Stanford University Press.

ROSENBLAT, ANGEL 1954 *La población indígena y el mestizaje en América*. Vol. II. Buenos Aires: Editorial Nova.

SICROFF, ALBERT A. 1960 *Les Controverses des statuts de pureté de sang en Espagne du XVᵉ au XVIIᵉ siècle*. Paris: P.U.F.

TUMIN, MELVIN M. 1952 *Caste in a Peasant Society: a Case Study in the Dynamics of Caste*. Princeton, N.J.: Princeton University Press.

— 1956 Cultura, casta y clase en Guatemala. *Integración Social en Guatemala*. (Seminario de Integ. Soc.)

VAN DEN BERGHE, PIERRE 1967 *Race and Racism*. New York: Wiley.

The Symbolic Role of Cattle in Gogo Ritual

PETER RIGBY

In this paper, I present an analysis of one aspect of the religion of the Gogo people of central Tanzania, East Africa.[1] My approach may appear at first sight to differ radically from Evans-Pritchard's treatment of a very similar problem in Nuer religion (Evans-Pritchard 1953, 1956), but my debt to him will be obvious in the following pages. Because of this, I begin with a brief discussion of Evans-Pritchard's statement of the 'identity', in symbolic terms, of men and cattle in Nuer religion.

I

Evans-Pritchard agrees with other writers on the Nuer that their religion is 'centred in the cow', and that Nuer values about cattle 'may almost be called religious'. But he quickly corrects the false impression created by these statements by emphasizing that 'there is . . . no evidence at all that cattle are venerated or in themselves are in any way regarded as guardian spirits . . .' (1956: 249). He does, however, take seriously the Seligmans' assertion that 'it is difficult to describe [the importance of Nuer cattle] to their masters or the love and care the latter have for their beasts, but it is certainly no exaggeration to say that it amounts to what psychologists would term "identification"' (Seligman 1932: 169; Evans-Pritchard 1956: 249).

This concept of 'identification', central in Evans-Pritchard's analysis, is both its strength and its weakness. It is not an easy concept to handle, particularly in the light of recent studies; and one must be prepared to become involved in technical psychoanalytic arguments. For example, he asks why Nuer men 'identify' themselves with oxen, by taking ox-names, rather than with bulls, and he leaves the question unresolved:

'The commonsense answer is that Nuer castrate all but a very few of their bulls, so that there would not be enough entire animals to go round, and this may be the right explanation' (Evans-Pritchard 1956: 254).

Peter Rigby

This kind of vagueness in Evans-Pritchard's discussion of cattle symbolism in Nuer religion has led, on the one hand, to very stimulating explorations of structural problems related to psychoanalytic interpretations (cf. Beidelman, 1966, 1968), and, on the other, to somewhat dubious psychoanalytic arguments based on Western clinical parallels (for example, Hayley 1968), or, in quite a different vein, to 'common-sense' explanations such as that of Schneider (1967; cf. Beidelman 1967).

The problem I wish to take up here is related to the question of 'identification', but not specifically to the question of 'why oxen'; although the different contexts in which oxen appear as opposed to other animals is an important part of the data. Instead, I examine in more general terms the significance of cattle, as a category of domestic animal, in Gogo religious belief and practice. As other domestic stock frequently take the place of cattle, other 'equations' must also be discussed, but these are subsidiary to the main problem. But first, one or two other points in Evans-Pritchard's analysis must be stated.

Apart from the idea of 'identification', Evans-Pritchard addresses himself to a problem which, to my mind, is far more important: that is, cattle (oxen) are a 'means of communication with the spiritual world'. This is clearly in keeping with Hubert and Mauss's classic analysis of the 'nature and function of sacrifice' (Hubert and Mauss 1898, trans. 1964: 97 *et passim*), and it is this point that I wish to develop in this paper.

In his first exposition of the problem, Evans-Pritchard states that this communication is achieved *through* identification (1953):

'. . . the ox a father gives his son at initiation provides him, through what Professor Seligman calls 'Identification' with it, with a direct means of communication with the spiritual world.'

Significantly (in 1956: 252), he omits the subsidiary clause, and leaves open the problem of how the communication is achieved. He still mentions 'ox-names' as providing 'the most striking example of, and evidence for, what Professor Seligman speaks of as "identification",' but it is no longer the basis of the communication with the spiritual world attained through oxen. I rather labour this point, because I suggest that Evans-Pritchard is not really concerned to explore what *he* means by 'identification', leaving the matter to Seligman's usage. Hence it may be assumed that oxen achieve communication between men and the spiritual world through processes other than 'identification', whatever the latter may mean. Evans-Pritchard does not really tackle this problem in sufficient depth, although he makes 'communication' the major conclusion in both the 1953 and 1956 versions (1956: 271):

> 'When . . . we seek to estimate what their cattle are to Nuer and how they see them, we have to recognize that they are the means by which men can enter into communication with God, that they are, as Father Crazzolara puts it, "the link between the perceptible and the transcendental".'

Note that it is 'cattle' as a general category, not specifically oxen, which are the means of communication. Bcidelman, as I have noted, has explored the problem of 'why oxen?' (1966), although he also considers why non-oxen are used in certain contexts, for example, mortuary rituals. In analysing the Gogo material here, I retain the broader concern of 'why cattle?' despite the fact that oxen feature most commonly in Gogo sacrifice.

II

Gogo society, like that of the Nuer, is best described as 'semi-pastoral'. There are very few 'purely' pastoral societies anywhere in the world, and the majority of those peoples called pastoralists in fact subsist to some degree upon the cultivation of grain crops, other economic activities, or the exchange of livestock for other commodities. Despite this, their cultural values frequently revolve around cattle or other livestock, and they possess what has been called 'the cattle complex' (Herskovits 1926; Schneider 1959; cf. Rigby 1967b, 1969, and in press). The Gogo are no exception.

The Gogo are a Bantu-speaking people who subsist primarily upon the cultivation of sorghums, bulrush millet, and maize, in a comparatively harsh environment (Rigby 1967b, 1969). They have herds of cattle, sheep, and goats, and although many homestead heads may no longer own large herds, they usually have some access to the products of livestock, for example through the trusteeship arrangements (*kukoza*) common among affines, kin, and neighbours. Middle-aged and elderly homestead heads, at the peak of their prestige and with homesteads at the point in their developmental cycle when they are largest, usually have big herds in their byres, as well as animals loaned out to trustees. Herds of sixty to two or three hundred are common, although the average herd is about eleven head.

259

The products of Gogo herds, milk, meat, blood, and fat, may not form a very large part of the Gogo diet; but they are, in fact, frequently consumed and are certainly the most valued foods. Other products, such as dung, urine, and hides are also important and appear frequently in ritual contexts. As is common with many other peoples, Gogo kill cattle (or sheep and goats) only in the context of sacrifice; but in most neighbourhoods, sacrificial occasions are very frequent. The products from animals which have died from 'natural causes' or disease are used, but these products belong to an entirely different category from those of animals which have been killed, i.e. sacrificed.

My main concern will be with the context of sacrifice. But in order to place the symbolic significance of cattle in the broader field of 'positional' meanings (Turner 1962, 1964) and so complete the picture, I also examine the ritual use and symbolic associations of some of the 'products' of cattle. The verbal associations which Gogo make concerning cattle are extended to their products, and this extension must be taken into account.

In everyday usage, Gogo frequently refer to people by terms relating to livestock, particularly cattle. This may occur in the normal use of certain kinship terms, as when a man and his wife's father address each other as *wandawo*, 'heifer', a term derived from Masai *entawuo*, 'heifer' (Rigby 1967b, 1969). This does not imply any 'identification' of in-laws with heifers! It merely conveys the idea that the two men have been in an exchange transaction involving heifers.

In other contexts, cattle terms used for people may carry a much more direct association of meaning between the category of person and the class of animal. Thus, young men may be referred to as 'bulls' (*zinghambaku*), as in the context of hoeing a field in a work party. Here, the reference is not simply 'customary usage', but relates the categorical opposition between the sexes to other binary pairs: in this case the oppositions between 'wild, uncultivated' on the one hand, and 'domesticated, cultivated' on the other, the former being associated with men, the latter with women (Rigby 1966a: 8). But men are never referred to by terms used for oxen or steers. Women are referred to by other cattle terms. For example, a woman who has had more than three children may affectionately be called '*mbuguma*' in conversation, *mbuguma* being a cow which has calved three times.[2]

Usages such as these are not elaborated any further, and may be taken as a general property of their cattle culture rather than as an aspect of the exegetical elaboration of symbolic meaning. Gogo do not have cattle songs as do many pastoral peoples, including the Baraguyu who live among the Gogo and other neighbouring Bantu peoples (Beidelman 1965). Cattle are sometimes praised for their beauty, and men may feel particularly attached to certain animals in their herds. But this does not prevent these animals from being given in bridewealth or other transactions.

Although cattle are 'men's business', they do not belong exclusively to the domain of men in actual control, use, and deployment. The homestead herd symbolizes the status and authority of the homestead head (*munyakaya*) as well as patrilineal inheritance and descent (Rigby 1967b, 1969). Each married woman, however, has certain rights in a part of her husband's herd. She uses the products of particular milch-cows which have been allocated to her 'house' (*nyumba*), and her sons inherit only 'house' animals; they have no rights in the beasts allocated to the houses of their paternal half-siblings. The calves belonging to a particular wife's part of the herd, and her small stock, are kept at night in the outside room (*ikumbo*) of her own wing of the homestead, separate from the animals allocated to the other wives. The task of milking cows belong to women, and they take the fresh milk to feed their own children. They make some into thick sour milk (*mhopota*) or skimmed sour milk (*masuce*), which their husbands and visitors may drink. The butterfat removed from milk is used almost exclusively by women, and they may occasionally sell it for petty cash.

Hence, although in jural terms men own and control cattle and other livestock, women have an important role in their use and deployment. Women therefore have certain rights in livestock, which can be upheld legally. These rights are not extinguished by the death of a husband, for, although a woman's sons inherit the herd, they cannot divide it up without her permission or until her death.

In ideal or categorical terms, however, cattle and their welfare are the concern of men. Control of the health and fertility of the herds is solely in the hands of men. Women intrude upon this domain only in specific ritual circumstances, and only because in these contexts role-reversal is the central symbolic component (see Rigby 1968a for a detailed analysis of such rituals).

III

The Gogo have a number of myths about the 'origin' of cattle and their relationship with men. It is essential to examine some of these myths before proceeding to a discussion of the symbolic role of livestock in ritual. I present two versions of these myths, the first a rather matter-of-fact, sparse one.

> Cattle used to be very numerous. They used to be wild animals (*nimu*), wild animals which lived in the bush. They used, in fact, to be buffalo (*mbogo*). One day, Cow heard the lion roar, and when it heard this, it fled to the homesteads of men, and went in. From then on these animals were known as 'cattle' (*ng'ombe*); but they are really just the same as the buffalo.

The elements of this rather bare tale may be expressed thus: (a) both men and 'cattle' existed before, but the latter were 'wild', 'things of the bush' (*nimu*) as opposed to 'things of the homesteads' (*mitugo*, the generic term for all domestic livestock, except the donkey). They originally had another form, and were 'buffalo'.[3] (b) They were frightened by the fiercest of all wild animals, the lion. (c) They fled to men for protection, and thence became 'cattle'. But they are still 'buffalo' in a sense; they therefore have an ambiguous identity, both 'domesticated' and 'wild'.

The second myth is more complex, and I summarize it here. I do not intend to compare the various versions of these myths in detail, in order to lay bare their structure (Lévi-Strauss 1962, 1963: 206–231 *et passim*, 1964, 1967a, 1967b, 1968, etc.). My concern in this context is rather to extract its basic symbolic message and relate this to the other contexts, particularly ritual contexts, in which cattle appear.[4]

> A divorced [or a 'widowed'] woman[5] was chased from the homesteads of men, banished from human society. The person wandered in the bush, and she had a male child. They met a lion and were very afraid. But the lion told the person not to be afraid, and asked her to nurse its children while it was out hunting. She agreed, and the lioness fed her while she did this, for a whole month.
>
> One day, a hyena came along and approached the person on the pretext of borrowing fire, for, it said, the rain was so heavy where it lived that the fire was always going out.[6] In taking the fire from the shelter that the human being had built, the hyena noticed the lion's children. Over a period of time, by playing upon the person's complete naïvety, the hyena eventually ate all the lion's children.

Realizing the possible consequences of her situation, the human being fled the lion's place with her child. They met many herds of animals in the bush, the hyenas themselves, the sable antelope, and they asked them all for help. But once the human beings said that they had a debt with lion (*cina mugawa na simba*), all the animals refused. Once the zebra heard the human's story, they protected her by placing her in the middle of the herd.

The lion traced the person there and asked for her, because the person had 'finished' its children. The zebra refused to give her up, saying that the person had sought refuge with them, so the human being was 'theirs'. The lion summoned its fellows and the lions and the zebra fought, the one lot biting, the other kicking. The lions were defeated.

The person was saved, and asked the zebra what they would like in turn. The zebra said they wanted nothing but a good place to graze. So the person took them to a great grass pan where there was unlimited, luscious grass, and the zebra were satisfied and told the person to 'return to her place'.

The person and her child set off to return the way they had come, both of them together. They slept at night in the bush, and one morning, when they came to the forest near their country, they came across a large wild animal sleeping, with its child nearby. The person first thought that it was a lion. But the beast woke up, came to look at the human being, then went back to its child. The person saw that it was harmless, so approached its offspring, thinking that she would take it home and care for it. She picked it up and carried it, the mother following along. When the person stopped, the beast stopped; but it did nothing to her. So they arrived at the homesteads.

The woman's fellow-humans said, 'Is that not what-ever-her-name-is who left here long ago? But what does she have?' She told them that it was her 'great wild animal' (*ilimu lyakwe*) which she had come across in the bush.

So she kept it for some time, until other similar beasts came in from the bush, the first being a male. The female's udders flowed with milk, and the person also began to drink it. Many more animals came in from the bush, she began to milk them every day; and she even saw how nice the milk was when it thickened. The person then began to share it with her fellow-human beings, who liked it. She said, 'These are cattle'. They began to reproduce. That is where they came from. Long ago, people did not have them.

The content of this myth may be expressed as follows. A woman (man?) is divorced (bereaved?) and rejected, with her child, by society. Whatever the alternatives, affinity is destroyed, and 'community' rejected (cf. Rigby 1968b). She is afraid of the bush and the animals, but the fiercest of them befriends her. She lives with lion, the most unambiguous symbol of the 'wild', caring for its offspring. But in her ignorance of the wild, she is duped by hyena, the most evil animal. Hyena is also considered to have ambiguous qualities: sexually hermaphrodite and an eater of carrion (cf. Beidelman 1961, 1963a). As a consequence, human being is rejected by all the animals except zebra, the 'wild animal' considered by the Gogo to be most friendly to men. Thus human being, having been associated with the 'most wild', lion, is now transferred to the care of an animal 'closer' to culture and human society, a game animal, zebra (cf. Leach 1964; and below). Furthermore, in the conflict between zebra and lion, zebra wins: a reversal of the normal consequences of unmediated, 'wild', conflict. Human being is saved, reciprocates, and is set on her way back to human society. Just as she is about to leave the bush and re-enter the cultural domain, she acquires man's most valuable possession. This possession ensures her reacceptance.

Cattle are again 'of the bush' but also 'of human society'; they retain their ambiguous quality of being associated with both the wild and the domesticated. Although the sex of the human being involved is not clear, the general burden of the myth is that it is a woman. Both the ambiguity in the beginning, as well as the emphasis on the feminine role, are deliberate and important. The 'person' in the story represents 'humanity' in general, versus the wild, as well as women as a category opposed to men. Cattle and women establish community, the former through being exchanged by men for women in bridewealth transactions. The equation is:

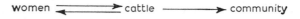

women ⇄ cattle ⟶ community

But there is another reason which I consider later. For the time being, I note that one aspect of the myth implies that a woman brought cattle to society, a reversal of what one would expect from Gogo categories in general. In mundane circumstances, cattle are 'men's business'.

IV

Gogo rituals may conveniently be classified into 'domestic' or 'private' rituals, and 'public' or 'communal' rituals. The distinction is not rigid; what are essentially domestic rituals may take on a public character in certain circumstances, and vice versa. Domestic rituals concern mainly the 'spirits of the dead' (*milungu*) or close kinsmen and affines, while communal rituals are concerned with the spirits of Gogo rituals leaders, who may influence the welfare of the whole ritual area (*yisi*, see Rigby 1966b, 1967b, 1968a, 1969). In each complex of rituals, the symbolic associations evidenced are somewhat different, and they are better treated separately.

Gogo have a notion of some 'power' or 'being' beyond, and greater than, the spirits of the dead. This notion is most frequently embodied in the concepts 'Cizuwa', which conveys certain qualities of the sun (*izuwa*), and 'Licanzi', about which I could find out very little (cf. Jellicoe 1967). Another mystical entity is 'Maduwo', a 'being' of uncertain sex but sometimes explicitly female. Maduwo is associated with whirlwinds and is said to carry off disobedient children. There are many stories about Maduwo, but also a great deal of scepticism. Gogo usually dismiss these stories as relating imaginary events which only happen to someone else, at a distant place, never to oneself or to one's kin, friends, and neighbours.

Neither Cizuwa nor Maduwo are, to my knowledge, ever invoked or have sacrifices made to them. They are remote, otiose. They do constitute one aspect of 'the other world', but do not directly intervene in the affairs of this world; and so they do not concern the Gogo (or us) very much.

The central postulate of Gogo religious belief is that there is a fundamental dichotomy and opposition between the 'world of the living' and the 'world of the dead'. Although Gogo have an ideology of patrilineal descent, the spirits of the dead (*milungu*) are not ordered into patrilineal categories, and Gogo do not conceptualize lineages as extending from one world to the other. Maternal and affinal *milungu* are as frequently invoked as any other category (Rigby 1969), although the *milungu* of one's father are the most important, and genealogical memory is normally greater on the patrilateral side. A crucial point is that the concept of *milungu* is always generalized; the idea of 'one *mulungu*' is not expressed in Gogo religious belief, although the term *mulungu* is now used for the Christian god (cf. Kiswahili *Mungu*). A person cannot have 'one spirit', only 'spirits'. An elder explained it this way:

> A person has many *milungu*; even when he dies, he has many *milungu*. So even if one name of a kinsman is selected as being the one who is interfering in the affairs of the living, one says 'The spirits of so-and-so have spoken' (*milungu ya nhendu yalonga*).

One contacts the whole 'world of the spirits' through sacrifice to the name, or set of names, of any dead kinsmen or kinswomen, as I show later.

A person does not enter the world of the spirits merely by death. Children and those who die unmarried and childless cannot achieve this entry, nor can people who die in certain ways. Traditionally, the bodies of those who were killed by lightning (*imuli*) or who died of contagious (*lona*) diseases were not buried, but thrown into the bush or left in the hollow trunks of baobab trees (*mipela*).

In order to achieve entry into the category *milungu*, one has to have descendants. It is one's heirs that give one a 'homestead', i.e. a gravestone. Gravestones (*vitenjelo*, sing. *citenjelo*) are called the 'homestead' (*kaya*) of the *milungu*, and most important sacrifices should take place at them, although this is not necessary for the large number of minor sacrifices. The noun *citenjelo* is derived from the verb *kutenga*, which is to place a pot of food on the ground so that a person may eat. The verb is used only for placing a *food* or *beer* pot in position: thus, '*unhenjeleje wugali*', 'put the food pot down so that I may eat'. Placing another container in the same position, such as a calabash, would require another verb, *kutuula*. *Citenjelo*, therefore, is the 'place where food is given' to the spirits of the dead.

The *milungu* are thus 'of the other world', but closely linked with the living world both by their recognition and constant propitiation, and by their constant interference in its affairs. The *milungu* of women are just as frequently involved in ritual situations as are the *milungu* of men. Another category of spirits, the 'evil spirits of the bush' (*masoce*), are feared, and Gogo have many stories about them; but they are never considered in any actual contexts to have interfered with the world of the living. They are relegated to the same sort of category of belief as is Maduwo.

Milungu interfere in the world of the living in a variety of ways. They make babies cry excessively to force the parents to give their babies particular names. They cause all sorts of minor accidents and even some major illnesses, although the latter are more usually thought to be caused by witchcraft and sorcery. The particular *milungu* involved in any case, and the reason for the mishap, are established by divination.[7]

When a child cries for the name of a particular ancestor, the name must be given with the gift of a goat or a heifer. A friend of mine explained:

The Symbolic Role of Cattle in Gogo Ritual

When a child cries for a name (*yalilila litagwa*), it is the diviner who tells the parents that the child has been 'troubled' (*yasinwa*) by a particular ancestor, so-and-so. He tells them that they must give the name to the child, with the gift of a goat. So they take the goat, cut a piece of skin from its ear, and tie this on the child. They also give the child the goat, which will be his from then on. When they are tying the piece of skin on the child, they call the names of the *milungu*, particularly the one which has affected the child.

One case of 'spirit-naming' involved the gift of a heifer:

Lubeli's young baby was burned by boiling water. Lubeli went to a diviner who told him, 'It is the angry spirits [*malungu*: the change of prefix from *mi-* to *ma-*, and therefore change of noun-class, denotes evil, angry, spirits] of your grandfather and his son's wife's father who have caused this. They want honey beer [*nghangala*, often used in sacrifice: see below] and they want you to cut the ear of a heifer and give their names to your child. And that heifer must become the property of the child'.

This, of course, does not involve the sacrifice of the animal; only the beer is sacrificed. But the animal given as a gift is also an element in the propitiation of the *milungu*; a gift in such a context is, in a sense, 'consecrated' to the spirits.

In more critical circumstances, such as those of severe illness or accident, the diviner may also identify the *milungu* as the cause. Both men and cattle may equally be afflicted by the *milungu*, as the following case illustrates:

Conya, the son of Njoliba, had a beer sacrifice. He made this sacrifice because, some time before, he had fallen ill. He went to a diviner who told him, 'It is the spirits of your "grandfathers and grandmothers",[8] they want "water" [i.e. sacrificial beer: see below] for they are "thirsty" (*wakaꞏuka*).' But Conya had become better without having the sacrifice, although he had promised it. Then all the children of his senior wife became ill, and the cattle began rejecting their calves, refusing to suckle them. So he went to another diviner who confirmed the first diviner's interpretation by 'catching' (*wakebata*) those same *milungu*. They were thirsty and wanted 'water'. So the sacrificial beer was prepared and given to the *milungu*, particularly Conya's paternal grandparents.

This again is beer sacrifice, although all major sacrifices should be cattle, mainly oxen, or small stock substituted for oxen. However, the frequency of relatively minor sacrifices is possible because beer is given. I discuss animal sacrifice in detail later; but even when beer is given, there are quite explicit associations with cattle, and between cattle and the *milungu*. Hence I describe beer sacrifice in detail.

v

Beer sacrifice (*wujimbi we misambwa*[9]) is the most usual way in which Gogo communicate with the dead. Beer given in sacrifice is not a substitute for an ox or other animal. It is a temporary, 'stop-gap' measure, and often an animal is promised to the *milungu* for a subsequent sacrifice. Thus, when Majima's son Mbalani, a young man of twenty-eight, contracted an eye complaint which troubled him for some time and seemed difficult to cure, his father held a beer sacrifice. Majima, his wife (Mbalani's mother), and others called on the *milungu* to cure Mbalani. For final emphasis, Majima poured beer a second time and said:

> Well father, here is your 'water', drink it together with your son's wife's parents [Mbalani's mother's parents], for I am still searching for your 'lung' [*lipupu lyenyu*: pieces of lung from sacrificial animals, together with liver, are given to the *milungu*: see below]. When I find it I will call you again.

In theory, therefore, animal sacrifice should follow. In practice, only very serious situations demand the sacrifice of an ox or other animal.

Beer for sacrifice must be specially prepared for the occasion, and the sacrifice must be held when the beer is exactly at the point when it is best. 'Second-day' beer (*majimbi ga mubitu*) is sour, and cannot be given to the *milungu*, nor can beer which is not fully matured. Further, it must be sacrificed in the early hours of the morning, just after sunrise and before the cattle have been driven out of the byre to pasture. The reasons for these procedures indicate the symbolic role of cattle in beer sacrifice.

There is an explicit association between the daily cycle of cattle-herding and the activities of the *milungu*. When I asked why beer sacrifices had to be held so early in the morning[10] one elder, very knowledgeable in ritual matters, told me:

> We sacrifice in the early morning because we say, 'The spirits of the dead are still asleep' (*milungu yikali yigonile*). If we wait until the sun has risen fairly high, we have allowed them to disperse; the spirits have left (*milungu yawuka*).

> If people delay then, early in the morning, they should wait until the evening, when the spirits have returned to the gravestones [and the cattle

have returned to the byre]. When the cattle go out to graze in the morning, the spirits have dispersed; they will not hear (*hodu milungu yeyagalai*; *siyohulika*).

A further explicit association is that between the sacrificial beer and the water given to cattle in troughs beside wells. I have noted that sacrificial beer can be, and usually is, in a ritual context, referred to as 'water' (*malenga*). Beer sacrifices are poured into a trough of mud or beer lees, made around a particular post in the homestead. The trough is called *mulambo*, the term used for troughs made near wells for watering cattle. This is not merely because *mulambo* is the generic term for all troughs in Cigogo; its use in the ritual context is deliberate and symbolic, as I show later.

As the officiant pours the beer into the trough, he calls the names of the *milungu* who have been identified for that occasion by a diviner. The officiant must be restrained by someone else, or he will pour all the beer away; one cannot be ungenerous to the *milungu*. Once the libation is complete, a breach is made in the trough so that the beer flows out in the direction from which the clan ancestors came. This breach is called *ideha*, which is the gate to the cattle byre, and therefore to the homestead.

The particular building post (*isumbili*) selected for the construction of the *mulambo* is one in the outside room (*ikumbo*) of the eastern wing of the homestead (*nyumba ye cilima*; see Rigby 1966a, 1967b, 1968a, 1969). This post is the architectural and ritual centre of the homestead, and is called *mhula ya kaya*, 'the nose of the homestead'. When a person is buried in the cattle byre to the west of this post, he lies with his head pointing eastwards, aligned with it. 'The nose of the homestead' is the physical locus of contact between the world of the living and the world of the dead in Gogo domestic rituals. It serves the same functions as the gravestones (*vitenjelo*). The only distinction is that, Gogo being a residentially mobile people (Rigby 1967b, 1969), a building pole which is also the 'nose of the homestead' is always available, wherever one has moved; the gravestone of one's father or other kinsman or affine may lie many miles away, its exact location forgotten in the tangle of memory and the regenerating bush.

These associations between cattle and *milungu* are admirably distilled in a statement made to me in discussion: 'Cattle drink at the troughs, and so do the spirits of the dead – together' (*Ng'ombe zikung'wera mumilambo, na milungu – hamonga*). Less expicitly, the behaviour of cattle is an indicator of the mood of the spirits, although the interpretation must still be verified by a diviner. This is a frequent occurrence, an example of which will suffice.

> Mugongo, a ritual leader, sacrificed both beer and a bull as a result of a serious omen: the cattle in his byre had been breaking out at night and running into the bush. He went to a diviner who told him that it was the *milungu* of his wife's parents who were responsible, and that he must hold a major sacrifice.

Why such behaviour in cattle is a portent of extremely serious misfortune will become evident as the analysis proceeds. Similarly, if wild animals like buck accidentally run into the cattle byre of the homestead ritual action must be taken. In this particular case, Mugongo sacrificed both bull and beer.

Although the interpretation is not explicit, the danger here clearly arises from the uncontrolled behaviour of cattle in their attempt to return to the wild at night. Cattle graze in the bush only during the day, in circumstances controlled by men. Their perverse behaviour in trying to go into the bush at night represents a confusion of categories, and hence ritual danger (cf. Douglas 1966). By the same logic, wild animal, in the byre signify the opposite confusion and hence ritual pollution (cf. Beidelman 1963b).

In all these contexts, there are explicit associations between men, cattle, and the spirits; there is no identification between them. Cattle provide, through these symbolic associations, a two-way means of communication. Their behaviour and afflictions can indicate the mood of the *milungu* to men; and the *milungu* are propitiated through the manipulation of the symbolic associations of cattle: an idea further elaborated to accommodate beer sacrifice. It is the health and prosperity of men and their children that are primarily at stake, although the welfare of livestock is also involved. Because cattle as a category already 'bridge' one boundary of classification, that between nature and culture as expressed in their myth of origin, they can also provide the link between men and the *milungu*: they are symbolically associated with both. I return to this point later.

The set of associations so far established are further illustrated in extracts from Majata's beer sacrifice:

> Majata opened the propitiation, 'Here is your "water" father. It is you *milungu* who are just sitting around [not doing as you should to protect us].

It is you who do nothing when the livestock bear offspring and then reject them. The livestock bear and reject their offspring while you only claim your "water"; well, here it is today, they are pouring it for you. And your fresh milk is also here, drink . . . From this point on, you will be looking from side to side, watching the cattle which reject their young. You *milungu*, who flung a goat into the fire, let the children's bodies be "cool" [i.e. let them be well].' Muyame, Majata's wife, then called the *milungu*, telling them that their 'milk' was there, and appealing to them to provide milk for her and her children, for she had been sorely troubled.[11]

In the context of domestic rituals, therefore, beer is sacrificed; but it is only a stop-gap measure, and cattle must be involved. It is the animal category 'cattle' that provides the logical link between the world of the living and the world of the dead in Gogo cosmology. When beer is given, there are direct associations with cattle: the beer is 'drunk' by the *milungu* from the cattle troughs, as water is drunk by cattle. The structure of beer sacrifice may be represented as follows:[12]

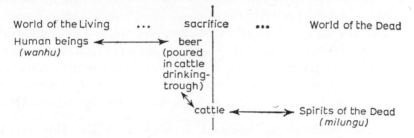

VI

Domestic rituals can, of course, involve animal sacrifice, and I have referred to one example in Mugongo's propitiation with bull and beer. In fact, the *milungu* may even select a particular beast which they want sacrificed to them, as illustrated in the following case:

The Gogo frequently move their herds many miles in search of good grazing and water, and these movements are called *kudimiza*. On one occasion, Mukunya, the son of Muswaga, moved his herd some thirty miles to a new area, necessitating about four nights in the bush. On the journey, one beast was lost for nearly two days, but was found again later. This ox was constantly giving trouble because Muswaga's *milungu* wanted its 'lungs' (*mapupu*, i.e. wanted it sacrificed to them). Mukunya could not hold this sacrifice until he returned home. However, even before he had moved his herd to the new area, his younger brother had been to a diviner to consult him on the safety of the move, and the diviner had warned him that the *milungu* of Muswaga, his father, would want the *mapupu* of that particular beast.

It is instructive to examine in some detail Mugongo's bull and beer sacrifice, which took place at Loje, southern Ugogo. I have stated that the ritual was precipitated by the behaviour of the cattle; some animals were breaking out of the cattle byre at night. However, as the sacrifice proceeded, it became apparent that some of Mugongo's children were ill with eye complaints, and some of the women in his homestead were having trouble with childbirth.[13] An appeal was thus made for help in all of these problems. And, for good measure, Mugongo added an appeal for good rains, a very common feature of all propitiation rituals, domestic or communal.

Owing to the fact that it was primarily the *milungu* of Mugongo's wives who had been identified as the cause of these harmful events, there was some problem as to how and where the rite should be carried out, and who should perform the main sacrifice. Siila, Mugongo's patrilateral cross-cousin and the main officiant, was late, and the cattle had gone out of the byre by the time he arrived at about 8.45 a.m. Although beer was being given, this fact was considered unimportant since an animal sacrifice was also to be made. The discussion over procedure is best told in the words of the participants (see the figure below):

MUGONGO (sitting in the homestead, sipping beer, to Siila): Now, cross-cousin (*baguma*), shall I call these *milungu* here in the homestead, or there at the gravestones [a few yards away, outside the homestead]? Because those *milungu* to be called are many; and even my wives' *milungu* are involved. Again, the kinsmen of my wives' have not come. So, my friends, tell me, where shall I conduct this propitiation?
SIILA: When you went to the diviner, what did he tell you?
MUGONGO: The diviner told me that it was actually the wives' *milungu* who were the real cause, and that my wives should go to their own kinsmen, brew sacrificial beer, and sacrifice an animal. They should sacrifice there, and call their own kinsmen's *milungu*. And I should sacrifice here and call my *milungu*. But my wives have few relatives at home, and none of them are even here. So I am asking your advice.
SIILA: You should go and sacrifice at the 'homestead of the spirits' [i.e. the gravestones] and call them there, including the wives' *milungu*. If they had been only your *milungu*, you could have conducted the sacrifice here in the homestead. But now that your 'affines' [*wakwizenjere*, see Rigby 1967b,

The Symbolic Role of Cattle in Gogo Ritual

Main officiants and milungu in Mugongo's propitiation

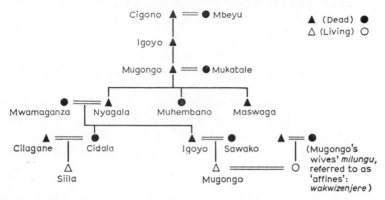

1969] are involved, you should go to the gravestones. They will all meet there (*wokwitanganila wose baho*).

The beer sacrifice was held first, each officiant taking some in his mouth and spraying it on the assembled company, particularly the children. Then they poured some on the gravestones while calling the *milungu*. Mugongo began by just calling a few names, 'Nyagala, Cigongo!' before Siila took over (see accompanying figure):

SIILA: Mbeyu! Wife of Cigono! You have afflicted the children! And this 'bull' [i.e. Mugongo] has, after divination, come to see you. You want 'water', you want 'lungs', so today he has brought them for you. This 'bull' has been to divination, and has seen that you have afflicted his children. You want 'water' and 'lungs'. So now let the children's bodies be cool. You have given your 'grandchildren' afflictions, and many have bad eyes and walk with them blinking and swollen. Let them walk well! . . . You, Sawako, Nyagala, and Mwamaganza, let the children's bodies be cool. And you 'affines', come and meet here!

Other officiants then took over and called the *milungu* for various things.

At the end of the libation, we all moved some fifteen feet away to a shade tree, to finish the sacrificial beer. All the beer brought out of the homestead to the gravestones had to be finished there. A black bull was brought to the clearing near the gravestones and killed, with one stab of a spear in the back of the head, by Mulawule, a young man who is Mugongo's *mutani* (joking partner; see Rigby 1968b). The elders took no notice of this activity. The killing, skinning, and cutting up of the sacrificial animal was done by young men (*wazelelo*) of the 'warrior' grade.

273

While the sacrifice was being prepared, the elders discussed a number of topics, including ritual procedures. Cigongolo, an elder from another neighbourhood who just happened to be around, asked Siila:

CIGONGOLO: Why do you people here begin with a beer sacrifice? Should you not call the *milungu* and give them the 'lungs' at the same time? Will you go back there again to the *citenjelo* and 'spray' (*kufunyila*) the children?

SIILA: Oh no, they won't all gather there again. The children are finished, because this other business is not difficult. One person who knows how to do the animal offering goes and gives it to them [the *milungu*], gives them their 'lungs'. Because there, when they poured the beer saying, 'Take your "water" and your "lungs", here they are,' they completed saying all that was necessary. And so the *milungu* have heard all. Now, when they have finished skinning the animal, one person who knows can go and give it to them . . .

CIGONGOLO: At home, we do not propitiate like that. We give the beer and the 'lungs' at the same time.

SIILA: So *that's* why you do not bear many children there! (Laughter) If *we* were to sacrifice for your wife, she would immediately become pregnant!

COGONGOLO: Oh, you liar. Would you sacrifice anything for my wife?

SIILA: But don't you hear it said that 'such and such a woman bore twins at Loje'? We don't hear this about your area. All we hear is that there are many barren women (*wagumba*) at your place, because you do not know how to sacrifice.[14]

Siila then left the group of elders and went over to the sacrifice. He took six small pieces of lung and six of liver (*itoga*). Sitting near the gravestones, he threw a piece of each in the four cardinal directions, east, south, north, and west, and the others 'up' and 'down'. These are the six aspects (*malanga mutandatu*, lit. 'six apertures') of the Gogo universe (Rigby 1966a, 1968a). He simply said, 'Now here are your "lungs" and your "liver", eat!' He did not call any of the *milungu* by name.

I have presented here only the bare outlines of a highly complex propitiation; but its main elements may be summarized as follows. A series of unhappy events, culminating in the abnormal behaviour of Mugongo's herd, needed to be rectified. The *milungu* of his wives, parents were identified as the main culprits, but their kinsmen could not handle the sacrifices. Hence, most of the *milungu* actually called were Mugongo's own; but the affinal involvement demanded that the sacrifice be held at the gravestones rather than in the homestead. It appears that the gravestones are a more effective locus of communication with a wider range of the *milungu* than the 'nose of the homestead', and the gravestones are normally used in animal sacrifice.

The use of the gravestones and the presence of a sacrificial animal made it redundant to use a 'cattle drinking-trough' for the beer sacrifice and also precluded the necessity for the cattle being in the byre. The beer was simply poured on the gravestones, and it was during this that the *milungu* were called; but constantly in the background was the impending animal sacrifice. This was a bull, as opposed to the more normal ox, and it was slaughtered in the manner usual to the Gogo. I was unable to find out exactly why a bull was sacrificed, but the little evidence I have points to the fact that it may have been considered responsible for the attempts to break out of the byre, and thus as having been 'chosen' by the *milungu*. The animal was 'given' to the *milungu* by Siila, the main officiant and Mugongo's patrilateral cross-cousin (see Rigby 1968b: 147–9, and 1969, for a detailed analysis of the ritual interdependence between cross-cousins).

Finally, although the precipitating event was connected with the behaviour of cattle, the central concern in the propitiation was with a whole range of domestic and physical problems, indicating the interference and unsettled mood of the *milungu*. The structure of Mugongo's propitiation may be expressed as in the accompanying figure.

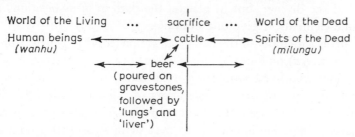

The presence of the sacrificial beast, just about to be given to the *milungu*, makes redundant the other complex of associations evident in purely beer sacrifice.

VII

I now turn to a brief discussion of the symbolic associations of cattle in communal rituals. There are a great number of diverse contexts here, but I have space to consider only two. The first is ritual activity connected with rainmaking and fertility, involving the ritual area (*yisi*) and the ritual leader (*mutemi*). The second is circumcision and initiation rituals, involving primarily the small neighbourhood or locality and certain categories of kin (cf. Rigby 1967c). Even these rituals are extensive, with local variations, and must await fuller analysis elsewhere; I merely select from them one or two examples of the symbolic meaning of cattle.

When the ritual leader holds the annual rituals for good rains and fertility in his country, a major part of the cycle is the *cidwanga* dance, *kuvina cidwanga* (also called *kuvina cigowe*). In this ritual dance, men and women come from all parts of the ritual area to dance in the cattle byre of the *mutemi's* homestead, the *ikulu* ('great place'). They wear strips of skin from a sacrificial black ox (or sheep) on their wrists. These are called *vigowe*, and men wear them on their right wrist, women on their left. This dance constitutes a public act of propitiation to the ritual leader's *milungu* as well as to all the *milungu* of the country (cf. Rigby 1968a: 157).

On another level, and more obscurely, the association between cattle, *milungu*, and the welfare of the whole ritual area may be established on the instructions of the rain diviners who must be consulted before any rainmaking and fertility ritual may take place. The details of such ritual instructions vary widely and may depend on the particular skills and whims of the diviner, but in general the pattern of associations retain the same elements. I give one example.

I went, as a member of the ritual delegation (*wanyalamali* or *wanyaku-jenda gandawega*), on four trips for rain, fertility, and protective medicines to a diviner who lived some forty miles away from our ritual area. On the first trip, just before the beginning of the rains when the diviner gave us medicated seeds to plant with ours, he also gave us several serious warnings. He is one of the best diviners and uses no material oracle in such circumstances, although he does have divining sandals for other situations. Here he simply 'dreamt' (*kulota*) our needs and problems.

We timed our arrival at his homestead for just before sunset: in fact, just as the cattle were returning to the byre. There were other clients from other areas there, and we slept in the cattle byre without discussing anything formal with the diviner. In the morning, after telling us what he would give us for the success of the crops and the fertility of our country during the impending rainy season, he said:

Further, [in my 'dreaming'] I went to your country and, when the rains had just begun and the first heavy storm had come, I found that the bush had become dangerous (*mbago yakalipa*). You will tell your people this: the bush had become dangerous. When the rains have just come, a lion will come to your country with three cubs; that is what they will see, those who walk in the wilds. So you go and tell your people what they are to expect.

The leader of our delegation asked, 'So what can we do with this dangerous wild animal?' The diviner said, 'Which wild animal?'

'The one you have just mentioned.'

'Oh, just a dog? That does not have any importance.'

'What do you mean, "It has no importance"? Will it not play with the lives of men?'

The diviner said, 'No, it will simply kill cattle.'

'So, if it destroys our cattle, that's all right?'

'Don't worry. We will "tie up" that wild animal.'[15] He then gave us detailed instructions on what we should do:

On the day that you see the tracks of that animal, a young man must take a spear and, with it, dig up some of the soil from the footprints. Then he should dig up soil from the hoofprints of cattle, in the same manner. He must also take soil from the footprints of a man, and from the tracks of goats. In other words, he must take soil from the tracks of all domesticated things (*zose zono zikudima muzikaya*, lit: 'all things that herd in the home-steads'). Then you should find five small pieces of a creeping grass (*madilo mahano*), mix them with the soil from those tracks, and put the mixture in five snail shells (*nghonze*). These five shells should be buried at all the 'apertures' of your country: one in the west, one in the east, one to the south, one to the north. And, finally, one should be buried in the middle. The people who should carry this out are a young man and a woman, both of whom should be left-handed . . .[16] When you have completed this work, those two young people should sleep at your homestead . . . and you should kill [sacrifice] a black sheep in their honour . . .

Here, then, the protection of a country from ritual danger, expressed in the presence of the fiercest of the wild animals, is achieved by another form of 'communication'. The soil from the footprints of cattle, men, and other domestic animals (the order is important) is physically mixed with the 'dangerous' soil from the lion's marks, thus neutralizing the latter. This 'de-fused' material is then placed on the boundaries of the country, to prevent any further dangerous incursions (cf. Rigby 1968a: 157–9). In this particular ritual context, the symbolic associations of cattle relate more to their significance in myth as outlined in section III above, than to their significance in the rituals of propitiation. It could, in fact, be said that this ritual activity represents, in an 'operational' context, the same symbolic meanings found in the myth of domestication. The same continuum between nature and culture is transformed from a set of cosmological categories into a manipulative ritual. I show later that these two contexts are logically and structurally related.

On the return of our delegation from the diviner, we went straight to the house (*nyumba*) of the delegation leader's senior wife. She took the medicated seeds we had brought for the country and placed the calabash in her inner room (*kugati*). She then brought out some stools, at which her husband remarked, 'Why do you bring stools? Bring the sleeping-skin (*nhyingo*).' She brought out a large black ox-hide, normally used as a mattress. We sat down on the skin. The senior wife then brought a gourd of water and a flywhisk. She used this to spray us with water, saying, 'What is the news of your journey? Let it be cool . . . Let the rains come.'

This minor rite is essential to 'cool' the ritual delegation from the dangers of their journey. The black ox-hide upon which the delegation sits has multiple symbolic significata. It first of all implies the presence of the *milungu* and a context of communication with them. It must be the unblemished skin of an ox which has been sacrificed on an important ritual occasion. It would be unthinkable to use the skin of an animal which had died of 'natural' causes.

Furthermore, the black skin represents rain clouds, and is therefore a symbol of good rains to come. One knowledgeable elder connected these ideas:

> When the delegation returns, they must first sit on a black sleeping-skin. The reasons are that we make the skin a symbol (*cikwihwaniciza*) of a rain cloud (*livunde*). One could say that it *is* a rain cloud.[17] They are bringing rain.

The leader of our delegation added:

> And that skin which is spread out for the delegation to sit on is not any old skin. It must be that of a sacrificial ox (*nghongolo nhemangwa*). It cannot be the skin of a beast which has just died, or which has been attacked by hyenas [*mabisi*, the most evil of wild animals: see note above]. It must be an ox which has been slaughtered 'in laughter' [i.e. for the good of men].

Even in such a minor part of the rainmaking and fertility cycle, then, cattle have an important symbolic role: they are the mediators between the world of men and the world of the spirits, as well as between men and nature. I must now turn to one final context, that of circumcision rituals, before I try to pull together the rather diverse threads of symbolic meaning in the material presented.

VIII

A great number of animals are sacrificed for each specific stage of the circumcision ritual cycle, and here the sex and type of animal are of far more explicit importance. In all the contexts discussed so far, oxen (or their substitutes) were sacrificed, with the exception of Mugongo's bull, for which there were special reasons.

The closing of one age-set and the opening of another is marked by the communal sacrifice of an ox.[18] These formal rituals have virtually ceased to exist, although some circumcision rites still take place on more or less traditional lines. I must therefore rely upon an elder's account, corroborated by others, of the opening and closing of age-sets:

> The men of the youngest age-set would gather together at a meeting and try to insist that more youngsters should be initiated into their set. The youngsters would refuse, saying that it was time to open a new set of their own [in which, of course, they would be the senior members as the set grew]. This often led to fighting, and the elders would come between the warriors and the uncircumcised youths and stop it. When they had stopped fighting, the age-set spokesman of the junior set would have to obtain a huge ox, which was sacrificed. This sacrifice ended their age-set recruitment, and they would divide the meat between their age-mates and the youngsters about to form a new set . . . Then they would take a strip of that ox's hide, one group holding one end, the other group at the opposite end. The elders would cut this strip, thereby formally distinguishing the age-sets . . .

The dividing of the meat and the cutting of the ox-hide provide the symbolic ritual sanction to a fundamental social transformation. The *milungu* are not invoked, but the social conflict is resolved by a religious act: the sacrifice of an ox.

In the context of the circumcision rituals themselves, there is a shift in emphasis from ritual communication with the *milungu* to ritual as an insurance against the untoward behaviour of nature. However, by implication, the *milungu* are interested and may become involved.

Peter Rigby

Before a circumcision rite takes place, the *milungu* need not be consulted. However, diviners are consulted to ensure that the correct ritual state (*mbeho swanu*) is present. I have explored the concept of *mbeho* in some detail elsewhere (Rigby 1968: 158–60 *et passim*), and do not discuss it here. I simply record what one informant told me, which turned out on subsequent investigation to be a correct description of the normal procedure:

> When we go to the diviner [for a decision on holding the circumcision rites], we go only to see what the ritual state of the country is, not to propitiate the *milungu*. When the children are initiated, you may see one who is being troubled. You will then go again to another diviner. He may tell you that this particular child is being troubled by angry spirits (*malungu*, see note above), and only then will you know that it is the spirits affecting him. But if that original diviner you went to was a really good diviner, he would have told you, 'You may be shocked by some occurrence as you proceed, and it will be the *malungu*. If this happens, you must return here at once.'

The parent who takes the responsibility for organizing circumcision rites in any area is normally the father of several sons who have reached the age of circumcision. He provides the first sacrifice, *ng'wisacibalu*, 'the sacrifice that "throws down" (establishes) the circumcision enclosure (*cibalu*).' *Ng'wisacibalu* is a steer or an ox or, occasionally, a sheep:

> That beast, *ng'wisacibalu*, is for the ritual state (*mbeho*) of the circumcision enclosure: it 'cools' (*yikupoza*) the place [i.e. rids it of ritual danger].

Another beast, also a steer, is provided by one of the fathers of the initiates. This is given to the operator (*munghunga*) the night before he begins, and is called the *muvugo*, 'the cooked thing' (from *kuvuga*, to cook sorghum porridge). But it is not merely a payment; it is a sacrifice which must be made before the success of the operations can be assured; and it must be killed there and eaten as a sacrifice. The meat is shared out to all present, the elders and young initiated men who will care for the initiands during the rites.

Just before the actual circumcision, another sacrifice is offered. This is usually a sheep which has been castrated while young (*nhule*), and is therefore equivalent to an ox; but a steer may be given. The operator first feeds this animal some medicines. This is the only *formal* act of consecration I have come upon in all Gogo sacrifices, although by

The Symbolic Role of Cattle in Gogo Ritual

definition, all sacrificial offerings are consecrated by the mere act of sacrifice: the victim passes into the 'religious domain' (Hubert and Mauss 1964: 9–11 *et passim*).

This sacrifice is called *nyamuwumbu. Nyamuwumbu* means 'a thing with the quality of *muwumbu*'. *Muwumbu* is a spreading leafy tree (*Lannea stuhlmanii*), about 20 feet high when mature. It is used in various medicinal contexts, but its principal qualities are best expressed in a Gogo statement about the tree:

> *Muwumbu* is a tree with dark bark and foliage, but inside it is red. If you strip off some bark and soak it in water, that water will become red, like blood (*malenga gagalya gakuwa nha sakami*).

The trunk also exudes a red latex.

But the tree itself, part of the 'wild', of nature, is not used in the rituals. The sacrificial animal, itself a part of domestic culture, represents also the natural qualities of the *muwumbu* tree. The informant who made the statement I have just quoted continued:

> And so those knives of blood (*imimaje ya sakami*) are 'cooled' in the chyme of the animal they call *nyamuwumbu*. Even long ago they never used the tree itself; it is just the 'name' (*litagwa*) of the sacrificial animal. They kill the animal there, where they are circumcising, and they skin it. When they have finished the operations, they plunge those 'lions' [circumcision knives] again and again into the chyme, 'putting out the fires' [of ritual danger] (*wakuzimizya*).

Another elder put it in a somewhat different way:

> That sacrificial animal they call *nyamuwumbu* because they take those circumcision knives and plunge them into its chyme, to 'cool them' (*kupoza*). They call those knives 'lions'.

I may summarize, then, as follows. The 'separation' of the initiates from society (Van Gennep 1908) is accomplished by physically transferring them to the 'wild', for the circumcision enclosure is built in the bush. Although its ritual safety must be ensured by sacrifice and the use of medicines, the central act of the rite is ripe with danger, both physical and ritual. The circumcision knives are identified with 'lions' (the wild), and these attack the initiates; blood is spilled. The dangerous ('hot') situation thus created must be 'cooled'. The initiates are part of the wild now; 'natural' medicine is used to achieve the cooling: the *muwumbu* tree whose chief qualities associate it with blood and the clotting of

281

blood (the red latex).[19] But men do not use the natural object in this way. Nature is too dangerous and uncontrolled; so men manipulate it through the intermediary of the sacrificial ox or sheep. The therapeutic qualities of the *muwumbu* tree, a part of 'nature', impinge upon the world of men through the mediation of the sacrificial animal; and the sacrifice enables men to manipulate the 'natural' qualities of the *muwumbu* tree through a symbol which embodies both nature and culture.

So too with the other sacrifices of the circumcision rituals. There is the *nzeku ye mafuta*, 'steer (or goat, *mhonde*, or sheep, *nhule*) of the fat', whose fatty soup and meat 'strengthen' the initiates and constitute their 'reintroduction' to eating, for they have up to now taken only medicines and they have fasted. This sacrifice must be given by the 'mother's brothers' of the initiates (*wakuku'ze*). The animals are killed when the camp for instruction and recuperation (*ikumgo*) has been built near the homesteads, and the initiates have moved there. Towards the end of the rites, when the initiates, now called *wanyamuluzi*, are about to be 'readmitted' into society by the ritual washing-off of their covering of white clay, the 'ox (or steer) of the great logs (*nghongolo ya matinde*)' is given by the agnatic kin of the initiates, their 'fathers'.[20] This sacrifice is consumed mainly by those young men and elders who have cared for the initiates, and who have 'carried the huge logs' to the circumcision enclosure for the fires kept burning there all the time.

This is not the place to analyse the total structure of Gogo circumcision rites and their complex symbolism. But the conclusion can be drawn that, at all the critical stages of these rites, cattle, or their associated substitutes or products, provide the only means of symbolic communication between men and the 'natural' and 'supernatural' worlds. The conjoined forces of the domain of 'nature' and the domain of the 'spirits' must be controlled to ensure the completion of the most difficult and dangerous rite of passage in Gogo society.

IX

The two questions, 'Why cattle?' and 'Are there any common structural principles which can be established for the diverse contexts of cattle symbolism in Gogo religion?' are really two sides of the same coin (cf. Strathern and Strathern 1968).

I am concerned with three basic oppositions in Gogo symbolic classification (cf. Rigby 1966a):

The Symbolic Role of Cattle in Gogo Ritual

domesticated	wild
(culture)	(nature)
men	spirits
world of living	world of dead

These are strong oppositions in Gogo thought, but they are not simple. The two domains are in each case distinct, but they interpenetrate in certain circumstances (cf. Hubert and Mauss 1964: 99 *et passim*). This interpenetration can be *controlled* by men only through the use of an intermediary. The intermediary is the sacrificial victim. Man himself cannot be the intermediary, for, if he were, he would have to destroy himself. This extreme solution is approached in some societies in the institution of human sacrifice; but, even where this existed, it was confined to rare and highly critical circumstances, and obviously cannot be an answer to the problems of everyday, mundane communication between the domains. But the fact that the Gogo select cattle as their sacrifice, as their intermediary between the world of men and the world of the spirits, is not merely because cattle are their most valued property. It is, rather, a logical consequence of their categorization of the universe, of their cosmology (Rigby 1966a, 1968a, 1968b). Cattle are both a medial category as well as an extension of men (culture) and of the wild (nature). Let me explain this further.

In the cattle origin myth, the logically and emotionally satisfying dichotomy between culture and nature is shattered at the beginning. Affinity (community: cf. Rigby 1968b: 151–3, and above; Douglas 1968) breaks down, and 'man', in this case represented by an ambiguous but predominantly female figure, is cast into the wild. I have already noted that this is consistent with two facts; (a) that it is only an ambiguous figure that can achieve this transition from culture to nature and back, and (b) that women and cattle are exchanged to create affinity and hence 'community'.

At first, the reversal is complete: 'man' is completely assimilated with the wild in the role of nurse to the most fierce wild animal, lion. But man cannot survive there and is duped by hyena, also of ambiguous status. Hyena 'reverses the reversal' by using a cultural artefact, fire, as an excuse for the deception. After another incident of reversal, in which zebra win their war with lion, 'man' is helped back to society by a game animal (cf. Leach 1964: 37 *et passim*). Man takes the first step to domesticating animals when he (or she) leads the zebra to good

283

pastures. When he leaves the zebra, it is therefore a simple step to domesticate the next, and even milder, animal he comes across. Thus, the simple opposition 'culture/nature' is transformed in the myth into 'areas of social space in terms of "distance from [man] ego" ' (Leach 1964: 36). The opposition may now represented as a continuum:

```
Man  . . . .  cattle  . . . .  zebra  . . . .  lion
(culture        (livestock)      (game)        (wild animal
                                                 – nature)
```

The Gogo myth of the origin of cattle clearly places them in an intermediary position, together with other less controllable things, in what otherwise is a simple binary opposition. It is, therefore, a straightforward logical transformation, arising out of Gogo categories themselves, to apply this model to the final pair of binary oppositions, viz, the world of the living: world of the dead: : men: spirits. This logic is plainly illustrated in all the ritual contexts described in this paper.

It may be added that the structure of Gogo religious belief here is simply a particular manifestation of a universal problem. As Leach states (1964: 38–9):

'Religious belief is everywhere tied in with the discrimination between living and dead. Logically, *life* is simply the binary antithesis of *death*; the two concepts are the opposite sides of the same penny; we cannot have one without the other. But religion always tries to separate the two. To do this, it creates a hypothetical "other world" which is the antithesis of "this world". In this world, life and death are inseparable; in the other world they are separate. This world is inhabited by imperfect mortal men; the other world is inhabited by immortal nonmen (gods). The category god is thus constructed as the binary antithesis of man. But this is inconvenient . . . To be useful, gods must be near at hand, so religion sets about reconstructing a continuum between this world and the other world.'

In the continuum constructed in Gogo religion, cattle have the central position. They already bridge the gap between nature and culture in Gogo categories; they are thus logically able to bridge another gap, between this world and the other world. The simple binary pairs men: spirits: : world of the living: world of the dead are thus transformed in Gogo ritual and belief into:

```
    men    .. .. ..   cattle  .. .. ..      spirits
(world of living)                        (world of dead)
```

The Symbolic Role of Cattle in Gogo Ritual

The ambiguous category 'cattle', embodying both nature and culture, is thus 'specifically credited with the power of mediation between gods and men' (Leach 1964: 39).

For the Gogo, this is not just a conceptual scheme. It is applied constantly, almost every day, in the numerous rituals, minor and major, which are such an important part of Gogo life. Apart from the material presented in this paper, I describe in detail elsewhere a situation in which cattle-herding is the central component in role-reversal rituals in Ugogo (Rigby 1968a), rituals which are directed towards ridding the country of ritual pollution. Again, the same symbolic themes are applied in a different form. Such frequent application in recourse to ritual action requires some flexibility. Once the continuum is accepted, any number of variations may be played upon it; but cattle always retain the central position. Hence, other domestic animals may be substituted for cattle, or beer may be given as a stop-gap sacrifice:

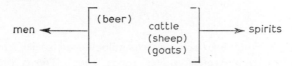

The beer can be offered as a sacrifice, but only in connexion with the symbolic and mediatory role of cattle. This association is strongly supported by the fact that sacrificial beer is always referred to as 'water'; the *milungu* drink beer from the 'cattle trough', just as cattle drink water from it, 'together'.

I have not yet mentioned one essential quality of all such 'liminal' or mediatory categories: taboo (Leach 1964: 39; Douglas 1966 *passim*; Turner 1964). Are Gogo cattle taboo? The answer, surprisingly, is yes. For they are subject to the most far-reaching taboo in Gogo society; they may never be slaughtered unless they are sacrificed to the spirits of the dead. This taboo is not elaborated exegetically; there is no need for exegesis when the taboo is built into the very structure of Gogo categories themselves.[21]

I conclude, therefore, by suggesting that it is in the context of sacrifice that the symbolic significance of cattle in Gogo religion is predominant, an idea directly derived from Evans-Pritchard's brilliant exposition of the role of cattle in Nuer sacrifice. In this context, I have no quarrel with Hubert and Mauss's general statement on the 'unity' of procedure beneath the diverse forms of sacrifice (Hubert and Mauss 1964: 97).

'This procedure consists in establishing a means of communication between the sacred and profane worlds through the mediation of the victim, that is, of a thing that in the course of the ceremony is destroyed.'

But this bare statement does not take full account of the symbolic meanings which may be attached to sacrifice; in the Gogo case, to cattle. These symbolic meanings can be established only by an analysis of the great variety of contexts in which cattle have symbolic meanings, and this includes both myth *and* ritual, and by an attempt to expose their common structure. This must then be related to the general cosmology of Gogo society as expressed in its structure of dual symbolic classifications. The simple oppositions characteristic of these classifications are transformed by myth and ritual into logical continua, or 'gradients', by the intrusion of a third, medial, category, which ensures men's control of the interference of one set in the other.

NOTES

1. Other aspects of Gogo religion, cosmology, and social structures are discussed in Rigby (1966a, 1966b, 1967a, 1967b, 1967c, 1968a, 1968b, 1969); see also Mnyampala (1954); Schaegelen (1938); Claus (1911). I am grateful for comments on earlier drafts of this paper from Professor T. O. Beidelman, Dr Adam Kuper, Mrs Zebiya Rigby, and Mr Gideon Senyagwa.
2. This certainly does not have the derogatory connotations of 'that old cow' in English!
3. The Nuer also state that cattle and buffaloes were once the same (Evans-Pritchard 1956: 269; cf. Beidelman 1966: 48, n. 8).
4. I collected several versions of this story, all very similar to that originally published in a collection called *Zimbazi ze Zifumbo, Nhandaguzi, ne Zisimo ze Cigogo*, edited by 'J.E.B.' (probably the Rev. J. E. Beverley of the CMS Mission, Mpwapwa) for the SPCK in 1901 (cf. Carnell 1955). This version was republished in another collection, *Mutumwa Simba*, by the Central Tanganyika Press and Longmans Green, London, in 1953.
5. The beginning of the story appears to be deliberately ambiguous about the way in which the marriage was destroyed (death or divorce) and the sex of the person who is eventually banished. Throughout the text the word used is *munhu*, which denotes a person of either sex. At first, immediately after the destruction of the marriage, the person is left *mwigane*, a term used only when referring to unmarried men (*igane*, the dormitory room attached to homesteads for unmarried youths and

visitors to sleep in). However, thereafter the person has a child (*yakawa kusawa mwana wa cilume*), the verb *kusawa* being used only for women. Also, the person is asked to 'nurse' (*koca*) the children of the lion, another exclusively feminine verb. For convenience, I use the female form in English, and discuss the significance of this ambiguity in detail later. I am grateful to Dr Richard Mazengo for his comments on this point.

6. Although fire does not have a really central place in this myth, it is interesting to note its intrusion. Lévi-Strauss, by making a 'culinary motif' one of the three basic elements of mythology, implies that ideas about fire are basic to all mythological systems (Lévi-Strauss 1967b).

7. Gogo resort to divination for the slightest of reasons; it is a pivotal activity in Gogo ritual action. However, I am not concerned directly with it here.

8. All kin of the second ascending generation *and beyond* are referred to by the same terms: *wakuku* for males ('grandfathers' and *wamama* for females ('grandmothers').

9. The term *misambwa* is very widely used in eastern Africa for various categories of spirits and rituals, but this is not the place to go into comparative details. It is important to note, however, that the word is used only in this context in Cigogo, and does not imply a general category of spirits.

10. When an ox or other animal is to be sacrificed, it is not necessary for the ritual to be held very early in the morning: see below.

11. Two points may be noted here: (a) the familiar way in which the *milungu* are addressed; there is no feeling of 'religious awe' or worship (cf. Rigby 1966b: 285, n. 38). (b) At this propitiation, beer, milk, and sweet beer (*masika*) were all poured for the *milungu*.

12. From his reading of the material, Dr Adam Kuper put forward an alternative interpretation: 'beer' would form one of a pair of oppositions, 'beer/cattle' in the following series:

beer	cattle
agriculture	pastoralism
women	men
affines	agnates

Hence, beer and cattle would both be mediatory categories of a complementary kind, and the structure of beer sacrifice would then appear as follows:

World of the living	sacrifice	..World of the dead
Human beings	beer	spirits of the
(*wanhu*)	(cattle)	dead
		(*milungu*)

It does not appear to me, however, that this interpretation is supported by the other evidence cited in this paper; I thus present it simply as another possibility.

13. Cf. (Rigby 1968a: *passim*), for other contexts in which the process of childbirth is affected and ritual action must be taken: again, ritual concerning the herding of cattle.

14. Siila and Cigongolo are actually members of clans which are joking partners (*watani*), and some of this conversation is a consequence of this relationship: see (Rigby 1968b). On the status of twins, see (Rigby 1966a, 1968a).

15. In the conversation, the diviner is attempting to show that events dangerous to normal men can easily be controlled if they heed his instructions.

16. For the ritual significance of left-handedness among the Gogo, see Rigby (1966a: 10–11, 1968a).

17. Hayley (1968) would say that this is an 'identification', a 'primitive symbolic equation': 'In the symbolic equation . . . the symbol substitute is felt to *be* the original object, whereas the symbol proper is felt to *represent* the object' (p. 266). This is a distinction derived from Western clinical materials, and its application to the Gogo material would be totally unjustified. When the Gogo say, '*Kotya lyo livunde*', 'You could say that it *is* the cloud', they are simply stressing a strong symbolic association; they are not proposing a 'symbolic equation' between mattresses and rain clouds!

18. Gogo age-sets are modelled on the Baraguyu system (Beidelman 1960), with the important exception that there is no closed period of several years in the recruitment of Gogo age-sets. As soon as a new Baraguyu set is opened, the Gogo, who have been continuing their initiations into the previous set, simply close the latter and open a new one.

19. I am not here concerned with the complex problems of circumcision rituals *per se*, and the obvious intrusion of colour symbolism (cf. Turner 1962, 1966, *et passim*).

20. There is some confusion as to whether this sacrifice should be an ox or steer, or a bull. The general consensus is for the former, but I came across one case of a bull (*nghambaku*) being taken as *matinde*. This may indicate local variations, but I did not inquire at the time.

21. Cf. the Kachin classification of cattle as 'polluted food', which may only be eaten in the context of sacrifice (Leach 1964: 57).

REFERENCES

BEIDELMAN, T. O. 1960 The Baraguyu. *Tanganyika Notes and Records* **55**: 245–78.
— 1961 Hyena and Rabbit: a Kaguru Representation of Matrilineal Relations. *Africa* **31**: 61–74.
— 1963a Further Adventures of Hyena and Rabbit: the Folktale as a Sociological Model, *Africa* **33**: 54–69.
— 1963b Kaguru Omens: an East African People's Concepts of the Unusual, Unnatural, and Supernormal. *Anthropological Quarterly* **36**: 43–59.
— 1965 Some Baraguyu Cattle Songs. *Journal of African Languages* **4**: 1–18.
— 1966 The Ox and Nuer Sacrifice. *Man* (n.s.) **1**: 453–67.
— 1967 Rejoinder to Schneider, H. K. (1967). *Man* (n.s.) **2**: 299–300.
— 1968a Some Nuer Notions of Nakedness, Nudity and Sexuality. *Africa* **38**: 113–31.
— 1968b Some Hypotheses Regarding Nilo-Hamitic Symbolism and Social Structure. *Anthropological Quarterly* **41**: 78–89.
CLAUS, H. 1911 Die Wagogo. *Baessler Archiv*, Beiheft 2. Berlin: Reimer.
CARNELL, W. J. 1955 Four Gogo Folk Tales. *Tanganyika Notes and Records* **40**: 30–42.
DOUGLAS, M. 1966 *Purity and Danger*. London: Routledge and Kegan Paul.
— 1968 The Social Control of Cognition: Some Factors in Joke Perception. *Man* (n.s.) **3**: 361–76.
EVANS-PRITCHARD, E. E. 1953 The Sacrificial Role of Cattle among the Nuer. *Africa* **23**: 181–98.
— 1956 *Nuer Religion*. Oxford: The Clarendon Press.
HAYLEY, A. 1968 Symbolic Equations: The Ox and the Cucumber. *Man* (n.s.) **3**: 262–71.
HERSKOVITS, M. J. 1926 The Cattle Complex in East Africa. *American Anthropologist* **28**: 230–72, 361–80, 494–528, 633–64.
HUBERT, H., AND MAUSS M. 1964 *Sacrifice: Its Nature and Function*. London: Cohen and West. Translated from the French 'Essai sur la nature et la fonction du sacrifice', *L'Année sociologique*, 1898.
'J.E.B.' (ed.) 1901 *Zimbazi ze Zifumbo, Nhandaguzi, ne Zisimo ze Cigogo* London: SPCK.
JELLICOE, M. 1967 Praising the Sun. *Transition* **31**: 27–31.
LEACH, E. 1964 Anthropological Aspects of Language: Animal Categories and Verbal Abuse. In Lenneberg, E. (ed.), *New Directions in the Study of Language*. Cambridge, Mass.: MIT Press.
— 1967 (ed.) *The Structural Study of Myth and Totemism*. ASA Monographs 5. London: Tavistock Publications.
— 1968 (ed.) *Dialectic in Practical Religion*. Cambridge Papers in Social

Anthropology No. 5. London and New York: Cambridge University Press.

LÉVI-STRAUSS, C. 1962 *La Pensée sauvage*. Paris: Plon. Translated as *The Savage Mind* (1966). London: Weidenfeld and Nicholson.

— 1963 *Structural Anthropology*. New York: Basic Books.

— 1964 *Le Cru et le cuit: Mythologiques*, Vol. I. Paris: Plon.

— 1967a 'The Story of Asdiwal'. In Leach, E. R. (ed.), *The Structural Study of Myth and Totemism*. ASA Monographs 5. London: Tavistock Publications.

— 1967b *Du Miel aux cendres: Mythologiques Vol. II*. Paris: Plon.

— 1968 *L'origine des manières de table: Mythologiques Vol. III*. Paris: Plon.

MNYAMPALA, M. 1954 *Historia, Mila na Desturi za Wagogo wa Tanganyika*. Dar es Salaam: The Eagle Press.

Mutumwa Simba, 1953 London: Central Tanganyika Press and Longmans Green.

RIGBY, PETER 1966a Dual Symbolic Classification among the Gogo of Central Tanzania. *Africa* **36**: 1–17.

— 1966b Sociological Factors in the Contact of the Gogo of Central Tanzania with Islam. In Lewis, I. M. (ed.), *Islam in Tropical Africa*. London: Oxford University Press (for International African Institute).

— 1967a Ugogo: Changes in Local Government and the National Elections. In Cliffe, L. (ed.), *One Party Democracy*. Nairobi: East African Publishing House.

— 1967b Time and Structure in Gogo Kingship. *Cahiers d'études africaines* **28**: 637–658.

— 1967c The Structural Context of Girls' Puberty Rites. *Man* (n.s.) **2**: 434–444.

— 1968a Some Gogo Rituals of 'Purification': an Essay on Social and Moral categories. In Leach, E. R. (ed.), *Dialectic in Practical Religion*. Cambridge Papers in Social Anthropology No. 5. London and New York: Cambridge University Press.

— 1968b Joking Relationships, Kin Categories, and Clanship among the Gogo. *Africa* **38**: 133–155.

— 1969 *Cattle and Kinship among the Gogo: a Semi-Pastoral Society of Central Tanzania*. Ithaca, New York, and London: Cornell University Press.

— in press Pastoralism and Prejudice: Ideology and Rural Development in East Africa. In Belshaw, D. G. R., and E. H. Brett (eds.), *Public Policy and Rural Development*. Nairobi: East African Publishing House.

SCHNEIDER, H. K. 1957 The Subsistence Role of Cattle among the Pakot and in East Africa. *American Anthropologist* **59**: 278–300.

— 1959 Pakot Resistance to Change. In Bascom, W. R. and M. J. Herskovits (eds.), *Continuity and Change in African Cultures*. Chicago: University of Chicago Press.

— 1967 Correspondence *Man* (n.s.) **2** : 299.

SELIGMAN, C. G. AND B. Z. 1932 *Pagan Tribes of the Nilotic Sudan*. London: Routledge and Kegan Paul.

STRATHERN, A. AND M. 1968 Marsupials and Magic: A Study of Spell Symbolism among the Mbowamb. In Leach, E. R. (ed.), *Dialectic in Practical Religion*. Cambridge Papers in Social Anthropology No. 5. London and New York: Cambridge University Press.

TURNER, V. W. 1962 Three Symbols of *Passage* in Ndembu Circumcision Ritual. In Gluckman, M. (ed.), *Essays on the Ritual of Social Relations*. Manchester: Manchester University Press.

— 1964 Symbols in Ndembu Ritual. In Gluckman M. (ed.), *Closed Systems and Open Minds*. London: Oliver and Boyd.

— 1967 *The Forest of Symbols*. Ithaca: Cornell University Press.

VAN GENNEP, A. 1908 *Les Rites de passage*, Paris: Émile Nourry. Translated by Monika B. Vizedom and Gabrielle L. Caffee as *The Rites of Passage*. London: Routledge and Kegan Paul (1960).

© Peter Rigby 1971

291

The Political Structure of the Trio Indians as manifested in a System of Ceremonial Dialogue

PETER RIVIÈRE

In that model of ethnographic description and insight, *The Nuer*, Professor Evans-Pritchard has shown with his characteristic clarity how the feud operates as an institutionalized means of social control. He also indicates that the incidence and duration of the feud are closely interlinked with the social structure; the feud rarely occurring and being quickly resolved among the closest kin and co-residents, while on the tribal boundaries, where the lack of joint commitment makes mediation difficult, the feud lapses into warfare. In this essay[1] I wish to follow Professor Evans-Pritchard's lead and to examine how far the forms and usages of a type of verbal duelling, referred to as ceremonial dialogue,[2] can be used as evidence for the existence of an underlying structure.

In this exposition I give firstly a general ethnographic background of the Trio, with emphasis on those aspects important for the understanding of ceremonial dialogue; second comes a description of the dialogue itself; third is indicated how ceremonial dialogue reflects and is reflected in other Trio institutions; and, finally, there are some comments of a more general and comparative nature.[3]

I

The Trio are a group of approximately 650 Carib-speaking Amerindians who live on either side of the Brazil–Surinam frontier. This is a head-water region both for the rivers which flow south through Pará to the Amazon and those which run north to the Atlantic. The water-divide is not marked by any continuous line of hills or mountains, and, except for the occasional peak of black rock towering above the forest, the terrain mainly consists of low hills divided by myriad small streams in the dry season and extensive swamps in the wet season. With the exception of a few small areas of savannah, the entire region inhabited by the Trio (almost 100,000 square miles, of which to all intents and purposes they are the sole inhabitants) is covered with tropical forest.

In its major features Trio culture shows no important variations from the Guiana 'culture area' (*vide* Gillin 1963). They are tropical forest cultivators whose main subsistence crop is bitter cassava produced by slash-and-burn farming techniques. However, hunting, fishing, and collecting have an important part to play in the diet and occupation of the Indians. The average size of Trio villages is also in keeping with other tribes in the interior of the Guianas but it is necessary to describe in slightly greater detail the particular settlement pattern of the Trio and the composition of their villages.

Traditionally,[4] the average Trio village contains 30 people with an upper limit of about 50 people. The villages are relatively scattered and isolated; there is rarely less than a half-day's walk between them and sometimes more than four days' march. If one plots the village sites in terms of days' march apart, a clear pattern emerges. First, there are the individual villages; second, a number of villages which lie less than one day's march from each other. This settlement grouping will be referred to as an *agglomeration*. The distance between the nearest villages of two different agglomerations is about two days' walk. The third grouping in the settlement pattern, which will be referred to as a *group*, is formed from a number of agglomerations. The nearest villages of different groups are four or more days' walk apart. All Trio villages are divided between only three groups, and these groups are coincidental with the three main river basins which form the area occupied by the Trio. Furthermore, stretches of savannah as well as watersheds help in the separation of the groups. This settlement pattern, as well as having spatial and topographical diagnostic features, has an attendant social element. An individual is likely to find 70 per cent of his nearest kin and affines in his own village, about 80 per cent in his own agglomeration, and 98 per cent within his own group.

However, certain words of caution must be introduced here. First, the Trio do not explicitly recognize these various settlement units inasmuch as they have no terms for them other than that for a village. Accordingly, one could be accused of imposing certain artificial distinctions on the material, but the criteria discussed indicate that there is some form of reality in this pattern and it will be shown that the use of ceremonial dialogue reflects Trio awareness of it. A second cautionary note is that this description provides a static view of what is a highly fluid situation – villages are not permanent and their populations also are mobile. While these are interesting features of the Trio, it is not necessary to consider the full implications of them in the study of ceremonial dialogue because, although any particular dialogue is concerned with changing the individual *status quo*, the pattern of its usage reflects the overall *status quo* and thus the socio-political structure at any given moment. A static view of this institution does not therefore detract from an understanding of it, but the reader should remember that it is a dialogue, and that this means interaction which, in turn, implies change.

A Trio village is an autonomous unit, but not one that contains any clearly recognizable political institutions. Political relationships are expressed in the same way as kinship relationships, and are in most cases inseparable from them. A village leader lacks any formally invested authority, and his position depends on his own ability to gain and maintain cooperation among his villagers. Since political ties are kinship ties, a man's position in the network of village kinship ties will indicate his structural suitability for the role, but after this it is a man's own ability that counts. There is wide scope for the politically ambitious, however, and the man who founds a village is its leader. The test of successful leadership is the size of the village, since there is no way in which a leader can coerce people into staying there. The village of a good leader is populous and relatively stable; the village of a poor leader will gradually lose its inhabitants until it is too small to exist as an independent unit.[5]

Social control within the village is little more than the obligations and rights of kinship. The leader, because of his position at the centre of a nucleus of kin who form the core of any village population, is in a better position than anyone else to manipulate the social relationships, and thus maintain a balance between the individual interests in the village. Tension within the village tends to arise from accusations of adultery or failure to fulfil certain kinship obligations. The failure to fulfil kinship obligations is frequently the result of a shortage of food, particularly game, which is then not distributed in the conventionally expected manner.[6] An economic shortage is expressed in social terms which, in turn, have political repercussions. The first sanction directed at an individual or part of the village population that fails to fulfil its obligations is gossip, which, in its most virulent form, becomes an accusation of sorcery. An open accusation of sorcery within the sphere of a single village would inevitably result in violence, but there is circumstantial evidence to suggest that such situations rarely occur because a village will have divided before this point is reached (cf. Rivière 1970). Mobility of population is a vital safety valve for reducing socio-political pressure.

Population movements mainly take place within the sphere of the agglomeration either as a social or as a geographical entity; that is to say, an individual or small group may leave one village and join another in the same agglomeration, or a slightly larger number of people may hive off to form a new village in the same general area. It should be noted that not all movement is the result of friction and many individuals and families move around within the agglomeration, visiting friends and relations and exploiting the different economic resources which the various villages offer. Because such a high proportion of those living in a single agglomeration are related by either genealogy or marriage, relationships within an agglomeration are in the first place little more than an extension of those to be found in a village. However, because each village is an autonomous unit, and may consist partly or entirely of Indians who have left a neighbouring village in an atmosphere of marked hostility, the relationships between villages of the same agglomeration are not invariably characterized by friendliness. The true picture is one of shifting alliances, so that at any one moment village A, B, and C may exist in an atmosphere of cooperative interdependence, while villages D and E share a similar relationship between themselves but one of marked hostility towards A, B, and C. The pattern may then shift so that the two groups become A, D, and E; and B and C. The most important political mechanism for realigning the villages in different alliances is the dance festival, an event which at one level permits the participants to forget and forgive old animosities but which at another level is the source of much new ill-feeling.[7] The participating villages at a dance festival mainly come from the same agglomeration, so there is for these villages a ritualized means of resolving outstanding conflicts.

Where there is hostility between villages it is normally expressed in terms of sorcery; both strangers and enemies are normally suspected of sorcery. To understand the relationships between villages it is necessary to discuss further the question of sorcery. For the Trio all sickness and death are the result of sorcery; no man dies unless he has been cursed. A relatively high proportion of the Trio die from sickness or disease which have exotic origin and are spread by infection and contagion.[8] It is therefore not surprising that the stranger is regarded with suspicion as a potential sorcerer, since the appearance of sickness so frequently follows in the footsteps of a visitor. There is at the same time a great tradition of hospitality in the area (without which, given the size, nature, and population density of the region, there would be little or no movement) but this is not contrary evidence to the suspicion that centres on the stranger but simply a different aspect of the same attitude. The only prophylaxis against being cursed is to be open, friendly, conforming, and cooperative. Hospitality, therefore, is a safeguard against sorcery and has its foundations in fear rather than kindness.

The closer villages are to each other in terms both of kinship ties and geographical distance (there is a close correlation between these two factors) the more means there are of mediating disputes between their inhabitants. With more distant villages, the connexions that help to maintain social control weaken and finally disappear. The villages of the same agglomeration are the most closely knit, since an individual can expect to find a very large proportion of his kin and affines within its boundaries. On the other hand, only two per cent of his relations exist in neighbouring groups. These units are not, however, absolute and agglomerations may well have more ties with the neighbouring group than with other distant agglomerations of their own group. Even so, there is some justification for regarding these units as more or less watertight compartments since ties across boundaries are formed by marriage and such unions are unstable in comparison with the enduring brother–sister relationship.

Thus ties of kinship outside an agglomeration are normally too weak to act as mechanisms of social control. Gossip is also ineffective in this wider environment. The conventional attitude towards visitors and strangers, particularly towards strange visitors, is one of suspicion tinged with fear – an attitude which, in its turn, engenders a practice of hospitality as a safeguard against sorcery. While the conventional hospitality permits communication between traveller and host, it is an inadequate mechanism for ordering any more effective interchanges. It is here that the institution of ceremonial dialogue comes into play.

II

There are three forms of ceremonial dialogue, and the difference between them is not simply an observable variation in behaviour but a terminological distinction made by the Trio themselves. The Trio criterion for the distinction is the 'strength' of the talk, and the same principle will be applied here.

It is perhaps stretching the definition too far to label the weakest of these talks as a ceremonial dialogue but I have included it for a number of reasons. These are that it is readily distinguishable from everyday conversation, it shows in embryonic form features of the stronger talks, the Trio distinguish it by a special name, and it fits into the general scheme I am going to draw up. *Tesʌmïken*,[9] as this form of the ceremonial dialogue is called, is readily distinguishable from everyday speech both by the speed at which it is carried on and by the continual and formalized response of *irʌrʌ* (that's it) by the listener which gives the conversation a slightly staccato effect.[10] While these are the features which distinguish *tesʌmïken* from everyday conversation they also indicate its relationship with the two stronger forms. It is also distinguished from the other dialogues in a number of ways. It is not marked by any particular formality, both men and women use it, they may be sitting or standing, two or more people may be involved, and they will almost certainly be acquainted or related. It is used to tell people what one is going to do, or what one has done when it involves something out of the ordinary or when the participants have not seen each other for some time. It is used to relay news between friends, and for when one is going on a journey or has returned from one. For example, I have seen this talk used by a man and his wife on returning from a two-week trip in conversation with the man's half-sister and his wife's half-brother. On exceptional occasions it may be used between affines who know each other well but conventionally should not speak to each other. Thus I saw a man use it with his mother's half-sister's husband who was laid up with a wounded leg, and at another time this same injured man used this talk with his wife's sister's daughter's husband. It may also be used between individuals in close daily contact when some particular emphasis is required. Thus I have heard an Indian talking *tesʌmïken* with his mother when he was trying to persuade her to pay attention to the missionaries' teaching.

The two other forms of ceremonial dialogue are collectively called *turakane*, business talking or talkers, which is a word also used for visitors. It is derived from the verb ʌ*turaka*, to talk business or to do barter. The main feature of these dialogues, and one which clearly distinguishes them from *tesʌmĭken*, is that they are competitive. They are also marked by a far greater degree of formality, and the easiest method of exposition is to start with the most formal and strongest talk in which these features are most clearly visible.

The strongest talk is called *nokato* and is almost the exclusive preserve of men. It is said that a man and a woman but never women alone can participate. The dialogue takes place between two men and normally in the middle of the village square.[11] The two men sit on stools facing slightly away from each other.[12] The stools are an important part of the ceremony since they are a symbol of maleness and formality. The original stool, so the myth runs, was carved out of rock, the symbol of eternity and endurance, which are important features of the ceremonial dialogue.[13] The Trio word for being well, in the sense of being in good health, is *karime*, and it also means strong, but further than this it means hard and long lasting. Thus someone who is well is strong and enduring, and a person who is good at ceremonial dialogue has his talk described as *karime*, which combines the sense of strength and length. The ceremonial dialogue is a verbal duel which is won by the man who can go on arguing longest. A dialogue between two men, both of whose talk is *karime*, may well go on for 24 hours. The loser is the man who runs out of words first, and when he can no longer reply he picks up his stool and leaves the village square.

During the dialogue the participants take it in turn to speak for a period of about ten minutes. The dialogue is made up of short rhyming sentences, the rhyme being achieved by ending every sentence with the same word. There are two possible endings, one *kara* and the other *tʌme*, which can be used according to the preference of the speaker and seem to lack any meaning other than their purpose of providing rhythm.[14] The listener responds by making a low murmuring grunt at the end of each short sentence.

The words and phrases used in these dialogues are said to be archaic. Informants claim that the words used in ceremonial dialogue were used in everyday speech by their grandfathers. Whether this is true or not it is quite observable that normally helpful informants have great difficulty in explaining the exact meaning of either words or phrases which occur in ceremonial dialogue. Thus the dialogues are not merely stylized in form but their actual content does not belong to everyday speech. There is, therefore, in ceremonial dialogue the use of an esoteric language in which meaning appears to play a secondary role. All informants, both young and old, agree that the old men have the strongest talk, and that young men do not know the use of *nokato*. There is a very clear correlation among the Trio between age, wisdom, and experience; the word *yumme* covers all these ideas and it is also used for a fruit which is ripe and ready for eating. The younger men, including one young village leader, never admit to speaking *nokato*, but it would appear that they mean that they cannot speak it fluently since the old men who know it say that they started to learn at an early age, at about twenty years old. It is also quite clear that for the majority of young men and women of all ages, much of the contents of the ceremonial dialogue makes no more sense than it does to me.

Further than this, and in agreement with it, is the unanimous opinion that an old man would always defeat a young man in the ceremonial dialogue. This, to some extent, is clearly a conventional attitude, and one old man pointed out as having particularly strong talk (he is the oldest Trio man I met) is obviously too far into his dotage to have carried on a ceremonial dialogue for any length of time. The conventional and assumed ability for the old to out-talk the young does not mean that the former have unbridled control over the latter, who have certain compensating mystical sanctions. An old person is good to a younger one because the former's soul is weak, and should the younger man die while his soul is still strong then the soul of the younger man will be more powerful than that of the elder man in the other world (*entu*, literally source, but when unqualified it refers to the soul source or reservoir).

Nokato is the strongest and most formal form of ceremonial dialogue, the slightly weaker and less formal talk is *sipʌsipʌman*. Younger men know and use it, and a number of women are also said to know it, and on occasions to have used it. Although the Trio classify it with *nokato* as *turakane* it has a number of features reminiscent of *tesʌmĭken*. It lacks the constant repetition of the rhyming ends, although some sentences or groups of sentences will end in *kara* or *tʌme*. The response is sometimes the grunt, but just as often the *irʌrʌ* response of *tesʌmĭken*. The participants normally sit on stools but not invariably, and this conclusion is supported by the fact that women may take part and they do not use stools.[15]

The feature of *sipʌsipʌman*, and this is implicit in its classification as a form of *turakane*, which aligns it with *nokato*, is its basically competitive nature. One can now go on to consider when and by whom ceremonial dialogue is used.

III

Ceremonial dialogue is used between strangers or kin and acquaintances between whom the relationship has temporarily lapsed. It has three main purposes: to receive visitors or announce one's arrival in a village, to trade, and to obtain a wife. These situations will be considered in turn although, as will be seen, they overlap each other to some degree.

When a stranger arrives in a village he is allowed and given the opportunity to explain himself. To understand this one must bear in mind what has already been said about attitudes to strangers. All strangers are regarded with suspicion – hostility mixed with fear – because strangers are the people who curse and who bring sickness, two things which are very close together in Trio thought. In his own agglomeration an Indian is known and his qualities of friendliness and cooperativeness are recognized.[16] These are the characteristics which are not simply the prophylaxis against sorcery but the indication that one is not a sorcerer. These qualities are not immediately recognizable in the stranger, nor are they taken for granted. The ceremonial dialogue allows the stranger, in forceful terms and under cross-examination, to claim his good intentions, to explain who he is and what he is doing. The content of such dialogue is a continued repetition of the fact that he is a good man, he is friendly, he is not a sorcerer, he is not ill, and that he does not bring colds with him. His opponent, normally the village leader, will throw doubt on his intentions by saying that other visitors had enjoyed their hospitality and yet cursed, that some had brought colds and people had died, and that other travellers had tried to take their women. In the course of the conversation the two sides will also take the opposite stand: the visitor will ask his hosts not to curse him and the hosts will assure the visitor that they are not sorcerers. The other main content of the 'reception' dialogue is the passing of news which, while important in its own right, also serves as further justification of the stranger's integrity since if those you know have accepted him then it is safe for you to do so.[17]

Most journeys are made for one of two reasons, trade or marriage.

However, many young Indians make extensive journeys without either of these aims in mind simply for adventure and out of curiosity – just to see, as one Trio put it. The same informant went on to explain that young men are not afraid and that fear comes with experience, nor are people afraid of young men because they are inexperienced i.e. cannot curse. He described how as a young man he travelled widely but that on one journey some people threatened to kill him, accusing him of sorcery, and that after that he travelled rarely but stayed in his village and was fierce to strangers.

There is not much that needs to be said about trade. Here the ceremonial dialogue has strong affinities with the institutionalized haggling of the market-place, and in the absence of any set values the ceremonial dialogue acts as a mediating device and a means of regulating the disputes that are the invariable concomitant of such open bargaining. Within the agglomeration there is no use for ceremonial dialogue in the field of exchange, since the obligations of kinship render it superfluous. Between those residentially and socially close no record is kept of what is received and given.[18] At the very most *tesʌmĭken* will be used when the request is outrageous enough to question the good faith of the relationship. The important article of trade among the Trio is the hunting dog, and, if one leaves out women, the single most valuable item in Trio culture. The value of a good dog is more than its worth as a hunting-aid,[19] since it is the main currency used to obtain manufactured objects from outside, mainly from Bush Negroes who act (or acted, since the trade is disappearing) as middlemen between the Indians and the 'Western' culture of the coast. Ceremonial dialogue does not enter into the trading relationship between the Trio and the Bush Negroes but instead another form of Trio institution is adapted for the purpose.

This is the Trio trading practice whereby some Indians, usually the older ones but not all of them, have specific trading partners (*ipanawa*) in distant villages. These partnerships are more or less permanent alliances once they are entered into, even if no exchange takes place over some years. Between *ipanawa* a close account is kept of what is exchanged but there is, at the same time, a high degree of trust involved since payment for a particular item is frequently long delayed. It is this trading practice which forms the basis, at least among the Trio, of the extensive trade routes which are a feature of the interior of Guiana. Ceremonial dialogue is still a feature of the bargaining between *ipanawa* but it is this practice without the ceremonial dialogue which forms the basis of the Trio trade with the Bush Negroes.[20] It might be noted here that the Trio also state that ceremonial dialogue is a Trio institution and that they do not use it with other people, Amerindian or otherwise.[21]

Conventionally the relationship term employed between Trio *ipanawa* is *pito*, a reciprocal term, which, although it can be defined genealogically, is not a term used for close kin or affines. The best definition for the term is classificatory brother-in-law or male cross-cousin and the use of this term between *ipanawa* gives further indication of the closeness of trade and marriage in Trio thought.

The use of ceremonial dialogue in obtaining a wife needs to be discussed in a little more detail. Marriage among the Trio is prescribed with a category of women which includes both cross-cousins but also all unrelated women until or unless they are classified by a term which places them in a prohibited category. A preference is stated for village endogamy, but in fact because of the high mobility within the sphere of an agglomeration this is the basically endogamous unit. While there is no definite rule of post-marital residence, there is a tradition of matrilocal residence but the tendency is for brothers and sisters to stay together – a practice made possible by marriage with the sister's daughter.

If a man marries a closely related woman there is no formality; no brideprice is paid, brideservice is negligible and barely distinguishable from the duties of kin, and the pre-existing nexus of relationships is not disturbed but simply strengthened. For a man who marries outside his own agglomeration, the situation is slightly different. He has to win his wife by ceremonial dialogue which he carries on with the father or some other male relative of the woman. On how well the suitor does in the dialogue will depend such things as the size of the brideprice, length and intensity of the brideservice, place of post-marital residence, and his status among his affines. Since it is mainly young men who marry away from home, the suitor normally comes out of the ceremonial dialogue rather badly for he will almost certainly be competing with a much older and stronger man. He will probably get his wife but at the price of long and strenuous brideservice, which will automatically be coupled with matrilocal residence. The lot of the in-marrying stranger is not a happy one, since he will find himself in an avoidance relationship with most of his new neighbours. Once a man is married he no longer resorts to ceremonial dialogue when he wishes to communicate with his wife's kin, with whom he should not converse directly at all, but through the medium of his wife. The avoidance relationship takes over as the means of mediating or preventing potential disputes and the degrees in which the severity of the avoidance is applied parallels the strength of the ceremonial dialogue used. The less well the participants are known to each other the more severe or stronger these institutionalized forms become. Finally, it might be noted that all strangers (and not simply unknown Trio) are regarded as a threat to a village's female capital and it is not surprising that the two most clearly defined forms of behaviour that exist in Trio culture should be concerned with their most valuable asset and its relationship to the outside world.[22]

IV

Enough has now been said to indicate the circumstances and the reasons for the use of ceremonial dialogue, but it will be useful to relate this usage to the Trio settlement pattern described above. What is described below is a consensus of various informants' opinions on this subject, and there are one or two interesting variations that will also be considered.

First, as has been mentioned, ceremonial dialogue is not used within the boundaries of the agglomeration. The Trio say that they do not use ceremonial dialogue with their *imoitĭ*, a term which implies relationship through co-residence. Co-residence is an important factor in the ordering of Trio relationships, even to the point where it may become confused with genealogical relationship, that is to say no clear distinction is made between them. Through mobility of population this may mean that virtually everyone inside an agglomeration will be classified as an *imoitĭ*.

The various informants agreed that they would use the weaker talk, *sipʌsipʌman*, with those of a different agglomeration of the same group, and the stronger talk, *nokato*, with people who lived further away, in one of the other two groups. It is interesting that, although I collected a number of independent accounts of the use of ceremonial dialogue, I received from all sources the same overall picture. It is probably safe to say that the picture is an idealized one, and that if it had been possible to observe ceremonial dialogue in practice there would have been numerous instances which did not fit the described behaviour.

It is worth considering at this point some of the variations on the main theme which I heard. One informant describing a journey stated that on coming to a village one evening he used *nokato* but that the following morning he spoke *sipʌsipʌman* with his hosts. This does make some sense since one would hardly expect the talk to become stronger as the parties got to know each other better and it is significant that the informant said 'next day', because the Trio consider that friendship comes through passing the night together.[23]

If the use of both types of dialogue in the same situation can be explained in the context of the ideal model, the situation in the second set of exceptions is not so clear. This concerns the use of ceremonial dialogue to ask people to dance festivals, and informants do not agree on whether invitations to such functions involved ceremonial dialogue or not; some said it does and others that it does not. One must assume that both answers are correct, and that in some cases ceremonial dialogue is used and in others not. I cannot be certain of what follows because I failed to follow up this particular line of inquiry since I did not notice the variations until I got home, but two possible explanations present themselves. First, that invitations to other villages of the same agglomeration are made informally and only those villages located in other agglomerations which are invited are asked formally. Alternatively, the ceremonial dialogue is used in asking those villages of the same agglomeration with which the host village is on bad terms. These seem to be the two most likely solutions and both fit in with the general scheme of interpretation since in both cases the ceremonial dialogue is used where there is an uncomfortable amount of social distance.

The third set of exceptions refers to women using ceremonial dialogue. One should note for a start that the situations in which a man uses ceremonial dialogue are barely appropriate for a woman. Women do not travel alone and therefore there is never any need for them to take part in a reception dialogue. Women do not trade, nor, as far as I have any record, do they take part in a dialogue relating to their daughter's marriage. It has already been stated that conventionally women are not expected to know ceremonial dialogues very well, nor do they sit on stools. All this suggests that a woman does not carry on ceremonial dialogues with a stranger, and the very few examples of women using ceremonial dialogue which I was able to collect bear out this assumption. An informant stated that a woman would be most likely to use ceremonial dialogue with her brother, and one of the recorded cases involves this relationship. The other case concerned a woman and her brother's son, and the woman's aim was to obtain meat from him which is not a normal obligation of this relationship. However, the presence of the brother–sister relationship in this context is not without interest, since the relationship is the pivotal one in Trio social organization and there is considerable and enduring social and economic interdependency between a brother and a sister. For the individual this relationship is as vital as the communication between villages is for Trio society as a whole. Unfortunately, I do not know the actual situations in which these dialogues occurred, but it would seem that its usage in this way fits with the function of the dialogue as a means by which communication is made possible either by mediating a new relationship or by re-forming an old one which has fallen into temporary abeyance.[24] Among close kin *tesʌmïken* is the usual talk employed but it is possible that in particularly important situations a stronger form has to be adopted.

In summary, the function of ceremonial dialogue is mediation in situations that are likely to give rise to conflict. Such situations are most likely to arise between those who are unrelated, and this fact is recognized by the increasing formality of the ceremonial dialogue in direct proportion to increasing social and physical distance. The boundary of the ceremonial dialogue is coterminous with Trio territory, and implies that its participants accept certain values and conventions. It is in the coincidence of Trio political and moral boundaries that the similarity between the feud and ceremonial dialogue is most apparent.

Evans-Pritchard defined the boundaries of the Nuer tribe as the point beyond which the feud turned into warfare, since there no longer existed the moral commitment to resolve the dispute. For the Trio every effort is made to prevent the dispute occurring and this is quite evident from the employment of ceremonial dialogue in situations which are *potentially* disruptive and among people between whom there is *likely* to be a clash of interests. This interpretation is fully in keeping with other facets of Trio culture and attitudes; the Trio like to keep things 'cool', they manifest a dislike of strong emotions, and put considerable value on moderation in all things.

Ceremonial dialogue is not a phenomenon unique to the Trio, and besides describing the Waiwai variety Fock has listed a number of other people among whom some similar institution would appear to exist (1963: 216–30). However, by distinguishing between ceremonial dialogue and the weeping greeting or mourning wailing, he indicates that the first is almost entirely restricted to the area north of the Amazon. This may be a valid distinction but it does overlook the importance of speech in the politics of many tribes south of the Amazon. To quote but two examples, among the Tupian Urubu, hard speech is an ideal of chiefship (Huxley 1963: 88); and for the Shavante oratory is an essential part of political success and a skilful chief will be able to have potential conflict talked out (Maybury-Lewis 1967). However, the only description of ceremonial dialogue which allows any comparison with that of the Trio is Fock's account of the Waiwai. While there are many similarities between the Waiwai *oho* and the Trio *turakane*, particularly in their content and function, there are some interesting differences which can be correlated with certain differences in social organization.

The most obvious difference is that there is only a single type, and presumably strength, of the *oho*, and this would appear to be used indiscriminately between co-villagers, between people from different villages, and even between those from different tribes. It is, of course, possible that there are variations in both strength and length which are not terminologically distinguished, but which still exist and are implicitly recognized. However, there is one institution, that of affinal avoidance, which shows a similar weak development. It has been mentioned that the Trio make almost exactly the same structural distinctions in their use of affinal avoidance as they do in their use of ceremonial dialogue. The Waiwai, who make no explicit structural distinctions in their use of ceremonial dialogue, have only weakly developed affinal avoidance – it is limited to the relationship between the wife's mother and her daughter's husband (ibid: 201). The Waiwai form of ceremonial dialogue clearly indicates that their view of their own society is different from that which the Trio have of theirs. First, Fock states 'The Waiwai tribe is not a political unit' (ibid.: 233), and his reason for this is that there is no one who represents the Waiwai as a tribe. Regardless of whether or not this is an adequate definition of a political unit, this claim is supported by the Waiwai use of ceremonial dialogue with other local tribes. This fits with certain features of their social environment since they are a small group living intermixed with a number of other groups, both Carib- and Arawak-speaking, with whom they have continual interaction. However, if the Waiwai do not express socio-spatial distinctions by means of the *oho* chant, it would appear that its use does reflect a socio-political organization, an administrative hierarchy within the village, which is absent among the Trio (ibid.: 208).

Peter Rivière

There are clearly some intriguing differences between Trio and Wai-wai social structure, but these are not likely to be revealed by restricting comparison to the obvious functional similarities of similar institutions. This is not meant to be a comparative study and, while I intend at some later date to attempt such a study of the tribes in the interior of Guiana, here I wish merely to stress that the full meaning of a particular institution can be reached only by examining its associated ideas and behavioural manifestations, and then by viewing them all as an aspect of the total social structure.

NOTES

1. This article is based on information collected during a period of field-work among the Trio in 1963–4. My field researches were sponsored by the Research Institute for the Study of Man, New York, to which organization I wish to acknowledge my continued gratitude.
2. The term "ceremonial dialogue" was introduced by Niels Fock to describe a similar institution among the Waiwai Indians, the western neighbours of the Trio (cf. Fock 1963). It would only lead to confusion to introduce a new term for this institution.
3. Certain aspects of Trio social organization are dealt with summarily in this paper but the evidence for any unsupported statement will be found in Rivière (1969).
4. This paper is written in the ethnographic present but in fact much of the traditional settlement pattern had disappeared as a result of missionary activity by the time I reached the field. The pattern which I use here is constructed from the account of Schmidt (1942) and my own field data. The detailed work of this reconstruction will be found in Rivière (1969: chapter VI).
5. The most permanent village of which I have a record lasted for at least twenty years under the same leadership and more or less on the same site. It finally ceased to exist as a result of missionary activity.
6. There is a further judgement on the quality of leadership in this; a capable leader is one who chooses a good village site and organizes successful hunting and fishing parties. In times of genuine shortage he will have to have the ability to weather and resolve the conflicts to which the shortage gives rise.
7. Cf. Goldman (1962: 202 sqq.). The very orgiastic nature of the dance festival gives rise to accusations of adultery and the movement of people allows the spread of any infection in the area, and suspicion of sorcery results.

8. As recently as 1952 and 1958 Protasio Frikel found Trio villages in which 25 and 17 Indians respectively had recently died from 'flu (1960).

9. Trio vowels are pronounced thus: a as in c*a*r; e as in p*e*t; i as in m*e*; o as in d*o*pe; u as in b*oo*t; ʌ as in c*u*p; and ɨ is a flat u.

10. It is not possible to confuse this form of talk with everyday conversation. After I had been among the Trio a few days only and while busy writing in my hammock, my attention was drawn to it by the change in rhythm of the conversation going on around me.

11. As far as I can make out, the dialogue did not *have* to take place in the village square, but it usually did so. Most ceremonial dialogues take place in the dry season, which is the time of year when the Trio travel; accordingly, the weather is usually suitable for the dialogue to take place in the open. Furthermore, the village square is a symbolically more appropriate place for ceremonial dialogue than the house, the former being a man's place and the latter a woman's.

12. Even when I persuaded two Indians to carry on a ceremonial dialogue for recording purposes they insisted on sitting slightly turned away from each other.

13. Besides wooden stools, the only item regularly used as a seat is the old shell of a land turtle. For comments on the symbolic value of this see Rivière (1969: chapters XI and XII).

14. A brief extract from one of my numerous recordings runs thus:

> *Wʌepha kara* (I have come)
> *kure wae kara* (I am good)
> *napono se wae kara* (things I am wanting)
> *ʌemirɨ se wae kara* (your daughter I want)
> *yipɨme iye wae kara* (my wife, I want)
> *yiwʌri me iye wae kara* (my woman, her being, I want).

It would be possible to substitute *tʌme* for *kara* throughout without making any difference to the sense.

15. Conventionally women do not use stools, but I have seen elderly women sit on them when no man was present except myself.

16. This does not mean that no one of the same village or agglomeration is regarded as being a sorcerer, but it is rare and the Trio prefer to think the best of the people whom they know. For further discussion of this point see Rivière (1970).

17. The Trio word for news is *eka*, which term is also used for name among the more westerly Trio. A range of meaning which reflects the journalist's adage that people are news. Among the Trio who live at the eastern end of the region the word for name is *etɨ*.

18. This form of exchange is equivalent to that called 'generalized reciprocity' by Sahlins (1965). Trade outside an agglomeration, whether with Trio, other Indians, or even those of different ethnic background, tends to correspond to Sahlins' 'balanced reciprocity'. There is no form of exchange, other than raiding, which can be classified as Sahlins's third form, 'negative reciprocity', although not all balanced reciprocity is free of a little cheating.

19. Possession of a good hunting dog adds to an Indian's prestige and also to his success as a hunter which, in turn, is a source of prestige.

20. Trade with an *ipanawa*, Trio or Bush Negro, is a form of delayed exchange, and it maybe months, even years, before an original payment is repaid.

21. One might imagine that the linguistic nature of the dialogue would automatically prevent its use across tribal boundaries, which in this area are usually dialect or language boundaries, but Fock claims that the Waiwai use ceremonial dialogue with members of other tribes and quotes Barrère on the Galibi to the same effect (1963: 220, 238). The Trio conception of ceremonial dialogue as a purely intra-Trio institution is, therefore, a means by which they express the notion of their political unity.

22. I have demonstrated elsewhere (Rivière 1969) how these institutions reflect one of the fundamental distinctions which the Trio make, that between inside and outside, and the extent to which the Trio use these categories in ordering their world.

23. When informants defined the word *imoitï* for me they invariably introduced the idea of passing the night together. Furthermore, the Trio lack a word for family or for those who share a house, and in response to my attempts to find one informants used expressions such as *yitawʌrʌken* which literally means 'my very own dawning ones', in other words those who have woken up with me and thus have spent the night with me.

24. I am grateful to Sr Roberto Da Matta who pointed out to me that *tesʌmïken* may be used to separate people as well as to bring them together. This certainly makes sense of the use of this talk when people are leaving on a journey or in the case when a son used it to his mother. In the majority of cases, however, its function is undoubtedly that of reuniting people.

REFERENCES

EVANS-PRITCHARD, E. E. 1940 *The Nuer*. Oxford: Clarendon Press.
FOCK, N. 1963 Waiwai: Religion and Society of an Amazonian Tribe. Copenhagen: *Danish National Museum, Ethnographic Series*. No. 8.

FRIKEL, P. 1960 Os Tiriyó. Belem: *Boletim do Museu Paraense Emilio Goeldi, Antropologia,* No. 9.

GILLIN, J. 1963 Tribes of the Guianas. New York: *Handbook of South American Indians* 3: 799–860.

GOLDMAN, I. 1963 The Cubeo: Indians of the Northwest Amazon. *Illinois Studies in Anthropology.* No 2. Urbana: University of Illinois Press.

HUXLEY, F. J. 1963 *Affable Savages.* London: Hart-Davis; New York: Viking Press, 1957.

MAYBURY-LEWIS, D. 1967 *Akwẽ-Shavante Society.* Oxford: Clarendon Press.

RIVIÈRE, P. G. 1969 *Marriage among the Trio.* Oxford: Clarendon Press.

— 1970 Factions and Exclusions in Two South American Village Systems. Pp. 245–55, in Douglas, M. (ed.), *Witchcraft Confessions and Accusations,* ASA Monograph 9. London: Tavistock Publications.

SAHLINS, M. D. 1965 On the Sociology of Primitive Exchange. Pp. 139–236 in Banton, M. (ed.), *The Relevance of Models for Social Anthropology.* ASA Monograph 1. London: Tavistock Publications.

SCHMIDT, L. 1942 Verslag van drie Reizen naar Bovenlandsche Indianen. Paramaribuo: *Department Landbouwproefstation in Suriname.* Bulletin No. 58.

The Genealogical Method in the Analysis of Myth, and a Structural Model

ERIC TEN RAA

Beyond tradition lies the horizon of pure myth which is always seen in the same time perspective (Evans-Pritchard 1940: 108).

The material which I propose to discuss in this paper[1] is the creation myth of the Sandawe of central Tanzania, a small people of non-Bantu stock who speak a click language which may be Khoisan, and who are organized in exogamous patrilineal clans. In doing so I hope to arrive at a better understanding of the meaning of the myth through the use of a genealogical analysis of the relationships between its heroes which, in turn, may lead to some new insights into the structure of myth, problems of mythical inversion, and the nature of mythical creation. The Sandawe creation myth is a tale of extreme simplicity, a fact which renders it particularly suitable for the kind of analysis which I propose to carry out on it. The simpler the tale, the smaller the danger that some significant detail may have been overlooked.

I. THE PROBLEM

To begin with we have to consider the scope of the myth. A creation myth is obviously an oral document which gives us a representation of the creation of the world, mankind, and the animals, but, as is the case with other creation myths, some versions of the Sandawe myth are more comprehensive than others, because they also seek to explain the origins of the various tribes which people the world, and how it came about that some animals behave the way they do. Notwithstanding this difficulty, the Sandawe myth does not offer us serious problems of delimitation of the material, because in its simplicity it tends to stick fairly closely to its subject-matter. Actually the explanations of tribal diversity throw an interesting sidelight on what the myth seeks to convey, and they will therefore be included in our consideration. Explanations of why animals behave the way they do, however, will be treated as side-issues. The reason for this is that the myth essentially concerns humanity, not the animal kingdom.

Second, we have to consider the form of the myth. The form in which the Sandawe myth is told is the same as the form in which historical traditions are told, but different from the forms of animal fables and miraculous stories; for this reason we have to decide whether myth and historical tale do not perhaps fall into the same category of oral tradition. Sandawe animal fables and miraculous stories are told in a form which is partly sung. Indeed, the telling of such stories tend to a considerable degree to be centred upon the songs which are sung in it; rather than the narrative itself it is the songs which convey the essence of the stories' protagonists. A good story ought to have a song. The song portrays the actors, and it might well be argued that the songs *are* the actors. But in mythical and historical tales the situation is quite different: these do not contain songs but, instead, they depend for their proper effect entirely upon the spoken text. Thus we see that the Sandawe myth and historical tale have an important form-element in common. And seemingly (but not in actual fact, as we shall see), they have even more in common than form alone. Historical tales are told in praise of the deeds of great magicians and other heroes, or of the founders of lineages and clans, or even of whole clans in their opposition to enemies. In a similar manner, stories like the creation myth may *seem* to be told in praise of a creator or a culture hero. Thus we are faced with a curious apparent correspondence between both the *form* in which myth and history are told, and the apparent *purpose* of the two. Both depend for their proper effect on the precision of the spoken word rather than on the poetry of a song, and both also seem to have for a purpose the commemoration of someone's deeds. But a closer look will soon convince us that this is not so and that, instead, the purposes (or functions) of myth and history actually display an important difference. This difference is important enough to make us decide that the two in fact belong in totally different categories.

The best we can do to gain a clear insight into the issue is to divert our attention for a moment away from the Sandawe scene and to consider Professor Evans-Pritchard's analysis of Nuer mythology. In *The Nuer* (1940: 108) he writes, 'beyond tradition lies the horizon of pure myth which is always seen in the same time perspective'. What he in effect does is to separate clearly pure myth from historical tradition.

The Analysis of Myth

The two are quite different from each other, he finds, in that they are based upon different kinds of time. And he continues to present us with a very illuminating discussion of the concept of mythical time (ibid.).

'It will have been noted that the Nuer time dimension is shallow. Valid history ends a century ago, and tradition, generously measured, takes us back only ten or twelve generations in lineage structure, and if we are right in supposing that lineage structure never grows, it follows that the distance between the beginning of the world and the present day remains unalterable. Time is thus not a continuum, but is a constant structural relationship between two points, the first and the last persons in a line of agnatic descent. How shallow is Nuer time may be judged from the fact that the tree under which mankind came into being was still standing in Western Nuerland a few years ago!'

The matter of the different aspects of time has been further illuminated by Feierman. Historians, he points out, make a similar distinction between two different kinds of time, i.e. the one they refer to as non-reversible time and the one they call reversible time. Events in a story which have happened at a given moment in its time-sequence are irretrievably located in the past. This is the non-reversible time to which students of history are accustomed. But there also exists another mode of thought about time, common to most religious conceptions. This is the time of eternal meanings; in this kind of time in Christian thought, for example, Christ can be in the world today. This is reversible time.[2]

From yet another, purely theoretical, angle the two have been separated by Lévi-Strauss in his well-known structural analyses in which he removes from the body of a myth its diachronic element – the sequence of time – in order to find the timeless core of the myth: that is, the message which it seeks to convey. Thus he finds that the diachronic element in a mythological tale is the factor which makes it possible to *tell* the myth. In other words, the diachronic element is simply a technical expedient in the process of conveying the message of which it forms no integral part.

Thus we see from the Nuer material as well as from general theory that pure myth and history have quite different purposes. Christian mythology is mainly theological, but the Nuer material shows us that myth is also socio-political. As Evans-Pritchard puts it, 'actual inter-relations of a political kind are . . . explained and justified in mythological interrelations', and he then continues to point out that Nuer mythology does this by explaining the relations between aristocratic clans and large stronger lineages living with them, or by bringing into some social relationship the ancestors of different lineages or clans (1940: 234). This reminds us of Lévi-Strauss's attempts, in 'La Geste d'Asdiwal' (1967), to isolate several kinds of message from the body of the myth, or to demonstrate the existence of several mythical levels which can be separated by analysis. This is a matter to which I also propose to pay some attention, but not until I shall have presented the analysis of my material. At the moment we shall therefore not consider the economic, geographical, and other messages contained in myth, or even its socio-political implications. What matters at this juncture is that, like the Nuer myths and other myths of the beginning of the world, the Sandawe creation myth appears to be a *social* document. This, then, is the basic assumption from which we shall develop our argument. This does not mean that our myth is not also a tale of the beginning of the world, the way the Sandawe see it. But it is not history; in fact, it is the very antithesis of history. It is based on a totally different concept of time, and 'time' as we know it in a historical sense is used in it only as a technical expedient. Unlike historical tales it is told simply to convey a social message, not as a commemorative tale in praise of some ancient hero.

In order to arrive at the core of our discussion we now have to consider the matter of variations. Is there a 'true' version of a myth?

That which I have referred to as non-reversible time is history, and because historical truth gets condensed and distorted in oral tradition, and sometimes mixed up with pure myth, it may be argued that oral tradition and true history are mutually exclusive. In order to remain true, historical texts would have to be handed down from generation to generation in a totally unaltered form, which is impossible. But on the other hand, myth, the timeless story, *can* be told in different forms because it is symbolic. Symbolism implies a rendition of values by analogy and by simile, by allegory and by parabole; we may therefore call it poetic representation, a representation which carries symbolic truth. Thus we find that historical truth depends on literal, prosaic representation, but symbolic truth allows for many different versions, and indeed thrives on variation.

Every storyteller tells a story in his own manner, in his own choice of words, according to his own viewpoint, and according to his own interpretation. Now, his interpretation may be a matter of very minor importance because usually his aim is to render the story as he has heard it rather than to render it with a particular purpose in mind, with a particular slant to it which is aimed at a specially selected member of the audience. Such instances do occur even though they may be rare.[3] But if a story is told for a particular purpose, then it is not surprising to find that one particular angle of it is stressed or even distorted.

But also if, as is normally the case, the story is told for no other reason than to provide entertainment for a general audience, the storyteller will naturally bring out his story the way he sees it. And each story-teller's vision of each particular passage may differ from that of another. He may have been struck by one particular aspect of a name, an action, or a theme, which he then renders according to his own insights. In this way we may collect different versions of a myth which not only show individual variation, but may also *disagree* with one another in detail.

Evans-Pritchard has noted that 'it is, of course, well known that there is much variation in the telling of the same folk-tale by different persons, but [that] not much has been said on this topic in respect of African folk-tale. Usually the best variant is published' (1964: 103). And, indeed, the exceptions are few. A notable one is W. H. I. Bleek, who as early as 1864 presented four Hottentot versions of the origin of death together with a fifth, a Zulu version, which shows much resemblance (1864: 69–73; 14). Another is Evans-Pritchard himself, who has devoted at least one whole paper to the presentation of five different versions of a Zande tale (1964).[4] In a more theoretical vein Lévi-Strauss has remarked that 'if a myth is made up of all its variants, structural analysis should take all of them into account' (1963: 217) and he points out that repetition helps to show up structure, arguing that in terms of their function variations may be likened to repetition in language (*passim*; 229 ff). Thus he finds that 'there is no single "true" version of which all the others are but copies or distortions' (ibid.: 218).

The question now arises, does not our argument that different versions may *disagree* with one another, contradict Lévi-Strauss? If we look at it closely we shall see that in fact it does not. I have already stated that myth represents symbolic truth, i.e. a many-faceted general truth rather than the factual truth of a time sequence. This appears to be in complete agreement with Lévi-Strauss, and to support his dismissal of the notion that versions might perhaps represent 'copies and distortions'. Mutually clashing versions must not be placed in a single

317

category with 'copies and distortions'; this may be done, as we have seen, in the case of factual history but not in the case of myth. Thus we find ourselves in agreement with Lévi-Strauss's theme in *Le Cru et le cuit*, that a piece of music may be played by many members of an orchestra, each of whom plays a different tune at the same time yet in harmony with the others, even though the individual notes which they play may be at variance with each other, and even clash. Like music, myth is poetry. Although there may be no single 'true' version of the myth, there *is* always a single 'true' main theme in its total representation.[5]

But how can we distinguish the 'true' main theme of our mythical orchestra? We can never listen to an orchestra of storytellers and appreciate the message which their myth contains; all we hear are the different versions. How then do we decide which parts of the myth belong to the main message and which are individual overtones? If we accept the proposition that a myth is a social document it follows that it expresses social values rather than historical fact, and if this is true we may use our knowledge of society to decipher the mythical message, since the one reflects the other. And because myth places its protagonists in certain social relationships to one another, as Evans-Pritchard has suggested, we ought to have a look at those relationships and decide which versions conform with social reality and which do not.

In a nutshell, we may now state our problem as follows:

(a) The totality of the myth as it is told (read: our material) consists of message plus time-sequence. With the aid of Evans-Pritchard's analysis and Lévi-Strauss's technique we can separate out the message.

(b) But the message is many-faceted and often contradictory. We have to find its main theme. This I propose to do by setting up the genealogies of the myth's protagonists, showing the nature of their relationships. Those sets of relationships which are socially acceptable can then be recognized as expressing the myth's social message, and those sets which are not must be relegated to the status of deviant versions or individual overtones. But these individual overtones cannot be simply discarded; they form a valid part of our material, and our interpretation will therefore also have to take the deviancies into account and explain them.

The Analysis of Myth

II. THE MATERIAL

Versions of the Sandawe creation myth have been recorded by Demp-wolff (1916), Bagshawe (1925), van de Kimmenade (1936), and myself. The first version to be presented here is my translation of van de Kimmenade's account of the myth in French (1936: 407). In fact it is a mixture of the Sandawe myth and van de Kimmenade's own exegesis, but it forms a good point of departure because it covers the main points of the myth succinctly.

Version No. 1

There is in the country a tree called *gélle*: this is the baobab. It is known that this tree lasts for centuries, it is often hollow and its cavity is sometimes so large that one could put a table and a bed in it. The Sandawe do not say who has made the baobab, but they let everything that exists come out of it. *Ma Túnda* (is this a name which is given to God?) stands in front of the baobab. Then a hyena emerges from it, which he lets go, than a sheep which he keeps; and then a woman with two children. *Ma Túnda* asks her: 'Where is your husband?' – 'My husband,' says the woman, 'is in the tree.' The man comes out of it. After that all sorts of animals come out of it, which *Ma Túnda* lets go except a cow and a chicken, which he also retains.

The next version, by Dempwolff (1916: 144–5), covers more or less the same ground but it is more elaborate, having been taken down in the vernacular before Dempwolff translated it into German. In order to avoid the pitfalls of double translation I present this version in an English translation which I have made from Dempwolff's vernacular text, not from his German translation.

Version No. 2

At first Matunda emerged from the inside of a baobab tree; God opened the gate, and then he stood on the earth. When he had stood up completely he stood at the opening. While he stood [there], then the hyena ran out first. And he let it go, and [the hyena] ran away. And then sheep came out, and he stopped them and held them fast. And immediately afterwards a woman with children came out. And now he held them fast and he inquired: 'Where is your husband?' – 'He is inside the house.'

And he too came out, and [Matunda] held him fast. And then all the creatures came out; then the cattle came out and he held them fast. And then all the creatures together came out in turn: then the snake came out, and he let it go and it ran away; and then the lion came out, and he let it go; and then the leopard came out, and this one he let go; and the rhinoceros came out and he let it go; and the elephant came out and he let it go; the buffalo came out and he let it go; and the gazelle came out and he let it go; all the birds came out and he let them go [but] the chicken he held fast; and the giraffe came out and he let it go; the eland came out and he let it go; and the zebra came out and he let it go; and all the [other] animals came out and he let them go.

The next version, also by Dempwolff (1916: 144), adds little to the previous one. In fact it gives rather less detail but it mentions some animals which have not been mentioned in the previous texts. As in the previous case, the following is my translation of Dempwolff's vernacular material.

Version No. 3

The Great One [was called] Matunda. The Great One, Matunda, emerged from the inside of a baobab [tree]. Matunda [then] opened it, and then a hyena came out [but] he left it alone and it ran away. But a sheep he prevented [from running away]; that one he caught, that one. And then a woman came out with two children, and then a man came out. And then cattle came out, they came out from the inside of the baobab, and then goats came out from the inside of the baobab, chickens came out, and then donkeys came out, all of whom had been inside. And then hares [came out], and then birds, and then dwarf antelopes came out from the inside of the baobab, and then impalas, and then ostriches, and then all the animals came out from the inside of the baobab.

The version which follows next is one which has been recorded by Bagshawe in English (1925: 63);[6] in this version there are elements present of the justificational type of myth which tell us why the hyena behaves the way it does, and why women have menses. It identifies the creator with the sun and his wife with the moon, while at the same time giving him a name which shows the sun to be his child: *Matunda Nxussu* means the Creator's (female) Child.

Version No. 4

Matunda Nxussu, now the sun and his wife Quabso, now the moon, came from inside a hill and begot 4 sons and 4 daughters. When those were old enough their father again opened the hill and let out the animals warning them to catch the herbivora but to let the carnivora go past. After the cattle and sheep came the hyena and the children made a mistake and tried to catch it 'which is why the hyena is always looking over its shoulder', and in the confusion many useful animals escaped. Matunda Nxussu received of everything else himself, but gave to his wife the task of arranging for the propagation of the various species 'which is why certain physical functions of women follow the age of the moon'. The children quarrelled and scattered, and because they obeyed the moon, their women had very many children, and all the tribes were founded.

The following version, which describes the Sandawe Garden of Eden, was recorded by myself in 1966. The full vernacular text, which has not been published before, is presented in the appendix.[7] This time the sun is referred to as the Creator's male child (the son of Mathunda).

Version No. 5

1. Very long ago the sun, who was the son of Mathunda, lived in the north, in [the country of] Omı.
2. In those olden days the earth was very beautiful and cool, and the ruler of the earth was the moon.
3. When the son of Mathunda looked up and saw the moon he loved her very much, and he followed her to the south, there where she lived in the sky.
4. And he said: 'Her I shall marry.'
5. When Mathunda saw her, the moon lived in the sky, and he climbed up, and he married her.
6. And when it was dark they stayed in a hill. They stayed [there] very long.
7. When they had stayed [there] many days, then she, the moon, gave birth to several children, four male children, and also four female children.
8. When they had been born they stayed [there], and they grew up.
9. And then their father opened up the hill again, and the children came out from the inside.
10. And then their father opened up the hill again, and all the animals came out.

11. To begin with, the elephant came out, who is the great one [among] all the animals.

12. And then giraffes, and then lions, and then kudus, and then donkeys, all the animals, and they went [away].

13. And presently cattle came out, and goats, and sheep, and chickens, and then the children's father spoke thus to his children: 'Catch them.'

14. And then the children caught them, and they tied them up, [but] all those [other] animals, they let them go and they went away.

15. When the cattle and also the chickens had finished coming out, then the hyena came out.

16. When the children were on the point of catching it, then their father said: 'Leave it alone, she is a bad one. She is a cow without horns.'

17. And she too, the hyena, was afraid of the children who [tried to] catch her, and ran away, and in running away she ran with her head turned back [looking] furtively over the shoulder.

18. For that reason the hyena always looks back furtively over the shoulder until today.

19. When the children had let all the animals go, then all these [i.e. the game of the bush] were Mathunda's, and the cattle, dogs [and] goats were of Man's children.

20. And as for the hyena, that one was a bad one, she indeed was a witch.

21. And when Father the Sun and also Mother the Moon do not see her (i.e. during pitch-dark nights), it is then when she comes out and walks about, because she is a witch.

So far our texts have been concerned with the act of creation itself and its attendant conditions, but some other versions include the emergence and distribution of mankind. The following text is my translation of a version collected by Dempwolff in 1910 (1916: 145).

Version No. 6

This Matunda lived by a rock; and he built a house [there] and he killed a black cow and sacrificed it. Now the other people [also] sacrifice, because God made the opening. And now he reared people, he reared many people, and then there were many. Now then when there were many, then this one went to Burunge, that other one went to Gogo, and yet another went to Hi, and yet another went to Mbugwe and others still went to Konongo and these others went to Taturu and yet another went to Iramba. And then the earth had enough people. But these [some] others have remained, and our [people] too [remained] here, our forebears were left [here]; they reared us, and now then our forefathers reared us. It was enough, and then there were many.

The version which follows next is one which I collected in 1966. The vernacular text is presented in the appendix.

Version No. 7

1. Long ago, this Mathunda lived in [the country of] Tl'ééna, alone and without a wife, hunting animals.
2. And when he saw the moon, he saw her as a very beautiful girl. And then he followed her and climbed up [into the sky] and married her.
3. And they lived at a large rock, and the moon, she gave birth to many children.
4. When she had borne them, then Mathunda slaughtered a black cow, and the moon then made rain and the country became beautiful.
5. And until now the people make [rain] sacrifices.
6. And then Mathunda opened up the rock and all the children followed one another out and went [on their way].
7. When [the children] were getting up she, the moon, said: 'You must follow my words, you must follow my way; and you too must go and bear many children.'[8]
8. And the children went and they built their homes, they went, and they followed the words (instructions) of the moon.
9. And in their child-bearing, too, they follow the days of the moon until now.
10. And they stayed [for a long time]. When they had stayed, they gave birth, they gave birth to very many children, and the people multiplied very much, and the country became filled.
11. But now they quarrelled, and they split up.
12. Some went to the north, and then these became Barabaiga, and some went to the south; as for them, they became the Gogo, and some went to the east; they became the Burunge, and others went to the west; as for them, they became the Rimi.
13. Now then, they who stayed behind here, they became the Sandawe.
14. And their children, too, followed the words (instructions) of the

323

moon, and they gave birth very much, and all the tribes were founded, and the whole earth became filled with people.

The last version was also collected in 1966. The vernacular text is presented in the appendix. Here the Creator is the child of the sun, and the name of the first man to be created on earth is given as Wangu.

Version No. 8

1. In the very remote past the sun and the moon, who was his sister, lived in the sky.
2. This Mathunda was the sun's son, and he opened the rock and all the animals came out.
3. And a woman came out, and there she stood. And a man came out whose name was Wangu, and he came out and there he stood.
4. And then Mathunda took as a wife her who was Wangu's sister and married her, and the other (Wangu) married this other woman (Mathunda's sister).
5. And they lived [there]. And while they lived [there] the sun was completely drying up the country, and the wells were further and further away, and they herded their cattle going to the wells, going on and on.
6. When this Mathunda had gone, then he came close to the well and made the cattle go in, and they drank, they drank very much in the water until they had finished it [all].
7. Presently then, Wangu let in all his cattle. When they had entered [the well] there was no water at all; in the well the water had completely disappeared.
8. He said: 'Ah, this what-not, he has finished up all the water!', and he was furious, and here then their friendship broke up.
9. And they quarrelled, and when they had quarrelled Mathunda's clansmen went hither and Wangu's clansmen went thither, and they brought forth many children, and all the clans were founded and arose, and then it was enough.
10. Yes, and until today the sun goes on drying up the country very much.
11. And here it is finished.

In addition to the eight texts now presented I have collected the following information in respect of the contents of the myth:

(a) The 'proper Sandawe name' for the creator is not *Mathunda* but *Barãse* or *Baránse*.[9]

(b) The sun and the moon are also referred to as twins (*pasa*).

(c) Mathunda lived by a tree which stands in northwestern Sandawe country. According to one informant it is situated in the neighbourhood of Kongí, according to another near Mungé. Yet others say that mankind was created at the rock of Namulé.[10]

(d) After Mathunda had quarrelled with Wangu he moved to another place where he built his house, reared his children, and lived until he died.

Finally, Dempwolff (1916: 147) also supplies some additional information (part of which is also contained in our texts):

> 'The man who emerged from the baobab was called 'Wangu. By marrying each other's sisters, he and Matunda became double brothers-in-law. While digging a well, and also while herding cattle, Matunda deceived 'Wangu, for which reason he had to pay him a fine of two cattle. Later one of Matunda's wives died in childbirth, and at the subsequent autopsy it was found that her unborn child was female. Matunda then had to pay 'Wangu a further fine of ten cattle.'

III. THE ANALYSIS

A. To begin with we have to remove from the myth the diachronic element, that confusing sequence of events in which the storytellers tell it to us: first, the ante-creational sequences of the creator going up into the sky before he marries the moon and begins his act of creation, or simply standing by a tree and creating on the spot; then, the sequences of creation itself, the question who came first, the woman (or women) and her (or their) children or her (or their) husband and the animals, and which animals came first, the wild or the domestic; and finally, the post-creational sequences of events in which either the people began to multiply immediately or Mathunda and Wangu first herded their cattle to the well, after which they quarrelled, separated, led their people off in different directions, and so laid the foundations of all the different clans and even of the peoples of the world.

Having removed the time-sequences and being left with the timeless facts which we can place next to each other for evaluation, we still have left enough on our hands to keep ourselves busy. Since society is an ordered system its creation must have been effected in an orderly manner and not in a haphazard, disorderly manner. Basing ourselves on the assumption that the myth is a representation of the way in which human society is made and a justification of the way in which it is organized, our principal task will therefore be to discover the nature of the relationships which make up that society.

B. The cast of the actors in our myth consists of the sun, the moon, the creator Mathunda, the first purely human male Wangu, and the two women whom they marry. And as supers there are also the women's offspring and assorted animals. All the principal actors are cast in the form of living people, and their play produces human society in the Sandawe image. This society is based on the marriages which Mathunda and Wangu contract with each other's sisters, and it is therefore the nature of these marriages which we have to discover in order to find the principal message of the myth.

Before we begin our analysis proper we have to clarify the image of one of the principal actors. Is the sun a man or a woman? The myth suggests the former, but the fourth version gives his name as 'the Creator's (female) Child', which obviously implies feminity, even though the same version also presents him as the moon's husband. The reason for this apparent contradiction is to be found in the habit of the Sandawe language to treat all celestial bodies as feminine. Even the everyday words for 'sun' (‖ *'aká-su*) and for 'moon' (*!áb-so*) – which is rendered by Bagshawe in his version as *Quabso* – embody the feminine suffix *-su*. We may therefore be satisfied that the sun of our myth is a male actor.

C. Having cleared up this point, we may now proceed to consider the roles of Mathunda and Wangu in the play, and at once we are struck by the fact that the nature of Wangu's relationships with the other members of the cast is quite unambiguous, but that in the case of Mathunda they are controversial. We shall first consider the case of Wangu, whose primary relationship is with the moon. In all versions of the myth Wangu either emerges from a tree or a hill or a rock, or he is born by the moon while she lives at that place with her husband – that is, in all those versions of the myth in which Wangu puts in an appearance, and that is by no means all of them. Versions 4, 5, and 7 state explicitly that the moon lived at a large rock and gave birth, although these versions do not directly refer to Wangu. All they do is to confirm that the tree (or the hill or the rock) is identical with the moon's womb. But in versions 1, 2, and 3 Wangu is clearly the first human male to be born on earth from the womb of the moon, even though he is not mentioned by name in those versions. He is mentioned by name only in version 8 and in the additional information supplied by Dempwolff. There can be no doubt that genealogically Wangu's relation to the moon is that of a son to a mother.

Mathunda's primary relationship, on the other hand, is with the sun and it is subject to considerable controversy, a controversy which appears to be a tripartite one: (1) the myth's versions disagree as to his seniority in respect of the sun; (2) they also disagree on whether it is he or the sun who marries the moon; and (3) it is not clear whether he or the sun, as the moon's husband, had been previously related to her or not ('is her brother' or merely 'is her husband'). These three questions all contain factors which affect Mathunda's (and his sister's) status in the cast, and therefore also the status of his (and Wangu's) marriage. For that reason we have to investigate carefully the various possibilities which they have to offer us.

1 *The question of Mathunda's seniority.* In the first version of the myth Fr van de Kimmenade asks whether Mathunda is perhaps identified with God. Versions 1, 2, and 3 all suggest that this might possibly be the case: he effects the act of creation on his own, like an independent supreme creator. And in version 4 the sun's name 'Creator's Child' suggests that Mathunda is the sun's father, which would clearly place him into a divine position. Version 5 seems to confirm this: it actually states in so many words that the sun is Mathunda's son, and Mathunda would therefore indeed occupy the position of the sun's father. But version 7 identifies Mathunda with the sun, while version 8 expressly describes him as the sun's son. In version 6 Mathunda is not identified with the sun but differentiated from God and appears to be his inferior: he makes a sacrifice, obviously to a superior being and presumably to God, and it is God who makes the opening of creation and not Mathunda; instead, the latter's role is merely confined to procreating. Thus, in deciding which type of relationship between Mathunda and the sun fits in best with the myth's main theme, we are faced with three alternative possibilities: either Mathunda is the sun's superior, or he is identical with him, or he is his inferior.

2 *The question of who marries the moon.* At the factual level the first version of the myth leaves the question open, yet it seems to be

Mathunda who marries the moon because it is he who opens her womb, the tree. The second version is not clear in this respect because it speaks of Mathunda's own emergence from the womb before he begins to create, and the same is the case in the third version. Version No. 4 is also ambiguous: the sun's name *Matunda Nxussu* implies that he is Mathunda's son, but the name may also be interpreted as representing the name of the creator, just as *Quabso* is the name of his wife; such an interpretation would identify the creator with the sun and his wife with the moon, and this is indeed what the tenor of this version seems to be. If this interpretation is not accepted, then the sun and not Mathunda would be the moon's husband. Version 5 is equally ambiguous. In the opening sentences the sun is the moon's husband, the moon being married to Mathunda's son, the sun. But in the fifth sentence the one who marries the moon is shown to be Mathunda himself, being identified with the sun. Yet in the nineteenth line the two are separated again while in the closing line the sun, and not Mathunda, is said to be the moon's husband. Version 6 does not comment upon the situation, but in version 7 it is clearly Mathunda who is the moon's husband and starts to procreate with her. Version 8, again, is not clear on this point. Once more we see that the moon's position is unambiguous: she is a wife and mother and the symbolic source of life. But the identity of her husband remains to be clarified.

3 *The question whether Mathunda or the sun, as the moon's husband, had been previously related to her ('is her brother').* In versions 4 and 5 Mathunda (or the sun) and the moon simply are (or become) husband and wife, and version 7 strongly suggests that Mathunda is a stranger from the north who happened to see the moon, took a fancy to her, and became her husband. On the other hand, the Sandawe say that the sun and the moon are heavenly twins (*pasa*) and version 8 of the myth contains a statement to the same effect: it says that they are brother and sister. The other versions are silent on this point, but it compels us to consider the possibility that the moon and her husband, whatever his identity may be, had been previously related.

If we now look at the marriages of Mathunda and Wangu we see that the categories of relationship to which their wives belong vary according to the status which is ascribed to Mathunda. What we have to do, therefore, is to draw up all the possible genealogies of the myth's actors. We can do this by computing the three possible seniority levels

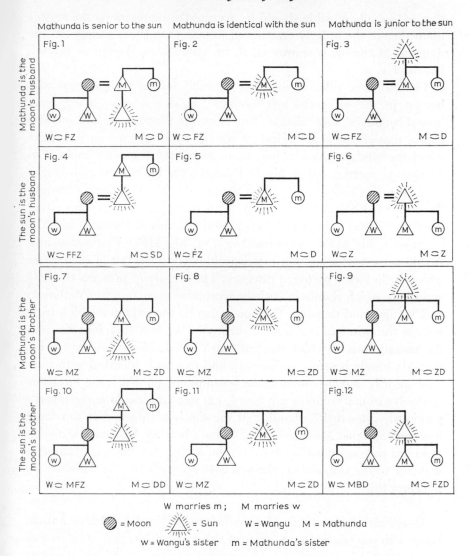

Mathunda is senior to the sun   Mathunda is identical with the sun   Mathunda is junior to the sun

Fig. 1	Fig. 2	Fig. 3
W⊂FZ M⊃D	W⊂FZ M⊃D	W⊂FZ M⊃D
Fig. 4	Fig. 5	Fig. 6
W⊂FFZ M⊂SD	W⊂FZ M⊃D	W⊂Z M⊃Z
Fig. 7	Fig. 8	Fig. 9
W⊂MZ M⊃ZD	W⊂MZ M⊃ZD	W⊂MZ M⊃ZD
Fig. 10	Fig. 11	Fig. 12
W⊂MFZ M⊃DD	W⊂MZ M⊃ZD	W⊂MBD M⊃FZD

W marries m;   M marries w

⊘ = Moon   △ = Sun   W = Wangu   M = Mathunda

w = Wangu's sister   m = Mathunda's sister

of Mathunda (question 1: does he belong to a generation senior, identical with, or junior to the sun?) with the alternative possibilities of identity offered by question 2 (is he or the sun the moon's husband?) and question 3 (is he or the sun the moon's brother?). This computation gives us twelve possible genealogies. Once we have drawn these up we can see which genealogy results in marriages which are in accordance with social realities among the Sandawe and which are not. Only those that are socially possible should be accepted as representing the myth's main theme: the orderly creation of human (Sandawe) society. In the diagram Mathunda is shown as *M*, his sister as *m*, Wangu as *W*, and his sister as *w*.

The Sandawe rules of marriage prohibit unions with women who belong in the categories of 'mothers', 'grandmothers', 'daughters', 'granddaughters', and 'sisters', but from the diagram we can see at a glance that all the genealogies, except the twelfth, result in marriages which the Sandawe consider incestuous and therefore socially impossible. Mathunda marries either his D ('daughter'), his SD ('grand-daughter'), his Z ('sister'), his ZD ('daughter'), his DD ('grand-daughter'), or his FZD ('cross-cousin'). Wangu, on his part, marries either his FZ ('mother'), his FFZ ('grandmother'), his Z ('sister'), his MZ ('mother'), his MFZ ('grandmother'), or his MBD ('cross-cousin'). All these categories are non-marriageable except the last of each series which is, in fact, a *preferred* category. Thus *Figure 12* presents the only genealogy which results in socially acceptable marriages for Mathunda and Wangu, and therefore this must also be the only one which truly reflects the principal message of our myth. We may therefore discount the assumptions on which the first two vertical columns are based, i.e. that Mathunda is senior to the sun, and that he is identical with him. And we may equally discount the assumptions on which the top three of the horizontal columns are based, i.e. that Mathunda is the moon's previously unrelated husband, that the sun is her previously unrelated husband, and that Mathunda is the moon's brother. Instead, the myth's principal message must be based on the assumption that (1) Mathunda is junior to the sun, and (2) the sun is the moon's brother. How do we interpret this?

1 *Mathunda's junior status*: Mathunda is not divine but a mortal human being who was the first man on earth although not the first to be *created* on earth; this is confirmed by his proper Sandawe name which is not *Mathunda* but *Barãse* or *Baránse* which means The First (I shall refer later to the meaning of the name Mathunda).

2 *The sun is the moon's brother*: The sun and the moon represent different lineages and there are pre-existing ties between them: they are related like brother and sister. Mathunda, the child of the sun's lineage, marries a daughter of the moon's lineage and Wangu, the child of the

moon's lineage marries a daughter of the sun's. Both marry daughters of lineages with which their own families are already standing in an affinal relationship, lineages which are not complete strangers, not unknown quantities, but groups which can be counted upon as being friendly because of pre-existing affinal ties with them.

Thus the principal message of the myth appears to be that the orderly system which society is, should be based on pre-existing ties and obligations, and that the marriages – on which the system's continued existence depends – should also be contracted in an orderly manner and with predictable quantities: hence the ideal of the cross-cousin marriage. The Sandawe have a relaxed, joking relationship with their cross-cousins whom they address and refer to as joking partners (*dáya*). Cross-cousin marriages do not create new and untried affinal relationships, instead they re-cement existing ones. They are the only marriages which do not interfere with the principle of lineage or clan exogamy, while at the same time also being based on pre-existing relationships between the partners.

Now we can also better understand the roles of the sun and the moon: they are not mere individuals but they represent whole families, lineages, or clans; the myth portrays them as celestial beings because, after all, lineages include the ancestors whose spirits are in the sky. In addition, it now becomes clear why the myth sometimes refers to the sun as the child of Mathunda and to Mathunda as the child of the sun or to both in a combined identity: Mathunda and the sun are both children of the same lineage, the sun's and Mathunda's, and either of them may therefore be seen as a child of that lineage. In the same sense either Mathunda or the sun may be portrayed as the moon's husband. Such a portrayal equally means that either of them, as a representative of their lineage, marries a female member of the moon's lineage.

The mythical level at which the creation of human society takes place is the level of the marriage of Mathunda and Wangu with each other's sisters, not that between the sun and the moon. What the 'marriage' between the sun and the moon really represents is the creation of affinal ties between the lineages to which Mathunda and Wangu belong, and these ties pre-exist to their double marriages. At the level of these marriages it is the *existence* of the partners' affinal relationships that counts, not their *creation*. The 'marriage' between the sun and the moon creates a symbolic 'brother–sister' relationship between their lineages, and it is not a marriage between individuals at all. It is not a marriage between

331

the person Sun and the person Moon, nor is it a marriage between the person Mathunda and the person Moon. With this, then, all the apparent contradictions between the myth's versions have been solved. They simply present different aspects of the same thing.

But there is more to the myth than that it merely explains the makings of an ideal society. It not only explains the existence of various lineages, clans, and even peoples, but also the existence of differences and discord between them. The most obvious portrayal of this we see in the quarrel between Mathunda and Wangu, and the settlement of their differences gives rise to the Sandawe legal system of fining. But the more subtle differences in the characters and propensities of Mathunda and Wangu we see exemplified in the 'maleness' and the 'femaleness' of their respective lineages. From Mathunda's point of view the 'maleness' of his lineage appears to imply superiority. His lineage has the power and the initiative (he creates), but it is also hostile (he cheats) and foreign (he arrives from the north). Wangu's 'female' lineage, on the other hand, is the passive one (the moon's womb has to be opened), but it is also more peaceful (Wangu is cheated) and represents the native element of the Sandawe people (Wangu emerges as the first Sandawe on Sandawe soil). The roles of superiority and inferiority become reversed if they are seen from the other's point of view: the moon precedes the sun as a ruler of the sky, she is beneficial and the possessor of innate fertility, she makes rain while the sun scorches, and at creation Wangu takes possession of the domestic animals while Mathunda's part are the game animals. But this position is reversed again when Mathunda proves to have cattle after all and waters them before Wangu does. Thus we see how the myth expresses the prejudices, antagonism, and even outright hostility between the members of the different clans. Yet, in spite of all this and notwithstanding their prejudices, they need each other for the continuation of human society: the moon's fertility is ineffective without the sun's procreative powers, and the sun's procreative powers are of no use without the moon's fertility.

The person Mathunda is more controversial than Wangu. While Wangu was born on earth and is purely human, Mathunda's origins remain shrouded in mystery. His origins are so mysterious that he is capable of being identified with the sun in its way up into the sky while he marries the moon. As a human being his origins are equally mysterious: he is of northern (read: unknown) origin. The northern land

The Analysis of Myth

from which he arrives is identified as Omí, which is empty bushland where the Sandawe like to go hunting, or as Tl'ééna, which is properly the name of the large volcanic cone which dominates the northern sky beyond Omí and is officially known as Mount Hanang. Omí and Tl'ééna may represent the nebulous Sandawe past when the tribe were hunters, and yet another association with the sky, respectively. And in his identification with the sun Mathunda is associated with the destructive heat of the dry season when the sun dominates the northern sky, while the moon in its association with the south and the rainy season represents life-giving fertility. Wangu, on the other hand, is merely the human issue of the moon's womb. Thus we see that Mathunda has cclestial associations which Wangu lacks. Mathunda represents spiritual values, Wangu earthliness. Yet, according to the principal message of our myth Mathunda's status is less than divine, and the additional information on the myth expressly states that he is only a mortal human.

The name Mathunda is not Sandawe but Bantu, and apparently of wide currency. Tastevin (1936: 407) points out that the Baganda call their creator *Ka Tonda* and that the Yaundé of the Cameroons call him *En Tondo bõ* which, he says, is 'évidemment le même mot'. According to Kohl-Larsen (1956: 45), *Itunda* is the form in which he has been adopted by the Tindiga as a sort of Goliath, and according to the same writer (1937: 26) *itunda* is the name for the baobab tree among the Isanzu. The meaning of the Bantu name *Ma-Tunda* is 'progeny', cf. the Swahili word *matunda*, 'fruits', and the Kimbu *ku-thunda*, 'to create' (ten Raa 1969: 25). The Sandawe seem to have adopted him and his myth from their northwestern neighbours, the Bantu-speaking Rimi, whose creation myth runs closely parallel to the Sandawe one: von Sick has recorded its essential features (1915: 45) which resemble our version No. 3 plus some of the additional information. The only real difference is that the Rimi *Matunda* descended from the sky on the rainbow. After completing the creation of mankind, the Rimi creator, like his Sandawe counterpart, stayed on earth, where he died.[11]

Thus we see that the person of the Sandawe creator is at once of celestial origin and earth-bound, that he is supra-human yet mortal, aggressive yet productive, beneficial yet cheating, foreign yet Sandawe. Whether the controversial nature of his character is due to a deliberate inclusion of *animus* in his *anima*, or whether this is merely the result of the Sandawe taking over a Bantu fertility symbol (the benevolent, creative Rimi sun: see Jellicoe 1967) onto which they have grafted the idea of a foreign creator (identified with the hostile Sandawe sun), is quite immaterial. What matters is that the resultant Sandawe creator is an expression of Sandawe cosmology, and that his marriage lays the foundation of Sandawe society. He is an ambiguous figure who operates at the cosmological level and at the same time at the sociological level of myth.

The side-issues of the Sandawe myth need hardly be mentioned. Its explanations of the distinction between domestic and wild animals, why the sun scorches the earth, why women have menses, why people sacrifice, and why the hyena is a witch and behaves the way it does, all these are self-explanatory.

IV. THE MODEL

We have seen that a myth consists of a message plus the technical expedient of telling it; to the latter part we may also refer as the *projection* of the mythical image. A projection is something which operates between two planes in such a manner that it creates on one of them an image that is derived from the other. A projection therefore represents a relationship, and the type of relationship it represents is one of communication between that which is conveyed (the pure myth) and the perceiver (the audience or the analytical interpreter). Now, we have already distinguished between two levels of myth, and the question arises whether these levels are communicated in the same way. My contention is that the result of this communication depends on the angles at which the different levels of the mythical message are projected, and that these angles may vary with the planes which they occupy in relation to the perceiver. If these planes differ, then the projected images will differ accordingly. We therefore have to consider now the matter of the mythical levels.

A useful point of departure is provided by the distinction which Lévi-Strauss makes between various mythical levels in the story of Asdiwal. He distinguishes between the geographical, techno-economic, sociological, and cosmological levels of the mythical message (1967: 13), which he uses to construe the myth's underlying system of meaning. Now a system of levels is, by its very nature, eminently suitable also to show the structure of myth itself. In order to do this we have to be certain what our levels are, and if we look at Lévi-Strauss's schema closely we shall see that we have to modify it somewhat. He refers to his 'levels' also as aspects, frameworks, schemata, and orders of mythical presentation. Apart from the terminological confusion which this involves it may be argued that his scheme of things also mixes aspects too freely with levels.

In our Sandawe myth we can distinguish similar categories: we can isolate geographical, economic, legal, and sociological aspects of the mythical message. The first centres upon the northern origin of man, his movement to the south, and his final dispersal; the second centres upon man's acquisition of domestic animals; the third upon the origins of his fining system; and the fourth, and most important, upon the relationships between man and his fellow-men. This group of aspects we have already referred to as the *sociological* level of myth. But we can also distinguish magical, spiritual, theological, and cosmological aspects of the mythical message. Of these the first centres upon womanhood deriving its fertility from the moon by the forces of similarity; the second centres upon Mathunda's sacrifices; the third is perhaps as nebulous as Sandawe divinity is itself; and the fourth and most all-embracing centres upon man's relationship with the seasons, time, eternity, and the cosmos in general. To this group of aspects we have referred as the theological and also as the cosmological level of myth. Since the cosmological aspects appears to be the most all-embracing we shall henceforth refer to this level as the *cosmological* level only. Here I would like to remind the reader that I do not intend in any way to detract from the value of Lévi-Strauss's pioneering analysis. Rather, I am building upon it; if anything, this should enhance its value, not diminish it.

A point of stress is that we have here two groups of aspects which do indeed operate at different *levels*. The first group represents aspects of relationships which operate at the natural level: these are the relationships between man and his natural surroundings. The second group represents the aspects of those relationships which operate at the supernatural level: these are the relationships between man and his supernatural surroundings. But the crucial question is, are these levels operating in parallel planes or not? Does the supernatural level operate in a plane which is higher but parallel to the natural level? At first sight it may seem so, but a closer look will convince us that this is not the case. For what is the nature of the mythical message which is projected from its two levels of operation? Is it something static? We must assume that it is not, because, as we have already seen, a message, too, involves a relationship between two points. Thus both levels of the message involve relationships between man and something else, which is some aspect of man's natural surroundings in the one case, and of his super-natural surroundings in the other. From this it follows that the two levels of the mythical message cannot run parallel but instead must converge on one point: man. And therefore, if one level operates in the horizontal plane, the other must operate at an angle to it, i.e. in an ascending plane.

If we now project our schema of mythical structure on paper we see that the levels of the message form two legs of an angle, at the junction of which stands man. This is the mythical version of man, who is a counter-projection of the audience into myth and who thus occupies the pivotal point in his own contemplation of himself.

We note from our diagram (*below*) that the projected message from

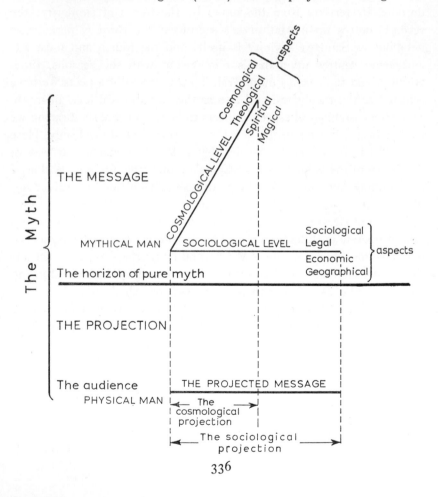

the sociological level differs from the cosmological projection. While the sociological projection is life-size, the cosmological one is foreshortened.

Next, we have to look at the problem of mythical inversion, a concept which has become well known from the explorations into the structure of myth by Lévi-Strauss and others, but which has also given rise to a certain amount of puzzlement and doubt. These doubts have recently been the subject of discussion in a paper on the meaning of myth by Mary Douglas (1967), who feels that common sense militates against some of the models of symmetry and inversion which have been set up. To English anthropologists they seem rather far-fetched, she notes, adding that 'we are being asked to suspend our critical faculties if we are to believe that myth mirrors the reverse of reality' (ibid.: 59). Yet several notable students of myth – apart from Lévi-Strauss himself – have felt it necessary to explain some otherwise inexplicable aspects of myth in terms of inversion. One admirable explanatory construct of this kind has been set up by Middleton, who concludes that Lugbara myth represents its mythical beings of creation as inverted beings (1954: 190). From his analysis it seems that it is the mythical distance which produces a sort of inverted image, which to Douglas's common-sense approach must look rather like the unreality of a mirage, and an upside-down mirage at that. With specific reference to the mythical relationships between the first people created, Sally Falk Moore holds that 'any myth about the creation of man which postulates a single first family is bound to give rise to some incestuous riddles' (1964: 1310). Since incest is the reverse of the real social ideals reflected by myth this means that she, too, acknowledges the principle of mythical inversion. She does recognize that the two incestuous original individuals stand for symbolic filiation. She quotes Firth's statement that 'Kinship is fundamentally a reinterpretation in social terms of the facts of procreation and regularized sex union', but she then continues: 'But if one moves from the realm of structure to the realm of symbolism, the contrary can be true.'

But is this assumption really necessary? Douglas suggests that it is not in the case of the Tsimshian, and I maintain that it is not in the case of the Sandawe. In fact there is no evidence at all that the Sandawe see their mythical heroes of creation as inverted beings. Rather the opposite appears to be true. The additional information collected about the myth shows us that the Sandawe see Mathunda very much as a human being, even though his origins are shrouded in supernatural mystery

337

and in some versions he is identified with the sun. He built his home on earth, herded his cattle, quarrelled with Wangu, moved to some other place where he reared his family, and died. The fact that mythical distance causes him to be projected as *different* from ordinary human beings does not make him an *inverted* being. And the 'brother–sister' marriage between the sun and the moon does not represent an incestuous inversion of social realities either: since the sun and the moon represent lineages rather than individuals, there is no question of incest. The marriage stands for any number of marriages between the lineages, and the relationships between them are therefore relationships of affinity, not of incestuous individuals. In other words, they represent the principle of clan exogamy rather than of sibling incest. Now, this is clearly also recognized by Falk Moore, yet she finds it necessary to postulate that the symbolic (or mythical) presentation of this situation may be the opposite from social structure. Could there perhaps be something wrong with the symbolic presentation in myth of social truth? It does not seem likely; common sense militates against it. And besides, if we were to accept such a supposition, then we would also have to abandon our basic assumption that myth is a social document. The only alternative, then, is that there must be something wrong with our perceptual interpretation of that symbolic presentation. And, as our model suggests, this is indeed the case and is due to the difference caused by the projection of messages from different mythical levels.

Marriage ties can be either exogamous or endogamous; there are no other possibilities. If, then, we assume that theoretically the possibilities are equal for both, we would have to draw a vertical line through the middle of our model, to separate the two. Now all marriages between mythical man and those partners who are projected in his own half of the diagram would appear to be incestuous, while his marriages with partners projected in the other half would appear to be exogamous. If we now look at the diagram (*below*) we see that his marriages projected from the sociological level of myth appear exogamous, while those projected from the cosmological level appear incestuous, even though in reality the social distances between the marriage partners are the same. The marriages between the sun('s lineage) and the moon('s lineage) are really as properly exogamous as the marriages between Mathunda and Wangu and each other's sisters. But there is no inversion; all there is, in fact, is a difference in projection caused by the foreshortening of the mythical image. It is the same process of foreshortening

338

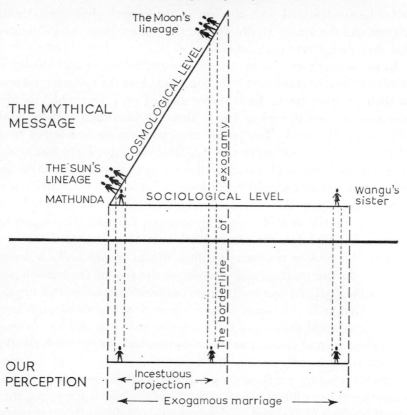

which reduces the images of whole lineages at the cosmological level, to the size of mere individuals.

The diagram (*above*) also shows us why Mathunda is so easily identified with the sun's lineage: they stand at the same spot or, at least, very close to one another. Mathunda represents mythical man, and in that capacity he stands at the junction of the two mythical levels. Because of this, he may be identified in two ways. Such a double identification is not possible in the case of Wangu, nor is it in the case of the moon. It would be impossible to identify the purely human Wangu with the purely celestial moon. While Wangu's place is exclusively in the sociological level of the myth, the moon's is exclusively in the cosmological level. The proper place of neither of them is controversial. Mathunda, on the other hand, stands with one leg in the sociological and with the other in the cosmological level of myth. Although he is human and mortal in the sociological level, he becomes superhuman and celestial

339

when he is identified with the sun in the cosmological level. Unlike Wangu and the moon, Mathunda and the sun are controversial figures, and they merge into each other.

In my recent paper on the Moon as a symbol of life and fertility in Sandawe thought (1969:26) I was concerned with the cosmological level of their creation myth. In it, I commented on a text which is here presented as part of version No. 5, that 'the Creator is initially called the son of Mathunda, but in the final sentence he is referred to as Mathunda himself. Usually the Sandawe do not clearly distinguish between the precise identities of the Creator, but an informant has stated that the text should really have referred to him as the son of Mathunda only in the last sentence. From this it would follow that Mathunda is the creator before he becomes the sun. The sun is his creation and therefore the son of Mathunda.'

What this passage presents us with is not an inversion. All it does is to show up the controversial position of the sun in the cosmological level of the myth. At this level the sun is the son of Mathunda's lineage, just as Mathunda is a son of the sun's lineage at the sociological level. The cosmological analysis of the myth also shows us that the moon is not a controversial entity, just as the sociological analysis shows us that Wangu is not a controversial person.

At this juncture we should realize that what we are in fact talking about now is two different levels of mythical *analysis*. It transpires, then, that if we wish to analyse two different levels of the myth we must also apply two different levels of analysis. In a single analysis the different projections clash with each other and even seem to present inversions. To a Sandawe listener the different projections of his myth do not clash at all. This is because he does not analyse them; instead, he just takes them in. Analysing two different levels is like shutting one eye and then the other, and looking at the projected image from two different angles. The Sandawe listener does not shut one eye, instead he uses his binary vision and lets his brain combine the different images. The informant who told me that the text of one version of the myth should really have referred to the sun as the son of Mathunda had in fact, in his discussion with me, taken over the one-sided approach which my Western-type analysis had forced upon him. Now, this is quite in order if we wish to look at the cosmological content of the myth only, and at the time I had indeed been concerned with Sandawe cosmology only. In a study of cosmology the analysis of the corresponding level of myth can give us valuable information. But when we analyse myth itself or, rather, the totality of myth, we have to analyse both levels of the myth. If, in this context, we stare ourselves blind on one level only, then we are bound to see an image which clashes with reality and which, in turn, may lead us to believe that what we are seeing is an inversion of the truth.

V. SUMMARY AND CONCLUSION

A. *The Method and Its Results*

It is far from me to contend that I have proven any general validity of our mythical model; its validity will first have to be tested on other myths, and its *general* validity may never be proven. Nor do I contend that all myths have necessarily two different levels. Quite conceivably some myths possess no more than a single level. A myth which is purely and simply a theological one would not possess a sociological level at all, but be entirely confined to the cosmological level. And a myth which is purely and simply a social document would not have a cosmological level. Our Sandawe creation myth, we have found, is more than just a social document because it also has a cosmological level. Therefore we have now to admit that our original assumption – that myth is a social document – has been rather too narrow and that we have to re-formulate it accordingly: in its fully developed form myth is a socio-religious, or rather, a socio-cosmological document.

I also wish to make no exaggerated claim on behalf of the genealogical method in the analysis of myth. In the first place it simply could not be applied to myths that do not contain material that lends itself to genealogical analysis. Myths that operate exclusively at the cosmological level are obviously unsuitable, but myths that operate at the sociological level may also not lend themselves to it. If, for example, a myth is limited to the economic aspects of the sociological level – which have no base in kinship relationships – then it will have to be subjected to an economic analysis. And, second, if we do find a myth of the suitable type, the chances are great that there will not be a sufficient number of versions at our disposal, so that we cannot base our analysis on the totality of the myth. In the case of our Sandawe creation myth, we have been particularly fortunate in that we have had access to as many as eight different versions plus some additional information, but we would be hard put to it to find many other creation myths from different peoples in an equal abundance of material.

Yet it has been shown convincingly, I believe, that the genealogical method *can* be fruitfully used to analyse out the principal social message from a myth. By using the method we have been able to eliminate all the 'secondary messages' or 'individual overtones' which do not form part of the principal social message, but deviate from it and even clash with it, And then, in taking account of these and tracing their origins to a different mythical level, the method has pointed the way to the formal separation of the two main levels of myth and to a recognition of the differences between them. As a result we have been able to set up an explanatory model of myth. This model, in its turn, explains why some of the myth's protagonists are controversial figures while others are not. The controversial figures are controversial, we find, because by standing at the junction of the different mythical levels they belong to both of them while at the same time they also merge into each other. And finally, our model suggests an explanation why some students of myth may have found it necessary to postulate mythical inversions where there are none, in order to account for incongruities in the results of their analyses. In fact, there is nothing wrong with their analyses proper, our model suggests, but the difficulty lies in their perception of a mythical image which appears to them different from what it is. It appears different because it has been foreshortened in its projection from a different and more distant mythical level. The wrong *kind* of analysis has been used.

B. *The Meaning of the Levels and of Mythical Creation Itself*

We have found that the *cosmological* level conveys the message of the innate (feminine) fertility of the human race as symbolized by the moon, which has to be activated by the aggressive (masculine) creative act of the sun and Mathunda. Although the resulting sun–moon marriage seems to be incestuous, being a union between two members of a single first family, it is in fact not incestuous because at its own mythical level it represents the regularized procreative union between lineages, which are exogamous. The *sociological* level conveys the message of the ideal social organization which emerges from Mathunda's act of creation and his subsequent marriage; this social organization is based upon cross-cousin alliances, because such alliances represent the only form of marriage that is based upon the principles of exogamy as well as upon existing filiation, and therefore it provides the answer to man's quest for security while at the same time avoiding incest. In addition to this, the sociological level expresses the Sandawe ideal of patrilocal residence: the moon's womb is placed there where Mathunda's home is located.

The two levels are combined into a single image of mythical creation through the binary vision of the Sandawe tribesman, who looks at both levels at the same time. What in effect he combines is the eternal values of the cosmological level with the ideals of his contemporary social surroundings. Thus the story of creation, which is the product of this combination, stands at the junction between cosmic eternity and social reality. It is the position of creation at this juncture which enables us now to recognize its true nature: creation is not an absolute beginning, even though the binary view makes it seem to be. In fact it is preceded by an eternity of non-evolution. In this eternity all the materials for a successful evolution of society are already present, but its evolution is not set in motion until the act of creation has been completed. Rather than a beginning, creation is therefore a transition. It is a transition from an eternal, amorphous condition to a contemporary, living reality.[12]

APPENDIX

No vernacular texts of versions Nos. 1 and 4 (van de Kimmenade's and Bagshawe's) are available, but the vernacular material of versions Nos. 2, 3, and 6 has been published (Dempwolff 1916: 144-5). Of versions Nos. 5 and 7 (my own) some excerpts have been published (ten Raa 1969: 25-9). The complete vernacular texts of these versions, as well as the vernacular text of version No. 8, are presented hereunder.

Version No. 5

1. Útaa úriǐ lóo'lo ǁ'akásu Mathúnda nǁoowe súkúma'tea íewa, Omíts'aa.
2. Útaa n!ee hewéts' !'úma úraa hlawé hàà tínkase, hàà !'úmakimèè ba'ásúǔs'ki !áb'so.
3. Mathúnda nǁwe hía !áb'soa ǀ'ánk'na ǀángei' paa úraa méénasu, paa khuats'aχámatenaa ǁ'àásu, ǁó' hés'wa tl'únguts'sa íe'tenaa.
4. Paa ká': "Heesu ǀ'uúes'."
5. Mathúnda hía ǀeei', !áb'so tl'únguts'sa íye, paa ké, paa ǀ'uk'ésu.
6. Tuéesi' aà gáwata'a nee. Úra' neewa.
7. Hía neewaioi' n!ee deétheai', sa hésu !áb'sõsu nǁóókosa habaméwa, máχa nǁóóko hakáχ, hàà thámés' nǁóókokí hakáχ.
8. Hìà habaǐgi' aà neewa, aà ǁanáwa.
9. Paa hesó tatá tl'eséa gáwãga n!oowe, paà nǁóóko kíta'tseà ǁaats'.

10. Paa hesó tatá tl'eséa gáwãga n!oowe, paà tshuu tshíaà ‖aats'.
11. Táŋsi' n|waá tu' tshuu tshíakimèè ba'ásengaa.
12. Aà tsámasuà, aà |atsúaà, aà g!okómíaà, aà dóróaà, tshuú tshía, paà ní'.
13. Hleési' aà humbuá tu', haà hlaá, haà inzálú, haà kókó, paa n‖óókó tatá íχaa n‖óókósakimèè imbó: "N!áá'wakwe."
14. Aà n‖óókoa n!aa'waà, aà hī|'awaà, haχwé tshuu tsíaχẽ bikhimaà pa ní'.
15. Húmbuχ kókóχkíaà tuú !'ókasi' aa thékéléa tu'.
16. Hía n‖oókoá n!aa'wasakiméai' paa hesó tatáa ka': "Miméékwe, hésu aχásus'ga'. Hésu humbuũsu tlanasús'ts'e."
17. Saa thékélékiaá n‖óókó n!aa'wa'õsa n|ooa thá, aa thásats'ki k'waétheesu k'eéts'k'eèts'sã tha.
18. Hewékimèèsa thékélé n!ee tsía dlo'ónasa k'eéts'k'eèts' dímenaaki.
19. N‖oóko híà tshuuχẽ bíkhikééwai' hleé' hewéχé Mathúnda'wai' hleé' hewéχé Mathúnda'wai' haa húmbuú, káakã, hlaã hewéχé máχa n‖ookó'wai'·
20. Ha thékéléki' haásu aχásusuũs' hesú khamba misábésus'.
21. Haa tatá ‖'akásũχ íyo !áb'sokí |ángetsesósi' saa túũ hísísa weré, misábésus'- sakiméésa.

Version No. 7

1. Útaa lóo'lo' Mathúnda Tl'ééna'tea íewa, ts'éχea thámetsùséts'ea, tshuúa !ínewa.
2. Pa hía |eéi' !áb'so, n‖oókotsu hláwetheèsua |aágesu. Paa ‖áasua |ánk'na keeiõ paa |'úésu.
3. Aà dī ba'áthets'à' neewa. Sa !áb'soa n‖óóko deéthe'sa habamé'wa.
4. Hísa habái' paa Mathúnda humbu k'ank'ara wak'aa, aa !áb'soa tl'oã'sa n/uí'aa, paa !'úma hlawé.
5. Hàà iswénaaki n/omóso phum'phu'séwa'a.
6. Pa hleé' Mathúnda dīnga n!oowé pa n‖oóko tsíaà ‖aáts', pa ní'.
7. Híà neẽ hángai' sa !áb'soa kis'sa: "Tsí imbókwe ‖á'awá, tsí ‖oókwe ‖aa ní'kweẽ sīnkiaa n‖óóko deéthe habaa.
8. Aà n‖óóko ní'aa hesó khoo'à' tlí'waa, níã' !áb'soa imbóts'ià' ‖'aá.
9. Hàà hesó habaats'inki !áb'so n!eea ‖'aá'wá iswénaaki.
10. Aà neewa. Hía neewaiói' aa habá, n‖oóko úrī deéthea habá, pa n|omóso úraà deéyóó pa !'úmakia !õnts'.
11. Aà hleési' sóka, aà n|īka.
12. Hésoa' súkúma'tena'a ní', hlé' héso Thathuru, aà hésoa khuats'aχáma'- tena'a ní', hésoki Wágogo, aà hésoa thoóna'tena'a ní', héso Búrúnge, aà hīsa n‖eéna'tena'a ní', hésókí Tsueéso.
13. Hleé' héso ó' tíkinats'ísõso, heso Sandawé.
14. Aa hesó n‖oókõsokia !áb'so imbóa ‖áá'wá, sa úra' habá, pa boyo tsía tútúu, pa !'úmakíá n|omósoa !õnts'.

The Analysis of Myth

Version No. 8

1. Útaa lóolo'si' ‖'akásu haa !ábiso hewé hlisusũs' tl'únguts'a' nee.[13]
2. Héu Mathúnda' ‖'akásu n‖weẽ, paa dĩga n!oowé, aà tshuúkía tsía tu'.
3. Sa thámeswa tu', sa ‖ó'sa n‖ume, Paa n|omésea tu', hewé ‖oã ka' Wángu, paa tú' paa ‖ó'a n‖ume.
4. Paa hleé' Mathúndaa thámesũsa siye héswa Wángu hlísúsũswa |'uuwe, paa hewáa thámesũ tẽswa |'uuwe.
5. Aà nee. Hía' neeioi' ‖'akásuki téhlaa !'úma nee hi‖'íts'eyóó pa ‖'aa ítha íthawankimeèyoó, aχ húmba' ‖'áana'a kesẽ niĩ ní'yóó.
6. Héu Mathúnda hía hik'ĩ ‖'aa ó'a béébawakái' paa húmbua n‖eewaka, aχ ts'ee ts'eeyóó ts'áants'a, aχ tóu.
7. Hlé'si' Wángu húmbuχea n‖eewaka. Hía n‖eeioi' ts'áa tlakí; ‖'aánts'a ts'áa téhlaa tlakí.
8. Ka': "Ah, héu ma'alé ts'áa tshíaa tóuts'e", paa k'itl'é, kwa ó'kea hesó wamookia |'áwa.
9. Aà bónkíwankí, hía' bónkíwankioi' Mathúnda n‖aakoχe ónthena'a' ní'ĩ aχ Wángu n‖aako ónthena'a' ní'i' aχ n‖óóko deéa' habaméwakee kwaχ n‖aako tsía tutuúwa hánga, aχ tleéa.
10. Ee, haa dímenaaki ‖'akásu úr'sa !'úma iyẽ hi‖'íséwaa.
11. Ó'a tshèèkíge.

NOTES

1. I wish to record my gratitude to the Nuffield Foundation whose generosity has enabled me to undertake the field research on which this paper is partly based, and to Professor K. O. L. Burridge and Mr Garrett Barden for their constructive comments on it. This paper has originally been read in the form of a seminar paper at the AASA conference held a Canberra in May 1969.
2. This passage I derive largely from a remarkable seminar paper read by Mr Steven Feierman at the University College, Dar es Salaam in 1966, on the subject of the royal myth of the Wakilindi of Usambara, Tanzania.
3. The telling of stories with a particular purpose is discussed in my *Society and Symbolism in Sandawe Oral Literature* (in press).
4. Outside Africa, notable examples of presentations of variants are provided by Boas's four versions of the myth of Asdiwal on which Lévi-Strauss has based his well-known analysis (1967). Burridge has given us four versions of a Tangu myth of which he also presents a sociological analysis (1957).

345

5. As Leach (1967: 2) points out, each of the four gospels in the New Testament also tells 'the same' story yet they are sometimes flatly contradictory on details of fact.

6. I thank Miss T. N. Bagshawe of Salisbury for permitting me to quote this version from her father's private diaries. I have also quoted it in my paper on Sandawe moon symbolism (1969).

7. But I have published excerpts from this text, and also from text No. 7, in my paper on Sandawe moon symbolism (1969).

8. In my paper on Sandawe moon beliefs I have translated the verb *hanga* as 'going out', but 'getting up' is more precise.

9. Von Luschan (1898: 343) mentions the name *Mairangu* but this appears to be a corruption of the Bantu *mu-lungu* or the Sandawe *warongo*, both of which mean 'divinity' or 'God'. The meanings of the names *Mathunda* and *Baránse* will be discussed later.

10. The last-mentioned version can be explained as belonging to a particular clan myth. The Namulé clan traces its origins to an ancestor who settled by the rock and reared his family there.

11. But there also appear to be important differences in the mythologies of the two peoples. At the cosmological level of myth, the roles of the Rimi sun and moon, in particular the sun, show significant differences from their Sandawe opposite numbers (ten Raa 1969: 51–2).

12. In addition to distinguishing between the cosmological and the sociological levels of the mythical message, it may be argued that it is also possible to distinguish two separate levels of mythical explanation. This distinction can be made in terms of an *effective cause* (Mathunda creates the world) and a *formal cause* (Mathunda's and Wangu's marriages and the ensuing system of social relationships give the world its social shape).

13. Usually the sun carries the feminine gender suffix (*hesú* instead of *hewé*). The masculine gender is used here to stress the sun's identity as a male person.

REFERENCES

BAGSHAWE, F. J. 1925 *Private Diaries*, VIII (M/S).

BLEEK, W. H. I. 1864 *Reynard the Fox in South Africa, or Hottentot Fables and Tales*. London.

BURRIDGE, K. O. L. 1957 Social Implications of Some Tangu Myths. *Southwestern Journal of Anthropology*, **12** (4): 415–31.

DEMPWOLFF, O. 1916 Die Sandawe: Linguistisches und ethnographisches Material aus Deutsch-Ostafrika. *Abhandlungen des hamburgischen Kolonial-Instituts* **34**, Reihe B, Bd. 19.

The Analysis of Myth

DOUGLAS, MARY 1967 The Meaning of Myth, with Special Reference to 'La geste d'Asdiwal', In Leach, E. R. (ed.), *The Structural Study of Myth and Totemism*. ASA Monograph 5. London: Tavistock Publications.

EVANS-PRITCHARD, E. E. 1940 *The Nuer*. Oxford: Clarendon Press.

— 1964 Variations in a Zande Folktale. *Journal of African Languages*, **3,** Pt. 2: 103–34.

FALK MOORE, SALLY 1964 Descent and Symbolic Filiation. *American Anthropologist* **66**: 1308–20.

FEIERMAN, STEVEN 1966 Seminar paper on *Habari za Wakilindi*, University College, Dar es Salaam.

JELLICOE, M. 1967 Praising the Sun. *Transition* **6**: 27–31.

KOHL-LARSEN, L. 1937 Issansu-Märchen. *Bässler-Archiv* **20**: 1–68.

— 1956 *Das Elefantenspiel*. Kassel.

LEACH, E. R. 1962 Genesis as Myth. *Discovery* (May).

LÉVI-STRAUSS, C. 1963 *Structural Anthropology*, trans. by L. Jacobson and B. G. Schoepf. New York: Basic Books.

— 1964 *Mythologiques: Le Cru et le cuit*. Paris: Plon.

— 1967 The Story of Asdiwal. In Leach, E. R. (ed.), *The Structural Study of Myth and Totemism*. ASA Monograph 5. London: Tavistock Publications.

MIDDLETON, JOHN 1954 Some Social Aspects of Lugbara Myth. *Africa* **24,** (3): 189–99.

TASTEVIN, C. 1936 Présentation. In van de Kimmenade, M. Les Sandawé (territoire du Tanganyika Afrique). *Anthropos* **31**: 395.

TEN RAA, W. F. E. R. 1969 The Moon as a Symbol of Life and Fertility in Sandawe Thought. *Africa* **39,** (1): 24–53.

— in preparation *Society and Symbolism in Sandawe Oral Literature*. London: Cass.

VAN DE KIMMENADE, M. 1936 Les Sandawé (Territoire du Tanganyika Afrique). *Anthropos* **31**: 395–416.

VON LUSCHAN, F. 1898 Beiträge zur Ethnographie des abflusslosen Gebietes in Deutsch-Ost-Afrika. Pp. 323–81 in Werther, C. W. (ed.), *Die mitterleren Hochländer der nördlichen Deutsch-Ost-Africa*. Berlin: Paetel.

VON SICK, E. 1915 Die Waniaturu (Walimi); ethnographische Skizze eines Bantu-Stammes. *Bässler-Archiv* **5,** Heft 1/2: 1–62.

An Anthropological Approach to the
Icelandic Saga

VICTOR W. TURNER

This article is essentially a tribute to the greatest living British anthropologist, Professor Evans-Pritchard of Oxford University, who in 1950
had the temerity to declare in his Marett Lecture, in face of the struc-
tural-functionalist orthodoxy of most of his colleagues that he regarded
'social anthropology as being closer to certain kinds of history than to the
natural sciences' (Evans-Pritchard 1950: 198). This view provoked a
storm of protest from the majority of British anthropologists, who held
to the position formulated by the late Professor Radcliffe-Brown and
his followers, including Evans-Pritchard in his earlier days, that the
behaviour and interpersonal relationships observed during fieldwork
by anthropologists should be 'abstracted in the form of structural
relationships between social positions and groups and these structural relationships (should) further be abstracted in the form of separate
systems: economic, political, kinship, etc.' (van Velsen 1967: 130). Comparison between such timeless and abstract structures elicited from the
rich variety of cultures in different parts of the primitive world was
thought to be in thorough accordance with 'scientific method'. History,
according to Radcliffe-Brown, in societies without written records or
about which written documents by alien investigators were not available,
could never be anything but 'conjectural history'. Such guesses were
almost worthless and much time and energy could be saved, as both
Radcliffe-Brown and Bronislaw Malinowski asserted, if stress were laid
on exposing the functional interconnexions between social positions and
institutions as they existed in the 'ethnographic present', in the here-
and-now of anthropological investigation, or even, as we have seen, in a
timeless milieu of structural relationships. Indigenous tales about the
past were considered pseudo-history or 'myth', and, at least in Malinowski's view, had the main social function of providing a charter and
justification for *contemporary* institutions and relationships between

349

positions and groups. Much understanding of the nature and functioning of certain kinds of social system was undoubtedly obtained by the
use of this so-called 'synchronic method'. But it led to a widespread
devaluation of historical research by British anthropologists, even where
an abundance of written documents was available, as in West Africa
and India, for example. Since Evans-Pritchard's Marett Lecture in 1950,
and even more pronouncedly since his Simon Lecture at Manchester
University in 1960, the trend has been in considerable measure reversed.
A stream of historical studies by anthropologists, particularly in
African tribal history, has rushed from the presses in the past few years.
Professor Jan Vansina, now at Wisconsin University, has even been able
to show us how the formerly despised oral tradition can be handled as
reliable historical evidence, if it is critically assessed in relation to other
sources of knowledge about the past; as he writes (1965: 7–8),

> '[Oral tradition] . . . has to be related to the social and political structure
> of the peoples who preserve it, compared with the traditions of neighbor-
> ing peoples, and linked with the chronological indications of genealogies and
> age-set cycles, of documented contacts with literate peoples, of dated natural
> phenomena such as famines and eclipses, and of archaeological finds.'

He also recommends the comparative use of linguistic evidence (ibid.:
180–1). Vansina, whose fieldwork was conducted from 1952 to 1960, was
undoubtedly influenced by Evans-Pritchard's 1950 Marett Lecture and
by the controversy that followed it, and perhaps even more powerfully by
Evans-Pritchard's historical study, published in 1949, *The Sanusi of
Cyrenaica*. A recent British example of Evans-Pritchard's pervasive
influence is the publication of a volume of historical studies by anthropologists entitled *History and Social Anthropology* (Lewis 1968). In the
United States the great Californian anthropologist, A. L. Kroeber, also
stressed, even before Evans-Pritchard, the importance for anthropology
of the historical approach (Kroeber 1935: 558), and the recent book *An
Anthropologist Looks at History* (Singer 1966) is a testimony to his
sustained interest in the matter.

When I heard Professor Evans-Pritchard deliver his Simon Lecture
'Anthropology and History' (1961) at the University of Manchester in
1960 I remember being deeply impressed, and oddly moved, when he
said (ibid.: 13):

> 'An anthropological training, including fieldwork, would be especially
> valuable in the investigation of earlier periods of history in which institu-

tions and modes of thought resemble in many respects those of the simpler peoples we study. For such periods the historian struggles to determine a people's mentality from a few texts, and anthropologists cannot help wondering whether the conclusions he draws from them truly represent their thought.'

For example, 'can an Oxford don work himself into the mind of a serf of Louis the Pious?' (ibid.: 14). I was impressed by this because it was largely through studying an early period of history that I had become addicted to anthropology. This period was the Icelandic Commonwealth, from Ingolf's settlement at Reykjavik in A.C. 874 to A.D. 1262 when the Icelanders of their own free will in solemn parliament made a treaty of union with the King of Norway in which they accepted, at last, his supremacy. I had come green to these white pastures as an under-graduate just before World War II when I studied under Professor Chambers, Dr Batho, and Dr Hitchcock, all of whom had been students of W. P. Ker, author of *Epic and Romance* (1967) and *The Dark Ages*, whose ruling passion was Icelandic literature. I was moved by Evans-Pritchard's words because they revived for me and made suddenly pal-pable not only my years of fieldwork among the Ndembu tribesmen of Central Africa, but also nights in the British Army when I had read E. V. Gordon's *An Introduction to Old Norse* – full of potent extracts from the Icelandic sagas – by torchlight under my blankets to evade the sergeant's baleful eye. On my return to civilian life, it was partly a desire to work in a live society not too dissimilar to ancient Iceland that made me switch from English to anthropology. But Evans-Pritchard vividly revealed to me the possibility of applying my anthropological experience and thinking to the very literature that had sent me indirectly to Africa.

Indeed, in this case it was not at all a matter of 'determining a people's mentality from a *few* texts' (my emphasis). The texts here are many and rich and full of the very materials that anthropologists rejoice in when vouchsafed to them by informants in the field. I shall say something about the nature and reliability of these texts in a moment, but would first like to make clear why they are of theoretical concern to me. In my African work I had proposed to analyse some important events which arose in village life, and which I called 'social dramas', as possessing a regularly recurring 'processional form' or 'diachronic profile' – in other words crisis situations tended to have a regular series of phases. They usually began with a breach of rule or norm and led, typically, to a rapidly ramifying cleavage, bringing about opposition between the largest groups that may be involved in the dispute, it may be between sections of a village or segments of a chiefdom. In Ndembu society, the small tribal group in Zambia I lived among for two and a half years, cleavage is accompanied by a set of adjustive and redressive procedures, ranging from informal arbitration to elaborate rituals, that result either in healing the breach or in public recognition of its irremediable character. I had derived the 'processional form' of the 'social drama' from data I had collected during fieldwork among the Ndembu of Zambia (formerly N. Rhodesia). These data, if not 'historical' in type, were at least 'microhistorical', in that they related to chains and sequences of events over a time, however limited, rather than to events coexisting at a given time. A large part of my data consisted of direct reporting, but I was forced at times to rely on accounts by informants of happenings in the village past. I made a virtue of necessity by placing in an analytical central position the very bias of my informants. For the main 'aim of the "social drama" is not to present a reputedly objective recital of a series of events; it is concerned, rather, with the different interpretations put upon these events, and the way in which these express nuanced shifts or switches in the balance of power or ventilate divergent interests within common concerns' (Epstein 1967: 228). My intention was that if 'facts' were examined from different points of view, and discussed with different informants, the extended case would take on a multidimensional aspect: the individual parties would be more than mere names but become characters in the round whose motives would become intelligible not only in terms of personality or temperament, but also in terms of the multiple roles they occupy simultaneously or at different times in the social structure or in transient factional groupings. In all this there was the notion that social events are spun into complex patterns over time by custom and will, and especially by conflicts of customs and wills and collective wishes and needs to resolve those conflicts. It was not long before I began to look for comparable data in other societies, for I was convinced that each society had its own variant of the social drama form. Each society's social drama could be expected to have its own 'style', too, its aesthetic of conflict and redress, and one might also expect that the principal actors would give verbal or behavioural expression to the values composing or embellishing that style. I was not in favour of 'abstracting separate structural systems, economic, political, kinship, legal, etc.' from the unitary yet phased movement of the social drama. A distinct aim of this study was to compare the profiles of dramas in different societies, taking into account such aspects as their degree of open-endedness, their propensity to regression, the efficiency of their redressive procedures, the absence of such procedures, the degree to which violence or guile were present in crises, and many more besides. Yet when I wrote my book there was a dearth of such information except in the works of some of my colleagues in the Central African field – and even there it was not systematically presented or related to relatively constant features of the social context. But if cross-cultural studies appeared to be 'out', cross-temporal studies were feasible. The writings of historians are bulging with 'social dramas', narratives of successive events that can be fitted without Procrustean violence into the schemas outlined earlier. But I was not sufficiently temerarious to tackle the data presented and handled by professional historians. Then I suddenly remembered my early predilection for Icelandic literature – indeed, it could well have served as the unconscious, or, at any rate, preconscious model for the 'social drama'. I had read most of the sagas available in English translation and had once had a smattering of Old Norse that could be revived, if necessary. And the sagas were nothing but connected sequences of social dramas. From them could also be inferred, so I thought, many features of ancient Icelandic social structure and economics – enough to provide a preliminary frame for the 'phase developments'.

The more I thought about using the sagas as collections of data comparable to my African extended cases, the better I liked the notion. It seemed to me, too, that since there was an abundance of 'native writings relating to the settlement and early history of Iceland' (as Vigfusson and Powell partly subtitle their *Origines Islandicae*) it might even be possible by examining the sagas in proper time-sequence to plot the successive stages of the development of effective adjustive and redressive procedures and this from the very foundation of Icelandic society. Icelandic scholars will readily perceive how naïve I was and how little I then knew of the jagged and treacherous terrain of Icelandic saga origins and datings. Nevertheless, I am still confident that, with due precaution, anthropologists can make a positive contribution to Icelandic studies, and in doing so sharpen their own understanding of social processes – for through the saga medium Icelandic society is portrayed as in constant change and development, though with certain repetitive and cyclical aspects.

Before examining a saga as a set of social dramas, which may be regarded as both indices and vehicles of changes in the structure and personnel of the social arenas to which they refer, let me sketch in briefly something of the salient Icelandic settings in space and time. Iceland itself contains about 40,000 square miles – one-fifth as large again as Ireland – but except for the narrow strip of coast 'between fell and foreshore' and along several river valleys there are few places suitable for settlement. Huge Jökulls or ice mountains back most of the coast. Iceland contains over a hundred volcanoes, a quarter of which have been active in historical times; fields of lava cover hundreds of square miles and hot springs or geysers are numerous. In brief, about six-sevenths of Iceland's area is unproductive, wild, and inhospitable; barren cold rock intermittently laced with inner fire. Owing to the position of the Gulf Stream, however, the climate, considering the latitude (63°–67° N.), is quite mild and humid. The weather seems to have been rather better during the saga period, for there is no mention of floating ice to the south at the time of the first settlement. There appear, too, to have been richer natural resources in wood and pasture. Shortage of wood was, nevertheless, a constant problem in the sagas. Men would voyage to Norway or Britain to load up with building-timber, and some of the bitterest feuds, such as Njal's Saga, began with quarrels between thralls over the precise boundaries of woodlands. Today, apart from small stands of mountain ash and birch, there is hardly any woodland to speak of in Iceland.

The early settlers took land around the coast, sailing without haste from one creek or bay to another to find good unoccupied land. Many sagas mention quarrels over land only a few generations after this original 'land-taking'. It has been calculated that about 5000 such settlements were recorded in the so-called colonizing period between A.D. 870 and 930. Many of these records appear in the *Landnamabok*, an early masterpiece of historical scholarship, by Ari Thorgilson the Wise, a cleric who wrote in the first half of the twelfth century. Since the settlers often came with married children and servants, it is likely that by A.D. 930 something like 30,000–50,000 people (the larger figure is Sir George Dasent's estimate) were living on about 6,000 square miles of utilizable land, much of which was sheep and cattle pasture. Three hundred years later, during the so-called 'Sturlung Age', it has been estimated by Einar O. Sveinsson that the total population was 'about 70,000–80,000' (Sveinsson 1953: 72). By that time there was much vagrancy, and mention is made of large numbers of itinerant seasonal or day-labourers. It seems likely that the carrying capacity of the land, or critical population density, had been exceeded, in relation to the means of subsistence and cultivable percentage of land then available. The present Icelandic population of about 200,000, about half of which lives in Reykjavik, depends largely upon commercial fishing for sale in the international market, and could not survive on farming and small-scale fishing alone. But it would seem that during the main saga period, around the turn of the first millennium, there was already pressure on land, or at any rate on certain categories of scarce resources, such as woodland and pasture, and that this pressure was one major source of the conflicts described in the sagas in terms of personalities, and such values as honour and shame.

Why did the settlers come to this bleak island in the first place and where did they come from? The answers to these questions shed much light on the form of the social dramas in the saga literature. The emigration from Norway, where many of the earliest settlers came from (though some came indirectly, stopping for a while in Scotland, Ireland, the Orkneys or Shetlands before moving on) was undertaken by many chieftains and kinglings to escape the over-rule of King Harald Fairhair, who sought to impose centralized monarchical rule on all Norway. As W. P. Ker had said (1967: 58): 'Iceland was colonized by a picked lot of Norwegians; by precisely those Norwegians who had . . . strength of will in the highest degree.' He points out that 'political progress in the Middle Ages was by way of monarchy; but strong monarchy was contrary to the traditions of Germania, and in Norway, a country of great extent and great difficulties of communication, the ambition of Harald Fairhair was resisted by numbers of chieftains who had their own local following and their own family dignity to maintain in their firths and dales'. The first Icelanders, in fact, were intractable, 'reactionary' aristocrats who refused to make themselves tenants or vassals of any king. This political and spatial disengagement made them a highly self-conscious group, who, as Ker says, began their heroic age 'in a commonwealth founded by a social contract' (ibid.: 59). Individuals came together to invent a set of laws and to try to set up jural procedures to make them work; it was not the movement of a group already possessed of a joint polity. The result was that, again in Ker's words, 'this reactionary commonwealth, this fanatical representative of early Germanic use and wont, is possessed of a clearness of self-consciousness, a hard and positive clearness of understanding, such as is to be found nowhere

else in the Middle Ages and very rarely at all in any polity' (ibid.).
From the anthropological point of view this self-recognizant clarity
what Ker calls 'dry light' makes them excellent informants about the
growth of their institutions – as set off from those of Norway – and
about their cumulating relations with one another.

As A. Margaret Arent has well expressed it (1964: xvi):

> 'in the founding days, the sovereign power lay in the hands of the *godar*,
> chieftain-priests who fulfilled both political and religious functions. A
> *goði's* authority extended over those who paid dues and worshipped at his
> temple. In exchange for this privilege and the *goði's* protection, these
> followers pledged him their allegiance and support. These quite naturally
> were the farmers and neighbors in his immediate vicinity. The number of
> *goðar* was limited and the title was generally hereditary. The farmers
> reserved the right to choose the *goði* whom they wished to follow, but
> loyalty to a certain one usually became more or less habitual. The relation-
> ship was thus one of mutual trust and agreement – the old Germanic code
> of loyalty between chieftain and followers. The years of the Commonwealth
> saw the establishment of the *Althing* (A.D. 930), a democratic parliament
> with a strong aristocratic base. The *goðar* automatically became members
> of the ruling bodies of parliament (the legislature and the judicature) and a
> Lawspeaker was elected to recite the laws at the meeting of the *Althing*
> which took place once a year on the plains of Thingvellir in the southwest
> of the country. As time went on, the *goði's* obligations became more political
> than religious, his power territorial.'

There was no centralized authority over and above the *goðar*. The
Althing, and the local *Things* for each of the Quarters into which Iceland
was divided, had no punitive sanctions behind them; men met there to
seek compensation for wrong or homicide, but there was no organized
state to back their claims with force even when plaintiffs were awarded
compensation *consensu omnium* – indeed, as we shall see, much depended
on how many supporters a plaintiff could get to 'ride with him' to
Thingvellir or recruit on that spot, if he were to have a hope of even
obtaining a hearing.[1] This weakness in the politico-legal structure – due
to the self-conscious independence of *emigré* aristocrats who had fled
centralized monarchy – left much leeway for internal and localized feuds,
and, in the Sturlung Age particularly, led to power politics on a large
scale and personal aggrandizement by the rich at the expense of the
small farmers. It may well have been directly due to the lack of centralized political authority that Icelanders put so much stress on personal

dignity, honour, and loyalty, and especially on the obligations of kinship. Since the courts had no mandate to carry out sentence, one had to take the law into one's own hands. One result was that even fancied slights might lead to bloodshed and homicide, for this sector of the culture became, as it were, overloaded with value emphases to compensate for the lack of sanctioned legal procedures. It was left to the plaintiff himself to enforce outlawry, fines, and settlements, and a good deal of the saga literature is taken up by accounts of how these things were done. There one can clearly see that if too much is left to personal honour, dishonourable deeds often result. The tragedy of the Commonwealth is the gradual corruption into oligarchy of its own principle of honourable, aristocratic independence from supreme overlordship – and doubtless the terrain with its natural barriers to easy communication was a factor here, though it must be said that Norway was equally rugged yet generated a kingship.

How far may the sagas be regarded as recorded history rather than historical fiction, as works of creative imagination inspired by the past? The problem is a real one, for though the sagas purport to tell of the ninth, tenth, and eleventh centuries, they were actually composed in the thirteenth century, the turbulent Age of the Sturlungs. Anthropologists may well suspect that several important social and political aspects of that age have been foisted by the sagamen upon the earlier events. Sveinsson (1953: 2) has eloquently described the Sturlung period (named after an important lineage):

> 'By this time the power of the individual chieftains has multiplied; one man may rule entire districts or quarters. . . . Some of the chieftains are possessed of greater wealth than their grandfathers dreamed of, others must provide for their initial establishment by forcible means. A considerable number of the common people are destitute. . . . All is restless motion. In earlier days . . . a man might send to the nearest farms for help in a fight with others of the same district or hostile visitors from a neighboring one. Now forces are levied from whole quarters for expeditions into other sections of the country. Instead of skirmishes there are pitched battles.'

One might comment on this that Njal's Saga, which professes to describe events around A.D. 1000, also tells of 'forces . . . levied from whole quarters', for example, the followers of Flosi who came to burn down Njal's homestead and household were drawn from the southern and eastern quarters. On the other hand, virtues are extolled in the sagas about early times which appear to have grown tarnished in the Sturlung

Age, personal integrity among them. Here, again, anthropologists might suspect that, as in Roman accounts written in the Empire about the Republic, a process of idealizing the past was going on. Thus both present reality and idealization may have distorted the picture presented by the sagas of the early Commonwealth. On the other hand, the Sturlung history itself, written by Sturla almost contemporaneously with its events, has the form and vividness of the sagas about earlier times. As W. P. Ker has said (1967: 252):

> 'The present life in Sturla's time was, like the life of the heroic age, a perpetual conflict of private wills, with occasional and provisional reconciliations. The mode of narrative that was suitable for the heroic stories could hardly fail to be the proper mode for the contemporary factions of chiefs, heroic more or less, and so it was proved by Sturla.'

My own view is that there were so many major continuities between the earlier and later years of the Commonwealth, at the basic levels of kinship and territorial organization, mode of subsistence, forms of adjudication and arbitration, and norms governing relations between individuals and groups, that sagas treating of both the earlier and later periods can be regarded equally as models of and for Icelandic social life as it lasted over several centuries. I do not think we have as anthropologists to concern ourselves too much with the problem of whether there was a highly developed oral art of saga-telling before the sagas were written down (the so-called 'Freeprose' theory), or whether the sagas were from the outset deliberate works of art, making considerable use of written sources (such as Ari's *Landnamabok*) as well as oral traditions (the so-called 'Bookprose' theory). The written sagas are clearly master-products of Icelandic society, which from the beginning contained a relatively high proportion of literate men, and we can thus regard them as authentic expressions of Icelandic culture. In many ways, too, early Icelanders are the best anthropologists of their own culture, they have the sober, objective clarity about men and events that seems to belong to the Age of Reason rather than the Ages of Faith. When they show, in saga form, how institutions came into being and disputes were settled, I am inclined to believe that they were reporting facts. Nevertheless, the sagamen are not 'sociologically' conscious of the contradictions and discrepancies in their own principles of organization, and regard the conflicts and struggles resulting from them as the effects of either Fate or personal malice. And, as in today's Africa, though to a lesser extent, witchcraft is sometimes invoked to explain mischance. It should also be said that though the sagas were written well within the Christian era in Iceland, many were about pre-Christian times and customs. Moreover, in the thirteenth century most sagas were written not by learned clerics but by laymen. Ari Thorgilsson, whose 'exact history . . . precedes the freer and more imaginative stories, and supplies some of them with their matter, which they work up in their own (less strict) way' (Ker 1967: 248), was indeed a priest, but he wrote in the twelfth century, which intervenes between the times portrayed in the sagas and the time of their writing. Other priests wrote sagas and histories after Ari and in his sober manner in the twelfth century. By the thirteenth century it is evident that some crucial change had occurred in the relationships between Churchmen and laity. To understand this change we must go back to the beginning of the Christian era in Iceland. Iceland's conversion to Christianity was characteristically pragmatic. As narrated in *Njal's Saga* and Ari's *Islendingabók*, it resolves into a collective decision taken at the Althing in A.D. 1000 to accept Christianity in order to prevent a radical cleavage in Iceland itself between Christians and pagans, and to facilitate trade and avoid conflict with the peoples of Europe, most of whom by that date had been converted. Individuals might continue to sacrifice to the Norse gods in private – and this was stated in A.D. 1000 by the Lawspeaker Thorgeirr at the Althing – as long as their public worship was Christian. One consequence of this was that, although 'organized paganism never revived', as Professor Turville-Petre points out (1953: 68), neither were pagan ideas excoriated as diabolic. The nobler pagan standards of conduct, which gave the feuds moral stature, continued to be effective—such as *drengskapr*, manly excellence, or a sense of honour. Such ethics, of course, did little to make peace, and, as Sveinsson has said (1953: 129), 'one saga could outweigh a hundred sermons'. Many of the *goðar*, or chieftain-priests, were ordained as Christian priests, and continued to exercise both sacred and secular functions, though sacredness was now interpreted in Christian terms. Priests, and even bishops, could and did marry and raise families. It took quite a while for Rome to exercise effective centralized authority over the isolated Icelandic Church 'out there' in Ultima Thule. In the permissive twelfth century, according to Einar Sveinsson (ibid.: 116–17),

'men in holy orders, the ordained chieftains not least, were the leaders in the intellectual life of the country, and they combined, in one way or another, a native and foreign way of thinking; these "learned men" naturally were the first to employ writing. But . . . there were also at this time a number of laymen who were but little affected by ecclesiastical influences and lived and moved in native learning. By 1200 knowledge of reading and writing had become not uncommon, at least among the chieftain class . . . (and, also, apparently among some gifted commoners) . . . There is no reason to suppose that literacy had declined by 1200, in the very springtime of the saga-writing of the laity, and . . . was far more widespread in Iceland than abroad. But just at that time, around 1200, the ecclesiastical and the secular separate.'

The Church orders priests to give up chiefly powers, enjoins celibacy on them, and in general raises them above other men as sacrificing priests in terms of the definitions of the Lateran Council of 1215.

'The Church thrusts away the laity, as it were, and the spirit and taste of the secular chieftains prevail. The laity now use their knowledge of writing to express that spirit. They inherit the critical spirit of the twelfth century (exemplified by Ari), and it becomes one of the principal forces in the intellectual life of many of them, whereas about the same time the Church encourages veneration of saints and belief in miracles and thus becomes the main pillar of belief in the marvellous. The literature of the nation undergoes great changes in the turn-of-the-century generation. The antique style, the style of the twelfth century, which has a certain very agreeable clerical flavour, is now replaced by the pure and limpid classical sage-style, which thus belongs to the Sturlung Age, while in the hands of monks and zealous clerics the clerical style moves towards what was fashionable abroad: long-winded rhetoric and sentimental prolixity are its characteristics from now on.'

Despite a clearly detectable anticlerical and chauvinistic note in Einar Sveinsson's work generally, I think that he here makes the point well that the prose sagas are mainly the product of laymen of the 'chieftain class'. This structural perspective may partly account for the interest in and knowledge of pagan matters shown in the sagas and for their almost purely pagan attitudes to conduct – I say 'almost' because in *Njal's Saga* particularly there are clear marks of Christian, even hagiographical, influences.

The major sagas, then, are the products of Sturlunga lay and chieftainly literate thought, reflecting on the written deposit of traditions about the early generations of the Commonwealth and, no doubt, on the oral traditions of great families as well. Such thought, kindled by creative fire and endeavouring to give meaning to an age full of outrage, has given us a series of peerless social dramas which yield us insight into the inner dynamics of Icelandic society before its 'disastrous submission' to the Norwegian Crown.

The saga I wish to examine in anthropological terms is *The Story of Burnt Njal*, recently described by Professor Turville-Petre of Oxford University, in his Introduction to the Everyman Library edition of Sir George Dasent's classical translation, as 'the finest of Icelandic sagas, and . . . one of the great prose works of the world' (1957: v). Its author seems to have lived in the late thirteenth century and to have been a learned man who had read not only most of the known sagas but many lost ones as well. Turville-Petre (1957: vii) believes that the outline of the story is 'undoubtedly founded on fact, and the chief events described took place in the last years of the tenth century and the first of the eleventh'. The author clearly lived much of his life in southern Iceland, for his knowledge of its features is intimate. *Njal's Saga* is preserved in some fifty or sixty manuscripts, the oldest of which date from the first years of the fourteenth century. It may be said to be the *fine fleur* of the saga age and the culmination of Icelandic literature. It is also the paradigmatic social drama of the Icelandic Commonwealth, containing if not resolving all its contradictions.

NJAL'S SAGA

Njal's Saga is an anthropological paradise. Its very liabilities in the eyes of most Icelandic scholars, who tend to be literary historians or critics, are anthropological virtues. W. P. Ker, for example (1967: 185) points out that 'the local history, the pedigrees of notable families, are felt as a hindrance, in a greater or less degree, by all readers of the Sagas; as a preliminary obstacle to clear comprehension'. But he is ready to admit, superb scholar that he was, that 'the best Sagas are not always those that give the least of their space to historical matters, to the genealogies and family memoirs' (ibid.: 185). Of course, anthropologists, with their practical immersion in small-scale societies with 'multiplex' social relationships, i.e. where 'people interact with the same sets of fellows to achieve several purposes, familial, productive, educational, religious, organizing' (Gluckman 1965: 256), attach great importance *precisely* to genealogical connexions, for kinship as such, in societies of this type, is often the spine or main trunk of articulation of many kinds of social relationships, economic, domestic, political, and so on. Social relationships are otherwise undifferentiated, for there is little scope for specialization; and kinship, as Gluckman says (ibid: 54) involves a general obligation on people to help and sustain one another, whatever may be the precise field of activity. Kin, of course, fall into different categories of relationships by birth, marriage, and even fosterage, which entail varying obligations. With this peculiarity of the anthropological approach in mind, it will surprise no one that the Norse sagas have never been comprehensively studied in terms of the kinship systems so completely deployed in the so-called 'family sagas', such as the *Laxdoela Saga* (which follows a set of linked and contiguous localized lineages over many generations from the first settlement, and in which types and degrees of kinship and affinity crucially influence behaviour), *Haward's Saga*, *Vatzdaela Saga*, and *Njal's Saga* (to cite but a few). For few who read tales primarily for literary enjoyment would undertake such hardy work!

It has often been pointed out how in the sagas great heed is paid to particular individuals and how the mysteries of individual life are hinted at. This stress should be complemented by a study of the social positions occupied by individuals in kinship, territorial, and political structures, and in the roles played by them in what anthropologists call 'action-sets' – quasi-groups that emerge in response to the pursuit of particular and limited goals – in the Icelandic case, for example, in feuds and litigations. From this point of view intuition and personal sensibility should be buttressed by a cool consideration of the genealogies and social geographies so richly supplied us by the sagamen. I am, of course, in no way arguing that the behaviour of the saga actors is *determined by*, or is the *effect of*, social factors such as genealogical position, systems of values, institutionalized political roles, and the like. I am only saying that these actors enter into relations with one another in 'social fields' that are in important ways structured *inter alia* by such factors. Their importance is such that it seems that quite often kinship obligations compel personal friends to fight one another.

I have mentioned the term 'field'. Let me now try to define it more precisely, throw in yet another term from political anthropology, 'arena', relate these to 'social drama', and then look at some of the rich data of *Njal's Saga* in terms of these concepts and their interrelations. A 'field' is composed of the actors directly involved in the social processes under examination. Its social and territorial scope and the areas of behaviour it implicates change as additional actors enter and former ones withdraw, and as they bring new types of activities into their interaction and/or abandon old types. It is often convenient initially to characterize a field when its actors are more or less at peace with one another or when the processes in which they are engaged are leading back to some previously established state. An 'arena' may be described as 'a social and cultural space around those who are directly involved with the field participants but are not themselves directly implicated in the processes that define the field' (Swartz 1968: 11). Thus in *Njal's Saga* there are a number of 'fields', each being defined by a process, or set of linked processes, such as seeking vengeance and/or going to law to obtain compensation. There are several 'arenas' also, the largest being geographically coterminous with the southern and much of the eastern quarters of Iceland and sociologically with their local political leadership patterns. In this socio-geographical arena there are a number of persons and groups that do not directly take part in field activities yet still exert a powerful influence on field behaviour. It is perhaps useful, too, to talk about 'field' and 'arena' *contents*. 'Field' contents include the values, meanings, resources, and relationships used, generated, and articulated by the actors. 'Arena' contents refer to values, meanings, and resources possessed by the actors but not directly employed by them in the purposive processes which activate the field.

'Social dramas' represent, so to speak, the time axes of fields. More than this, they open up the psychological dimension because they throw into relief the feelings, attitudes, and choices of individuals, as well as the relatively constant and consistent, or 'structural', aspects of arena and field. They also indicate where principles of organization are likely to be situationally inconsistent, discrepant or opposed, or even radically contradictory (as in the Icelandic case of pagan and Christian attitudes to revenge-killing in the *Sturlunga Saga*). The social drama, in short, shows how people actually live in arenas of a particular type, how they pursue their ambitious or altruistic ends in them, and how, through significant choices made by important individuals or groups, the arena structure may itself be changed.

Njal's Saga, as it has come down to us, quite naturally leaves the structure and properties of field and arena implicit – clearly, its intended audience is expected to have knowledge through personal experience of the institutionalized background and the kinds of values and motives that influence and appraise deeds. But, for the anthropological investigator, 'field–arena' is more than a mere background; it is a theoretical construct, developed out of the study of many societies possessing widely divergent cultures. For the audience and actors Icelandic, or even Nordic culture is a 'natural' background, Icelandic society merely 'the way men live'. Anthropologists know that other men live in quite other ways, and their task is to show how this particular Icelandic arena is constructed in terms that would allow for comparative study with the arenas of other cultures. I have said that kinship was an important, almost 'irreducible' principle of Icelandic social organization, but this does not tell us what the specific rules of Icelandic kinship are, or how kinship is connected with other structural principles.

Anthropologists who try to study process and history without accounting for structural considerations are just as one-sided as the traditional structuralists who neglected process and history. Thus we can learn much about the Icelandic saga from Radcliffe-Brown, whom we earlier noted as one of the fathers of British structuralism. In the Introduction to *African Systems of Kinship and Marriage* (Radcliffe-Brown & Forde 1950), he has pertinent things to say about Teutonic kinship which bear on *Njal's Saga* (which he mentions but misspells! though his reference is almost the only one in anthropological literature to Iceland). He points out how in some Teutonic societies at least, 'there existed large house-communities under the control of a house-father or house-lord, of the type of what it is usual to call the patriarchal family. Sons continued to live with their father under his rule and daughters usually joined their husbands elsewhere [a form known as 'virilocal marriage' V.T.]. But although the patrilineal principle was general or usual, it was not always strictly adhered to. Thus in . . . *Nyal's Saga* [*sic*] the house-community of old Nyal included not only his wife Bergthora and his three married sons but also a daughter's husband, and, with children, men-servants, and others, the household numbered some fifty persons' (ibid.: 17–18). But while the core of the local group was a group of patrilineal kin, in matters concerning blood vengeance and *wergild*, which is the indemnity that is required when one person kills another, a wider range of kinsmen was involved. This was what the Anglo-Saxons called the *sib*, defined by Radcliffe-Brown as 'computable cognatic relationship for definite social purposes'. One's *sib* in Anglo-Saxon England, or in Iceland, was not a group but a range of persons focused on oneself. If one was killed the *sib* would receive the *wergild* or indemnity.

Commonly, the inner circle of an individual's *sib* included his father and mother, his brother and sister, and his son and daughter. Beyond that various degrees of kin were recognized. Anglo-Saxons appear to have included within the *sib* all the descendants of the eight great-grandparents. The situation in *Njal's Saga* is fairly flexible. Much seems to depend in this society of individualists on whether the principal kinsman of a victim of homicide, on receiving *wergild*, makes a personal decision to divide it among other members of the deceased man's *sib* or not. A big man will get his own way. Those who seek vengeance for a slaying, however, form a varied band, hardly equivalent to a *sib*, but united by diverse ties of kinship, affinity, neighbourhood, political affiliation and friendship. Here politics, or better, politicking, rather than kinship duties alone, seems to play the major role. One musters support from any quarter where it may be had. But the fact that a wide range of kin, on both the killer's and the victim's side, are made visible at each homicide, is an important 'arena-characteristic' of old Icelandic society. How many actually enter the 'field' of purposive *wergild* or vengeance action depends on many other factors, political, economic, and psychological. Such factors become apparent as the 'social dramas' succeed one another to make up at last the total 'saga'.

Other arena characteristics I should mention are territorial and political organization. Since we have from Ari information about the first 'land-taking' we can plot the process of territorial settlement. The first settlers sought out the will of the gods by throwing into the sea just off Iceland the sacred pillars of the high seat (*ǫndvegi*), brought from Norway and watching where they drifted ashore. Next they viewed or 'kenned' the land by climbing the nearest point of high ground. After that the land was ritually 'hallowed' by surrounding it with a ring of bonfires. Hallowed land became the settler's own and its boundaries were then marked by natural or artificial landmarks or beacons. The next step was to demarcate house and farm buildings, and 'town' or home fields. The chieflings who were first settlers built a *Hof* or temple for the gods, where blood sacrifices were made at important rituals and festivals. These priest-chiefs were the first *goðar*, whom we mentioned earlier. Their first step, after settlement, was to allot portions of land to kinsmen, followers, and friends – as is told at length in Ari's *Landnamabók* and the *Laxdoela Saga*. The first tracts were so huge that plenty was left for followers of the priest-chieftains. As time went on and land became occupied, the power of the *goðar* was often much reduced, since their followers were free to stay or go. As in New Guinea today among the so-called 'big men', a *goði's* influence depended on such things as physical strength, personal fame, and skill at arms, just as much as on birth and inherited wealth. A man's power might wane with age, feuds would take toll of his children and kin, while younger *goðar* might wax in power and influence around him. The very attribute which gave him most fame, generosity in providing feasts for his own people and other neighbours, and helping them to pay debts and *wergild*, might be that which impoverished him most decisively. Giving to win and keep followers depletes wealth and loses followers. Thus much depended on a man's present achievements and less on his past glories or family fame. The main sanction against his abusing his powers were that his Thing-men might leave his temple and join another *goði's*

The *goði* had the right to call together the *Things*, or meetings of the people, at stated times, to discuss public business and where suits at law might be taken up. As priest he hallowed the *Thing*, and proclaimed peace while it was in session, he was chief magistrate presiding over the meeting, he named judges and superintended the proceedings. In summary, he was leader of the district of his *goði*-ship, giving protection in return for allegiance. But another man, if strong enough, could build a new temple in his district and subvert his followers. The possession of a temple and personal power, based on numbers, organization, and resources, were all he needed as a title to his office. One even reads of *goði*-ships being bought and sold.

The picture we have at about the end of the first few generations of occupation is of a number of little priest–chiefdoms all round the coast of the island, under the influence, rather than the power, of *goðar*, who at stated times convened their adherents and retainers to meetings for the settlement of matters of common concern. Alongside the *goðar* were important secular household heads, some of whom aspired to *goði*-hood. Each *Thing* or meeting was independent of the others, and quarrels between them could only be settled by treaty or battle – as between sovereign powers. Here the local *goði* represented the community in what may be termed its 'foreign relations' and tried to come to a settlement with his fellow *goðar*. But even when Ulfljot made a code of laws for Iceland, and Grim Goatshoe his brother found a southern site at Thingvellir for an *Althing* or general assembly of Icelanders in A.D. 929–930, one cannot assert that an Icelandic *state* had come into existence. Even at the *Althing* almost everything depended not on the law code – though this was manipulated in litigation to give a gloss of legitimacy to the acts of powerful men and to enlist support from the uncommitted – but on how much force a man could muster when it came to a showdown. Issues and grievances could be ventilated at the *Althing* but the settlement of issues was left effectually to the parties concerned and men continued to 'seek their rights by point and edge' (*med odde ok eggjo*), as Njal once lamented.

Njal's Saga is mainly a matter of 'point and edge' despite Njal's own creation of a Fifth Court, to be held at the *Althing* 'to steer the law and set men at peace'. I have counted the killings in Njal – they amount to 94 in the 330 pages of the Everyman Edition. Some take place out of Iceland, but most are intimately connected with the chain of feuds that compose the saga. One wonders how reliable this figure is when one considers Sveinsson's comment (1953: 72) that the number of men killed in battle or executed between 1208 and 1260 (in the so-called 'turbulent' Sturlung Age) has been computed at around 350 or about 7 per year – in a total population of 70,000 or 80,000. Quite possibly, the more sanguinary sagas had as one function that of the cautionary tale – they warned against what might happen if people did not respect the rules of kinship and neighbourhood relations. In reality, many more feuds may have been settled peacefully than bloodily. But the extremism of Njal's saga throws into high relief the normal and fitting. There is in the case of Njal's household what might be called an almost unnatural stress on, or overevaluation of the father–son bond, at the expense of other *sib* and affinal ties, which are radically undervalued, as where Njal's sons kill their almost 'saintly' foster-brother Hauskuld, the *goði*, whom Njal himself had set up in his office. Njal's sons, even after marriage, continue to reside not only on their father's land but in his very homestead. This solidarity was one cause of their deaths – had they not lived together and fought together they would not have been burned together. ('The family that yearns together, burns together.')

The plot of *Njal's Saga* may be divided into three parts, each a separate narrative, yet interlinked like the phases of a great ritual. The first describes the heroic deeds at home and abroad of Gunnar of Lithend, and how his wife Hallgerda and Njal's wife Bergthora nearly set their households against one another, by 'egging on' their thralls and servants to kill one another. Bergthora even involves her sons in the killings at last. But Njal and Gunnar remain firm friends and settle the homicides by *wergild* not retaliation. The first part ends with the killing of Gunnar in his home after having been exiled for a series of killings in self-defence. The second section begins when Njal's oldest son helps Gunnar's son avenge his father's death, and continues, through a chain of killings, counter-killings and attempts at settlement and reconciliation, to the burning of Njal, his wife, children, a grandchild, and many servants in their homestead, by Flosi, who has taken up the task of avenging Hauskuld the *Goði*'s death. Flosi is accompanied by many who seek vengeance on Njal's sons for kinsmen slain by them. The final part narrates the retribution exacted on the Burners by Kari, Njal's son-in-law, whose wife perished in the flames. Kari harries the Burners over Iceland and even pursues them over the sea; he slays Gunnar Lambisson, a Burner, at the very feast-board of Jarl Sigurd of the Orkneys. The saga virtually ends with the reconcilation of Flosi and Kari, who goes on to marry Flosi's brother's daughter, and has a son by her whom he calls Flosi.

W. P. Ker remarks (1967: 190) of *Njala*: 'It carries an even greater burden of particulars than *Eyrbyggja* (another family saga); it has taken up into itself the whole history of the south country of Iceland in the heroic age.' The 'south country' mentioned is the arena for the field of social relations formed by the ultimate confrontation between the Burners and Njal's faction at the slaying of Hauskuld. Indeed, since Njal's burning raised suits in two Quarter Courts and then in the Fifth Court of the *Althing* it could be said to have had all Iceland as arena. Strangely, although it deals primarily with killings between the patrilineal residential cores of 'house-communities', the saga's main sequence of events begins with a quarrel between unrelated women, Bergthora and Hallgerda, and ends with reconciliation between unrelated men, Kari and Flosi.

Kari, though unrelated by birth to Njal and his blood-kin, indeed, not even an Icelander but an Orkneyman, is linked by marriage to them, as is Bergthora, Njal's wife. Hallgerda is linked by affinity to the opposite faction, as is Flosi. Thus connexions by marriage may serve as either disruptive or unitive factors in the relations between 'house-communities' and sets of linked 'house-communities'. In the case of the women who are incorporated into patrilineal core-groups by virilocal marriage and spend most of their post-marital lives in their husbands' communities, rising to the status of matriarchs, concern for the honour of these local, particularistic groups becomes a ruling passion. They are not concerned with the wider groupings, such as District, Quarter, or Iceland, but foment local conflicts with their sharp taunting tongues. But men, through their participation in juridical and legislative action on a wider scale than the local, may exert their influence as in-laws to reconcile disputing house-communities rather than exacerbate their enmities. Even when they are inimical to both parties to a dispute, like the sinister Mord Valgardsson, who provokes Njal's sons to kill Hauskuld by deceitful words, ill-wishing men have to couch their mischievous intentions in the honeyed language of the common good. But the women have no such inhibitions. When Hallgerda hires Brynjolf the Unruly to cause trouble among Bergthora's servants, early in the saga, she says to him (referring to Atli, one of Bergthora's men): 'I have been told that Atli is not at home, and he must be winning work on Thorofsfell.' [He was cutting wood there.]

'What thinkest thou likeliest he is working at?' says Brynjolf.
'At something in the wood,' she says.
'What shall I do to him?' he asks.
'Thou shall kill him,' says she.

Nevertheless the killings of servants for which these women are responsible are relatively small beer. The bulk of the saga is made up of long social dramas. As social drama the first phase, that of 'breach' of regular norm-governed relationships is usually a killing, the next phase, 'crisis', sees the mobilization of factions, either to take revenge and defend against it, or to seek compensation; if the drama continues to the phase of bringing in 'redressive procedures', these may either be of an informal kind, as when Njal and Gunnar privately decide to offer one another compensation for the slain thralls, or involve formal measures ranging from 'self-doom', where a plaintiff is conceded the right by his opponents to name the kind and extent of damages he thinks fair, through recourse to local and District *Things* to the *Althing* of Iceland and the 'Fifth Court' in it. *Njal's Saga* begins with simple breaches of order, minor crises, and informal redress, mainly at the level of relations between household-communities in a small region of the South Quarter, which cumulate, despite temporary settlement and redress, until finally the 'breach' is the killing of a *goði* who is also a good man, the 'crisis' involves a major cleavage between factions consisting of the major lineages and *sibs* in southern and south-eastern Iceland, and the parties seek 'redress' at the *Althing* and Fifth Court. *Njal's Saga* shows pitilessly how Iceland just could not produce the machinery to handle major crises, for inevitably the *Althing* negotiations break

369

down and there is regression to crisis again, sharpened crisis, moreover, that can only be resolved now by the total defeat of one party, even its attempted annihilation. The art of the literary genius who took the oral and written traditions and wove them into the saga we now have reveals for us how the bitterness of the early household feuds, which Njal and Gunnar had the authority to keep formally within local bounds, nevertheless trickled through the rivulets of many small crises into what might have been a national crisis had there been a nation. The fact that there was no nation was represented by the absence of national laws with teeth in them, the teeth of punitive sanctions jointly applied by the leading men. Thus local feuds which could be only transiently contained by enlightened individuals generated forces over time which sundered Iceland and revealed the weakness of her uncentralized, 'acephalous' polity. Strong individualism can only be kept in bounds by strong centralized institutions. It seems, however, that *Njal's Saga* was written after Iceland had accepted Norwegian overlordship and Norway's king, and it may have been partly written to show how the traditional Commonwealth had no means of keeping the peace. Patently, *Njal's Saga* reflects the experience of the Sturlung Era. The saga relates, in terms of personalities, the story of a society. Njal succeeds in keeping local peace for a while but cannot curb his own sons, who disobey him in order to carry out their mother's will. Yet the greatest men of Iceland hang upon his words when he proposes to establish general legal machinery, such as the Fifth Court, and give him support. The irony of the saga is that it is through the continual disobedience of his own sons, who undertake revenge killings against his will, that the final disasters come about, exposing the impotence of Icelandic redressive institutions. Njal is shown as a man who always seeks peace and is forever trying to set up social devices for keeping it. For example he fosters Hauskuld, whose father Thrain has been slain by Njal's grim and blackly humorous son Skarphedinn, precisely to reconcile the lad and his kin *with* Skarphedinn, and Njal's other sons, Helgi and Grim. For a time this seemed to work and, as the saga says, 'Njal's sons took Hauskuld about with them and did him honour in every way.' Njal later had the Fifth Court make him a *goði*. But in the end Skarphedinn slew Hauskuld, and thus made the burning almost inevitable. For a time it seemed that Njal and Flosi who took up the suit for Hauskuld's slaying would come to terms about compensation but at the last moment Skarphedinn offered Flosi an unforgivable insult that could only be wiped out in blood. A society organized at its only effectual level, the local level, on kinship, and especially on patrilineal kinship, cannot cope with larger, more impersonal, national relationships and issues. Thus the very power of agnation, of the paternal bond, compelled Njal to stand by his sons and indeed suffer death with them, although they had wilfully brought that death about by flouting his advice and ruining his efforts to create peace-maintaining machinery above the local level.

With the hindsight of the post-Sturlung period *Njala's* author is portraying for us the fate of a social order, of the old Germania transported to an inhospitable island where Teutonic nomadism was slowed down and halted by lack of adequate cultivable or pastoral land – save for the ultimate adventurers like Eirik the Red and Leif Erikson who discovered the New World. All the structural contradictions were left in the 'laboratory experimental' conditions of Icelandic isolation to shake the polity to pieces. The settlers were aristocrats of the ancient breed, who fled to a 'ruined land of sphagnum moss' to continue the old ways, even the old verse forms, in terms of the old attitudes which had elsewhere vanished before Christendom and chivalry. The sagas, especially *Njal's Saga*, chronicle, step by step, the suicidal character of that last stand.

Yet it was perhaps, by another paradox, the very fact of Germania's projection into the new literate age by four centuries that made Icelandic literature possible. The constrast between the new polities abroad, observed by vigilant and highly intelligent Icelandic travellers and vikings, and their own ancient acephalous polities, based on kinship and local organization of a small-scale character, made for an almost self-mocking self-awareness, and for W. P. Ker's 'dry light'. Yet aristocratic prideful obduracy kept the old order – or was it disorder? – going, and let us remember that some of the results were major literature as well as a high homicide rate.

I will have to conclude where I would like to have begun by pointing out that the sagas read like exceptionally well-filled ethnographic records and diaries, written by an incomparable literary artist. I would have liked to have begun by making a technical analysis in anthropological terms of the details of *Njal's Saga*, relating its copious genealogical materials to the siting of homestead owners on the map and pointing out how the meticulous descriptions of such things as seating order at wedding feasts reflect the social structure also visible in the patternings of genealogies and settlements. At the wedding of Gunnar and Halgerda, for example, not only were the different kinds of kinship, affinal, and territorial relationships in which the guests stood to Gunnar represented in their placing round the festal table, but the shape of things to come was simultaneously represented by Njal's party's placement on one side of Gunnar and the foremost Burners' on the other – a clear indication of the importance of structural links and divisions for the development of the feud. Literary critics would assent to W. P. Ker's words that in Njal 'the essence of the tragic situation lies in this, that the good man is in the wrong, and his adversary in the right' (1967: 190–1). The anthropologist would see the situation less in ethical terms. The Icelander compelled by structural ties to take up a vengeance suit has a similar role to that of a mature man in an Ndembu village in Central Africa (Turner 1957: 94). Such a senior villager is compelled sooner or later to take a stand on the question of succession to the headmanship. A person who tries to avoid pressing the claim for that office vested in his very membership in the village kinship structure, when the old headman dies is subjected to intense pressure from his close kin and children to put it forward. If he should still fail to do so, there occurs a displacement of the locus of conflict, not a resolution or bypassing of conflict. Instead of leading a group of kin against the representatives of other pressure groups or factions, he becomes the target of criticism and even scorn from members of his own group. At some point in the social process arising from succession he is compelled to turn and defend himself, whatever his temperament or character, however 'good' or 'bad' he may be. As I wrote, 'the situation in an Ndembu village closely parallels that found in Greek drama where one witnesses the helplessness of the human individual before the Fates: but in this case the Fates are the necessities of the social process'. *Mutatis mutandis* the same basic situation prevailed in Iceland, and this is pithily revealed in *Njal's Saga* in its accounts of how men reacted to the rules forcing them to take part in the feud. Icelandic social structure never resolved the opposition between forces making for centralization and forces making for decentralization, between extreme individualism and family loyalty, between kinship and citizenship and, perhaps, also, between a bare subsistence economy and the aspiration to an aristocratic style of life. There may well have been increasing pressure on effective resources at that subsistence level which exacerbated disputes between adjacent *goðar* and their followers over scarce resources, such as timber and meadows, and activated other structural and cultural contradictions. A host of cultural considerations I have not been able to mention are relevant here; Njal, the man of peace was a Christian but Icelandic standards of conduct remained vindictively pagan; it is constantly hinted that he was somewhat effeminate – his enemies called him mockingly 'the Beardless Carle' – for if pursuing vengeance is defined as manly, seeking reconciliation with one's foes must be unmanly, and so on. But ultimately, for the author of the saga, Njal seems to symbolize the Commonwealth itself. This is perhaps best reflected in the celebrated scene when the burning begins. I must quote (from Dasent's translation):

> Flosi (from outside) said to Bergthora, Njal's wife, 'Come thou out, housewife, for I will for no sake burn thee indoors.'
>
> 'I was given away to Njal young,' said Bergthora, 'and I have promised him this, that we would both share the same fate.'
>
> After that they both went back into the house.
>
> 'What counsel shall we now take?' said Bergthora.
>
> 'We will go to our bed,' says Njal, 'and lay us down; I have long been eager for rest.'
>
> Then she said to the boy Thord, Kari's son, 'Thee will I take out, and thou shalt not burn in here.'
>
> 'Thou hast promised me this, grandmother,' says the boy, 'that we should never part so long as I wished to be with thee; but methinks it is much better to die with thee and Njal than to live after you.'
>
> An ox hide was thrown over the three of them, and they spoke no more.
>
> Skarphedinn saw how his father laid him down, and how he laid himself out, and then he said, 'Our father goes early to bed, and that is what was to be looked for, for he is an old man.'

For me, these laconic, ironic, heroic words epitomize the fate of the Icelandic Commonwealth, and its attempt to find peace and order. It could not live but it made a good end, so good that its failure to survive became immortal literature.

NOTE

1. In practice the system worked out as a balance of power between districts and land-holders; a majority decision of the *Thing* could only be enforced if you had power on the winning side. If you had not, the decision was unrealistic and probably some excuse was found to alter it.

Victor W. Turner

REFERENCES

ANDERSON, THEODORE M. 1964 *The Problems of Icelandic Saga Origins*. New Haven and London: Yale University Press.

ARENT, A. MARGARET 1964 *The Laxdoela Saga*. Seattle: University of Wisconsin Press.

EPSTEIN, A. L. 1967 The Case Method in the Field of Law. In Epstein, A. L. (ed.), *The Craft of Social Anthropology*. London: Tavistock Publications.

EVANS-PRITCHARD, E. E. 1949 *The Sanusi of Cyrenaica*. Oxford: Clarendon Press.

— 1950 Social Anthropology: Past and Present. *Man* **50**: 118–24.

— 1961 *Anthropology and History*. University of Manchester Press.

GLUCKMAN, MAX 1965 *Politics, Law and Ritual in Tribal Society*. Oxford: Blackwell.

GORDON, E. V. 1927 *Introduction to Old Norse*. London: Oxford University Press.

KER, W. P. 1967 *Epic and Romance*. New York: Dover Publications.

KROEBER, A. L. 1935 History and Science in Anthropology. *American Anthropologist* **37**, No. 4, Pt. 1 (Oct.–Dec.): 538–69.

LEWIS, I. M. (ed.) 1968 *History and Social Anthropology*. ASA Monograph 7. London: Tavistock Publications.

RADCLIFFE-BROWN, A. R., AND DARYLL FORDE (eds.) 1950 *African Systems of Kinship and Marriage*. London: Oxford University Press.

SINGER, MILTON (ed.) 1966 *An Anthropologist Looks at History*. Berkeley and Los Angeles: University of California Press.

SVEINSSON, EINAR O. 1953 *The Age of the Sturlungs: Icelandic Civilization in the Thirteenth Century*. Ithaca: Cornell University Press.

SWARTZ, MARC (ed.) 1968 *Local-level Politics*. Chicago: Aldine.

TURNER, V. W. 1957 *Schism and Continuity in an African Society*. Manchester: Manchester University Press.

TURVILLE-PETRE, E. O. G. 1953 *Origins of Icelandic Literature*. Oxford: Clarendon Press.

— (ed.) 1957 *The Story of Burnt Njal* (trans. by Sir George Webbe Dasent). London: Dent, Everyman Library.

VANSINA, JAN 1965 *Oral Tradition*. Chicago: Aldine.

VAN VELSEN, J. 1967 The Extended-case Method and Situational Analysis. In Epstein, A. L. (ed.), *The Craft of Social Anthropology*. London: Tavistock Publications.

VIGFUSSON, GUDBRAND, AND F. YORK POWELL 1905 *Origines Islandicae*. 2 vols. Oxford: Clarendon Press.

Nuer Priests and Prophets

Charisma, Authority, and Power among the Nuer

T. O. BEIDELMAN

. . . I was no prophet, neither was I a prophet's son; but I was an
herdsman, and a gatherer of sycamore fruit: and the Lord took
me as I followed the flock, and the Lord said unto me, Go prophesy
unto my people . . .   Amos 8: 14–15

He was an hairy man, and girt with a girdle of leather about his
loins.   2 Kings 1: 8

Evans-Pritchard readily concedes his great debt to French sociology, perhaps the greatest single influence being that of Lévy-Bruhl. Of course, the works of Durkheim and his followers Mauss, Hubert, and Hertz also provide an important theoretical framework but even here Evans-Pritchard appears to have rejected or ignored many aspects of these works. For example, today the French sociological classics exert an enormous influence in the structural analysis of myth, ritual, folklore, and cosmology, yet these lines of analysis are never touched upon by Evans-Pritchard. He utilizes such concepts as asymmetric polarity as devices for presenting data, but not as keys for apprehending the basic intellectual principles by which a society's values and ideas are ordered. Still less is he concerned with interrelating such cosmological categories with social groups.

German thinkers have played even less part in Evans-Pritchard's thought, though such men as Marx and Weber have had a lasting impact on sociology, probably as great or even greater than Durkheim himself. Still less is Evans-Pritchard concerned with such writers as Freud and Jung, though their works provide important groundwork for many of the basic theories originated by Durkheim and his school regarding the relation of ideology to emotions and expressive behaviour.

To some extent this neglect may be due to Evans-Pritchard's own deep absorption with explicating one broad Durkheimean problem, the interdependence between ideology and social norms.[1] But these have almost always been within the scope of particular societies, rather than in terms of any general notions or theories pertaining to many or most societies.

In this essay[2] I hope to clarify certain ethnographic facts reported for the Nuer of the southern Sudan and thereby illustrate the richness of data collected by Evans-Pritchard and others who worked among the Nuer. However, this essay has two broader aims as well: (1) by applying certain principles of structural analysis of the symbols related to leadership, I try to indicate some of the ambiguous values attached to such persons. In this, I merely continue along one analytic path initiated by Durkheim and his followers. (2) By applying certain Weberian notions to data primarily collected by researchers with a Durkheimean slant,[3] I hope to suggest indirectly how the notions of these two masters may complement one another and sharpen analysis of certain religious and political institutions. These mainly involve the interrelationships between power and authority and the ambiguities and difficulties involved in distinguishing between the two.

I contrast two types of Nuer leaders, ritual experts (priests) and prophets. For one reason or another, these men become outstanding on account of being credited with powers over or relations with the supernatural. In the course of making my points about these social statuses, I also consider very briefly some aspects of other Nuer known for their supernatural connexions: minor medicine men, suspected ghouls, and prominent men who make sacrifices. I contend that certain socially significant features of ritual experts (priests) and prophets become clear if we consider them in terms of Weber's contrast between legitimate and charismatic (non-institutionalized) authority, and in terms of the more basic political distinctions between authority and power, to which this Weberian model is ultimately related. Since I have already written extensively on these issues elsewhere (1966a; 1968) I do not develop these points here. It is a tribute to the richness of the Nuer data that sufficient material is available for an analysis so alien to the researchers' original intentions.

I

Evans-Pritchard describes the Nuer prophet and priest (ritual expert)[4] as two very different social beings. Prophets may, according to him, be said to assume their positions voluntarily and individually, whereas priests are born into lineages whose adult men may, at least theoretically, exercise priestly functions. Yet prophets are not thought of by Nuer in this way: they are called by Spirit. Prophets hold diffuse but highly unstable power; priests hold very narrowly defined but lifelong authority. Priests speak for men to God; prophets speak for God to men; but both operate in social affairs which are both political and religious. Evans-Pritchard suggests that the priesthood is a more traditional, purely Nuer institution, whereas prophetism is a more recent development, perhaps due to the influence of neighbouring peoples and to the upheavals caused by the arrival of Arab and European traders, raiders and conquerors (E-P 1956: 303-4; 308-9). Yet the influence of neighbouring peoples, especially the Dinka, seems to have such a long history among the Nuer that one wonders how safely this may be assumed. Furthermore, if one reviews the material available on these two types of leader, one finds many similar features shared by both; furthermore, there seems to be a tendency for Nuer prophets to spring from priestly lineages and sometimes for prophetic and ambitious individuals outside such lineages to try to assume priestly attributes (cf. sections IV, VII, and VIII of this paper). To put it in Weber's terms, Nuer priests sometimes widen and strengthen their authority by assuming charismatic powers more often associated with prophetic figures; and Nuer prophets try to convert their charismatic powers into a more routinized authority. The interdependence between authority and power, between institutionalized and individualized powers, presents problems in the analysis of leadership in any society. In an acephalous political system such as the Nuer, which Evans-Pritchard once paradoxically described as ordered anarchy, this interdependence is especially complex.

In his attempt to analyse authority, Weber constructs a number of pure heuristic models which probably cannot be found unalloyed in any society, but which correspond in varying degrees to the complex hybrid sets of political relations present everywhere (1947: 328). As defined by him, pure charismatic authority exists only in a kind of nascent state, since, in order to execute orders and maintain purposeful interaction, leaders must routinize or stabilize their powers into some kind of more legalized and rationalized set of rights and procedures (1947: 364). Therefore, although charismatic persons tend to arise as exceptional and revolutionary individuals, if they are successful in securing the support of others, they become leaders and founders of corporate groups rather similar to the groups from which they sprang. Conversely, traditional, conventional persons with authority retain their power only so long as this is effective through their individual powers and skill to achieve their authorized ends, that is, the goals of the collectivity – whereas a charismatic leader may often define new goals. But successful charismatic authority is converted into routinized authority of a more traditional cast, and successful traditional authority always requires some of the attributes of charisma (Weber 1947: 364, 382). Although Weber writes of charismatic authority and traditional authority, it is clear that the activities with which he is concerned may also be contrasted in terms of the distinctions between authority and power.[5] We generally consider authority to be legitimized power and though power and authority are very complexly related, it is often useful to distinguish between them analytically in order to grasp the nature and problems of leadership and the control of others. Power without authority lacks stability and continuity; authority without power cannot long secure obedience and soon falls into desuetude. Such propositions are commonplace enough, but the complexity of their implications, even in relatively simple societies, is often underestimated. To demonstrate my contentions I now consider the Nuer data in more detail.

II

Nuer priests and prophets often serve as mediators in the affairs of various social groups which are in conflict with one another. This medial function, in turn, relates to the fact that such leaders are thought also to stand as intermediaries between men and God (Spirit). Thus, to make sense of these activities and attributes of Nuer priests and prophets, one must have some grasp of the basic features of Nuer cosmology.

We are told that for the Nuer the most fundamental cosmological division is that separating Spirit (*kwoth*) from the world of Creation (*cak*) in which man (*ran*) dwells (E-P 1956: 3, 144). The essence of Spirit is its ethereal, undifferentiated, infinite nature transcending the different categories of Creation. Its essence is therefore unmanifest and unknowable to Nuer. Nuer know Spirit only in its manifestations through finite vehicles which partake of Creation yet in some respects are thought to stand outside Creation. An object or act that holds attributes of a particular category partakes of Creation; but the more this same object or act is viewed as fitting into two or more such

378

categories at once, the more it resembles Spirit whose essence is its transcendence of single categories.[6] The convergence of categories, due to the convergence of two or more ideological model systems, in certain objects, persons, occasions, or acts is the common feature of all ritual behaviour. The symbolic interrelation of moral men and oxen provides rich examples of this (Beidelman 1966a).

All social ordering within the world of man seems to spring from an initial dichotomization between Spirit and Creation. When Spirit passes into the sphere of Creation it brings pestilence, lightning, sterility, possession; but it may also bring supernatural prowess, fertility, victory in battle, rain, etc. Sometimes Spirit intrudes negatively for no reason apparent to men, but sometimes this is due to men failing to observe proper rules ordering their lives, to fail to observe *thek* (respect). They may have failed to follow certain customary rules related to proper awareness of status within and towards various groups in society or in nature; or they may have committed immoral acts which led to serious conflicts in these relations. I suggest that these immoral acts and the confusion of social categories are seen by Nuer as one and the same. In a sense, too, the transcendence of Spirit into the world of nature also represents a kind of failure of Spirit to observe the distinctions (*thek*) between the two. But whether this confounding of order is due to the inexplicable temporary interference of Spirit or due to the errors and accidents of men, the effects are the same: both spheres of existence are out of joint and only ritual activity can put matters right again. Until that time, failure to observe *thek* may subsequently lead to misfortune or, in serious cases, to an illness called *nueer*, a form of dysentery (Howell 1954: 45).[7]

Thus, all Nuer religious activity relates in some way to the problems of dissolution and redefinition of such symbolic categories. However, not all such acts are aimed simply at reseparating such categories which have become confused. As Hubert and Mauss observed in their essay on sacrifice and as Evans-Pritchard echoes (1956: 4), religious rites often centre upon a paradox; one sometimes purposely confounds such categories in order to induce the presence of the supernatural in the sphere of men and then one may formally manipulate these symbolic attributes of Spirit within a certain pattern which eventually expresses a clearer separation of them from men. The inverted behaviour of Nuer prophets is an example of this other kind of religious activity, in which a person deliberately attempts to conflate categories of symbolic attributes in order to partake of the dangerous powers of Spirit. In doing so, a prophet's conduct often very closely resembles that of anti-social ghouls or witches or asocial madmen.[8] However, in many other Nuer religious acts, the reverse is true and Nuer symbolically separate categories of things, persons, and acts which somehow have become blurred and ill defined. In either type of religious activity, whether it be a deliberate confusion of categories or a separation of them, certain symbolic forms and acts appear time and time again.

Before proceeding to a more involved discussion of these points, perhaps an example from Nuer ritual behaviour may illustrate what kind of ambiguous relations I mean which can both separate yet also connect things. I use as my example the attributes and associated behaviour of a minor Nuer ritual expert, one who has certain powers to control crocodiles and prevent them from harming men and livestock.[9]

Evans-Pritchard reports that certain Nuer respect (*thek*) crocodiles; he sometimes refers to Nuer having crocodiles as totems (1954a: 33). Now this connexion between a group of humans and a species of wild animals is thought to have been brought about by a twin birth in which one twin was the ancestor of such humans and the other of crocodiles. Nuer also regard the birth of twins as a manifestation of Spirit. The deceased common ancestor appears to be the spirit sacrificed to on certain occasions involving the relations between these saurian humans and their crocodile counterparts. The descendants of these twins are expected to avoid one another in that such humans should not slay crocodiles, while crocodiles in turn should not kill these persons or their livestock. If crocodiles were to interfere with these saurian humans, sacrifice by a saurian Nuer might be made to the eponymous spirit common to both these Nuer and crocodiles but if this still did not re-achieve such reciprocal separation, the humans might begin to disregard their own obligations and hunt crocodiles, sell their hides, etc. Conversely, if these saurian humans killed crocodiles without such provocation, they might face supernatural punishment through derangement, illness, or misfortune such as producing monstrous children with saurian physiognomies. Yet so long as such relations are properly observed, saurian men stand medially between their fellow-humans and fellow-crocodiles in that they may sometimes sacrifice in order to make a river safe for all humans and their stock against crocodiles. Crocodiles stand towards these saurian humans as a category of natural or bush creatures, different from other wild animals, for such ritual does not lead other animals to refrain from harming men. Their common lot with their fellow-Nuer leads these men to restrict the ordinary behaviour of crocodiles which must then refrain from devouring not merely their saurian brothers but all humans. To say when certain Nuer *thek* crocodiles that they 'respect' them, therefore, hardly conveys all the ambiguous processes at work. Three sets of categorizations operate at once, even though, in a strict sense, these may appear to be somewhat contradictory: all men are distinguished from all wild creatures of the bush including crocodiles; saurian men are categorized with crocodiles; saurian men stand medially between other men and crocodiles.

By Nuer definition there are persons throughout Nuerland who claim to stand between men and Spirit. By definition this involves the regulation and control of extraordinary events or states, viz., all manifestations of Spirit within Creation, including the potential supernatural disorders which may result from social conflict. To some extent any Nuer who performs a ritual act temporarily assumes some such medial status between men and Spirit. Certain men such as leeches, diviners, curers, possess specialized and more enduring powers along this line. Various ceremonial or ritual experts possess such powers within fairly specialized spheres of action; and a few Nuer prophets of varying degree of power and fame are thought to possess especially awesome and far-ranging gifts of this nature.

There is some moral ambiguity in any ritually defined status. This is partly because such ritual persons tend to connect hostile or ambivalently related persons or groups and that their connexions with the supernatural consequently need not be viewed from the same moral perspective by each of the persons or group so involved in their activities. In their most pronounced forms, these characterize persons outside the normal measure of social roles: whether these novel or extraordinary roles are seen as admirable or execrable, creative or malevolent, seems to depend upon how such persons relate to those who judge and define them within their community.[10]

III

Nuer recognize a number of ritual experts or priests whose rights to office are usually inherited agnatically. The most prominent of these is the *kuaar muon* (priest of the earth), sometimes referred to by Nuer as *kuaar twac* (priest of the skin) on account of the leopard- or serval-skin worn over their shoulders and right arms.[11] Such men are thought to stand in a mystical relationship towards the soil, the earth. Being closely connected to the earth on which all Nuer live and from which all Nuer and their livestock gain sustenance and which represents the widest possible Nuer value, these priestly men are thought in some sense to stand in a kind of medial position between all Nuer groups; furthermore, through their roles as sacrificers such men also have a mystical connexion with Spirit, as manifested in the sky, the only other all-inclusive physical entity. Such men purify acts of homicide, pollution resulting from failure to obey prohibitions operative during a feud, and serve as the main mediators in settling feuds and in payment of bloodwealth (E-P 1934: 49; 1956: 293–8; Howell 1954: 45, 84). They also may administer oaths in certain disputes where their mystical relation with the soil is thought to cause illness to any false witness (E-P 1935: 37–9; 1956: 297–8). Such priests also remove pollution caused by close incest and by failure to observe certain other important prohibitions and they may dissolve any such incestuous unions which may have inadvertently taken place. Priests of the earth are said to have settled warfare between different Nuer tribal groups (Howell 1954: 58), but it is not clear whether this may have also been due to other social qualities as well. No Nuer should carry his spear into the presence of a *kuaar muon*, presumably out of respect for his peacemaking attributes (Howell 1954: 44), though perhaps for sexually symbolic reasons. It appears that such priests may also have been actually connected with certain raiding preparations and have the right to a cow after a raid (Seligman: 216–17).

A *kuaar muon* stands in a relation to the earth very much like that of any other Nuer towards his totemic counterpart: just as in the case of the saurian Nuer described above, so too the *kuaar muon* must show respect (*thek*) towards the earth, which is simply to say that his relation towards it is expressed by both notions and acts of avoidance and of sacred interconnexion. He must avoid pot-makers lest their wares crack and he avoids direct contact with the soil on some occasions;[12] he may anoint the earth and seeds if crops are poor, and, like a twin, he is buried separated from contact with soil (E-P 1934: 45–6; 1956: 291). He may put earth on his head to weaken the enemy before a raid (Seligman: 216). Apparently for similar reasons, he may be asked to conduct minor ritual for rain, but this is said not to be widely credited by Nuer (E-P 1956: 298).

If such a priest's instructions are flouted, it is said that he may curse by slaying an ox and then rubbing off all the hair from its head (E-P 1934: 51),[13] or he may simply invoke a curse onto the soil where a person stands (E-P 1956: 291; 1949e: 288–9); apparently such curses are greatly feared (E-P 1934: 46–7). The curse of an earth-priest slain by persons who failed to respect his authority was thought especially harmful (cf. E-P 1945: 58 ff).

Evans-Pritchard reports that such priests of the earth conduct ceremonies of purification for any serious act of sin or pollution (1956: 289–90). However, he goes on to imply that the seriousness is defined with relation to difficulties involving two or more different agnatic groups, viz., problems related to close incest, feud, and other serious disputes. There seems little point repeating his ethnographic descriptions here since these rites are already well described (ibid.: 293–7). However, there are certain broad symbolic aspects of these rites which are neglected by him and these require further discussion. In such rites the priest of the earth stands between the groups involved and in this sense he may be thought of as outside each. From one perspective he may be said to transcend all groups and thereby partake of all, but from another perspective he may be said to conform properly to none. This medial role, then, is ambiguous with positive (uniting, sacred) aspects but also with negative (confusing, polluting) ones. The homicide often resides with or near the priest who thus comes into contact with the disorderly, polluting aspects of homicide, symbolically represented by the homicide having his person and homestead untended until the resultant feud is settled. But the priest also provides the means by which such pollution may be removed and social conflict resolved. Below I discuss how Nuer sometimes symbolically represent manifest Spirit, the most powerful medial phenomenon they know, through certain black and white objects; it is surely no accident that the black and white pied-crow is also called *kuaar*, for if no *kuaar muon* is available to cleanse a polluted homicide, he may cleanse himself by slaying such a bird, removing its upper beak and licking it. Just as the human priest cleanses by inverting enacted order (drawing blood from the slayer who is himself polluted by having drawn blood), so the homicide cleanses himself be breaking respect (*thek*) with the pied-crow. For Nuer should respect all birds and never eat them and should especially respect the pied-crow which is associated with rivers (symbolically medial for Nuer) and with Buk, the mother of Deng, the most powerful of the air-spirits associated with some of the greatest Nuer prophets (E-P 1934: 98; 1956: 31–2).

With a homicide, a state of feud or negative reciprocity is established between the kin of the slayer and the slain; this may only be dissolved by the payment of bloodwealth which is in turn converted into bride-wealth (positive reciprocity) for the ghost. So long as the feud is in effect, those involved must observe dietary prohibitions almost identical with those established by affinity. Furthermore, the payment of bloodwealth is equated with bridewealth, since it procures a wife for the slain's ghost (cf. E-P 1947: 187-8). Elsewhere I discuss in detail the structural and symbolic parallels for Nuer between the pollution of affinity and the pollution of feud (Beidelman 1968).[14]

Besides such priests of the earth, Nuer recognize other ritual experts: it is not clear whether *kuaar thoan* (priests of the serval) are the same as priests of the earth (priest of the leopard). Howell reports that serval-priests settle disputes between earth-priests (1954: 44), whereas in eastern Nuerland this is done by a commoner (*dwek*). But Evans-Pritchard reports that such settlements are reached by members of aristo-cratic clans (1956: 293). Nuer also recognize cattle-priests (*kuaar ghok*) who are connected to nearly all aspects of cattle fertility, health, raiding, pasturage (E-P 1935: 49-55). They can also curse cattle, causing an offending man to become sick from drinking milk or using the hides of his own herd which are thought to adhere painfully to his flesh. Cattle-priests must be buried in fresh cattle manure. They bless by aspersion with milk and cannot accept cattle in compensation for adultery with their wives (E-P 1956: 300-1; Howell 1954: 30; Lewis: 80). They have many ceremonial duties related to the establishment and naming of age-sets, initiation redefining men's relations towards cattle. Evans-Pritchard suggests that despite the importance of cattle for Nuer, such cattle-priests are far less influential than earth-priests (1956: 302), yet elsewhere he describes some cattle-priests with very great influence who become prophets (1935: 50-3).

There are other Nuer ritual leaders of far lower standing and influence than these who are more usually simply entitled *gwan* (owner), rather than *kuaar* (priest): for example, *kuaar yik* (priest of the mats) may also be called *gwan yik*; such a person moderates disputes between affines arising when a wife dies during her first childbirth. (Apparently, this corresponds to some extent with a situation of feud requiring bloodwealth to remove pollution.) Other such ritual experts are *gwan muot*[15] (owner of the spear) who performs rites before hunting and raiding; *kuaar biedh* (priest of the fishing-spear) who performs rites to protect fishermen; *gwan nyanga* or *gwan thoi* (possessor of crocodile or grass) who performs rites against crocodiles and for fishermen (cf. discussion above on saurian Nuer); *kuaar juaini* (priest of grass) who also protects fishermen; *gwan pini* (owner of water) who performs anti-flood ritual; *gwan keca* (possessor of the durra-bird) whose ritual drives off these pests (E-P 1956: 302–3). Besides these, Nuer also recognize very many minor ritual specialists such as curers, leeches, owners of medicine bundles, diviners, etc.

IV

The basic sociological features are fairly similar for all such priestly persons, so that if one understands the means by which earth-priests function, one may grasp the fundamentals for their lesser counterparts.

In analysing priestly Nuer, Evans-Pritchard makes a number of statements which seem contradictory both in terms of themselves and in terms of the ethnographic evidence. Thus, he first presents the earth-priest simply as a sacralized referee, implying that he is only able to effect settlement when all of the disputants have already desired this:

'In situations of *nueer* in which hostile feelings are not aroused, as when twins are born or a person is killed by lightning, the head of the family or its master of ceremonies officiates. These are family and lineage affairs. So, whereas the *gwan buthni* [master of ceremonies] acts in sacrifice on behalf of an exclusive social group, the leopard-skin priest for the most part performs sacrifices in situations in which two groups are opposed to one another and which therefore require a person unidentified by lineage attachment to either to act on behalf of the whole community. The priest thus has a central position in the social structure rather than in religious thought, for his priestly functions are exclusive not because, on account of the sanctity of his office, only he can perform sacrifices, but because representatives of neither party to a dispute can effectively act in the circumstances obtaining. As he entirely lacks any real political authority or powers it is understandable that he could not carry out his functions unless during their performance his person was sacrosanct. The presence of a priesthood adds nothing to the dominant ideas of Nuer religion. It is rather these ideas which give to a political role its necessary attributes. Put in another way, the Nuer have priests who perform certain politico-religious functions but their religion is not intrinsically a priestly religion' (E–P 1956: 300).

To concede that a mediator must have secured some willingness on

385

the part of the disputants before he can mediate, and even to concede that he may be endowed with certain mystical attributes, is still not to discount any important informal power on his part due to his tact, skill and, more important, due to his own ties to the two groups involved.

Evans-Pritchard further describes earth-priests in terms which resemble those sometimes associated with the qualities of a Roman Catholic priest:

> 'In whatever circumstances a priest acts as intermediary between men and God the virtue which gives efficacy to his mediation resides in his office rather than in himself. Consequently, it does not matter what sort of a person he is, socially, psychologically, or morally. The virtue derives from the office having been established by God at the beginning of things as part of the social order' (ibid.: 299).

Yet elsewhere he himself observes:

> '. . . although their powers are hereditary, and although all members of a priestly lineage can, therefore, act in a priestly capacity, in practice only certain families do so, and these families can function as priests wherever they happen to reside' (ibid.: 292).[16]

Still elsewhere, he includes cattle-priests along with earth-priests in this generalization (1935: 51); indeed, in an earlier paper he seems to contradict his later view. I prefer his relatively unreflective and more empirical view when the author had just returned from the field rather than his later, more considered conclusions:

> 'Although, on account of the limited range of his functions, the cattle-expert has on the whole far less social influence than the land expert, nevertheless his sacred character, his ritual powers and their economic consequences, give him hereditary prestige and peculiar opportunity for clutching the reins of power. As I have already observed, when speaking of the land-expert, inheritance of ritual powers gives a man privilege of opportunity but whether he seizes his opportunity or not depends on his character. As a general rule unless a *wut ghok* is also a leader by temperament and ambition he has the limited importance of a magico-religious expert, but there are examples of men who have achieved great reputation and real executive power' (E-P 1935: 51–2).

One would probably also be safe in assuming that such men were never mere youths, but rather older men, more skilled in the tactics of moderation and lobbying perhaps with a considerable following built up through the years by offspring, affines, and clients. Seligman cites a myth relating earth-priesthood with seniority (Seligman: 207).

Much of Evans-Pritchard's argument is based on the situation as he observed it on the borders of the Lou and eastern Jikany tribal groups, which had few earth-priests, but other tribal groups such as the Gaawar, Lak, and Thiang are reported to have many such families. Furthermore, these are reported to come from the aristocratic or dominant lineages of these areas (Howell 1954: 29). This requires very different interpretation from that which Evans-Pritchard provides where he observes that in most areas such earth-priests are not of dominant clans because they should be scattered so as better to perform their levitical functions and should not have strong affiliations with any of the contending groups which are usually of the local aristocratic clan (1956: 292). To be fair, one should note that he does record an earth-priest who was a member of a dominant clan (1956: 108) and states that earth-priests are said to descend from Gee, who is also said to be the ancestor of the most important Nuer clans (1956: 114). This interpretation of such priests as a minority fits in with Evans-Pritchard's report that members of earth-priest lineages may not intermarry, whereas Howell doubts this (E-P 1934: 45; Howell 1954: 84). Lewis attempts to resolve the apparent contradiction by suggesting that the disagreement between Coriat and Evans-Pritchard over the relative importance of earth-priests (cf. E-P 1934: 44–5) can be resolved if we realize that earth-priests gained spokesman (*ruic*) status with political influence in those areas where they belonged to dominant lineages, but that in areas such as those where Evans-Pritchard worked (e.g. Lou), they were weak and had no such opportunity to make political capital out of their priestly roles (Lewis: 83). Evans-Pritchard himself observes that such earth-priests were especially sought for help by members of small settlements or lineages with little support elsewhere; it seems reasonable to assume such factors might lead to the development of factions supporting such men (E-P 1935: 39). In one dispute he describes the earth-priest settling the case who was also a prophet (E-P 1956: 111).

But we know that one famous lineage of earth-priests which provided the prophets Ngundeng and Gwek was of Dinka origin (Coriat: 221–2); however, this may be due to their status as a sister's son's lineage towards an aristocratic clan (Alban: 200–1; Willis: 200–1),[17] for Evans-Pritchard shows how earth-priestly status is associated with such relationships (cf. E-P 1935: 48; Beidelman 1966a; 1968). In any case, skilful and tactful mediation and the explication of a wide range of kin affiliations would seem of great value in conducting such affairs, while the office itself seems to offer an excellent vehicle for a politically ambitious person.

We know that such priestly office has often provided means for even wider powers such as those held by a spokesman (*ruic*) or prophet (*gwan kwoth*, possessor of Spirit). Both Howell (1954: 30) and Lewis (80) comment on the tendency for spokesmen to spring from such priestly lineages of various types, so that we see that early administrators may have oversimplified the situation but were not entirely naïve in assuming some kind of 'chiefly' attributes to such priests. I suspect also that their political influence may have been considerably greater in areas further from the borders where Evans-Pritchard did not do research, since the British authorities had harshly suppressed such activities wherever they were able during the decade prior to Evans-Pritchard's visit. Lewis (82) also observes that an earth-priest may further enhance his status through the use of magic (*wal*). The most famous of Nuer prophets, Ngundeng, and his son Gwek who succeeded him, were earth-priests (Coriat: 221–3; Lewis: 80); Ngundeng is also said to have begun to exceed his strictly levitical functions when a smallpox and rinderpest epidemic ravaged the Lou Nuer. He ceremonially 'buried' these plagues in the earth and when this met with great success, his fame surpassed that of a mere priest (Alban: 201). Fergusson appears to use the term *chief* with reference to spokesmen and/or priests, and *kujur* or *witchdoctor* with reference to men possessed by certain forms of Spirit; he describes an unusually influential cattle-priest named Gac Jaang[18] who became a prophet who used magic to increase his power and influence (1935: 52–4). Howell reports that certain earth-spirits (*kwoth piny*) such as *biel* of the cattle-pegs, are associated with a cattle-priest (*wut ghok*) and presumably may possess him. Fergusson describes two sons competing to inherit their father's power, engaging in competitive claims to magico-prophetic prowess (1921: 151) and describes a Nuer leading his group off from the rest of his section under his charismatic claims to 'witchcraft' (ibid.: 154).

Thus, priestly Nuer sometimes seek to augment their power and influence through charisma both in terms of political manipulation as expressed by spokesmanship and leadership in raids, and through claims to more diffuse supernatural powers, often of a fatidical nature. Among the Nuer, magical powers cannot be sharply distinguished from some of the attributes of prophets; all Nuer prophets possess such magical attributes regarding healing, warfare, fertility, and the establishment of a reputation as a magical curer or sorcerer requires certain charismatic powers over neighbouring Nuer. Conversely, non-priestly Nuer possessed of certain political or supernatural advantages sometimes attempt to legitimate these powers through becoming priests. There is little written on this, but Howell does note that aspiring experts try to assume a leopard-skin and thus become earth-priests (1954: 216), and Lewis (81) contends that commoners could be given such status through a rite of drinking milk from a gourd into which everyone spat. Certainly Evans-Pritchard provides the most revealing remarks of all:

> '. . . persons who do not belong to a priestly family can become priests, transmitting their powers to their children, by what the Nuer call *tetde*, by hand. This means that such a man is given a leopard-skin by a priest and told to carry out priestly services. In some myths of origin of the Jikany tribes the leopard skin was given by the ancestors of the dominant lineages to their maternal uncles that they might serve as tribal priests. The structurally opposed lineages of the clan were then in the common relationship of sisters' sons to the line of priests, which thus had a mediatory position between them' (1956: 293).

This fits in nicely with what we know of the symbolic power and ambiguity of affinal relations among the Nuer and with the ambivalent relations between sisters' sons and mothers' brothers (cf. sections V and IX), but it is not easy to accommodate this with Evans-Pritchard's earlier assertion that the office of priest is utterly independent of other social attributes, personal characteristics, or statuses. It further suggests that Nuer are likely to become priests only if they also occupy somewhat favourable positions within the lineage framework.

V

All adult Nuer men have some contact with Spirit in view of their right and duty to conduct sacrifice. But some Nuer have more prolonged and intense contact than others and these are said to be possessors of Spirit (*gwan kwoth*), though it would be more nearly correct to say that they themselves are possessed. In the most dramatic forms of Spirit possession, famous prophets, such a man is described as being like a sack or bag (*guk*) filled with Spirit. But ethnographic and historical reports indicate that prophets are only Nuer possessed like many others but who have succeeded in securing wider social endorsement of their peculiar status as mediators between men and Spirit (cf. section VI).

T. O. Beidelman

Any Nuer may be possessed by Spirit; such status is not inherited although it does tend to pass down certain lineages, and influential prophets tend to come from priestly lineages. Though many Nuer are possessed by Spirit in its more minor forms and many more own medicine and fetishes[19] most important and serious types of possession involve air-spirits.[20] Men possessed by lower, earth-spirits, but who nurse greater ambitions, tend eventually to be possessed by air-spirits as well. Indeed, prophets with any pretensions to power may be possessed by manifold spirits. Evans-Pritchard contends that many of the most prominent air-spirits are of Dinka origin, but considers that the air-spirit *col wic* (lightning and its victims) is of undisputable Nuer origin. Many of these air-spirits are associated with illness, epidemics, warfare, misfortune, streams, floods. None appears purely benevolent. Perhaps Nuer simply project all problematical, divisive aspects of their culture on to Dinka, just as they project many negative aspects of domestic affairs onto women (cf. Beidelman 1966a).

Unlike priests, Nuer prophets must manifest anomalous, extraordinary attributes to demonstrate the validity of their claims to a new and unusual authority.[21] We have seen that Spirit manifests itself through a confusion or dissolution of the ordinary. This can take the form of illness, mental derangement, inversion, peculiar behaviour (E-P 1956: 33), but how then does one distinguish the signs of Spirit from the symptoms of evil forces or madness? Indeed, Evans-Pritchard reports that initially Nuer say that they have difficulty distinguishing between a madman or epileptic (*gwan noka*) and a prophet (1956: 44). They are what Weber calls 'charismatic berserks' (1952: 97). Confirmation of a prophet's calling is mainly through the public evaluation of the kinds of acts the nascent prophet claims to have performed after his strange behaviour begins – and by his success in curing, bringing fertility, removing epidemics, divining the future, bringing rain, cursing opponents, and, in the past, ensuring victory against neighbouring peoples raided for livestock and captives (Coriat: 225–7; Alban: 220–1; Jackson 1929: 130; E-P 1949e: 289; 1956: 299, 308; Willis: 199; Seligman: 233–4). As in the case of Judaic prophets (Weber 1952: 87–8, 90–117), these leaders' functions as 'warrior ecstatics' seem especially important.

Evans-Pritchard observes that the ambitious nature of prophets is unlike normal Nuer who would want to avoid Spirit. Whenever a prophet actively seeks such possession, and some do, certain of his

390

fellow-prophets and neighbours deeply resent this or, at the least, entertain highly ambivalent feelings towards him (E-P 1956: 307). Crazzolara recounts cases of men who gained considerable power in this manner (1953: 164), and even describes several such men in one locale competing with one another for control of certain spirits. He implies that each may seek to intimidate his competitors, but that his success in this depends on the kinds of supporters he finds and the factions these may involve (159, 165; cf. also E-P 1935: 60). But this ambiguity is an attribute of all aspects of Spirit as far as Nuer are concerned.[22]

VI

When a Nuer wishes to be possessed, as in the case of a seance, he may put skins over his head since darkness (perhaps to induce lack of discrimination between categories) facilitates possession; similarly air-spirits are sometimes thought to descend in storms particularly at night (E-P 1956: 35–6; Crazzolara: 162). Smoke may be blown into a witch's eyes to remove his power, and blindness and curing of blindness are somehow related to such powers (Fergusson 1921: 149, 151). Percussion is necessary to contact Spirit. Nuer make use of rattles and clapping and every air-spirit has its consecrated drums (E-P 1956: 35–6, 51). A spirit is sometimes said to shake the possessed by the hair (Howell 1952: 87), and we find Nuer prophets unique among their people for their long, unkempt hair and beards – which in normal Nuer would be groomed or shaved except when in a state of pollution due to mourning or homicide.[23] In this, polluted Nuer resemble prophets in their restricted sexuality, but about this we cannot be sure since the exact prescriptions against sexual relations for persons in mourning, involved in a feud, and undertaking sacrifice or prophecy are not made clear by any of the sources dealing with the Nuer.

A person who is possessed by Spirit may become sick, but aspiring prophets exhibit more dramatic symptoms than this. Such a person may dribble, drool, maintain a vacant stare, or act like an epileptic. He may engage in long but pointless tasks such as spending hours arranging shells into designs on the ground in the bush; he may spend long periods in the wilderness; or he may even eat excrement or ashes.[24] Prophets may speak in tongues,[25] go into trances, fast, balance on their heads, wear feathers in their hair,[26] be active by night rather than by day, and may perch on rooftops. Some sit with tethering pegs up their anuses[27] (E-P 1934: 57; Jackson 1929: 91, 130; Coriat: 236; Huffman: 52, 53).[28] Prophets are also described as having the powers of levitation and transformation into animals (Coriat: 236). Until the raids they endorsed were carried out successfully in the eyes of those involved, some newly possessed prophets, still unlegitimized, sometimes abstained from cow-milk and only drank goat-milk,[29] apparently an inversion of ordinary manly behaviour (Crazzolara: 163). Similar inverted behaviour also seems to have characterized some ritual experts or priests (E-P 1934: 49, 53–4), but since these sometimes strove to become prophets, we cannot be sure that this is associated with expert or priestly status. This anomalous sexual status seems appropriate since the essence of Spirit (*kwoth*), in contrast to Creation (*cak*) and man (*ran*), seems likely to be thought of as sterile.[30] Although Spirit may convey fertility and health, it also conveys infertility, illness, and death, and a perfect and full submission to the morality associated with it runs counter to many of the vital aspects of Nuer society as it exists in Creation, a point I try to establish elsewhere (1966a).

Prophetic self-impalement on tethering pegs may be a form of latent homosexual behaviour;[31] ambiguous sexuality is a common feature of religious figures everywhere, including Christendom. John Middleton makes strikingly similar observations for a prophetic movement among the Lugbara of northern Uganda, a movement perhaps deriving from the area of the Nuer and Dinka and from the Mahdist movement (Middleton 1963: 99; cf. also Driberg). We know that when the famous Nuer prophet Gwek was slain while leading an attack against British colonial forces, he was found wearing a leather apron, a garment ordinarily associated with Nuer women who have borne children (Coriat: 237).[32] However, we cannot be sure here whether this was to mime women's behaviour or to cover the genitals or anus. We know that, among the Dinka, women's aprons are used to cover the exposed anus of a man, and, on sacrificial occasions, the genitals of an ox (Lienhardt 1961: 268, 269). Nuer ghouls (*rodh*) or witches are also sometimes associated with similar sexual inversions of clothing, women being accused of wearing leopard-skins and men of wearing leather pubic aprons, each normally worn by Nuer over their genitals in the presence of their affines (Howell and Lewis: 160; Beidelman 1968). A Nuer prophet who proselytized among the Shilluk had a bodyguard of women (Willis: 202). Old women past menopause and barren women are occasionally possessed and become minor prophets; although they cannot sacrifice, their sexual ambiguity allows them important connexion with Spirit (E-P: 308).

Although the theory of latent homosexuality mentioned above may be relevant to these data, the sexually ambiguous attributes of such prophetic persons seem more likely to be related to symbolic assumption of a kind of transcendent sexual autonomy. The status conferred by only one sex generates limitations: the dependence upon the opposite sex, and the resultant contradictory loyalties to several kin and domestic groups; the ideological associations of sexuality with the family, the passage of time and, ultimately, death, all often exemplified in the differences not only between the sexes but between parents and off-spring (cf. Leach: ch. VI). The confounding or blurring of ordinary sexual categories seems to suggest a status at once sterile and nonsexual, yet also supergenerative in its transcendence of the limits imposed by any simple sexual category. A prophet's important function as a 'warrior ecstatic' may relate to sterility; Fergusson describes a war leader being unable to keep living children because of his extraordinary bellicosity, which had mystical harmful effects (1921: 155).

Bodily deformation may also relate to gifts of prophecy and possession. We know that the prophet Gwek was squat, hunch-backed, and ugly (cf. Coriat).[33] In this sense, at least, prophetism is inherent in individuals. But it is thought by Nuer that some persons secure earth-spirits (*kwoth piny*), minor spirits, by going to Dinkaland and there giving up a limb or fingerjoint in exchange for such a connexion (Howell 1953: 87).[34] Though such deformation is achieved, it is irreversible and thus in a sense inherent.

Among the best accounts we have of Nuer prophets are those recorded by the administrator Fergusson in the 1920s and the reports of Coriat, Alban, and Willis dealing with the prophet Ngundeng and his son Gwek.

Even while a youth, Ngundeng is said to have exhibited abnormal qualities such as sacrificing to a goat and taking speech away from others (Coriat: 222). With his success at turning back epidemics, Ngundeng intensified his abnormal symptoms.[35] He fasted, went into trances, and perched on the roof of his cattle byre. Soon afterwards he ordered his followers to organize in order to erect an enormous pyramid to his spirits (Coriat: 222; for a discussion of pyramids in the southern Sudan, cf. below). Similarly, the two cattle-priests who turned prophets, Gac and his son Jaang, exhibited unusual traits even in childhood, thereby indicating their supernormal qualities (E-P 1935: 52–3).

Gwek, Ngundeng's son, is described as morose, misshapen, slavering, known for balancing upsidedown atop his father's pyramid. He too had an unusual origin, for his mother was barren until her husband, the prophet, made her eat medicines from a frog (*gwek*) by which she conceived (E-P 1935: 60); another reputed prophet-witch is said to have descended from a hartebeest, while another was associated with the liminal area between heaven and earth, with the moist *kot* tree, and with birds and grass (wilderness) (Fergusson 1921: 149, 151, 154). Gwek is also reported to have been a twin which, though not a prerequisite to prophetism, is certainly a status also associated with the manifestation of Spirit; Gwek was also associated with a type of wild goose (Jackson 1954: 164).[36] Gwek is said to have talked in tongues at night, could change himself into a goat, and assumed possession of his father's magical pipe. He is said to have trembled, foamed at the mouth, and screamed while prophesying (Coriat: 227).

Fergusson provides a dramatic instance of a Nuer becoming a prophet although he does not grasp the significance for Nuer of the events he describes (1930: 212–13):

'There is yet another war on. When my back was turned, an idiot called Dak Dthul, who used to be old Madi's chief songster,[37] was nearly killed by a thunderbolt which fell among his cattle. It appears he went off his head, and endeavoured to raise the country to attack the Dinkas and oust the Government. The Chief, Madi, however, opposed him, and his first effort failed. By degrees, he managed to win about fifty lads to join in his standard, and they set out to raid the Dinkas; but, on the way, their hearts failed them owing to their small numbers, and they returned. Once again he beat his war drums and called on the people to join him, but again they refused. He cursed them, and swore that there would be bloodshed for those who resisted him.[38] As bad luck would have it a fool, who was brandishing a loaded rifle, let it off accidentally, killing one of his own men and wounding two others. That was enough, in the eyes of the onlookers, to prove the truth of Dak's threat; and they all joined him, setting out there and then for the Dinkas, whom they surprised at night. They killed about 20, capturing something like 40 women and children and 2000 cattle, as well as destroying the Dinka villages. Dak excelled himself by killing two Dinka boys in cold blood and cutting them into little bits. He refused to allow his followers to take any of the captured stock, or women; and proved his madness by not only sacrificing cattle wholesale, but also by killing four of his own men.

One would have thought that such a succession of appalling acts would have sickened the people, but it merely served to augment Dak's reputation . . .'

Nuer consider lightning the most immediate manifestation of Spirit; its victims go directly to Spirit without mortuary rites and their descendants may be possessed by their spirits which are connected to that of the spirit of lightning (*col wic*). This spirit is also associated with rain, streams, spear symbols, and warfare (cf. E-P 1949a; 1953a: 58; 1956: 11, 46, 52–3, 57, 59–60, 205; Howell 1954: 86; Stigand 1919; Beidelman 1966a: 464). Such victims as persons possessed by a deceased victim, and those found unaccountably dead in the bush, are all associated with *col wic* and must be buried separated from the earth, in the manner of twins (E-P 1946: 234–5; 1954a: 31). Although these powers are not considered great, some Nuer believe that a person possessed by a *col wic* may bring rain by saying that he or she is thirsty (E-P 1956: 59–60; Crazzolara: 98).

Bearing these facts in mind, one finds Fergusson's account clearer. The allegedly senseless slaughter of stock makes sense as an expression of supreme power; we know of similar holocausts elsewhere, sometimes expressing diffuse and autocratic power (for example, among the Swazi, Beidelman 1966b: 398–9; and among the Xosa, Willoughby: 116–20; MacMillan: 341–2). Although such accounts may be distorted, even the alleged dismemberment of the Dinka youths may have been for war medicines, since we know that Nuer, possibly under the influence of Dinka, sometimes used such magic made from the corpses of enemies (E-P 1935: 58.)[39]

Evans-Pritchard contends that prophets are a relatively new feature of Nuer religious life, but many of the symbols and notions related to these, such as the ideas associated with *col wic*, seem basic to traditional Nuer thought, and that Nuer lineages usually propitiate at least one *col wic* (E-P 1956: 53). He associates Nuer prophetism with the rise of Mahdism but it is not at all clear what influence the dervish Mahdi may have had on a development of Nuer and Dinka prophetism (cf. E-P 1956: 308–10), though Emin Pasha is reported to have remarked that when Nuer and Dinka besieged Bor under the prophet Donlutj, they behaved like dervishes and wore rosaries (Gray: 161).

T. O. Beidelman

VII

It is certainly clear that Nuer utilize possession as a means to power. Certain barren and old women with no access to influence through sons may sometimes gain esteem in this way (e.g. Crazzolara: 162). A Dinka captured by Nuer went out of his way to acquire abnormal traits and thereby gain the reputation of being a prophet, presumably to better his own weak position; he became the prophet Dengleka (Seligman: 231–2). A common euphemism for a scorcerer is 'son of a Dinka' (Westermann: 123), with the connotation that such marginal persons are less socially integrated than purer Nuer.[40] It is also likely that Nuer believe that aliens sometimes have special knowledge of supernatural powers which Nuer themselves lack. This may perhaps be shown by their borrowing cults from such peoples as the Dinka and Shilluk, as indicated through the various citations in this paper, including the borrowing of magic, interest in new air-spirits and earth-spirits, and in prophetic cults using pyramids and sacred pools. Kir, one of the eponymous ancestors of the Nuer, is associated with a magical Dinka spear and references to Dinka are made even in formalized prayers by the associated clan (Jackson 1954: 166). The place of this spear seems the nearest thing Nuer have to a corporate shrine; Seligman reports that an earth-priest serves as the spear's custodian (Seligman: 214).

Evans-Pritchard seems to explain the bias towards spirit possession among Nuer lineages with obvious Dinka descent as due to such beliefs originating from the Dinka (1956: 29, 33). Such a historical explanation may well be valid, but it neglects certain possible sociological factors which would complement it. In the one case of such possession which Evans-Pritchard provides in detail, involving a lineage of Dinka origin, an elder seems to have used such possession to bolster his own control over junior kin; thus, even though a junior was ill, it was the elder who was possessed and who spoke the intents of the spirit thought to be causing the illness (E-P 1956: 36–7). Such Dinka lineages tend to be smaller and poorer than purer Nuer lineages, and are presumably still in the process of building up useful affinal and maternal ties with more respectable Nuer lineages. Such lineages would fall under the category of sisters' children's groups, a position structurally the same as that reported already of candidates for priesthood. This medial aspect of the sisters' child/mother's brother relation in Nilotic patrilineal societies has been commented on by others (cf. Lienhardt 1955). If this generalization is correct, one may assume that purer Nuer lineages have sufficient human and material assets to allow conventional, traditional assertion of authority, whereas Dinka-derived groups repeatedly require charismatic revival and possession to shore up an elder's authority. (At the risk of a forced analogy, it seems something like an episcopalian gentry and a revivalist proletariat in early nineteenth-century Midland England.)

To understand the influence of a Nuer prophet, we must also understand his relation to his supporters. Although a wide range of persons consult prophets, clearly the prophets' most important supporters are those least content with the *status quo*. While some prophets gained influence during times of turmoil due to disease or the arrival of the Egyptians and British, most seem to owe their fame to their ability to encourage young warriors to make successful raids on their neighbours for livestock and captives (E-P 1956: 45, 308; Fergusson 1930: 212-13; Crazzolara: 165-6; Willis: 201). I suggest that such supporters tended to be junior sons and sons of poor fathers, especially those from smaller, poorer lineages such as those with Dinka background. Such youths would often be anxiously seeking livestock for wives but would often be frustrated by their poorer lot. One could say that a prophet's influence arises from the powerlessness of the fathers of such youths. In a certain sense, the influence of prophets rests in part upon a kind of undermining of some aspects of the authority system, since youths were subordinated to their elder kinsmen through their need for livestock for marriage. Evans-Pritchard describes the cattle-priest and prophet, Gac Jaang, as one who encouraged youths to go on such raids but also as one famed for his abusive behaviour towards the fellows of his own age-set, presumably the fathers of such youths; this seems to be consistent with a prophet's abnormal reliance upon junior men not necessarily even agnatically related to him (E-P 1935: 53-4).

Coriat suggests that one of the main causes of some prophetic outbursts among the Nuer was the prophet's resentment and fear that growing local government influence would sap their authority (221); Fergusson seems to agree with this (1930: 264). The prophet Gwek encouraged raids on the Dinka for women and cattle and also encouraged an unsuccessful raid on a small police post (Jackson 1954: 169); at his fatal encounter with government troops his warriors numbered about three hundred (ibid.: 170).

A successful prophet would take a share in the booty of livestock taken in such raids. Evans-Pritchard describes some as patently greedy for

397

wealth (1935: 61). A famous prophet would be possessed by many different forms of Spirit and would try to marry a wife to each (Howell 1954: 216). Extra livestock was also needed by prophets to provide the extra sacrifices and food required to increase their prestige and cater to their followers (Crazzolara: 163). In the dervish period, prophets altered the custom of bloodwealth payments for certain Nuer, presumably for influential followers; they also allowed marriage with certain prohibited kin, perhaps another measure which would appeal to many of their younger adherents (Willis: 200). The only case of marriage to a sister's ghost which Evans-Pritchard recorded involved the prophet Deng, who secured bridewealth for this marriage from bloodwealth exacted from Dinka, a group one would have thought ordinarily not involved in such compensatory payments (1945: 12). In his endorsement of new norms and in his distribution of gifts and booty, the prophet rewards outside the routinized economic and religious system. And the very fact that a prophet's claims to authority lie outside legitimate and ordinary institutional principles relates to the intensity of the demands for obedience made upon his following.

Perhaps the most dramatic example of the support which some prophets received is furnished by the erection of the pyramid of Dengkur for the prophet Ngundeng (or Wundeng). His supporters are said to have worked an entire winter season building huts at Keij for accommodation of the food supplies and labour force for this project. Then over the next two years all who passed through the area brought some grain to be stored there. In the following four years Nuer built a great pyramid of earth forty to sixty feet high (Coriat: 223–4, photo). A spear decorated with an ostrich egg and ostrich feathers was mounted at its top (Jackson 1954: 160).[41] A pool, probably with supernatural associations such as those for certain other areas of the Nuer and Dinka (Fergusson 1922), was a short distance to the north[42] of the pyramid (Jackson 1954: 160). Elephant tusks and horns of a white bull, goat entrails, and bones were placed inside the pyramid and other elephant tusks decorated the base. The dimensions of this shrine are hardly in accord with accounts of the Nuer as a people never willing to become engaged in extensive and sustained cooperative labour. Stigand writes (1918: 118):

> 'It is said that about fifty years ago the Garjok women were smitten with childlessness and that for many years they bore no male children. At last, about 40 years ago, they made pilgrimages to Dengkur's mound in the Lau country, which had already obtained a reputation for sanctity. They

took presents of tusks of ivory, beads, cattle for slaughter, etc., with them, and it was at this time that the great collection of tusks, stuck in the earth around the mound and adorning its top, were acquired.'

Howell believes that such pyramids are probably of Dinka origin (1948), and describes an important Dinka shrine taken over by Nuer (1961), but various persons claiming supernatural prowess among the Nuer accumulate mounds of bone and ash from sacrifices and feasts and such mounds grow with an owner's influence (Willis: 202). Fergusson writes of one prophet's site:

'We then proceeded to destroy the stronghold which had been made at the sacred place whcre God is supposed to have descended to Earth. We found it littered with cows that they had sacrificed, and there were numerous signs of Kujur ceremonies which had been held on all the paths in order to insure that we should be wiped out . . .' (1930: 221).

These pyramids were quite probably associated with attributes of mediality such as lightning, pied-colours, and elephants. The elephant tusks may be related to the fact that Nuer seem to regard elephants as medial between man and bush and Spirit, with many human-like attributes; elephants are descended from a Nuer woman and thus stand as sisters' children to Nuer, and slain elephants are subject to many of the mortuary and homicide ceremonies and prohibitions usually associated with humans (Howell 1945).

The establishment of a sacred shrine seems vital to a charismatic figure. To attain wider power a prophet must secure a congregation to hear his words and witness his acts and then put these into effect. The shrine is ideally outside conventional social groups and hence may unite ordinarily disparate social sections.

VIII

Just as Nuer priests sometimes seek to strengthen their traditional authority by charismatic behaviour, so too Nuer prophets may seek to routinize their charismatic power by converting this power into corporate, more stable authority. As soon as a person is newly possessed, he faces problems of legitimization. I have indicated some of these above regarding curing, divining, and the need for carrying out successful raids. At the very outset, a prospective prophet must secure some public affirmation of his fatidical status. Crazzolara (163) discusses how a *pat* (percussion) ceremony is required to achieve this about two weeks after the man is possessed, the candidate informing people in outlying regions that they should attend the coming ceremony. One may assume that the size and composition of the attendance measures the initial scope for the new prophet's practice. As a possessed person, the aspirant makes a mud-shrine (*yik*) or windscreen (*buor*) for his spirit and secures drums and rattles for his ceremonies (E-P 1956: 48). As his success grows, he may take on more spirits and a larger following. Ultimately, he may become a *ruic naadh* (spokesman of the people) (Howell 1954: 31; Lewis: 81). Some prophets were *ruic*, such as Ngundeng and his son Gwek (Lewis: 79), but Lewis sharply disputes Evans-Pritchard's assertion that all prophets operated on a tribal level and were thus *ruic*. Prophets are only the most prominent of many possessed and supernaturally endowed persons. They may thus be placed along an analytical continuum ranging from petty herbalists and curers through persons possessed by minor spirits to aspirant prophets with the most grandiose claims. A prophet, as defined by Evans-Pritchard, seems to involve too narrow a range; a tribal-level prophet seems the only person to whom he would apply the term, whereas such a leader is simply one among a great number and is only distinguished by his particular success in exerting influence over an especially large area (Lewis: 82).

A Nuer spokesman sometimes tries to have his sons succeed him (Lewis: 80-1); this probably expresses a general Nuer trend towards agnatic succession to power, although Deng Liker of the Gawaar Nuer, while a son of a prophet, is described as having achieved his own leadership due to his fighting prowess rather than to the advantage of his birth (Willis: 201). Prophets often pass power to a junior agnate (much as do priests) (E-P 1956: 308-9); for example, Gwek assumed prophethood from his dead father, and on Gwek's death his younger brother took over (Alban: 200); the cattle-priest and prophet Gac was succeeded by his son, Gac Jaang (E-P 1935: 52-3); and the prophet Dwal Diu inherited his prowess from his father (Ben Assher: 162-3).

But although Nuer priests may become prophets and Nuer prophets, priests, the former process seems by far the more frequent. It may be that this is simply a distorted picture due to the kind of data that are reported, for the appearance of prophets, at least those with a warlike bent, was of far more concern to foreigners reporting on the Nuer. But there are good social-structural reasons to suppose that these processes were not of equal frequency. The assumption of prophetic, charismatic powers is far less bound to social status than is priestly authority.

Indeed, it may even compensate for a weak position within a lineage. But in a society such as the Nuer with complexly balanced lineage alliances and neighbourhood affiliations, any roles dependent upon references to such affiliations are difficult to achieve. In the case of priests, especially earth-priests, this involves their strategic positions mediating between several such groups. This would account for the greater difficulty in converting prophetic status (which confounds lineage loyalties) into priestly status, which is based rather upon mediating between these groups.

IX

In the preceding pages I have presented Nuer priests and prophets as different yet overlapping statuses sharing many features, grounded in more basic aspects of Nuer ideology and society. However, these under-lying features extend to far more than supernaturally oriented leaders of this exceptional nature. Before presenting my conclusions I therefore briefly consider two very different complementary sides of Nuer society: (1) I contrast these ambiguous but essentially social leaders with Nuer witches and ghouls who are for Nuer the epitome of antisocial beings; (2) I consider the ordinary Nuer elder in contrast to the more or less sacred and extraordinary nature of priests, prophets, and ghouls. Such a comparison illustrates the different moral evaluations set upon the exercise of power in Nuer society. It also suggests that figures with power cannot be neatly distinguished at all levels; there are certain ambiguous and negative aspects of power, even when judged as legi-timate, that suggest a subtle continuum rather than a set of clear categories of such social statuses and roles.

The Nuer believe in ghouls (*rodh*) or witches. These are inherently evil persons with malevolent powers who deliberately break some of the most important prohibitions in Nuer society. These offences seem to be the source of a ghoul's renewed supernatural strength and also his or her main source of pleasure. The status of a ghoul, like that of the greatest social and ritual leaders, is, in most though not all cases, achieved and not inherited, although there seems some tendency for ghoulishness to run in families (Crazzolara: 221; Howell & Lewis: 163). A ghoul's most striking characteristic is his interest in playing and fornicating with corpses. As typical for Nuer, sexual and alimentary symbolism are here closely linked (e.g. Howell & Lewis). Unfortunately, we lack good data on Nuer ghouls and other antisocial Nuer such as a person with an evil eye (*peth*) or a witch (*niah*). Evans-Pritchard makes only one brief mention of ghouls (*rodh*) in his study of Nuer religion (1956: 176). The best accounts of these and related persons are a rather unsophisticated essay by Howell and Lewis (1947) and a description by Crazzolara (212–21). There are some important and tantalizing attributes shared by ghouls, priests, and prophets. Ghouls are famed for the confusion and difficulties they cause, not unlike the difficulties caused by such prophet-priests as Ngundeng and Gac: they disobey relatives and ordinary leaders and break prohibitions (viz. break *thek*), the same means by which certain prophets gain extra power and acquire the signs of their calling. They may invert their proper social roles, invert sexual attributes, mutilate corpses, and break alimentary and sexual prohibitions (Howell & Lewis: 158–61). They seem to have some association with sisters' children (Howell & Lewis: 160; Crazzolara: 219); they convert others into ghoulishness by hurling clods of earth at them (Crazzolara: 220), an act rather like an earth-priest's curse; and like some prophets their sexuality seems jeopardized since they cannot produce offspring except on contact with graves and, as in one case reported, their female partner is compared with a barren cow (Howell & Lewis: 162). Like prophets, their connexion with some terrible manifestations of Spirit relates to a kind of sterility and like prophets, too, ghouls are active at night.

Priests and prophets, ghouls or witches, are all in some sense Nuer persons peripheral to the most established and conventional social statuses. They all, to use Weber's term, exhibit 'cultural hostility'. All are in some sense morally ambiguous, and, in the case of priests and to a lesser extent prophets, the basic assumption seems to be that these persons help their fellows and provide guidance towards socially approved ends which benefit others as well as themselves. In a sense, temporary unorthodox behaviour by priests and prophets achieves a new synthesis in terms of the most basic social norms. It also assumes that to the extent that some prophets were thought to use their powers for their own advancement and selfish ends, they also partook of witch-like attributes. This is consistent with the highly ambiguous and somewhat negative accounts sometimes provided regarding the interaction of Nuer prophets and their neighbours.[43]

In an earlier paper (1966a), I observe that really successful Nuer, those termed 'bull' (*tut*), who have large numbers of kin and clients dependent upon them, achieve their success only, in a sense, by the exploitation of various rights and obligations for their own ends. To put it another way, any person who gains outstanding influence in a society based on kinship, affinity, and clientship, does so by some form of 'wheeling-and-dealing', however subtle, among those persons related to him. Success is a measure of skilful betrayal of the ideal for the pragmatic and expedient. Men of this sort succeed only over a path of difficult and sometimes ruthless kin and neighbourhood politics; the line here between a local neighbourhood leader or 'bull' and a more important spokesman (*ruic*) is thin and only one of emphasis (Lewis: 80). The authority of all these men is only measured by their power and that, in turn, rests in large part upon the individual attributes of leadership and skills of personal politics, as much as upon the advantages of wealth and birth which often are not that exceptional for such leaders when compared with their neighbours in this theoretically egalitarian society. Earlier we learned that, while any men of a levitical lineage might perform priestly ceremonies, in fact only senior influential men did so and that only charismatic and ambitious men of this sort transformed such levitical into fatidical powers and authority; similarly '. . . women do not make [lineage] sacrifices and . . . though any man may do it only senior men who are fathers of families, "bulls" as the Nuer call them, do so' (E-P 1956: 287).

In a restricted sense, at least, we may regard a 'bull' as ambiguous in his use of power and yet 'traditionally authoritative' in his seniority within a lineage and neighbourhood; such a model somewhat parallels that of a priest or prophet. It is 'bulls' who sacrifice and thus mediate between Spirit and their agnatic dependants, just as priests and prophets stand between Spirit and even larger political groups. The larger and more diverse the groups connected and articulated, the greater the skill and charismatic leadership required of the person operating within (yet partly outside) the traditional scheme; and as the size of the groups increases, the kind of traditional behaviour prescribed becomes more and more vague and diffuse, more flexible. This parallels manifestations of Spirit which increase in potency as they increase in abstraction and unspecificity. For these reasons, both the charismatic force and the affective ambiguity of the figures involved may also increase along with social variety and scope of the group. Nevertheless, the essential model remains related to the basic problem of achieving practical power within a traditional system. The often described 'egalitarianism' and 'ordered anarchy' of the Nuer do not preclude power and social importance for certain leaders, though these individual celebrities and their respective followings may be ephemeral indeed.

The status of a 'bull', a ghoul, a priest, or a prophet is theoretically different but not always readily distinguishable when such labels are applied to actual data, whether case material or ideological formulations. Such persons are particularly difficult to label during their initial stages of prominence. This illustrates the subtle and ambiguous interdependence between negatively and positively valued moral acts, between legitimate and wrongful power.

X

In the introduction I drew a contrast between the work of Durkheim and Weber. In a sense this was an unfair dichotomization. In recent decades the term 'Durkheimean analysis' has often referred to an emphasis upon normative systems and a preoccupation with cultural ideology, along with a corresponding lack of interest in materialistic or psychological factors and a failure to consider innovations and the divergence from certain norms as processes outside the normal workings of society. In the analysis of authority and power, this had sometimes led to an emphasis upon the former at the expense of the latter. Conversely, the followers of Weber have often tended towards an overemphasis upon ideology as a tool by which certain elite groups control a society and, while the more abstract, formalistic quasi-autonomous aspects of a belief system are considered, this is rarely with real subtlety regarding their symbolic content. But the grounds for such stereotyped labels lie far more in the works of those who have mined the capital of the classical sociological tradition than in the nature of these founding fathers themselves.

The Nuer data suggest that certain revisions may be required in both Weberian and Durkheimean concepts of authority; although these might relate only to the Nuer case, it seems likely that this is true for many other societies as well. Weber's discussion indicates the ambiguity between authority and power, and his discussion of the charisma of office and of the legitimation of charismatic powers shows that he fully grasps the interplay between the various determinants of power and the efficacy and durability of authority. But Weber's concern seems mainly with the processes involved, with the ways by which various statuses are achieved, maintained, or lost. He presents these factors as means by which persons pass from one social category to another rather than in terms solely of certain medial or ambiguous social categories or statuses. A social anthropologist might contrast this to the works of van Gennep, where these very factors define a pivotal and crucial social status or, rather, a kind of interstitial non-status.

The Nuer data demonstrate similarities between priests and prophets and also, in some respects, parallels between both these and asocial or antisocial witches or ghouls. Evans-Pritchard defines Nuer priests in terms of formal norms but it is clear that priests are effective and influential because of powers not derived strictly from within such norms of office; Nuer prophets are charismatic but they are not peripheral to Nuer institutions in the manner suggested by Weber's description of a prophet as a revolutionary outside the normative, authoritative system. While prophets may be iconoclasts bent on a dissolution of a social system, this is always within some pre-existing social and ideological terms of that society, although this may be defined in rather broad and abstract terms. In the case of the Nuer, charismatic prophets do not seem so much innovators or revolutionaries as institutionalized leaders enabled to organize persons and groups which are only periodically significant or useful for members of that society. As Weber himself observes, any situation with demands beyond everyday routine has some charismatic foundations and thus any socially heterogeneous situation in which acts are not clear-cut partakes of this to some degree (1948: 245). In his analysis of witchfinders Bohannan seems to make a similar observation about the Tiv of Nigeria (1958). Perhaps these contrasts between institutionalized innovators and revolutionaries are merely questions of degree and terminology, but in any case the distinction is certainly one which must be kept in mind.

There are several ways by which one might reformulate analytical categories in order to deal with such situations. One may consider all positions of authority as ambiguous, manifesting actual power only in terms of the kinds of interplay between legitimately and non-normatively defined acts. This would be a corrective to Durkheim's handling of authority which underplays the factors of power and its implementation which are so stressed by Weber. One may reassess Weber's category of charismatic authority in his handling of prophets where he plays up the non-normative aspect of such men. At the least, one may posit a redivision of Weber's analytical category of charismatic leadership: (a) those who are revolutionary and clearly outside and opposed to the existing social system;(b)those who are in some sense institutionalized within the system, appearing regularly or periodically in a society in such a manner as to effect temporarily certain configurations within the system, but who in the long run may only provide a means by which certain inconsistencies or impediments between social ends and social means are ironed out. This is not to say that such persons may not at some point take on more revolutionary aspects and redirect activities and groupings into some irreversible new direction, but this need not be so of all prophets.

A comprehensive reassessment of the notions of Weber and Durkheim regarding prophets and priests is beyond the scope of this essay and beyond my own knowledge of these two masters. Rather this reconsideration of Nuer priests and prophets is presented as an approach to alternate ways of examining some of these perennial issues as they confront the social anthropologist. I hope also to have shown indirectly how overemphasis along one such analytical line may have influenced the way ethnographic data are handled.[44] It is to the great credit of researchers such as Evans-Pritchard that contemporary social anthropologists have seen that the problems raised by their own sometimes esoteric and exotic data relate firmly to the mainstream of sociological theory. The closed ideological system of Zande belief about witches and the struggle for power by Nuer priests and prophets hold lessons for all interested in contemporary issues of social theory; for such insights, we are permanently in Evans-Pritchard's debt. Without reference to the mainstream of sociology and psychology, however, social anthropology holds no lessons for us today; and without broadening social theory to include the odd and troublesome anthropological exceptions, modern social theories deprive themselves of one of the most powerful means at their disposal for refining and sensitizing their own analytical perceptions.

NOTES

1. It has been pointed out that although they were celebrated contemporaries in what is now regarded as the same discipline, neither Durkheim nor Weber cited each other's work (Tiryakian 1956). Similarly although Evans-Pritchard cites Durkheim and various biblical scholars and draws many contrasts between the ancient Jews and the Nuer, he ignores the

great sociological classic analysing priests and prophets, Weber's *Ancient Judaism*.

2. This is the third paper I have written reanalysing various aspects of Nuer religion; I hope eventually to present brief essays on other aspects of Nuer culture. The richness of Evans-Pritchard's data and the important issues which these raise provide ample grounds for labour by many future researchers. In the accompanying source citations, I have abbreviated Evans-Pritchard to E-P. I should like to thank Dr J. C. Crocker, Professor John Middleton, Dr Rodney Needham, Dr Peter Rigby, Professor Edward Tiryakian, and Rev. Philip Turner for reading and commenting on various drafts of this paper.

3. Evans-Pritchard's findings on the Nuer are Durkheimean in their concern with normative models, but, except for Lienhardt, none of the other authorities which I cite appear interested in such interpretations. Howell was a District Commissioner among the Nuer who later studied social anthropology with Evans-Pritchard. However, he displays a strong independence and often vigorously disagrees with his teacher. His own interests in problems of modernization and administration discourage such model-building and a holistic approach. Lewis was another colonial administrator among the Nuer; he read Evans-Pritchard's work and was associated with Howell. Fergusson was the first District Commissioner among the Nuer and was murdered by them some years before Evans-Pritchard's arrival. He writes without grasping the broader patterns of Nuer society, but with a keen awareness of current political movements and leaders with whom he was closely involved. Crazzolara was a Roman Catholic missionary who worked with the Nuer before Evans-Pritchard. Although he did not publish until long after his successor, his work takes no account of that of Evans-Pritchard. Much of the evidence collected by these other researchers seems to fit into a Weberian mould.

4. The literature is confused by the variety of terms used to describe such persons. In the earliest writings they are simply described as *witch-doctors* or *kujur*. Evans-Pritchard uses the term *priest of the earth*, but in his early writings he also often called them *leopard-skin chiefs*. He uses the term 'ritual expert' to refer to all of the many priestly persons among whom priests of the earth are only one category, though perhaps the most important.

5. Nuer seem to conceive of power and authority in 'zero-sum' terms, that is, power is held by certain persons only at the expense of someone else. Conflicts over paternal authority between genitors and paters, and competition between prophets and other ritual leaders seeking local influence, all suggest this.

6. Any phenomena may be assigned within a culture to an infinite number

of symbolic categories; if these are sometimes ambiguous, it is because certain phenomena are culturally conjoined in ritual, myth, joking, or ceremonies. The separation yet conjunction of men and natural species (such as crocodiles among the Nuer) is a cultural mental act. I doubt whether any truly satisfactory explanations for this existential connexion can be presented.

7. The problem of *thek* and *nueer* is very complex and merits a long paper; cf. E-P 1949c; 1956: 64–5, 79, 103, 129, 177–83, 241, 291; Howell 1954: 205; Beidelman 1968).

8. Similarly, it is a commonplace to say that a medieval person's definition of Joan of Arc as a saint or witch rested largely upon his adherence to French or English politics, but that in turn depended upon an important point: many on each side seem sincerely to have interpreted the same phenomena as having opposite yet similar significance, opposite in that these were related to good and evil, but similar in that these were clearly extraordinary for the same reasons and therefore had to be accounted for in terms of some supernatural agents, be they God or Devil.

9. A *gwan thoi* or *gwan nyanga* (possessor of crocodile or grass) is sometimes also referred to by the more priestly title of *kuaar*, e.g. *kuaar thoi* (E-P 1956: 67, 202); indeed, Howell merely terms these *kuaar thoi*, which he roughly translates as 'water expert', and seems to class these with other Nuer priestly types (1954: 9). For a delightful vignette on such a saurian Nuer, cf. Duncan (1948).

10. Thus, Evans-Pritchard relates: 'It is alleged, that in the old days, if a man died of magic his kinsmen would try to slay the magician (*gwan wal*), though I have not recorded a case of a magician having been killed. Nuer point out that a magician does not use his magic against persons in his own community but only against persons of other villages, so that it is not easy to revenge yourself on him since he will be supported by his village who regard powerful magic as of value to their community' (1940: 167).

11. The published data do not indicate what this may signify: for example, is this hand or arm concealed in a manner resembling the custom among the Meru (Needham)?

12. The avoidance of earth compares with certain prohibitions between a son-in-law and mother-in-law (E-P 1943: 3); cf. my comparison of the attributes of earth-priests and affines (1968a). Nuer initiates must also wear sandals to avoid the earth, and must also cover themselves with cloth to avoid Spirit (MacDermot: 378); this closely parallels Nuer treatment of other liminal persons (cf. next footnote and Beidelman 1968a).

13. This may relate to certain medial attributes of baldness or hairlessness.

For example, shaved and newly initiated Nuer are sometimes referred to as old and hornless cattle (*cötni*) and share many medial, sexual, and ritual attributes; the same term is applied to old baldheaded men (E-P 1936b: 241–3; Huffman: 29–32; Jackson 1929: 146; Kiggen: 63); for an extensive discussion of Nuer notions about hair, cf. Beidelman (1968: Part III). I note here that hairy liminality is illustrated by an earth-priest removing the pollution of homicide by shaving off the killer's hair (E-P 1956: 110, 297).

14. Although the logic of the symbolism is still unclear, the leopard – or serval-skin seems to symbolize medial, ambiguous status in the two situations where it is worn: among male affines and by an earth-priest. It may well be that the dappled quality of these pelts is symbolically equivalent to a Hopkinesque parallel in the pied-cow and pied-cattle. The notion of pied-divinity is also held by the Dinka and may even be of Dinka origin (Leinhardt: 46; Bedri: 50). Certain mystical properties seem inherent in the spotted skin itself. Thus an earth-priest may pass a skin to an offender who consequently is endangered; or an accused person may prove the veracity of his oath by sitting on a leopard-skin (Seligman: 215, 217). The black and white of the pied crow (associated with Buk, mother of the sky-spirit Deng), may possibly relate to the double aspects of sky: black (good rainclouds) and white (dangerous lightning). Buk is said to have a double nature relating to both sky and earth. The name Buk in Dinka refers to markings in black and white (E-P 1956: 31–2). The ostrich may be singled out for association with an air-spirit because the male is a black and white bird, for only the ostrich's plumage seems of mystical significance (ibid.: 30–1, 34, 38, 46). Variegation may also relate to the special attributes Nuer assign to pythons, to their association in turn with bees (E-P 1956: 67, 78, 82, 217–18), and may help explain their link as mother's brother to Deng (*ibid.*: 78). Curiously, Europeans, perhaps also viewed as highly ambiguous, are termed *kuaar* (priest) (E-P 1956: 291).

15. Seligman (217) refers to him as *ngul muot* and states that he must be of the owner-clan of the area.

16. Elsewhere he notes that all cattle-priests are of purely Nuer lineages and that, although any member of such a group might serve, in fact usually only senior men do so (E-P 1956: 300–1). Howell has compared this with similar Dinka priestly institutions (1951: 261–2, 272–3).

17. They were originally Bull Nuer of Dinka extraction; however, Ngundeng moved to the land of Lou Nuer and he and his kin married into that group (Alban), being, consequently, in the status of sisters' children.

18. This person may also be of Dinka origin; at least, we know that the word *jaang* means 'Dinka' in Nuer.

19. Howell contends that some Nuer secure earth-spirits by purchase and initiation (1953: 86).
20. For a detailed discussion of these issues and of the attributes of air-spirits and *col wic*, cf. E-P 1956: 28–62; 1953; 1949b).
21. Willis writes of Nuer and Dinka prophets as ". . . men who have a certain position by inheritance, but try to enhance it by assuming powers of magic . . ." (201). Abnormal behaviour is universally associated with prophets and is especially well described for Judaic prophets (Weber 1952: 286–7; Lindblom: 6–46). Lindblom observes that 'Madness when it comes from God, is superior to sanity, which is of human origin' (28).
22. I have already indicated above that, for Nuer, sacrifice is to contact Spirit in order to send it away, to be rid of it because of its dangerous and polluting attributes; Crazzolara emphasizes the malevolence of Spirit for Nuer by citing God's occasional envy and jealousy of any person with wealth and good fortune. He terms this malevolent aspect of God a basic notion (*Grundidee*) among the Nuer (1953: 95).
23. Compare this with hairy or shaved prophets in Israel (Lindblom: 68–9).
24. This inverted equation of ashes with food also occurs in certain Nuer ceremonies conveying a denial of some attributes of twin status (cf. E-P 1936a). Judaic prophets also partook of unclean foods (Lindblom: 171). One possible explanation might be that the prophet's mouth was thereby consecrated to liminality and thus made free for divine and extraordinary utterances.
25. Speaking in tongues may have some connexion with the disorder of lightning (E-P 1949a).
26. This may be seen from photos, but it is not discussed by any authority. However, this may relate to the medial qualities of birds which link Creation and Spirit. In Nuer legends supernaturally gifted persons are sometimes associated with birds and with the bush (Fergusson 1921: 151, 154). There are also photos of Nuer earth-priests with a feather in their hair (E-P 1956: pl. XIV; 1940: pl. XXIV).
27. I am unable to find any discussion of the tethering pegs though these appear in several Nuer ceremonies, and they may well stand for jural attributes. A cattle-peg sprite is associated with cattle fertility (E-P 1956: 98–9). Among the Dinka such pegs often stand for a shrine, yet we are not told why (Lienhardt 1961: 259–60). Nuer shrines seem to be marked by forked sticks or branches rather than by tethering pegs (E-P 1956: 114; but cf. ibid., pl. II).
28. E-P's earlier discussion of prophets (1935: 55–68) is more useful than his final analysis (1956: 292, 305–6).
29. Middleton informs me (private communication) that goats seem to hold inferior and somewhat negative or ambiguous symbolic positions over

much of the southern Sudan. Here and in later citations one finds prophets associating themselves with goats rather than cattle, whereas goats seem to be associated with women and cattle with men. This may relate to certain latent homosexual or sterile attributes of such persons. Judaic prophets also wore leather girdles and were associated with hairy garments, wilderness and liminality (Pederson: 110; Lindblom: 65-6). Goats are used to remove the pollution associated both with a possessing ghost and with homicide (E-P 1956: 38, 297). Curiously, the only persons allowed to eat a goat slain to remove a possessing spirit are a prophet and his two friends (songsters?) and some children – all persons outside the jural system involved (E-P 1956: 38).

30. I am grateful to Dr J. C. Crocker for his clearer formulation of this point which I probably made insufficiently clear earlier (1966a).

31. In my earlier paper (1966a: 456-7) I note the undercurrent of latent homosexuality in much of Nuer symbolic behaviour, a point first brought to my attention by Dr Kathleen Gough Aberle in 1955.

32. When he led his warriors into battle, Gwek held his magical pipe in his left hand and his magical fishing-spear in his right. The fishing-spear is well known to have mystical and ritual associations for the Dinka and we know that Gwek was of Dinka origins. The full meaning of this spear and pipe and their manual associations is unclear (Jackson 1954: 170), but pipe-smoking seems to convey certain prophetic prowess (E-P 1956: 37).

33. Jackson, long familiar and sympathetic towards the Nuer, found Gwek highly neurotic and very deformed physically (cf. 1954: ch. X). Evans-Pritchard tells us nothing about Nuer albinos, but Titherington shows a photo of a Dinka albino 'magician' (Pl. XX).

34. The only other case of such deliberate debilitation is in another situation reported by Howell (1954: 218), in which a man cut off a finger-joint to expiate the pollution of bestiality, an act with certain possible implications of witchcraft. Both bestiality and possession by spirits seem to involve some kind of pollution.

35. Middleton also describes the growth of prophetism among Lugbara during a time of terrible epidemics (91).

36. His goose-like attributes may relate to his glossolalia, for Nuong Nuer are said to be called twot after a type of goose with an unusual call, because of their trait of speaking 'a hitherto unknown tongue' (Fergusson 1921: 150).

37. Every important prophet has several songsters or assistants, apparently men possessing attributes of a lesser but similar nature to a prophet. We find a number of prophets who started as songsters for other prophets (Fergusson 1930: 212; Willis: 201; Coriat: 237; Crazzolara: 167). Judaic priests also had their special singers (Pederson: 188).

38. Evans-Pritchard maintains that the curse of prophets was an important aspect of their power (1949e: 289; 1956: 168); this was also important to priests and members of the same age-set (1956: 167–8).

39. Sexual mutilation may even have been important in Dinka prophetic and priestly beliefs (Bedri: 49).

40. Conversely, Dinka may refer to witches as Dor (Bongo), a tribe neighbouring them (Richards: 144).

41. We know that the ostrich is associated with a certain Nuer air-spirit (*nai*), while the spear-names and probably spears are associated with a fierce air-spirit (*wiu*) influential in warfare. Spears are also probably associated with *col wic*, the spirit of lightning. Elsewhere, I discuss the various mystical associations Nuer hold for spears (E-P 1954: 30–1; Beidelman 1966a: 457–9). We know too that earth itself holds some kind of mystical significance for the Nuer.

    The shrine at Luang Deng was consulted by both Dinka and Nuer (Lienhardt 1961: 100); this was marked by a pyramidal mound.

42. The west is an unpropitious direction for the Nuer and with one's back to the west one is oriented with the north to the left, another unpropitious orientation. Unfortunately, there is no information to indicate what, if any, symbolism is involved in the relative locations of the pyramid and pool. Dinka prophets who gained support from Shilluk, Mandari, and Nuer, as well as from their own people, were associated with spirits connected with pools and water (Fergusson 1922); this was also true of Lugbara spirit cults related to prophets (Middleton). One Nuer prophetic type was recognized by his having uprooted grass in the bush and having thereby created a pool (Fergusson 1921: 154).

43. Even the behaviour between ordinary Nuer and ghouls and witches may sometimes be difficult to distinguish; thus, a man with a connexion to a harmful totemic creature or thing (such as the saurian Nuer in the previous discussion) might be asked to deflect it from his group; but Evans-Pritchard relates an incident where an angry Nuer threatened to break his respect (*thek*) towards such a creature in order to harm the group out of spite (1949c: 232). Likewise, even God himself is thought of in certain highly negative terms (Crazzolara: 95).

    I am tempted to compare Nuer prophets to women in that they too are highly ambiguous socially, producing wealth and people (booty and captives in the case of prophets), yet destroying society through the conflict, dangers, and cross-cutting loyalties they engender. For a long discussion of this in terms of women, cf. Beidelman (1966a).

44. Elsewhere I suggest some reasons why many social anthropologists may be biased towards a Durkheimean model (1970: 503–4).

REFERENCES

ALBAN, A. H. 1940 Gwek's Pipe and Pyramid. *Sudan Notes & Records* **23**: 200–1.

ANONYMOUS 1921 The Reason for the Beir's Hatred of the Dinka. *Sudan Notes & Records* **4**: 51.

BEDRI, I. 1948 More Notes on the Padang Dinka. *Sudan Notes & Records* **29**: 40–57.

BEIDELMAN, T. O. 1966a The Ox and Nuer Sacrifice. *Man* **1** (n.s.): 453–67.

— 1966b Swazi Royal Ritual. *Africa* **26**: 373–405.

— 1968 Some Nuer Notions of Nakedness, Nudity and Sexuality. *Africa* **38**: 113–31.

— 1970 Some Sociological Implications of Culture. In McKinney, J. C. and E. Tiryakian (eds.). *Theoretical Sociology*. New York: Appleton-Century Crofts.

BEN ASSHER 1928 *A Nomad in the South Sudan*. London: Witherby.

BOHANNAN, P. 1956 Extra-Pocessual Events in Tiv Political Institutions. *American Anthropologist* **60**: 1–12.

CORIAT, P. 1939 Gwek, the Witch-Doctor and the Pyramid of Dengkur. *Sudan Notes & Records* **22**: 221–38.

CRAZZOLARA, J. P. 1933 *Zur Gesellschaft und Religion der Nueer*. Mödling bei Wien: Studia Instituti Anthropos.

DRIBERG, J. 1931 Yakan. *Journal Royal Anthropological Institute* **61**: 413–20.

DUNCAN, J. S. R. 1948 A Dry Season Trek. *Blackwood's Magazine* **264**: 352–6.

EVANS-PRITCHARD, E. E. 1934 The Nuer: Tribe and Clan IV–VIII. *Sudan Notes & Records* **17**: 1–57.

— 1935 The Nuer: Tribe and Clan VII (cont.)–IX. *Sudan Notes & Records* **18**: 37–87.

— 1936a Customs and Beliefs Relating to Twins among the Nilotic Nuer. *Uganda Journal* **3**: 230–8.

— 1936b The Nuer: Age Sets. *Sudan Notes & Records* **19**: 233–71.

— 1940 *The Nuer*. Oxford: Clarendon Press.

— 1945 *Some Aspects of Marriage and the Family among the Nuer*. Lusaka: Rhodes-Livingstone Institute.

— 1947 Bridewealth among the Nuer. *African Studies* **6**: 181–8.

— 1948 A Note on Affinity Relationships among the Nuer. *Man* **48**: 3–5.

— 1949a The Nuer Col Wic. *Man* **49**: 7–9.

— 1949b Two Nuer Ritual Concepts. *Man* **49**: 74–6.

— 1949c Nuer Totemism. *Annali Lateranensi* **13**: 225–48.

— 1949d Burial and Mortuary Rites of the Nuer. *African Affairs* **48**: 56–63.

EVANS-PRITCHARD, E. E. 1949e Nuer Curses and Ghostly Vengeance. *Africa* **19**: 288–92.

— 1953 The Nuer Spirits of the Air. *Annali Lateranensi* **17**: 55–82.

— 1954 A Problem of Nuer Religious Thought. *Sociologus* **4**: 23–41.

— 1956 *Nuer Religion*. Oxford: Clarendon Press.

FERGUSSON, V. 1921 The Nuong Nuer. *Sudan Notes & Records* **4**: 146–55.

— 1922 The Holy Lake of the Dinka. *Sudan Notes & Records* **5**: 163–6.

— 1930 *The Story of Fergie Bey*. London: Macmillan.

GRAY, R. 1961 *A History of the Southern Sudan 1839–1889*. London: Oxford University Press.

HOWELL, P. 1945 A Note on Elephants and Elephant Hunting among the Nuer. *Sudan Notes & Records* **26**: 95–104.

— 1948 'Pyramids' in the Upper Nile Region. *Man* **48**: 52–3.

— 1951 Notes on the Ngork Dinka of Western Kordofan. *Sudan Notes & Records* **32**: 239–93.

— 1953 Some Observations on 'Earthly Spirits' among the Nuer. *Man* **53**: 85–8.

— 1954 *A Manual of Nuer Law*. London: Oxford University Press (for International African Institute).

— 1961 Appendix [on the Luak Deng], pp. 97–103, in Lienhardt (1961).

HOWELL, P., AND B. LEWIS 1947 Nuer Ghouls. *Sudan Notes & Records* **28**: 158–68.

HUFFMAN, R. 1931 *Nuer Customs and Folk-lore*. London: Oxford University Press (for International African Institute).

JACKSON, H. 1929 The Nuer of the Upper Nile Province, Khartoum. *Sudan Notes & Records* **6**: 59–107.

— 1954 *Sudan Days and Ways*. London: Macmillan.

KIGGEN, J. 1948 *Nuer-English Dictionary*. London: St. Joseph's Society for Foreign Missions, Mill Hill.

LEACH, E. R. 1961 *Rethinking Anthropology*. London: Athlone Press.

LEWIS, B. A. 1951 Nuer Spokesmen: a Note on the Institution of the Ruic. *Sudan Notes & Records* **32**: 77–84.

LIENHARDT, R. G. 1955 Nilotic Kings and their Mothers' Kin. *Africa* **25**: 29–42.

— 1961 *Divinity and Experience*. Oxford: Clarendon Press.

LINDBLOM, G. 1963 *Prophecy in Ancient Israel*. Oxford: Blackwell.

MACMILLAN, W. M. 1963 *Bantu, Boer and Britain*. Oxford: Clarendon Press.

MACDERMOT, B. 1969 Proud Nuer Tribe. *Geographical Magazine* **41**, (1): 375–81.

MIDDLETON, J. 1963 The Yakan or Allah Water Cult of the Lugbara. *J. Roy. Anthropol. Inst.* **93**, (1): 80–108.

PEDERSON, J. 1940 *Israel: Its Life and Culture*. Vol. III. London: Oxford University Press.

RICHARDS, M. 1935 Bongo Magic. *Sudan Notes & Records* **18,** (1): 143–7.

SELIGMAN, C. G. & B. Z. 1932 *Pagan Tribes of the Nilotic Sudan*. London: Routledge.

STIGAND, C. H. 1918 Warrior Classes of the Nuers. *Sudan Notes & Records* **1**: 116–18.

— 1919 The Story of Kir and the White Spear. *Sudan Notes & Records* **2**: 224–6.

TITHERINGTON, G. 1927 The Raik Dinka of Bahr el Ghazal Province. *Sudan Notes & Records* **10**: 159–210.

TIRYAKIAN, E. A. 1966 A Problem of the Sociology of Knowledge: the Mutual Unawareness of Emile Durkheim and Max Weber. *Europ. J. Sociol.* 7: 330–6.

WEBER, M. 1947 *The Theory of Social and Economic Organization*. Glencoe, Ill.: Free Press.

— 1948 *From Max Weber: Essays in Sociology* (eds. H. H. Gerth & C. W. Mills). London: Routledge & Kegan Paul.

— 1952 *Ancient Judaism*. Glencoe, Ill.: Free Press.

WESTERMANN, D. 1912 The Nuer Language. *Mitt. Sem. Orient. Spr.* **15**: 84–141.

WILLIS, C. A. 1923 The Cult of Deng. *Sudan Notes & Records* **6**: 193–208.

WILLOUGHBY, W. C. 1928 *The Soul of the Bantu*. New York: Doubleday.

Bibliography

The Writings of E. E. Evans-Pritchard,

F.B.A., M.A.(Oxon.), Ph.D.(London), Hon. D.Sc.(Chicago),
Hon. D.Sc.(Bristol), Hon. D.Litt.(Mancun.)

Compiled by E. E. Evans-Pritchard
amended and corrected by T. O. Beidelman

AA   = *American Anthropologist*
AQ   = *Anthropological Quarterly*
AS   = *African Studies*
BFA   = *Bulletin of the Faculty of Arts* (Egyptian University, Cairo)
BSOAS = *Bulletin of the School of Oriental and African Studies* (University
           of London)
JAI   = *Journal of African Languages*
JRAI   = *Journal of the Royal Anthropological Institute*
SNR   = *Sudan Notes and Records*
TLS   = *The Times Literary Supplement*

1927   Preliminary Account of the Ingassana Tribe of the Fung Province.
       SNR X: 69–83.
1928a   The Dance. *Africa* I, No. 4 (Oct.): 446–62; republished (1965h).
1928b   Oracle Magic of the Azande. *SNR* XI: 1–53.
1928c   Avokaiya Fishing. *Man* XXVIII (March) 27: 37–8.
1929a   The Morphology and Function of Magic. *AA* XXXI: 619–41;
       reprinted pp. 1–22, in *Magic, Witchcraft and Curing* (ed. J. Middleton),
       Amer. Mus. of Nat. Hist., New York, 1966.
1929b   The Bongo. *SNR* XXI, No. 1: 1–61.
1929c   The Study of Kinship in Primitive Societies. *Man* XXIX (Nov.)
       148: 190–1.
1929d   Some Collective Expressions of Obscenity in Africa. *JRAI* LIX:
       311–32; republished (1965h).
1929e   Letter [Concerning acknowledgements for 1927; 1928b]. *SNR* XII,
       Pt. 1: 114.
1929f   Witchcraft (*Mangu*) among the Azande. *SNR* XII, No. 2: 163–249.
1929g   Review of *Les Azande ou Niam-Niam* by Mgr. C. R. Lagae. *SNR*
       XII, Pt. 2: 261–5.
1929h   Review of *The Spiked Wheel-Trap and its Distribution* by K. G.
       Lindblom. *SNR* XII, Pt. 2: 266–8.
1929i   Review of 'The Bari' by C. G. & B. Z. Seligman [article in JRAI
       1928]. *SNR* XII, Pt. 2: 268–71.
1929j   Review of *Zwischen Weissem Nil und Belgisch-Kongo* by H. Bernatzik.
       SNR XII, Pt. 2: 271–2.

1929k Review of *Nuer-English Dictionary* by Ray Huffman. *SNR* XII, Pt. 2: 272.

1929l Review of *West African Societies* by F. W. Butt-Thompson. *Africa* II, No. 4 (Oct.): 428.

1931a Sorcery and Native Opinion. *Africa* IV, No. 1 (Jan.): 22–55.

1931b Review of *The Red Men of Nigeria* by J. R. Wilson-Haffenden. *Man* XXXI (Feb.) 35: 31–2.

1931c An Alternative Term for Brideprice. *Man* XXXI (March) 42: 36–9.

1931d Mani, a Zande Secret Society. *SNR* XIV, No. 2: 105–48.

1931e Heredity and Gestation as the Zande See Them. *Sociologus* VIII, No. 4: 400–14; republished in (1962g).

1931–2 The Mberidi (Shilluk Group) and Mbegumba (Basiri Group) of the Bahr-el-Ghazal. *SNR* XIV, No. 1 (1931): 15–48; XV, No. 2 (1932): 273–4.

1932a Ethnological Observations in Dar Fung. *SNR* XV, No. 1: 1–61.

1932b The Nature of Kinship Extensions. *Man* XXXII (Jan.) 7: 12–15.

1932c Review of *Taboo, Magic, Spirits* by Eli Edward Buriss. *Man* XXXII (May) 154: 127–8.

1932d Review of *Roman Britain* by R. G. Collingwood. *Man* XXXII (Sept.) 254: 220–1.

1932e Al-Mastaqbil al-'Ilm al-'Ijtima'a [The Future of Sociology]. *Al-Ahram* [in Arabic].

1932–3 The Zande Corporation of Witchdoctors. *JRAI* LXII, No. 2 (July–Dec.): 291–336; LXIII, No. 1 (Jan.–June): 63–100.

1933a The Intellectualist (English) Interpretation of Magic. *BFA* I, Pt. 2: 1–21.

1933b Review of *The Origin and History of Politics* by W. C. McLeod. *Man* XXXIII (April) 193: 73.

1933c Zande Blood-Brotherhood. *Africa* VI, No. 4 (Oct.): 369–401; republished (1962g).

1933–5 The Nuer: Tribe and Clan. *SNR* XVI, No. 1 (1933): 1–53; XVII, No. 1 (1934): 1–57; XVIII, No. 1 (1935): 37–87.

1934a Review of *Fighting-Bracelets and Kindred Weapons in Africa* by K. G. Lindblom. *SNR* XVII, Pt. 2: 267.

1934b Review of 'Likundu die Sektion der Zauberkraft' by Hermann Baumann [article in *Zeit. f. Eth.* 1928]. *SNR* XVII, Pt. 2: 268–70.

1934c Lévy-Bruhl's Theory of Primitive Mentality. *BFA* II, Pt. 2: 1–26. republished in *Journal of the Anthropological Society of Oxford I*, No. 2 (1970): 39–60.

1934d Social Character of Bridewealth with Special Reference to the Azande. *Man* XXXIV (Nov.) 194: 172–5; republished in (1965h).

1934e [co-editor with R. Firth, B. Malinowski, and I. Schapera] *Essays Presented to C. G. Seligman*. Kegan Paul, London.

1934f Zande Therapeutics. In (1934e): 49–61.

1934g Imagery in Ngok Dinka Cattle Names. *BSOS* VII, No. 3: 623–8; republished in (1965h).

1935a A Trip to Dungul Oasis. *BFA* III, Pt. 1 (May): 24–49.

1935b Witchcraft. *Africa* VIII, No. 4 (Oct.): 417–22.

1935c Exogamous Rules among the Nuer. [A communication of a lecture given 20 Nov. 1934] *Man* XXXV (Jan.) 7: 11.

1935d Review of *The Uganda Journal* Vol. I, Nos. 1 & 2. *Man* XXXV (April) 61: 62.

1935e Review of *L'Afrique Fântome* by Michel Leiris. *Man* XXXV (April) 62: 62.

1935f Review of *Social and Psychological Aspects of Primitive Education* by J. M. Evans. *Man* XXXV (Sept.) 155: 143.

1935g Ethnological Survey of the Sudan, pp. 79–93, in *The Anglo-Egyptian Sudan from Within* (ed. J. A. de C. Hamilton), Faber and Faber, London.

1935h Megalithic Grave Monuments in the Anglo-Egyptian Sudan and in other Parts of East Africa. *Antiquity* IX, No. 34 (June): 151–60.

1935i Review of 'Die Bedeutung des Rindes bei den Nuer', by R. P. Crazzolara [An article in *Africa* 1934]. *SNR* XVIII, Pt. 1: 165.

1935j Review of *Some Nuer Terms in Relation to the Human Body, Book I, Pts. 1 & 2* by C. B. Soule. *SNR* XVIII, Pt. 1: 165.

1936a Customs and Beliefs Relating to Twins among the Nilotic Nuer. *Uganda Journal* III, No. 3 (Jan.): 230–8.

1936b Daily Life of the Nuer in Dry Season Camps, pp. 291–302, in *Custom Is King: Essays Presented to R. R. Marett* (ed. L. H. D. Buxton), Hutchinson's, London.

1936c Review of *Tramping Through Africa* by J. W. Roome. *Man* XXXVI (July) 70: 55.

1936d Review of *Pareto* by Franz Borkenau. *Man* XXXVI (July) 172: 125.

1936e Science and Sentiment: an Exposition and Criticism of the Writings of Pareto. *BFA* III, Pt. 2: 163–92.

1936f Zande Theology. *SNR* XIX, No. 1: 5–46; republished in (1962g).

1936g The Nuer: Age Sets. *SNR* XIX, No. 2: 233–71.

1937a Review of *Marriage Conditions in a Palestine Village* by Hilma Granqvist. *Man* XXXVII (Jan.) 23: 26.

1937b The Nuer Family [Abstract of a lecture given 26 Jan. 1937]. *Man* XXXVII (Feb.) 37: 34.

1937c Review of *Baluba et Balubaisés*. *Man* XXXVII (Feb.) 46: 38.

1937d Review of *The Web of Thought and Action* by H. Levy. *Man* XXXVII (June) 126: 102.

E. E. Evans-Pritchard

1937e Anthropology and the Social Sciences, pp. 61–74. *Further Papers on the Social Sciences*, London.

1937f Anthropology and Administration, pp. 87–90. *Oxford Summer School on Colonial Administration* (July), Oxford.

1937g *Witchcraft, Oracles and Magic among the Zande.* Clarendon Press, Oxford, pp. xxv + 558.

1937h The Non-Dinka Peoples of the Amadi and Rumbek Districts. *SNR* XX, No. 1: 156–9.

1937–8 Economic Life of the Nuer. *SNR* XX, No. 3 (1937): 209–45; XXI, No. 1 (1938): 31–77.

1938a A Note on Ingassana Marriage Customs. *SNR* XXI, No. 2 (Dec.): 307–77.

1938b Review of *A Tribal Survey of Mongalla Province* by Members of the Province Staff (ed. L. F. Nalder). *Man* XXXVIII (Jan.) 10: 13.

1938c A Note on Rainmakers among the Moro. *Man* XXXVIII (April) 49: 53–6.

1938d Some Administrative Problems in the Southern Sudan. *Oxford Summer School on Colonial Administration*, Oxford.

1938e Some Aspects of Marriage and the Family among the Nuer. *Zeitschrifs für vergleichende Rechtswissenschaft* LII: 306–92; republished as a monograph: *Rhodes-Livingstone Paper* 11 (1945). pp. 70.

1938f Review of *Sons of Ishmael* by G. W. Murray. *Africa* XI, No. 1 (Jan.): 123.

1939a Nuer-Time Reckoning. *Africa* XII, No. 2 (April): 189–216; republished as Bobbs-Merrill Reprint (1966), Indianapolis.

1939b Obituary: Arthur Maurice Hocart: 1884–March 1939. *Man* XXXIX (Aug.) 115: 131.

1939c Introduction, pp. xix–xxxiv, to *The Social Institutions of the Kipsigi* by J. G. Peristiany. Routledge, London.

1940a Bibliographical Note on the Ethnology of the Southern Sudan. *Africa* XIII, No. 1 (Jan.): 62–7.

1940b Obituary: Lucien Lévy-Bruhl, 1939. *Man* XL (Feb.) 27: 24–5.

1940c The Relationship between the Anuak and the Föri (Sudan). *Man* XL (April) 62: 54–5; republished in *SNR* XXIII, No. 2: 337–40.

1940d The Political System of the Anuak [Abstract of a lecture]. *Man* XL (May) 87: 73.

1940e Review of *Human Types* by Raymond Firth. *Man* XL (June) 120: 95.

1940f Review of *History and Science* by Hugh Miller. *Man* XL (Sept.) 177: 144.

1940g African Genealogies [A letter]. *SNR* XXIII: 201–2.

1940h *The Political System of the Anuak of the Anglo-Egyptian Sudan.* Monograph on Social Anthropology No. 4, published by Percy Lund,

Humphries & Co., for the London School of Economics and Political Science, London. pp. 164.

1940i [co-editorship with Meyer Fortes] *African Political Systems*, published by Oxford University Press, for the International African Institute, London; [co-authorship with Meyer Fortes] Introduction, pp. 15–23.

1940j The Nuer of the Southern Sudan, pp. 272–96, in (1940i).

1940k *The Nuer: A Description of the Modes of Livelihood and Political Institutions of a Nilotic People.* Clarendon Press, Oxford, pp. xiii + 271; reprinted as a paperback, Clarendon Press, Oxford, 1968; French translation, *Les Nuer*, Editions Gallimard, Paris, 1969 [Preface by Louis Dumont: i–xv]; Introductory, pp. 7–15, reprinted, Bobbs-Merrill.

1940l The Political Structure of the Nandi-Speaking Peoples of Kenya. *Africa* XIII, No. 3 (July): 250–67; republished in (1965h).

1940m [with M. Fortes] Memorandum on a Plan of Research into Problems of Modern Political Development in Africa. For the *Hebdomadal Council* vol. 175 (8 March) Oxford, 185–96.

1940-1 [with A. C. Beaton and T. H. B. Myners] Folk Stories of the Sudan. *SNR* XXIII, No. 1 (1940): 55–74; No. 2 (1940): 271–8; XXIV, No. 1 (1941): 69–84.

1941 Foreword, pp. ix–xi, to *The Moulids of Egypt (Egyptian Saints-Days)* by J. W. McPherson, N.M. Press, Cairo.

1943a Note of the Nasaires, in *A Note on the Alawites* (Security), M.E.I.C., G.H.Q., M.E.F. [Mimeographed].

1943b *The Place of the Sanusiya in the History of Islam.* British Military Administration, Cyrenaica; republished by British Military Administration, Tripolitania, 1945.

1944a [Editor] *Handbook of Cyrenaica* (reserved), G.H.Q., M.E.F.

1944b Tribes (Habitat and Way of Life), in (1944a), constituting Pt. VII.

1944c Tribes and Their Divisions, in (1944a), constituting Pt. VIII.

1944d *The Non-Sanusiya Orders in Cyrenaica.* British Military Administration, Cyrenaica.

1944e *A Note on the Zawaya of the Sanusiya Order in Cyrenaica.* British Military Administration, Cyrenaica.

1944f Arab Status in Cyrenaica under the Italians. *Sociological Review* XXXVI, Nos. 1–4 (Jan.–Oct.): 1–17.

1944a The Sanusi of Cyrenaica. *Africa* XV, No. 1 (Jan.): 61–79.

1945b The Distribution of Sanusi Lodges. *Africa* XV, No. 4 (Oct.): 183–7.

1945c *Biographical Notes on Members of the Sanusi Family.* British Military Administration, Cyrenaica.

1945d Cyrenaica [letter]. *The Geographical Journal* CV, Nos. 5–6 (May–June): 227–9.

1945e A Hymn [unsigned] and Arabic version, Nuzayyina Hadbē al- 'adida biāsmā' i allahi al-husnā [We Adorn this issue with the ninety-nine attributes of God] [unsigned], *Barqua Weekly Review*, No. 62 (3 March) (Benghazi); reprinted [in English], The Beautiful Names of God, *Blackfriars* 27, supplem. (1946): 1–3; reprinted *Muslim Sunrise* (1947) (Washington, D.C.), exact issue and date unknown.

1945–9 A Select Bibliography of Writings on Cyrenaica. *African Studies* IV, No. 3 (Sept. 1945): 146–50; V. No. 3 (Sept. 1946): 189–94; VII, No. 2 (June 1949): 62–5.

1946a Applied Anthropology. *Africa* XVI, No. 1 (Jan.): 92–8.

1946b Nuer Bridewealth. *Africa* XVI, No. 4 (Oct.): 247–57.

1946c Hereditary Succession of Shaikhs of Sanusiya Lodges in Cyrenaica. *Man* XLI (May–June) 51: 58–62.

1946d Italy and the Bedouin in Cyrenaica. *African Affairs* XLV: 12–21.

1946e Italy and the Sanusiya Order in Cyrenaica. *BSOAS* XI, Pt. 4: 843–53.

1946f Topographical Terms in Common Use among the Bedouin of Cyrenaica. *JRAI* LXXVI: 177–88.

1946g *Some Ikhwan and Other Sanusi Families*. British Military Administration, Cyrenaica.

1946h Social Anthropology. *Blackfriars* 27: 409–14.

1946i Obituary: G. O. Whitehead. *SNR* XXVIII: 242–3.

1946j The Cyrenaica-Tripolitania Boundary [Letter]. *The Geographical Journal* CVII, Nos. 3–4 (Mar.–April): 169–70.

1946k Review of *The King of Ganda* by T. Irstam. *Africa* XVI, No. 3 (July): 132.

1946l Review of *La Tente Noire* by C. G. Feilberg. *Africa* XVI, No. 3 (July): 207–8.

1946m Review of *The Dynamics of Clanship among the Tallensi* by Meyer Fortes. *BSOAS* XI (1943–6): 906.

1947a Bridewealth among the Nuer. *African Studies* VI, No. 4 (Dec.): 181–8.

1947b A Note on Courtship among the Nuer. *SNR* XXVIII: 115–26.

1947c Obituary: Jack Herbert Driberg 1888–1946 [with bibliography]. *Man* XLVII (Jan.) 4: 11–13.

1947d The Sanusi of Cyrenaica [Abstract of a lecture given 15 June 1946]. *Man* XLVII (Feb.) 19: 28.

1947e Artificial Deformation of Ox-horns in Southern Sudan [Letter]. *Man* XLVII (Feb.) 39: 36.

1947f Further Observations on the Political System of the Anuak. *SNR* XXVIII: 62–97.

1947g Review of *Paysans de Syrie et du Proche-Orient* by J. Weulerssc. *Man* XLVII (Oct.) 150: 136.

1947h Does Anthropology Undermine Faith? *The Listener* XXXVII, No. 954 (8 May): 714–5.

1947i [unsigned] Sociological Significance of Language and Culture. *Nature* CLX, No. 4059 (Aug. 16): 205–6.

1947j Review of *The Action of the Italian Government in Favour of the Libyan Agriculture. Africa* XVII, No. 1 (Jan.): 66.

1947k Review of *Le Bou-Mergoud* by M-L. Auboulog-Laffin. *Africa* XVII, No. 3 (July): 215.

1947l Review of *Knowing the African* by E. W. Smith. *Africa* XVII, No. 3 (July): 217–8.

1947m Review of *A Study of History* by A. J. Toynbee. *Blackfriars* 28 (June): 285–6.

1948a *The Divine Kingship of the Shilluk of the Nilotic Sudan.* The Frazer Lecture of 1948. Cambridge University Press, Cambridge. 40 pp.; republished in (1962g).

1948b Nuer Marriage Ceremonies. *Africa* XVII, No. 1 (Jan.): 29–40.

1948c Terminal Note to 'The Age-Set System and the Institution of "Nak" among the Nuer' by P. Howell. *SNR* XXIX, No. 2: 181–2.

1948d Nuer Modes of Address. *Uganda Journal* XII, No. 2 (Sept.): 166–71; republished, pp. 221–5, in *Language in Culture and Society* (ed. D. Hymes), Harper & Row, New York, 1964; and in (1965h).

1948e Review of *Religion and Culture* by Christopher Dawson. *Unitas* [unlocated].

1948f *Social Anthropology: an Inaugural Lecture delivered before the University of Oxford on 4 February 1948.* Clarendon Press, Oxford.

1948g A Note on Affinity Relationships among the Nuer. *Man* XLVIII (Jan.) 2: 3–5.

1948h Review of *Manual d'Ethnographie* by Marcel Mauss. *Man* XLVIII (June) 81: 69–70.

1948i Review of *Forme e soggetti della letteratura popolare Libica* by E. Panetta. *Africa* XVIII, No. 1 (Jan.): 70.

1948j Review of *Regime della Proprieta Fondiaria nell'Africa Italiana, Vol. I, Libia* by M. Colucci. *Africa* XVIII, No. 1 (Jan.): 70–1.

1948k Review of *Maze of Justice* by Twefik el Hakim. *Man* XLVIII (Sept.) 120: 106.

1948l Review of *The Influence of Islam on a Sudanese Religion* (by Joseph Greenberg). *Man* XLVIII (Oct.) 134: 122.

1949a Burial and Mortuary Rites of the Nuer. *African Affairs* XLVIII, No. 190 (Jan.): 56–63.

1949b Nuer Curses and Ghostly Vengeance. *Africa* XIX, No. 4 (Oct.): 288–92.

1949c Nuer Totemism. *Annali Lateranensi* XIII: 225–48.

1949d Luo Tribes and Clans. *Rhodes-Livingstone Journal* VII: 24–40; republished (1965h).

1949e The Nuer 'Col Wic'. *Man* XLIX (Jan.) 2: 7–9.

1949f Association of Social Anthropologists [A report of a meeting on 5 & 6 Jan. 1949]. *Man* XLIX (March) 30: 32.

1949g Review of *Kingship and the Gods* by H. Frankfort. *Man* XLIX (April) 53: 45.

1949h Two Nuer Ritual Concepts. *Man* XLIX (July) 96: 74–6.

1949i Anthropology and Colonial Affairs. *Man* XLIX (Dec.) 179: 137–8 [Summary of contributions by E. Evans-Pritchard and R. Firth to meeting 5 July 1949].

1949j *The Sanusi of Cyrenaica.* Clarendon Press, Oxford, pp. v + 240.

1949k Translation of an Elegy by Ahmad Shauqi Bey on the Occasion of the Execution of Sidi 'Umar al-Mukhtar al-Minifi. *The Arab World* 19 (Feb.).

1949l Nuer Rules of Exogamy and Incest, pp. 85–103, in *Social Structure* (ed. M. Fortes) Cambridge University Press, Cambridge; volume republished by Russell and Russell, New York, 1963.

1949m Review of *La Civilisation du désert* by R. Montagne. *Africa* XIX, No. 1 (Jan.): 79.

1949n Review of *Bibliografia de studi africani della missioni dell'Africa Central* by P. S. Santandrea. *Africa* XIX, No. 3 (July): 249–50.

1949o Association of Social Anthropologists. [Note of a meeting held on 28 and 29 September, 1949]. *Man* XLIX (Dec.) 183: 139–40.

1950a The Nuer Family. *SNR* XXXI, No. 1 (June): 21–42.

1950b Association of Social Anthropologists [Report on a meeting 6 & 7 Jan. 1950]. *Man* L (May) 74: 61.

1950c Ghostly Vengeance among the Luo of Kenya. *Man* L (July) 133: 86–7.

1950d Social Anthropology: Past and Present [The Marett Lecture]. *Man* L (Sept.) 198: 118–24. German translation, *Socialanthropologie gestern und heute*, see entry (1965g).

1950e Letter [On grasses in Nuerland]. *SNR* XXXI, Pt. 1 (June): 160–1.

1950f Marriage Customs of the Luo of Kenya. *Africa* XX, No. 2 (April): 132–42; republished in (1965h).

1950g Nilotic Studies [Presidential Address]. *JRAI* LXXX, Pts. 1 & 2: 1–6.

1950h Association of Social Anthropologists [Report on a meeting 29 & 30 Aug. 1950]. *Man* L (Dec.) 259: 163.

1950i Kinship and the Local Community among the Nuer. Pp. 360–91 in *African Systems of Kinship and Marriage* (eds. A. R. Radcliffe-Brown & D. Forde), Oxford University Press for the International African Institute, London.

1951a Some Features and Forms of Nuer Sacrifice. *Africa* XXI, No. 2 (April) 112–21; reprinted, pp. 133–57 in *Gods and Rituals* (ed. J. Middleton), Amer. Mus. of Nat. Hist., New York, 1967.

1951b Review of *Magic: a Sociological Study* by H. Webster. *Man* LI (April) 87: 52–3.

1951c The Institute of Social Anthropology. *The Oxford Magazine* LXIX, No. 17 (26 April): 354, 358, 360.

1951d Maine on Morgan [Letter]. *Man* LI (Aug.) 181: 104.

1951e The Shilluk King-Killing [Letter]. *Man* LI (Aug.) 202: 116.

1951f *Social Anthropology.* Cohen and West, London; English paperback edition, Cohen and West, London, 1967; US edition, Free Press, Glencoe; republished in USA as a paperback by Free Press, Glencoe, combined with (1962g) pp. vii + 134; Japanese translation, *Shakai Jinrui-gaku, Dobunkan,* Tokyo, 1963; Spanish translation, *Antropologia Social,* Nueva Vision, Buenos Aires, 1957; Arabic translation *Al-Antropologiya al-Ijtim 'iya,* Munsha'at al-Malarif, Cairo, 1958; Hindi translation, *Sāmajik Mānava Vijñan,* Rajkamal Prakeshan; French translation, *Anthropologie sociale,* Petite bibliothèque Payot, Paris, 1969 [postscript by Michel Panoff].

1951g *Kinship and Marriage among the Nuer.* Clarendon Press, Oxford. pp. xii + 183.

1951h Review of *The Lwoo, Pt. I* by J. P. Crazzolara. *Africa* XXI, No. 1 (Jan.): 81.

1951i Bridewealth: a Plea in Its Favour, the Importance of Exact Terminology [Letter]. *East Africa* III, 365 (Sept. 17): 12.

1952a Some Features of Nuer Religion [Presidential Address 1951]. *JRAI* LXXXI Pts. 1 & 2: 1–13.

1952b A Note on Nuer Prayers. *Man* LII (July) 140: 99–102.

1952c Obituary: Franz Baermann Steiner: 1908–1952. *Man* LII (Dec.) 264: 18.

1952d Review of *The Lwoo, Pt. II* by J. P. Crazzolara. *Africa* XXII, No. 1 (Jan.): 87.

1952e The Bibliography, pp. 182–98, in *The Nilotes of the Sudan and Uganda* by Audrey Butt. Ethnographic Survey of Africa: East Central Africa Pt. IV, Oxford University Press, for the International African Institute, London.

1952f A letter to E. E. Evans-Pritchard from L. Lévy-Bruhl with comments by E. E. Evans-Pritchard. *The British Journal of Sociology* III, No. 2 (June): 117–23; republished as: Lettre au Professeur Evans-Pritchard. *Revue Philosophique de la France et de l'étranger* CV (1957). 407–13.

1952g Foreword [with Fred Eggan], pp. v–vi, in *Structure and Function in Primitive Society* by A. R. Radcliffe-Brown, Routledge and Kegan

Paul, London; paperback edition, 1969; American edition, Free Press, Glencoe, 1965; Italian edition, *Struttura e funzione nella societa primitiva*, Jaca Book, Milano, 1968; French edition, *Structure et fonction dans la société primitive*, Les Editions de Minuit, Paris, 1969.

1953a The Nuer Conception of Spirit and its Relation to the Social Order. *AA* LV, No. 2, Pt. I (April–June): 201–14; republished as a Bobbs-Merrill Reprint; reprinted, pp. 109–26, in *Myth and Cosmos* (ed. J. Middleton), Amer. Mus. of Nat. Hist., New York, 1967.

1953b Nuer Spear Symbolism. *AQ* XXVI (n.s.)(Jan.): 1–19.

1953c The Sacrificial Role of Cattle among the Nuer. *Africa* XXII, No. 3 (July): 181–98; republished in abridged form, pp. 388–405 in *Cultures and Societies of Africa* (eds. S. & P. Ottenberg), Random House, New York, 1960.

1953d A Note on Ghostly Vengeance among the Anuak of the Anglo-Egyptian Sudan. *Man* LIII (Jan.) 3: 6–7; republished in (1965h).

1953e Bridewealth and the Stability of Marriage [Letter]. *Man* LIII (May) 122: 80.

1953f The Nuer Spirits of the Air. *Annali Lateranensi* XVII: 55–82.

1953g Review of *Blood-Brothers* by H. Tegnaeus. *Africa* XXIII, No. 2 (April): 170.

1953h Religion in Primitive Society. *Blackfriars* 34: 211–18.

1953i A contribution to Anthropology at Oxford. *The Proceedings of the five-hundredth meeting of The Oxford University Anthropological Society, held on Feb. 25 1953*. Holywell Press, Oxford.

1953j Foreword, pp. v–vii, in *A Manual of Nuer Law* by P. Howell, Oxford University Press for the International African Institute, London.

1954a The Meaning of Sacrifice among the Nuer [Henry Myers Lecture]. *JRAI* LXXXIV, Pt. 1 (Jan.–June): 21–33.

1954b A Problem of Nuer Religious Thought. *Sociologus* IV, No. 1: 23–41; reprinted, pp. 127–48, in *Myth and Cosmos* (ed. J. Middleton), Amer. Mus. of Nat. Hist., New York, 1967.

1954c Zande Texts [Letter]. *Man* LIV (Oct.) 260: 164.

1954d A Zande Slang Language. *Man* LIV (Dec.) 289: 185–6.

1954e Introduction, pp. v–x, and essay entitled "Religion", pp. 1–11, in *The Institutions of Primitive Society*. Blackwells, Oxford; German edition, *Institutionen in primitiven Gesellschaft*, Suhrkamp Verlag, Frankfurt am Main, 1967; Spanish translation, *Instituciones de la sociedad Primitiva*, Escuela nacional de antropologia y historia, Mexico, 1964.

1954f Introduction, pp. v–x, in *The Gift* by Marcel Mauss, Cohen and West, London; US edition, Free Press, Glencoe; US paperback edition, Norton Press, New York, 1967; German edition, *Die Gabe*, Theorie 1,

Suhrkamp Verlag, Frenkfurt am Main, 1968; U.K. paperback edition, 1970.

1954g Foreword, pp. ix–xi, to *The People of the Sierra* by J. Pitt-Rivers. Weidenfeld and Nicolson, London; US edition, Criterion Books, New York; US paperback edition, Phoenix (Univ. Chicago Press) Press, 1961.

1955a Zande Historical Texts, Pt. 1. *SNR* XXXVI, No. 2 (Dec.): 123–45.

1955b The Position of Women in Primitive Societies and in our Own [Fawcett Lecture]; first published in (1965), pp. 37–58.

1955c Review of *Zur Gesellschaft und Religion der Nueer* by J. P. Crazzolara. *Anthropos* L: 476–7.

1955d Review of *The Fate of the Soul* by Raymond Firth. *Man* LV (Nov.) 183: 171.

1955e Review of *Il Cannibalismo degli Asande* by R. Carmignani. *Africa* XXV, No. 2 (April): 202–3.

1955f Review of *Social Origins* by A. M. Hocart. *TLS* (Oct. 7): 591. [Unsigned].

1955g Obituary: A. R. Radcliffe-Brown. *The Times* (October 27), p. 14, column A, London.

1956a A History of the Kingdom of Gbudwe. *Zaïre* X, No. 5 (May): 451–91; No. 7 (July): 675–710; No. 8 (Oct.): 815–60.

1956b Zande Historical Texts, Pt. 2. *SNR* XXXVII: 20–47.

1956c *Sanza*, a Characteristic Feature of Zande Language and Thought. *BSOAS* XVIII, Pt. 1: 161–80; republished in (1962g).

1956d Cannibalism: a Zande Text. *Africa* XXVI, No. 1 (Jan.): 73–4.

1956e Zande Clan Names. *Man* LVI (May) 62: 69–71.

1956f Zande Totems. *Man* LVI (Aug.) 160: 107–9.

1956g *Nuer Religion.* Clarendon Press, Oxford, pp. xii + 336; UK paperback, 1971.

1956h Preface, pp. 11–13, to *Taboo* by Franz Steiner. Cohen and West, London; US edition, Philosophical Library, New York; Penguin paperback, 1967.

1957a Zande Historical Texts, Pt. 3. *SNR* XXXVIII: 74–99.

1957b The Zande Royal Court. *Zaïre* XI, No. 4 (April): 361–89; No. 5 (May): 493–511; No. 7 (July): 687–713.

1957c The Origins of the Ruling Clan of the Zande. *Southwestern Journal of Anthropology* XIII, No. 4: 322–43.

1957d Zande Border Raids. *Africa* XXVIII, No. 3 (July): 217–31.

1957e Zande Warfare. *Anthropos* LII, Nos. 1 & 2: 239–62.

1957f Zande Kings and Princes. *AQ* XXX, No. 3 (July): 61–90.

1958a Witchcraft Explains Unfortunate Events, pp. 277–81, and Consulting the Poison Oracle among the Azande, pp. 304–14; excerpts from

429

(1937g) in *Reader in Comparative Religion* (eds. W. Lessa & E. Z. Vogt), Row, Peterson & Co., Evanston.

1958b The Ethnic Composition of the Azande of Central Africa. *AQ* XXXI, No. 4 (Oct.): 95–118.

1958c An Historical Introduction to a Study of Zande Society. *African Studies* XVIII, No. 1: 1–15.

1958d Preface, pp. ix–xi, to *Tribes Without Rulers* (eds. J. Middleton & D. Tait). Routledge & Kegan Paul, London; UK paperback edition, 1970.

1958e Review of *Myth and Guilt* by Theodore Reik, *The Tablet* (March): 229–30.

1959a The Distribution of Zande Clans in the Sudan. *Man* LIX (Feb.) 24: 21–5.

1959b Review of *Cultural Anthropology: The Science of Custom* by Felix M. Keesing. *Man* LIX (March) 74: 53.

1959c The Teaching of Social Anthropology at Oxford. *Man* LIX (July) 180: 121–4.

1960a Religion and the Anthropologists [The Aquinas Lecture]. *Blackfriars* XLI, No. 480 (April): 104–18; republished in (1962g).

1960b The Sudan: an Ethnographic Survey, pp. 333–40, in *Culture in History: Essays in Honor of Paul Radin* (ed. S. Diamond), Columbia University Press, published for Brandeis University, New York; UK edition, Oxford University Press, London.

1960c The Azande [Letter]. *Man* LX (Dec.) 235: 182.

1960d A Contribution to the Study of Zande Culture. *Africa* XXX, No. 4 (Oct.): 209–24.

1960e The Ethnic Origins of Zande Office-Holders. *Man* LX (July) 141: 100–2.

1960f Zande Cannibalism. *JRAI* XC, Pt. 1: 238–58; republished in (1965h).

1960g Zande Clans and Settlements. *Man* LX (Nov.) 213: 169–72.

1960h The Organization of a Zande Kingdom. *Cahiers d'études africaines* IV: 5–37.

1960i [Unsigned] Review of *The Rites of Passage* by Arnold van Gennep. *TLS* (4 April): 236.

1960j Introduction, pp. 9–24, to *Death and the Right Hand* by Robert Hertz. Cohen and West, London; US edition, Free Press, Glencoe.

1960k Review of La Superstizione Zande by Gero (Filiberto Giorgetti). *Man* LIX (Dec.) 243: 185.

1960l The Wind of Change. Review of *A New Earth* by Elspeth Huxley. *The Sunday Times* (London) (3 July).

1960m Beyond the Congo. Review of *Year of Decision* by Philip Mason. *The Sunday Times* (London) (21 August).

Bibliography of the Writings of E. E. Evans-Pritchard

1961a Note [A Correction]. *Africa* XXXI, No. 2 (April): 184.

1961b *Anthropology and History* [Lecture delivered at Manchester University]. Manchester University Press, Manchester, pp. 22; republished in (1962g); Spanish translation, *Antropologia e Historia*, pp. 3–27, in *Nuestro Tiempo* 188 (February 1970), Pamplona.

1961c A Note on Bird Cries and Other Sounds in Zande. *Man* LXI (Jan.) 7: 19–20.

1961d Review of *Lewis Henry Morgan: American Scholar* by Carl Resek. *Man* LXI (Oct.) 206: 179–80.

1961e Zande Clans and Totems. *Man* LXI (July) 147: 116–21.

1961f Introduction, pp. 1–3, to *A Spanish Tapestry* by Michael Kenny. Cohen and West, London; US edition, Indiana University Press, Bloomington, 1962.

1961g The Religion of the Dinka [Letter]. *The Listener* LXVI, No. 1692 (Sept. 7): 355.

1962a Anthropological Research in the Southern Sudan. *Sudan Society* I (Sept.): 9–14.

1962b Review of *Essays in Sociology and Social Philosophy:* Vol. III, *Evolution and Progress* by Morris Ginsberg. *Man* LXII (May) 116: 72–3.

1962c Three Zande Texts. *Man* LXII (Oct.) 235: 149–52.

1962d Review of *Sources of Religious Sentiment* by Maurice Halbwachs. *Man* LXII (Oct.) 246: 156.

1962e Some Zande Texts, Pt. 1. *Kush* X: 289–314.

1962f *Zande Texts*, Pt. I. Oxonian Press, for All Souls College, Oxford, pp. 50 [Privately printed.]

1962g *Essays in Social Anthropology.* Faber and Faber, London, pp. 233; republished with (1951f) in US by Free Press, Glencoe; US paperback, 1963; UK paperback 1969.

1962h Ideophones in Zande. *SNR* LXIII: 143–6.

1962i Comment on: The Feet of the Natives Are Large: an Essay on Anthropology by an Economist, by Joseph S. Berliner. *Current Anthropology III*, No. 1 (February): 65.

1962j Étude d'une Religion primitive. Review of *Divinity and Experience* by R. G. Lienhardt. *La Table Ronde* No. 173 (June): 104.

1963a A Further Contribution to the Study of Zande Culture. *Africa* XXXIII, No. 3 (July): 183–97.

1963b Foreword, p. vi, and Some Zande Texts, pp. 1–21, in *Studies in Kinship and Marriage: Dedicated to Brenda Z. Seligman* (ed. I. Schapera). Occasional Paper No. 16, Royal Anthropological Institute, London.

1963c Some Zande Texts, Pt. 3. *Kush* XI: 273–301.

1963d *The Comparative Method in Social Anthropology* [Hobhouse Memorial

Lecture No. 33]. Athlone Press, for the University of London, London, pp. 30; republished in (1965h).

1963e Meaning in Zande Proverbs. *Man* LXIII (Feb.) 3: 4–7.

1963f Reply to Tom Harrison: Zande Texts. *Man* LXIII (March) 48: 46.

1963g Social Anthropology [Letter]. *Man* LXIII (May) 88: 77.

1963h Sixty-One Zande Proverbs. *Man* LXIII (July) 136: 109–12.

1963i Notes on Some Animals in Zandeland. *Man* LXIII (Sept.) 173: 139–42.

1963j The Zande State [The Huxley Memorial Lecture]. *JRAI* XCIII, Pt. 1: 134–54; republished in (1965h).

1963k [Unsigned] Review of *The Worship of the Sky-God* by E. O. James. *TLS* (Sept. 6): 676.

1963l [Unsigned] Review of *Sacrifice and Sacrament* by E. O. James. *TLS* (April 26): 293.

1963m Foreword, pp. vii–viii, to *Witchcraft and Sorcery in East Africa* (eds. J. Middleton & E. H. Winter). Routledge, Kegan Paul, London.

1963n Review of *Enquête démographiqu en milieu* (*Uele, Congo*) by N. Neven, J. de Petter, and H. Danakpali. *Africa* XXXIII, No. 2 (April): 164–5.

1963o Some Zande Folk-Tales, Pt. 1. *SNR* XLIV: 43–68.

1964a *Zande Texts*, Pt. II. Oxonian Press for All Souls College, Oxford, pp. 45 [Privately printed].

1964b *Zande Texts*, Pt. III. Oxonian Press for All Souls College, Oxford, pp. 45 [Privately printed].

1964c Zande Proverbs: Final Selection and Comments. *Man* LXIV (Jan.–Feb.) 1: 1–5.

1964d Foreword, pp. vii–viii, to *Sacrifice* by H. Hubert and M. Mauss. Cohen and West, London.

1964e Some Zande Texts, Pt. 3. *Kush* XII: 251–81.

1964f Some Zande Folk-Tales, Pt. 2. *SNR* XLV: 59–78.

1964g Two Zande Folk-Tales. *Man* LXIV (July–Aug.) 132: 105–9.

1964h Variations in a Zande Folk-Tale. *JAL* III, Pt. 2: 103–34.

1964i Four Zande Tales. *AQ* XXXVII, No. 4 (Oct.): 157–74.

1964j *Zande Texts*, Pt. IV. Oxonian Press for All Souls College, Oxford, pp. 34 [Privately printed].

1964k The Oxford Library of African Literature (co-editor with W. Whiteley and R. G. Lienhardt). Clarendon Press, Oxford.

1965a Some Zande Texts, Pt. 4. *Kush* XIII: 213–40.

1965b Some Zande Folk-Tales, Pt. 3. *SNR* XLVI: 50–66.

1965c *Zande Texts*, Pt. V. Oxonian Press for All Souls College, Oxford, pp. 32 [Privately printed].

1965d A Final Contribution to a Study of Zande Culture. *Africa* XXXV, No. 1 (Jan.): 1–7, 20.

1965e Some Zande Animal Tales from the Gore Collection. *Man* LXV (May–June) 61: 70–7.

1965f Four Zande Tales. *JRAI* XCV, Pt. 1 (Jan.–June): 44–74.

1965g *Theories of Primitive Religion.* Clarendon Press, Oxford. pp. x + 134; UK paperback edition, 1966; German translation, *Theorien über primitive Religionen*, Suhrkamp Verlag, Frankfurt am Main, 1968, together with (1950b).

1965h *The Position of Woman in Primitive Societies and other Essays in Social Anthropology.* Faber and Faber, London. pp. 260.

1965i Foreword to *The 'Soul' of the Primitive* by Lucien Lévy-Bruhl, pp. 5–6 (English translation of *L'âme primitive*, 1927). Allen and Unwin, London.

1966a Some Zande Folk-Tales from the Gore Collection. *AQ* XXXIX. 4 (Oct.): 265–87.

1966b Zande Trickster and Other Tales. *JAL* V, Pt. 2: 128–60.

1966c Twins, Birds and Vegetables [Letter]. *Man* I (n.s.), 3 (Sept): 398.

1966d Some Zande Texts: Part 5. *Kush* XLVII: 300–25.

1966e Foreword, p. 7; Prefazione, p. 9, to *La Superstizione Zande* by F. Gero (Tr. F. Giorgetti).

1967a Foreword, p. 5, to *A Bibliography of A. M. Hocart* by R. Needham, B. Blackwell for Institute of Social Anthropology, University of Oxford, Oxford.

1967b Azande, pp. 929–30, in *Encyclopaedia Britannica.* [A]

1967c Mangbetu, pp. 779–80, *in Encyclopaedia Britannica.* [M]

1967d Nuer, pp. 735–6, in *Encyclopaedia Britannica.* [N]

1967e Senusi, pp. 225–6, in *Encyclopaedia Britannica.* [S]

1967f *The Zande Trickster.* Clarendon Press, Oxford. pp. vi + 240.

1967g [Unsigned] Review of *A Diary in the Strict Sense of the Word* by B. Malinowski. *TLS* (Oct. 26): 1017.

1967h Social Anthropology and the Universities of Great Britain. *University Quarterly*: 167–81.

1967i Some Zande Texts about Family and Kin. *SNR* 48: 99–109.

1967j Zande Iron-working. *Paideuma* XIII: 26–31.

1969a Preface, pp. ix–x, to *The Observation of Savage Peoples* by Joseph-Marie Degérando (translated by F. C. T. Moore). Routledge and Kegan Paul, London.

1969b Zande Notions about Death, Soul and Ghost. *SNR* L: 41–52.

1969c The Perils of Translation. *New Blackfriars* (December): 813–5.

1969d Review of *African Religions and Philosophy* by John S. Mbiti. *Journal of African Religion* II, No. 3: 214–16.

1970a A Zande Funeral Custom. *Man* (n.s.) V, No. 1 (March): 126–9.

1970b Bergson and Witchcraft [Letter]. *Man* (n.s.) V, No. 1 (March): 131.

1970c Zande Bridewealth. *Africa* XL, No. 2 (April): 115–24.

1970d Foreword, ix–xi, to *Kings and Councillors* by A. M. Hocart, edited by Rodney Needham, University of Chicago Press, Chicago.

1970e *The Sociology of Comte: an Appreciation.* Manchester University Press, Manchester. pp. v + 26.

1970f Oxford's Scientists: Professor E. E. Evans-Pritchard. [An Interview.] *Zenith* VII, No. 3: 20–1.

1970g [Unsigned] Review of *Frazer and the Golden Bough* by R. Angus Downie. *TLS* (28 August): 945.

1970h Azande Exogamy and Endogamy [Letter]. *Man* V, No. 2 (June): 313.

1970i [Unsigned] Review of *Witchcraft, Sorcery and Social Categories among the Safwa* by Alan Harwood. *TLS* (28 August): 945.

1970j Review of *The Nature of Nomadism* by Douglas L. Johnson. *The Middle East Journal* XXIV, No. 2 (Spring): 241.

1970k Some Reflections on Mysticism. *Dyn* (The Journal of the Durham University Anthropological Society) I: 101–15.

1970l Preface, xv–xvii, to *Witchcraft in Tudor and Stuart England* by Alan Macfarlane. Routledge, Kegan Paul, London; US paperback, Harper Torchbooks, 1970.

1970m Social Anthropology at Oxford. *Man* V, No. 4 (Dec.): 704.

1970n *Zande Texts*, Pt. VI. Oxonian Press for All Souls College, Oxford, pp. 49 [Privately printed.]

1970o Social Anthropology at Oxford. *Journal of the Anthropological Society of Oxford* I, No. 3: 103–9.

1970p A Zande Matrimonial Problem. *AQ* XLIII, No. 4: 215–24.

1970q Sexual Inversion among the Azande. *AA* LXXII: 1428–34.

1970r Zande Conversation Pieces, pp. 29–49, in *Échanges et communications: mélanges offerts à Claude Lévi-Strauss* (eds. J. Pouillon and P. Maranda). Mouton, The Hague & Paris.

1971a Reigning and Ruling. *Man* VI, No. 1: in press.

1971b Recollections and Reflections. *The New Diffusionist* No. 2: 37–9.

1971c [Unsigned] The Political Order. Review of *Political Anthropology* by Georges Balandier. *TLS* (April 23): 469.

Index of Names

Abamalaki, 186
ABERLE, D. F., 102
ABERLE, K. G., 411n.
ADAMS, R. N., 247
Africa Inland Mission, 186
African National Congress, 23, 25
ALBAN, A. H., 387f., 390, 393, 400
Amazon River, 293, 306–7
American Negroes, 250
Andes, 234, 251
ANDRADE, R. G., 130
Apoh River, 209
Arabs, 37, 52, 118, 180, 195
ARENT, M., 356
Arikara, 162
Awatixa, 162
Awawaxi, 162
Aweikoma, 141–59
Azande, 19f., 179f., 194f.

Baganda, 186–7, 191, 195, 333
BAGSHAWE, F. J., 319f., 343(app.),
    346n.
Bantu, 34n., 259, 261, 333
Barabaiga, 323
Baraguyu, 261, 288n.
Baram River, 203, 208f., 212, 215, 224,
    226n.
BARDEN, G., 345n.
BARRÈRE, 310n.
BARNES, J., 1–17, 71n.
BARTH, F., 254n.
BATHO, 351
Batu Belah, 215
BEALS, A., 247
BECKWITH, M. W., 168f.
Bedouin of Cyrenaica, 71n.
BEDRI, I., 409n., 412n.
BEIDELMAN, T. O., 229n., 258f.,
    261, 264, 270, 286n., 288n., 375–415
Belgians, 180f.

BELTRÁN, A., 248
BEN ASSHER, 400
BERREMAN, G. D., 238–9, 247, 251,
    254–5n.
BLALOCK, H. M., 123
BLEEK, W. H. I., 317
BLOOMFIELD, M., 33n.
BOAS, F., 345n.
BOHANNAN, L., 38
BOHANNAN, P., 405
BONDEVIK, K., 6
Borneo, 203ff.
Borneo Evangelical Mission, 226n.
'Botocudo', 158n.
BOUGLÉ, C. C. A., 240, 247
BOURRICAUD, F., 247
BOWERS, A. W., 161–77 passim
BOXER, C. R., 57
Brahmins, 111f., 237
Brazil, 130, 141ff., 293
Brazilians, 141
Bremnes, 3–16
Britain, 354
British, 65, 118, 180–1, 236, 397
Buddhism, 1
Buganda, 191
Burma, 135
BURRIDGE, K. O. L., 345
Burungi, 323
Bush Negroes, 302f., 310n.

Cameroons, 333
CAMPBELL, D., 137
CAMPBELL, J. K., 225n.
CARNEIRO, R. L., 130
Castle Concordia, 57f., 64f.
Catholics, 4
Caxias, Duqe de, 142, 156, 157n.
Ceylon, 251
CHAMBERS, 351
China Sea, 204

435

Index

Chipepo Chieftaincy, 23, 24
Chisamu, 23, 24, 25, 28
Choma District, 22
Christians, 1ff., 21, 186ff., 238, 252, 359
CLAUS, H., 286n.
DE CLERQ, F.S.A., 61, 62, 63
COHEN, M., 231
COLBY, B., 247
COLLINS, B., 33n., 34n.
COLSON, E., 19–35
Columbus, Christopher, 254n.
Congo, the, 179
CORIAT, P., 387–98 passim, 411n.
COROMINAS, J., 234, 251, 254n.
COVARRUBIAS HOROZCO, S. DE.,
    234, 253, 254n.
CRANZ, F. E., 10
CRAZZOLARA, J. P., 391–9 passim,
    401f., 407n., 410n., 411n., 412n.
CROCKER, J. C., 407n., 411n.
Crow, 162, 254n.
CUNNISON, I., 71n., 119n.

DALE, A., 34n.
Dakota, 162
DAM, P. VAN, 63
DASENT, G., 354, 361
Dayak, 71n.
DEMPWOLFF, O., 319f., 322, 325,
    343(app.)
Denmark, 8, 11f.
Dervish, 117
DIJK, L. J. VAN, 66f.
Dinka, 82ff., 103, 111ff., 180, 377, 387,
    390ff., 409n., 410n., 411n., 412n.
DOLLARD, J., 254n.
Dominicans, 57
DOUGLAS, M., 135, 270, 283, 285,
    337
DOUGLAS, R. S., 212
DRIBERG, J. H., 199n., 392
DUMONT, L., 241, 243, 250f., 254n.
DUNCAN, J. S. R., 408n.
DURKHEIM, E., 135, 375f., 404f.
Dutch, 41, 54, 57–69
Dutch East India Company, 40, 57ff.

Eastern Orthodox Church, 8
Egyptians, 397
Egyptian Sudan, 180–1
ELLIOTT, D., 138
ELSHOUT, J. M., 206ff., 225n., 226n.
Emin Pasha, 180–1, 395
EPSTEIN, A. L., 16n.
Eta, 250
EVANS-PRITCHARD, E. E., 3, 19f.,
    22, 37f., 40, 80ff., 123f., 135, 157n.,
    161, 203, 225n., 232, 257ff., 266n.,
    293, 313ff., 349ff., 375–89 passim

FALK MOORE, S., 337f.
FEIERMAN, S., 315, 345n.
FELL, J. R., 26, 34n.
FERGUSSON, V., 388, 391, 393ff.,
    407n., 410n., 411n., 412n.
FERNANDEZ, F., 248
FIRTH, R., 71, 225n., 337
FOCK, N., 306f., 308n., 310n.
FORDE, D., 364
FORELL, G. W., 9
FORTES, M., 10, 119n.
FOX, J. J., 37–77
FRANCKE, 7
FREUD, S., 375
FRIKEL, P., 309n.

Gaajak Clan (Nuer), 87, 89
Gaawar Clan (Nuer), 82, 387
Galibi, 310n.
GALTON, F., 126
Gê, 141, 156
GEERTZ, C., 73n.
Germany, 8f., 12
GILLIN, J., 246, 247, 294
GLUCKMAN, M., 86, 361f.
Gogo, 257–91, 323
GOLDMAN, I., 308n.
GORDON, E. V., 351
GOUGH, K., 79–121
GRAAFLAND, N., 66–7
GRAY, R., 395
GREENLAND, D., 200n.
Guajira, 234, 251

436

Index

Index

Index

Index